DIGITAL WRITING RESEARCH

*Technologies, Methodologies,
and Ethical Issues*

NEW DIMENSIONS IN COMPUTERS AND COMPOSITION

Gail E. Hawisher and Cynthia L. Selfe, editors

DIGITAL WRITING RESEARCH

Technologies, Methodologies, and Ethical Issues

Edited by

Heidi A. McKee
Miami University

Dànielle Nicole DeVoss
Michigan State University

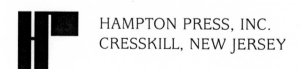

HAMPTON PRESS, INC.
CRESSKILL, NEW JERSEY

Printed in the United States of America

Library of Congress Cataloging-in-Publication Data

Digital writing research : technologies, methodologies, and ethical issues / edited by Heidi A. McKee, Dànielle Nicole DeVoss
     p. cm. -- (New dimensions in computers and composition)
  Includes bibliographic references and index.
  ISBN 1-57273-705-0 -- ISBN 1-57273-706-9 (pbk.)
1. English language--Rhetoric. 2. Report writing--Dataprocessing. 3. Research--Methodology. 4. Research--Morals and ethical aspects. 5. Scholarly electronic publishing. I. McKee, Heidi A. II. DeVoss, Dànielle Nicole.
  PE1478.D54 2007
  808.00285--dc22
                  2007007006

Hampton Press, Inc.
23 Broadway
Cresskill, NJ 07626

CONTENTS

FOREWORD

James E. Porter

The field of computers and writing has much to celebrate in terms of its research achievement. In 2003, the journal *Computers and Composition* commemorated its 20th anniversary with the publication of a double issue of the journal edited by this collection's co-editors, Dànielle Nicole DeVoss and Heidi McKee. The book series for the field is in its 17th year. The series started at NCTE as "Advances in Computers and Composition"; moved to Ablex in 1994 under the label "New Directions in Computers and Composition"; and is now housed at Hampton Press, where it is called "New Dimensions in Computers and Composition." The publication venue may have changed, but the editorial leadership has been steady and stellar. Under the expert direction of Gail Hawisher and Cindy Selfe, the series has published 20 volumes, with another 5 forthcoming (as of this writing). The Computers & Writing Conference met for the 22nd time in May 2006 at Texas Tech University, and in 2007 at Wayne State University in Detroit, Michigan. The field has a history, as well as a keen sense of its history, as chronicled in *Computers and the Teaching of Writing in American Higher Education, 1979–1994: A History* (Hawisher, LeBlanc, Moran, & Selfe, 1996). These publications, events, and historical benchmarks signify the existence of a robust field with a strong record of research and scholarly achievement. I am proud to have been a member of this community since 1988, my date of entry into the field.

And now we have the publication of another impressive collection, *Digital Writing Research: Technologies, Methodologies, and Ethical Issues*, the

21st volume in the book series, a work that includes 20 chapters (including the co-editors' Introduction) from a variety of researchers—some well established, most newer in the field—each of them contributing significant perspectives on digital writing research. I have waited a long time for *Digital Writing Research* to appear. Not because the authors, editors, or publishers were slow in producing it—not at all—but rather because the field of computers and writing has long needed this work. What distinguishes this collection is that its contributors are not merely reporting on the results of their research projects—although most do that, and that's important and helpful in its own right—but they are also focusing on methodology itself: raising important methodological, epistemological, and ethical questions about the nature of digital writing research, and offering us theories for understanding it and practical strategies for doing it. In this respect, *Digital Writing Research* represents a key developmental stage in the maturity of the field. This is what our field has needed: critical reflectiveness about its own methodologies and an awareness of its distinctive nature as a field of research. More on this in a moment. . .

The field of computers and writing has a long and strong record of research achievement—that's the good news. The not-so-good news is the fact that few outside the field know that. Our work is still not very much recognized, acknowledged, or respected by other fields. We have a public relations problem: Nobody outside our field cites us. Still, after all these years. Obviously that's a pretty gross generalization—you will think of plenty of exceptions to rebut it—but I stand by it; the claim is true as a generality. We don't get no respect—not from Communication, not from Education, not from Human–Computer Interaction (HCI) studies, and, still, not very much from Rhetoric/Composition.

Compiling evidence of neglect is tedious, discouraging work—not to mention that the job of a foreword is to praise, not complain—so I will not do much of that here. But just take a look at a few of the collections and journals in other fields that sponsor Internet-based communication research. You might think that a collection entitled *Internet Communication and Qualitative Research: A Handbook for Researching Online* (Mann & Stewart, 2000) would list *some* research from computers and writing. Wrong. In its 19-page bibliography citing 367 sources it does not list even one source from the journals *College Composition and Communication*, *Computers and Composition*, or *Kairos: A Journal of Rhetoric, Technology, and Pedagogy*, nor any of the books in the book series, nor any papers from the Computers & Writing Conference. The collection *Online Social Research: Methods, Issues, and Ethics* (Johns, Chen, & Hall, 2004)—consisting of 16 chapters, most of them by scholars in communication studies—likewise includes no citations from *Computers and Composition, Kairos,* or the New Directions/New Dimensions book series. None. I read fairly widely on Internet-based communication research, both print and online materials, and, unfortunately, in my experience these two collections are not exceptional or unusual in their neglect of our research.

We fare somewhat better (now) in composition studies, especially in recent years. Our research is regularly published in *College Composition and Communication* (see, for instance, DeVoss, Cushman, & Grabill, 2005; Hawisher, Selfe, Moraski, & Pearson, 2004; Hocks, 2003; Yancey, 2004). But in many ways our research is firewalled from mainstream composition research, treated as a quirky subspecialization for technogeeks rather than as a fundamental topic—for everyone in the field—critical to the understanding of writing. This is an aspect of our work addressed by the co-editors in their Introduction, where they list and describe other prominent collections absent of a focus on digital writing research methods and methodologies. A recent collection on composition research—*Research on Composition: Multiple Perspectives on Two Decades of Change* (Smagorinsky, 2006)—provides a representative example of what I am talking about. Although the collection advertises itself as a comprehensive historical perspective on composition research published between 1984 and 2003, it includes no distinct chapter on research in computers and writing. (Although, to be fair, Russell Durst's chapter on "Writing at the Postsecondary Level" does provide a brief statement on "Technology," pages 95–96, and Anne Beaufort's contribution on "Writing in the Professions" has a three-page discussion on pages 222–225.)

The absence of a distinct chapter per se does not bother me. What is significant here is not number of pages or citations. Rather, the problem is more epistemologically endemic than that: It is the overall failure of most chapters to acknowledge that computers and Internet technologies have changed composing. The chapters talk around questions of production and delivery. They review 20 years of research on student writers at different levels, research about classrooms, about teachers, about language proficiencies, about critical pedagogy, about assessment, about academic discourse, about textual features, about collaboration, and so on. But there is no serious, sustained review of research having to do with the technologies, materiality, production, or delivery of writing. Again, I don't find *Research on Composition* unusual in this regard. My view is that most research in composition, particularly in the past 10 years, neglects these aspects of composing.

Why? This might be a good question to ask at this point. There are lots of ways to answer that question, but I'll explore just one possibility here. In his book *The Function of Theory in Composition Studies* (2005), Raúl Sánchez claimed that the field of composition no longer focuses predominantly on studying composing practices, ironically. Sánchez attributed this to a kind of theory lust, encouraged by composition's affiliations with the English Department (and English literature and theory); with the humanist emphasis on the hermeneutic/interpretive function; and, particularly, with the recent upsurge of interest in "the politics of representation" (p. 4). Sánchez noted that "while the work of traditional English studies remains the teaching of textual interpretation, the work of composition has been the teaching of textual production" (p. 62). Sánchez thus urged composition to revive its focus on production and on writing as an act.

I agree with Sánchez's overall claims about composition studies and theory, and find them insightful. But at the same time I want to say to him: If you want to find out what happened to production, look at the field of computers and writing (which Sánchez neglects). Our emphasis on technologies of writing *is* a focus on production. But, like most in Rhetoric/Composition, Sánchez views technology from an instrumental standpoint: It might be a convenient vehicle for creating writing, but, like the typewriter or the pencil, technology is merely a "tool" in the instrumental sense—that is, a neutral medium, not a substantive factor affecting rhetorical dynamics or composing practices. And so it is simply not worth talking about.

The field of Rhetoric/Composition has yet to acknowledge, truly acknowledge, that changes and developments in writing tools have changed writing, literacy, and communication practices in fundamental ways—that, given how writing happens in the 21st century, *all* composition research needs to be computers and writing research. That's a pretty disturbing claim to make (it has, however, been made before, e.g., Hart-Davidson et al., 2004; WIDE Research Center Collective, 2005), and, obviously, we have a long way to go to convince Rhetoric/Composition of this viewpoint: that technology is substantively integral to, not incidental to, the activity of writing. Several of the contributors to *Digital Writing Research*—for example, Rebecca Rickly, and Susan Hilligoss and Sean Williams—explicitly challenge the field of Rhetoric/Composition to take digital research more seriously. But, in fact, the entirety of *Digital Writing Research* raises that challenge, implicitly, to the field.

* * *

Ah yes, *Digital Writing Research*. It may not seem like it, but I really am introducing the book, admittedly in a roundabout way. To understand the significance of *Digital Writing Research*, it is, I believe, necessary to see its historical emergence not only in the field of computers and writing but also vis-à-vis Internet research in other fields and vis-à-vis Rhetoric/Composition as a field of research inquiry. This volume answers a number of long-standing, troubling questions for the field: How is our research different and distinctive? How does it contrast with and contribute to Internet research in communication studies? What is its relationship to composition research? Should our research *matter* to anyone outside the field?

The key to understanding the significance of *Digital Writing Research* is encapsulated in this paragraph from the co-editors' Introduction, which I cite at length because it cannot be better said:

> As we hope is clear by our discussion of emergent technologies and the various contexts of their use, computers and other digital devices are not just tools for writing and communication. Digital technologies and the people who use those technologies have changed the processes, products, and contexts for writing and the teaching of writing in dramatic ways—and, at this current cultural, historical, and intellectual moment, it is imperative that our research approaches, our methodologies, and our ethical understandings for researching adequately and appropriately address these changes in communication technologies.

This statement articulates a challenge that is also an opportunity: Digital technologies are radically changing (have changed) writing—and our research needs to understand the dramatic scope of this change and to address that change. What I like most about this collection is that it pushes the research agenda forward: It recognizes the challenge and responds to it by providing a range of research essays that collectively mark a path for the field.

The chapters in *Digital Writing Research* show us, either implicitly or explicitly, that the definition of "writing" has changed in the digital age and that, consequently, our approaches to doing research need to change; we need a parallel and equally dramatic change in our notions of methodology. The contributors take up this issue in different ways. Susan Hilligoss and Sean Williams, for instance, point out that researching multimedia genres requires that we expand the notion of "text" to include visual images. We cannot just analyze words on paper. We must look at designs and images, video and audio, interfaces and infrastructures, and at the intersections between various media. Amy Kimme Hea systematically catalogues and provides critical reflection on specific challenges involved in doing research on the Web. Stuart Blythe shows us that doing research on online documents requires that we take a different approach to sampling and data coding. With print texts, defining the boundaries of a document is easier than for Web-based hypertexts (for which document boundaries are much harder to determine). Blythe's chapter provides a detailed analysis of how methods must be adapted to suit digital research. Colleen Reilly and Douglas Eyman convincingly argue that even our conventions for citation and methods for citation analysis need to change.

The technologies we are now using for data collection themselves raise methodological issues. Cheryl Geisler and Shaun Slattery discuss the use of video screen capture technology as a research tool—a tool that raises its own distinctive set of methodological and epistemological questions. Joanne Addison talks about the use of mobile technologies as a tool for research. These tools are not just neutral devices for collecting literacy artifacts; they change what data are collected. There are critical issues, particularly ethical issues, involved in using the tools, especially tools that enable a much higher degree of surveillance and intrusion than traditional methods ever afforded. Developments in technology certainly enable us to observe and capture more of the writing process—but should we? When research might cross the line into the realm of unethical surveillance is an issue Lory Hawkes explores in her chapter.

Digital Writing Research is characterized by a high degree of reflexivity about methodological and epistemological issues—and several chapters are particularly strong in this regard. Julia Romberger's; Iswari Pandey's; and Jacklyn Lopez, Joshua Burnett, and Sally Chandler's chapters each engage in theoretical reflection and raise political questions about the positionality of the digital writing researcher vis-à-vis participants. Kevin Eric De Pew makes a compelling case not just for the desirability of methodological triangulation, but for its *necessity*: Single-method research designs, especially those focused on text only, are not likely to capture the rhetorical dynamic of online communications. Kristine Blair and Christine Tulley examine the nature of research collaboration—focusing on the relationship between dissertation adviser and student. That's a common type of research collaboration, but not one that is often critically interrogated as thoroughly as Blair and Tulley do.

Collectively and implicitly, these discussions argue that methodology has to account for the local—"local" meaning the technological environments in which writing occurs. This view counters the modernist notion of methodology (and of theory, too) that views methods as a static given, no matter the location of the specific study: Methods are presumed to transcend location, participants, and, certainly, technology considerations. In *Opening Spaces* (1997), Patricia Sullivan and I tried to show that this abstracted, theoretical view of method was a limited and limiting view that would prevent us from seeing what was most significant in a given inquiry and that would impair our ability to affect change and improved conditions for participants. *Opening Spaces* was an invitation—a plea—for computers and writing researchers to reinvent method in ways that would allow them to conduct nuanced, complex, and useful studies. We argued this: You can't unreflectively buy methods off the shelf. You can't import the methodological assumptions of a conventional ethnography or case study into a study of online environments and expect that method to help you understand the dynamics of that environment or to yield valid (or, more importantly, useful) conclusions. You have to begin by massaging, adapting, reshaping, and remaking both the methods and the methodologies—and to do that you have to be critically self-reflective about methodology. In particular for the study of technology, you need be aware of the tendency for traditional methodologies, especially those influenced by humanist paradigms, to neglect, efface, or instrumentalize technology.

Computers and writing may be at an historical moment comparable to where feminist research was in the 1980s and early 1990s. At that point, feminist researchers were doing studies of women, certainly, yes—but was there such a thing as a distinctive feminist methodology? That was the question that Sandra Harding (1987), Liz Stanley and Sue Wise (1990), and others pursued: that is, was feminist research simply conventional research tools applied to the study of women? Or, did it actually represent a distinctive form of methodology and epistemology, an entirely different way of conceptualizing inquiry? The question has long since been answered: Feminist methodology is not simply research on, by, and/or for women, but rather it represents a distinctive epistemological framework and form of conducting a research inquiry, one that challenges the modernist and androcentric assumptions about the role of the researcher as objective, distanced, impartial, and knowledgeable expert observer. It is a perspective that now, fortunately, thoroughly permeates the conception of our relationships with research participants—even when the tenets of feminist methodology are not explicitly invoked.

Likewise, digital writing research should not be viewed merely as research about writing with technology. It should be viewed, rather, as changing the fundamental assumptions about methodology, particularly the humanist assumption that divides the human from the technological. Digital writing research takes a cyborgian view and a networked view of human communications. It is not simply old methods applied to new events or practices. It represents a new way of looking altogether—an approach that emphasizes the role of production, delivery, and technology in human communication, but even beyond that, acknowledges the hybrid, symbiotic relationship between humans and machines. What is exciting to me is seeing the field acclimating to this understanding of itself. Of course this is not the first or only instance of that in our field by any means (see Takayoshi, 2000, for example). But it is exciting to see it on the extensive level evident in *Digital Writing Research*.

To sum up the key epistemological breakthrough here: Doing digital writing research is not merely a matter of shipping old methods and methodologies to a new research locale—for instance, the Internet, the World Wide Web, synchronous chat spaces, virtual classrooms, and so on. Rather, technologically mediated research locales demand changes in method and methodology. What does it mean to study an electronic community, when the geographical and linguistic and relational parameters that constitute the traditional ethnographic community are not at all the same as those for a virtual community? What are we studying when we look at synchronous conversation: Are we studying the people, the communication dynamic, the technology, or all of the above? These are the sorts of methodological questions we need to be asking.

Digital Writing Research is useful, important, and innovative in a number of other ways worthy of mention:

- **Pragmatic**. In *Opening Spaces*, Pat Sullivan and I (1997) commented that, "One reason that we find the field of computers and composition an interesting site for critical investigation is that its members have always displayed a keen sensitivity toward practice, both the practice of teaching writing in computer-based environments and the situated uses of technology" (p. 25). This volume is no exception in regards to practice or pragmatism. Its numerous chapters offer useful advice for new researchers about the "how to" of research and plenty of examples and details from the contributors' own studies. Researchers on digital composing should definitely read William Hart-Davidson's chapter on time-use diaries and Stuart Blythe's chapter on data coding and sampling for online documents. Further, Rebecca Rickly's chapter offers both critical disciplinary questions and pointed practical issues in terms of graduate training in research methods.
- **Ethically vigilant**. All of the chapters show a commendable sensitivity toward the ethical issues involved in various methods and methodologies. But for a number of contributors—including Michelle Sidler, and William Banks and Michelle Eble—ethical questions are the primary focus of attention. As Sidler points out, the line between "public" and "private" discourse is not as easily distinguishable for

Web-based discourse as it is for print documents. Banks and Eble take us into the world of IRBs and show us the challenges of explaining and justifying digital writing research in terms of review criteria that don't quite fit our research approaches. Janice McIntire-Strasburg explores ethical (and legal) issues involved in doing research on multimedia writing.

- **Globally aware**. Several chapters push the field to develop a stronger global awareness in its research, a push that the field desperately needs. Beatrice Smith explores what it means to do ethnography in online work environments that cross national boundaries, that participate in a global information economy, and that "combine virtual and nonvirtual spaces." Ethnographers have to shift and adapt their approaches to study communication practices in these environments. As Iswari Pandey points out, qualitative research needs to develop a postnational perspective in order to understand the literacy practices of postnational subjects whose identities and locations cannot be described in conventional terms. But the perspective does not pertain only to the research participants. Researchers themselves need to develop what Filipp Sapienza calls a "transnational identity," and perhaps adopt multiple roles as well, in order to engage participants effectively.

- **Interdisciplinary**. I am impressed that the contributors reach beyond the typical disciplinary boxes that too often constrain our thinking to engage the work of other fields. The contributors in this volume cite and engage work in computer science, library science, management and organizational studies, education, communication, sociology, youth studies, literary and cultural theory, graphic design, HCI studies—and of course Rhetoric/Composition and computers and writing (for a good example of what I mean, see Colleen Reilly and Douglas Eyman's chapter). This is a sign of a maturing research field.

Most impressive of all, though, is the editorial work of Heidi McKee and Dànielle Nicole DeVoss—not only in terms of inviting and attracting an impressive lineup of researchers, in promoting and encouraging the emergence of *new* researchers, and in providing substantive editorial review, but, perhaps most importantly, in shaping and articulating the identity for this volume. Their Introduction is a major historical and disciplinary statement in its own right about the purpose and status of digital writing research. It provides an excellent overview not just of this collection but also of the field at large. It makes a compelling case for the importance of establishing a distinct identity for "digital writing research."

The title of this work may be the most interesting and daring editorial move of them all. It is significant that Heidi and Dànielle chose to label this work "Digital Writing Research" rather than "Computers and Composition Research" or "Internet Research" or "Digital Media Research." The terminology of the title presages a shift in the focus of the field—a shift that is neither innocent nor insignificant, as it signals a new identity and direction for the field.

Like its earlier predecessor terms—computers and composition, computers and writing—*digital writing* establishes that the focus of our field continues to be the activity of writing—the act of producing and distributing writing and the ways in which technology assists, promotes, impedes, and/or shapes that process. Many researchers in other fields study Internet behavior, computer-mediated communication, new media designs, and the like—but for more than 20 years it has been the field of computers and writing that focuses specifically on writing-with/in-the-technology. That won't change.

The term "composition" signifies our particular interest in composing processes and also our affiliation with composition studies; it identifies what has long been a primary research locale for the field—the first-year college composition course. But the shift to the word "writing" (which has been happening for some time now) reflects more accurately what our field has actually been doing: examining writing practices across numerous academic, public, and professional spaces, not just college classrooms. The ambiguity of the term "writing" is also an advantage: it could refer to the text itself, or to the process of creating the text, in both the technical and the intellectual senses of create (i.e., writing refers to inscription, handwriting, even keyboarding, but also to the imaginative, creative, and inventive components of that activity). Writing also specifies an action: writing TO someone in order to DO something—to thank them, change them, offend them, praise them, or inform them—and so highlights the rhetorical, performative dimension. Research in this field explores writing in all these varied senses.

The term *digital* signifies the dramatic shift from the analog and print world to a new kind of writing space altogether. Digital refers to computer-mediated technology, to be sure, but the term carries cultural connotations and avoids the instrumentalism implicit in terms like "computer" and "Internet." The focus of the field is not technology-as-machine but rather technology-as-cultural-space as well as technology-as-production-space, as a virtual environment in which humans live, not just a medium through which they talk.

And so *Digital Writing Research* is the perfect title for a work that celebrates the achievement of a well-established field while simultaneously pushing that field into a new identity. This volume makes a strong case for the distinctive and important nature of computers and writing research. It is time for other fields to notice this work—and this collection should make them take notice.

James E. Porter
Writing in Digital Environments (WIDE) Research Center
Michigan State University

INTRODUCTION

Heidi A. McKee
Miami University

Dànielle Nicole DeVoss
Michigan State University

A researcher committed to issues of labor as they intersect with technology seeks to conduct an ethnography of workplace culture in the customer service branch of a large multinational corporation. As she explores the sites at which she can enter the field to collect data, she realizes that there is no there there (as John Perry Barlow, 1996, might put it)—the workers are dispersed, spread across continents and countries. A single telephone number and email address distribute information to dozens of workers in multiple locales, spread across geographic distance and time zones. How then is she to define her research site and to locate herself and her participants?

A researcher analyzing representation and the ways in which individuals appropriate and subvert iconic figures on their personal Web pages gathers URLs of sites that look promising for research. During the course of his research, several of the key sites he is studying and writing about are taken offline by the Web authors. Faced with a nearly completed manuscript and a looming deadline, and knowing that even though these sites are offline

1

they have been archived by an Internet archive (http://www. archive.org, which saves and stores Web sites without permission), what should the researcher do? Revise his research and his manuscript to not include those now nonexistent sites, or go to the archives and continue his research?

Several teacher–researchers work on a collaborative project to code the multimodal elements in students' new media texts. Their goals are to better understand how these modes work and to develop more robust curricula for teaching the integration of multimodal elements in digital composition. As they explore different approaches for coding the data they have gathered, they wrestle with the way coding schemes used for verbal texts change shape and even fall apart entirely as they attempt to code "texts" that include audio (music, voiceovers, and more); movement (animation and video); textual elements; and other multimedia, multimodal aspects. Given the increased multimodalities in digital compositions, what coding schemes might they adapt for what types of texts?

A graduate student researcher has been a member of an online support group for diabetics for several years, sometimes lurking, other times posting when she finds another person's post particularly engaging or interesting. As she considers possible topics for her dissertation, she decides she would like to focus on the rhetorics of empowerment and agency in these group discussions. As she and her dissertation advisor discuss the study— and begin to prepare forms for her university's Institutional Review Board—they realize that they are not sure how to address her movement from participant to researcher in light of the online site of study. How will her shift in identity and participation potentially change the dynamics of the online support group? At what point in time will she need to identify her researcher role?

A researcher decides to conduct a critical discourse analysis of messages posted in discussion forums geared toward teenagers. Because the discussion forums are publicly available to anyone with access to the Internet, he decides that he does not need to seek permission from the individuals to research and use their online posts. He does, however, use pseudonyms when he refers to and quotes from their posts in his work. When he publishes his research in a print-based, peer-reviewed journal, he includes many direct quotations that, when entered into a search engine, could immediately provide the URLs to individuals' posts and thus explicitly reveal their identities. Has the researcher engaged in an ethical research practice? Has he appropriately negotiated issues of consent, anonymity, and privacy?

A researcher studying multimedia writing practices collects the files students created for their digital writing projects. In their new media essays, students frequently used copyrighted work—weaving together pieces of popular songs, images from advertisements, clips from movies, and complete texts of written publications. The researcher plans to publish her analysis of their work in an online journal, including sample student files. Does she need to secure permissions for the re-presentation of the copyrighted material contained in the students' projects?

A composition researcher who often studies computerized writing technologies and who often publishes in online journals, such as Computers and Composition Online *and* Kairos, *is preparing her tenure dossier. A requirement for that dossier is that she illustrate the "impact factor" of the journals in which she publishes. Neither of the online journals is rated by any citation database. The researcher knows of the value and importance of these journals to the computers and writing community, but how can she make the case to others who expect numerical representations of value? That is, what methodologies might she use to assess the impact factor of online journals?*

RESEARCH QUESTIONS IN A DIGITAL AGE

These scenarios and the questions they raise barely scratch the surface of the complications of digital writing research. Computerized writing technologies impact how and what we write, the ways in which we teach and learn writing, and, certainly, computers and digital spaces affect our research approaches. *Digital Writing Research* focuses on how writing technologies, specifically digital technologies, affect our research—shaping the questions we ask; the sites we study; the methodologies we use (or could use); the ethical issues we face; the conclusions we draw; and, thus, the actions we take as scholars, researchers, and teachers. In the chapters that follow, the authors analyze methodologies, technologies, and ethical approaches for researching digital writing and writers working in digital contexts. Although many of the chapters provide examples drawn from studies conducted or reviewed by the authors (e.g., studies of gay youths' blogs; research on information technology workers at a global, outsourcing company; studies of video gamers' literacy practices), the focus of each chapter is on articulating particular methodological and ethical approaches for conducting digital writing research.

The term *digital writing research* refers to research that focuses: (a) on computer-generated, computer-based, and/or computer-delivered documents; (b) on computer-based text-production practices (and we deploy *text* broadly here, to include multimedia artifacts); and/or (c) on the interactions of people who use digital technologies to communicate (McKee & Porter, in press). Because of the increasing digitization of writing in educational, institutional, and social contexts, all composition researchers, not just computer and writing specialists, need to consider methodological and ethical approaches to digital writing research. Further, the term digital writing research—rather than the more commonly used term *Internet research*—acknowledges that not all digital writing and related communicative acts and interactions occur on the Internet.

A set of core concerns sparked by earlier research and fueled by recent conversations and trends led us to gather the contributions collected here. The core questions that this collection addresses include many that the opening scenarios raise, but also such questions as:

- How have researchers adapted methodologies for digital writing research? For example, how might a researcher conduct an ethnography in an online community? What approaches are available for the coding of digital texts? What institutional obstacles impede a feminist, collaborative methodology when, for instance, researching and publishing digital work?
- What methods are being used by researchers studying sign systems beyond the textual? What research is being conducted on visuals? What methods are being used by compositionists for studying multimedia texts?
- How is a particular writing technology—for example, the Web, word-processing software, or handheld devices—being researched by computers and writing scholars?
- What constitutes appropriate human subject research in online environments? When is consent needed, especially when working in diverse cultural and technological forums? What new issues related to person-based research does writing in networked spaces create?
- How are computerized technologies, particularly global technologies, raising new (or remediating old) ethical issues related to privacy, individual rights, and representation?
- How have computers and digital spaces changed collaboration among researchers and participants?
- How have electronic journals and other methods of publishing writing research influenced our research directions and the distribution of research findings?
- Given the continually evolving state of technology and human interactions with and through technological affordances, what preparation do future researchers need? How might approaches

to research be discussed and integrated into research methods courses so as to include considerations of the digital?

These are just some of the questions addressed in various ways by contributors to *Digital Writing Research*. In developing responses to these questions (and others), contributors to this collection do not aim to create a strict "how to" for a particular research site or methodology, but rather they aim to provide a range of answers—and a range of further questions—that researchers might consider as they make methodological and ethical decisions. We see these not as responses that will rapidly become obsolete in the face of changing perspectives toward writing or evolutions in digital technologies, but rather as questions and answers that construct a framework to scaffold our research, our conversations, and our theorizing as we continue to wrestle with technological change and its impact on our teaching and research. It is our hope that these chapters—described in more detail below—will provide experienced researchers with the means to reflect upon various aspects of their research and will offer researchers new to composition studies or new to computers and writing research an introduction to possible approaches and related methodological and ethical issues.

Perhaps the most obvious impact of computerized writing technologies upon research practices occurs at the sites we now research and with the questions we currently ask. For this reason, we begin this introduction by briefly sketching a few of the contexts in which we now find ourselves as researchers—contexts that we realize are, of course, historically situated. We provide this overview as a means to situate the chapters in this collection and to argue that writing spaces and research contexts have indeed changed with the increasing move to digital technologies, and especially with the increasing move to communicate, and, specifically, write with digital technologies. After this discussion of changing writing spaces, we move to review previous discussions of methodologies and ethical approaches for conducting digital writing research. We close by describing each section and chapter in the collection.

DIGITAL WRITING SPACES: EVOLVING CONTEXTS FOR WRITING RESEARCH

We have witnessed dire warnings and exuberant predictions about the effects of digital technologies on society, culture, education, and individuals since the advent of the computer and with every digital technology since—from those designed to play and explore, to those designed to share and communicate. These warnings and predictions have been remediated in each digital device as it is introduced in the marketplace and integrated into our lives. Whether one welcomes or rues the integration—at times, saturation—of computerized and digital technologies in our lives and in our classrooms, what constitutes writing and what provides for the contexts for writing have indeed changed with these technologies.

These changes are, in part, a result of the ways in which digital writing technologies have converged in recent years. Never before, for instance, have writers (of certain economic classes and at particular institutions) had at their fingertips the means to integrate text and graphics (and, for the tech-savvy, animation, audio, video, and other elements) and to publish and widely distribute digital products to virtual spaces. Home computers are quickly becoming as ubiquitous (and, in some homes, as multiple) as televisions; cell phones are writing devices as well as talking devices (not to mention cameras, video recorders, Internet service providers, and video game consoles, to name just a few of the options available on today's cell phones). Even household appliances are becoming part of what Bill Gates identified in 1999 as the "everyone, anytime, anywhere" convergence of digital technologies—technologies connected in robust ways to one another, allowing users to connect across time, place, space, device, and media. Companies and academic institutions are producing myriad integrated products that span multiple facets of and tasks related to our everyday lives. What becomes most clear within this mix is that writing, composing, communicating, and meaning-making take place across a variety of both human and technological networks.

The Context: In Workplaces

It is obviously not just in the home and with cell phones that digitized technologies are changing the means and contexts of how we use writing. In the workplace, collaborations increasingly occur across global networks, bringing both positive and negative effects for workers and the communities in which they work. Within corporations, issues of email etiquette, appropriate use of instant messaging, and larger issues of workflow across digitized spaces are topics of seminars and employee training programs. Blogging is becoming an accepted workplace practice, so much so that one 2004 headline in *Fortune* magazine proclaimed that "it's hard to manage if you don't blog" (Kirkpatrick, p. 46).

The authors of *Writing: A Ticket to Work . . . or a Ticket Out*, a report providing data from a survey of industry leaders representing companies employing almost 8 million workers, noted that two-thirds of employees in North America have some writing responsibility (College Board, 2004). Importantly, what the report also delivered was information as to what has both increased and enhanced this responsibility for writing. Digital tools and electronic spaces are changing the amount and types of writing workers produce. Email, for instance, has perhaps caused the biggest changes in the ways in which writers communicate on the job. Relatively unknown in the North American workplace in the early-to-mid 1980s, email is now the primary mode of communication; as the report states, "in this electronic age, writing skills are critical. Because of e-mail, more employees have to write more often" (College Board, p. 14). Along with ubiquitous email and Internet use comes increased surveillance of writing and reading practices as well. Software programs often include surveillance capabilities that allow employers to closely monitor and track an employee's Internet use—how much time an employee spends reading and sending email, what Web sites the employee visits, how much time is spent on various Web sites, and whether the domains visited are work-related or not. This sort of surveillance creates, in some senses, a digital panopticon, where the work and communication patterns of employees are visible and trackable.

One of the most interesting ways in which workplace writing has changed shape—and a trend that will certainly continue to grow over the coming years—relates to the database-driven spaces of the Web. With the current boom of Web- and database-delivered documents, writing digital content often means producing dynamic document chunks distributed via queried databases. As Michael Albers (2000) described dynamic documents: "Multiple writers at multiple locations contribute information to a document database which then, upon reader request, dynamically generates a unique document fulfilling current reader needs" (p. 191). Writers thus face a careful and difficult negotiation of technology and rhetorical contexts that allow for information to become discrete, called-up pieces that require verification to ensure that they are coherent, consistent, and polished before they are embedded deep within databases for retrieval by users.

The Context: In Education

In education, the increased adoption of course-management software by administrators and information technology staff (among others) who have

a vested interest in the use of such systems has led to an increased movement of class materials and discussions onto templates and into digital
archives. Educational institutions continue to push for and shape the development of online classes, programs, and degrees, raising questions about
issues of delivery, agency, and ownership of materials in digital space. More
and more institutions are going wireless, allowing instructional spaces to
extend beyond the networked classroom and into common/open spaces
on campuses, into libraries, and across outdoor spaces.

The communication methods of teachers and students have also shifted. In addition to email, many instructors have adopted office hours via
instant messaging programs. The ways in which students communicate
with each other have likewise changed; students use blogs to post and
share materials and document their project processes. Students IM and
text message one another for status checks, to collaborate, and to coordinate group meetings. Students not only are using, but will increasingly be
required to use portable devices such as PDAs and iPods (see, for instance,
the Duke iPod project launched in the fall of 2004).

The modes for communicating are also changing student composi-
tions. As explained in the Conference on College Composition and
Communication (2004) "Position Statement on Teaching, Learning, and
Assessing Writing in Digital Environments":

> Increasingly, classes and programs in writing require that students
> compose digitally. . . . The expression "composing digitally" can refer
> to a myriad of practices. In its simplest form, such writing can refer to
> a "mixed media" writing practice, the kind that occurs when students
> compose at a computer screen, using a word processor, so that they
> can submit the writing in print. . . . Digital composing can take many
> other forms as well. For example, such composing can mean partici-
> pating in an online discussion through a listserv or bulletin board. It
> can refer to creating compositions in presentation software. It can refer
> to participating in chat rooms or creating webpages. It can mean cre-
> ating a digital portfolio with audio and video files as well as scanned
> print writings. Most recently, it can mean composing on a class weblog
> or wiki. And more generally, as composers use digital technology to
> create new genres, we can expect the variety of digital compositions to
> continue proliferating. (n.p.)

Writing is no longer confined (if it ever was) to standard letter-sized paper,
set with default margins, default font sizes, default font faces, and default
paragraph spacing. Digital videos, soundscapes, and visual essays are

increasingly common in writing curricula, both in first-year writing cours-es and in advanced seminars. Often the push for increased digitization of curricula comes not from administrators eager to make their programs "cutting-edge," but from the students themselves who—as the work of such literacy scholars as Cynthia Selfe and Gail Hawisher (2004) and Jonathan Alexander and Will Banks (2004) have shown—come to school with rich, diverse experiences in digital composing. Teachers thus wrestle with nego-tiating the multimodal literacies many students bring to the classroom with the often more traditional needs and expectations of writing program and other institutional administrators. Compounding these complications is, of course, teacher access to training, and, more importantly, to the time required to learn new digital writing technologies and to map research proj-ects through which teachers can study digital writing processes.

The Context: Changing Processes and Products

As writers in educational and other contexts have and are discovering, the processes and products of digital writing are often quite different from paper-based processes and products, mainly because digitized technolo-gies shift the ways in which composing takes place and change the effects that writing has on writers and audiences. Writing for and reading on screens, for instance, is very different from writing for and reading on paper. And screens certainly vary—the screen of a cell phone is different from the screen of a PDA; the screen of a typical desktop computer mon-itor is different from the screen of an information kiosk. Text also changes shape when it becomes part of a floating, yet-to-be-anchored mix of media elements, when sound intersects it and when images revolve around it. Cell phones allow speakers to capture a moment and distribute it instant-ly, with or without the context of voice or text message. PDAs allow us to write field notes, capture audio, and document other modes of communi-cation to be saved and perhaps moved, most often into another digital context.

Further, because of the connectivity afforded by digital spaces, audi-ences and writers can be related to each other more interactively in time and space. The ways in which composers can find, download, and remix media elements; publish their work; and gather feedback dramatically change with the power and speed of networked space. These tools change the way we do research, the way we produce "texts," the ways we approach authority and originality, and the way we deliver our writing—in fact, the very ways we conceive of authorship and publication.

Connectivity allows writers to access and participate more seamlessly and instantaneously within digital spaces and to distribute writing to large and widely dispersed audiences. Not only do the abilities for and spaces of distribution and delivery shift, but they also grow significantly. For instance, the number of online forums devoted to popular video games such as *Halo 2* and the *Grand Theft Auto* series are stunning in their numbers, and even more stunning in terms of production. Taking *Halo 2* as an example, hundreds of threads and hundreds of thousands of posts fill the pages of the official sites and forums and the many fan-built and fan-maintained forums. This cultural and social move to online spaces is occurring in the political arena as well, as seen by Moveon.org's extensive participation in the 2004 U.S. presidential election and as seen by the connectivity and organization of global groups of demonstrators protesting the World Trade Organization.

The Context: Digital Writing

We use the term *digital writing* rather than computers and writing or digital compositions so as to make an explicit argument for the changing nature of what it means to write and to be a writer in a world increasingly influenced by digitized technologies (McKee & Porter, in press; WIDE Research Collective, 2005). Embedded in our understandings of digital writing are implicit transformations. First, a transformed composing environment—writing mediated by software and produced on handheld and desktop digital devices. Second, transformed methods of authorship and ownership that perhaps rely more on pastiche, appropriation, and copying and pasting than ever before. Third, and closely related to the second, transformed notions of collaboration in writing processes and authorship. Fourth, transformed modes of delivery—writing not only composed through but distributed primarily via networks. Fifth, transformed modes of interaction, commentary, and participation, facilitated within and across networks and interfaces. The tools themselves are revolutionary, but the more important, more significant revolution occurs in the possibilities created for connection and communication—framed by convergence, interactivity, and multimodal meaning-making (Grabill & Hicks, 2005; Porter, 2002). Interactivity allows readers to interact with and at times coauthor texts in dynamic ways across networked spaces. And, for many modes and spaces, writers create documents and craft texts that draw upon multiple media elements and that require them to attend to the affordances and limitations of the spaces in which they publish and distribute their work.

As many scholars in computers and writing have noted, this context presses up against larger issues of intellectual property, plagiarism, access, credibility of sources, and dissemination of information—all of which orbit around digital writing practices.

As we hope is clear by our discussion of emergent technologies and the various contexts of their use, computers and other digital devices are not just tools for writing and communication. Digital technologies and the people who use those technologies have changed the processes, products, and contexts for writing and the teaching of writing in dramatic ways—and, at this current cultural, historical, and intellectual moment, it is imperative that our research approaches, our methodologies, and our ethical understandings for researching adequately and appropriately address these changes in communication technologies.

DISCUSSIONS OF RESEARCH METHODOLOGIES AND ETHICS FOR DIGITAL WRITING RESEARCH

Seeking Research Guidance

Composition Studies has a long history of examining research practices. A solid body of work has emerged since Richard Braddock, Richard Lloyd-Jones, and Lowell Schoer's ground-breaking 1963 *Research in Written Composition*, including:

- *Research on Composing: Points of Departure* (Cooper & Odell, 1978)
- *New Essays in Technical and Scientific Communication* (Anderson, Brockmann, & Miller, 1983)
- *Teacher-Researcher: How to Study Writing in the Classroom* (Myers, 1985)
- *Research in Written Composition: New Directions for Teaching* (Hillocks, 1986)
- *The Making of Knowledge in Composition: Portrait of an Emerging Field* (North, 1987)
- *Composition Research: Empirical Designs* (Lauer & Asher, 1988)
- *Methods and Methodology in Composition Research* (Kirsch & Sullivan, 1992)
- *Into the Field: Sites of Composition Studies* (Gere, 1993)

- *The Practice of Theory: Teacher Research in Composition* (Ray, 1993)
- *Writing in the Workplace: New Research Perspectives* (Spilka, 1993)
- *Ethics and Representation in Qualitative Studies of Literacy* (Mortensen & Kirsch, 1996)
- *Feminist Empirical Research: Emerging Perspectives on Qualitative and Teacher Research* (Addison & McGee, 1999)

Running almost tandem with this work was the emergent and robustly developing research in computers and writing. In 1975 in *College Composition and Communication,* Ellen Nold published "Fear and Trembling: A Humanist Approaches the Computer," the first article addressing computers within composition. Four years later, in 1979, Hugh Burns defended the first dissertation on computers and writing, *Stimulating Rhetorical Invention in English Composition through Computer-Assisted Instruction.* In 1983, Kate Kiefer and Cynthia Selfe launched the journal *Computers and Composition.* From the rich base of research done in the 1980s on the use of word-processing software, we know a good deal about composers' writing processes (see Hawisher, 1986, 1988, 1989). We also have studies from later in the 1980s analyzing different writing software (e.g., Beserra, 1986; Bridwell-Bowles, 1989; Bump, 1990; Cross, 1990; Cullen, 1988; Deming, 1987; Hawisher, 1988; Hawisher & Fortune, 1989; McAllister & Louth, 1988). Since those benchmark events and studies into word-processing and the use of early software programs, hundreds of studies on writing and the teaching of writing with computerized technologies have been conducted and their results have been published in a wide variety of books and journals—online and in print. From those initial studies of the use and impact of word-processing software and hypertext programs such as Storyspace and Hypercard to more recent studies of weblogs, instant messaging, and writing with portable devices, the areas of and foci for our research continue to expand as digital technologies evolve.

Although scholars and researchers have been exploring composing processes for many years, and some studies have addressed how composing processes shift with emergent digital technologies, there has been—and still continues to be—little extended and published examination by compositionists of the methodologies used and ethical issues faced when studying writing with/in digital technologies. For works published prior to the mid-1980s, the omission can perhaps be understood by the fact that computers were still not widely used by individuals in home, workplace, and educational settings. (Other fields, however, were exploring the impact of computers upon research practices much earlier than composition, as shown, for example, by the 1965 collection Dell Hymes edited on *The Use of Computers in Anthropology*.) But there may be another reason for this omission—the assumption among composition scholars that research practices for collecting data, reporting research, and handling ethical issues when studying nondigitized writing and writing contexts can be applied just as easily to the study of digital writing and writing contexts. Although certainly some research practices carry over, especially the underlying principles of a particular research approach—what Egon Guba and Yvonna Lincoln (1994) called the paradigms shaping questions of ontology, epistemology, and methodology—not all do because of the impact of computerized technologies on sites of and approaches for research. For example, the underlying principles guiding a particular research approach—such as in feminist research, with its explicit examination of gender in social, political, and educational systems; the commitment to use research to empower participants; and the willingness to subject the researcher to the same lens of inquiry (see Addison & McGee, 1999; Harding, 1987; Kirsch, 1999; Sullivan, 1992)—may not change when a researcher moves from studying nondigitized writing contexts to researching digitized writing contexts. But what may change is how those methodologies are enacted and what constraints digital research spaces impose or create for researchers.

The scenarios with which we opened this chapter raise just some of the questions digital writing researchers may encounter when adapting or developing methodological approaches for researching digital writing and studying writers working with digital technologies and in digital contexts. As Gail Hawisher and Patricia Sullivan (1998) commented when describing their search for methodological guidance to conduct research on an all-women email discussion list:

> Our work had much in common with other feminist studies in composition . . . but they could offer little guidance in the area of online research. . . . Neither was the metadiscourse about method in composition studies extensive enough to guide our decisions about structuring an approach to study a new domain—an e-space. (p. 176)

The dilemma Hawisher and Sullivan faced—how to adapt methodologies used in print-based writing research for digital writing research—is one that we feel most researchers studying in/on digital spaces are encountering or will encounter. It is our hope that this collection will serve as a productive contribution to discussions of how research methodologies have been or could be adapted to best address the continually evolving questions we seek to answer and the knowledge we seek to develop when studying writing on and in digital spaces.

Emerging Discussions and Ongoing Questions

Contributors in this collection borrow from and build upon the existing work that frames digital writing contexts. One of the first events spurring a discussion of methodologies for studying digital writing and digital technologies was not an article about research methodologies per se but rather a report about the effects of the interface on student writing: Marcia Halio's 1990 article "Student Writing: Can the Machine Maim the Message?" Halio claimed that the graphical interface of the Macintosh computer caused students to write less-effective essays with lower readability levels than those of MS-DOS users. Her claim, based upon observations of students using the software Writer's Workbench, spurred a great deal of discussion about what constitutes valid method and methodology within the field. Writing in a special section of the journal *Computers and Composition,* John Slatin and 19 other composition scholars critiqued Halio's study because it was "so seriously flawed by methodological and interpretative errors" (n.p.). In particular, the group of scholars critiquing Halio's study pointed out that the difference she found in students' written expression could have been caused by a number of factors and that Halio needed to consider individual writers' contexts and prior experiences with computers more fully. As they explained:

> A more useful study would provide additional detail about the University of Delaware students, their backgrounds, and the attitudes toward writing they brought with them into the classroom—in other words, information about the factors influencing the students' classroom performance and, indeed, their initial choice of which sections to take [e.g., the PC or Mac section]. Halio completely ignores information crucial to evaluating student writing—information about the student's racial, ethnic, and class affiliations, about their gender, and (not least, in this context) about their previous experience with computers. (n.p.)

Slatin et al.'s critique points to how uses of technology cannot be studied as if writers and technology exist in isolation. Their call for greater contextualization of data mirrors the move in the late 1980s and early 1990s in the broader field of rhetoric and composition toward more studies of writing and writers in context.

For example, in her extensive review of studies in the 1980s of word-processing software and writers' composing processes, Gail Hawisher (1989) noted that "little research has been completed that examines how computers interact with the departmental English program or the larger school curriculum as a whole" (p. 61), and she urged researchers to take up such work. Influenced by the emerging social constructionist understandings of knowledge, meaning-making, and research, Andrea Herrmann (1990) argued that "research methods for investigating the impact of computers on writers should encompass the larger social perspectives of writers working within various discourse communities" (p. 124). In particular, she advocated the use of ethnographic methodologies. A few years later, Billie Wahlstrom (1994), drawing from feminist theories and methodologies, noted the overly enthusiastic claims prevalent in many of the computers and writing studies conducted in the 1980s and early 1990s. She called for a more critical, feminist approach to research because "bringing a feminist perspective to the technologies of the writing classroom prepares us to discover other discontinuities, gaps, and silences" (p. 185).

The call for more feminist and more critical approaches to computerized writing technologies was common in the early 1990s and still influences research discussions today. In their key 1991 article "The Rhetoric of Technology and the Electronic Writing Classroom," Gail Hawisher and Cynthia Selfe described how, as editors reviewing submissions for *Computers and Composition*, they were concerned by "the uncritical enthusiasm that frequently characterizes the reports of those of us who advocate and support electronic writing classes" (p. 56). They called for more studies from a critical, sociocultural perspective examining how computerized writing technologies reinscribe social and political inequities and biases. Writing several years later, Pamela Takayoshi (2000) wondered if perhaps the issue with much research in computers and writing "lies not in the overwhelming positive nature of the stories but in reliance on *stories* themselves" (p. 127). She argued for the application of feminist research methodologies to complicate "teacher-told, person-based narratives" (p. 128). Takayoshi advocated an approach that fostered deeper explorations and examinations of power within multiperspective and often ambiguous narratives.

In addition to calls for applying particular theoretical approaches, a few researchers have, however, provided more explicit discussions of methodological issues. For instance, Marcia Curtis and Elizabeth Klem (1992), in their chapter "The Virtual Context: Ethnography in the Computer-Equipped Classroom," overviewed ethnographic approaches and described an ethnographic study they conducted. Curtis and Klem speculated that ethnography, a methodology that calls for entering a research site open to a variety of possibilities and research directions, may be too overwhelming for teacher–ethnographers working in technological contexts because of the fast pace at which the technology changes. As they explained:

> For many of us, the newness and change we face every day in our own
> computer classrooms may, indeed, feel overwhelming. And in our ver-
> tigo, it is natural for us to desire to secure ourselves both in and
> through research: to enter inquiry armed with hypotheses and read to
> "test whether," rather than to suspend expectation and simply ask
> "how." (p. 169)

Despite the allure of more deductive approaches to "test whether," Curtis
and Klem concluded that it is important for researchers studying computerized writing classrooms to conduct inductive ethnographic studies so as
to understand more fully how computers impact writing and the teaching
of writing.

Scott DeWitt (1996), reacting to the dearth of empirical studies of
hypertext and to the plethora of theoretical discussions of the potentials for
hypertext (e.g., Bolter, 1991; Landow, 1992; Lanham, 1993), called for
more empirical research on the use of hypertext in the context of the composition classroom, focusing particularly on how students read and write
with various hypertext programs. Following up on this call, DeWitt and Kip
Strasma (1999) edited the collection *Contexts, Intertexts, and Hypertexts*,
where teacher–researchers reported on their experiences integrating
hypertext into composition curricula. This collection was one of the first to
gather computers and writing research studies centered on one topic.
However, the collection was focused most fully on reporting research
results and not upon presenting and interrogating methodological
approaches.

In *Opening Spaces: Critical Research Practices*, Patricia Sullivan and
James Porter (1997) provided one of the most extended discussions to date
of methodological and ethical approaches for computers and writing
research—one that is frequently cited by contributors to this collection.
Drawing from feminist and postmodern perspectives on research, Sullivan
and Porter sought "to legitimize the problematizing of method" (p. 58).
They called for a critical research praxis that recognizes the multiple and
shifting subjectivities of researchers and participants and that recognizes
the impossibility that any methodology or any technology could ever be
value-free. As they explained:

> For the study of writing technologies, we advocate a view of research
> as a set of critical and reflective practices (praxis) that are sensitive to
> the rhetorical situatedness of participants and technologies and that
> recognize themselves as a form of political and ethical action. (p. ix)

Key to this praxis is that researchers strive to pursue an ethical approach that empowers research participants and that acknowledges the various political, material, and ethical contexts shaping the research, including the technological contexts. Sullivan and Porter argued that computerized technology must be accounted for by researchers, not only in terms of how technology shapes *what* is studied, but also *how* such studies are enacted. In the last chapter of their book, "Enacting Critical Research Practices," they addressed these issues more fully, describing what they called the "tensions between the technologies and particular research situations" (p. 170). They noted how for researchers who started working in less computerized times, it can be difficult to move to researching in computerized contexts (an issue discussed by other researchers, such as Curtis & Klem, 1992). One example they provide is of a classroom ethnographer who, in face-to-face discussions, can tape record and retrieve all participants' responses and who can know that all participants are engaged in hearing the same words spoken, but, when the discussion moves online, does not know which students are reading what posts or even if students are involved in the discussion at all because they could be online doing other things. If a researcher moves to track more carefully what students and teachers are doing online through such data-collection methods as retrieving online transcripts or including keystroke captures and videotaping screens (the technology available in 1997), then the amount of data collected can be potentially overwhelming. Because of the complexity of researching in digitized spaces, Sullivan and Porter emphasized that researchers should "embrace working across methodological interfaces" (p. 187), pursuing multiple methodologies while continually engaging in critical, reflexive practices.

Written just after the World Wide Web launched live and as it was just beginning to become ubiquitous, Sullivan and Porter's (1997) text does not address Web-based research. Web-based research has, however, been discussed in more recent publications, particularly those in technical communication studies. Laura Gurak and Christine Silker (2002), for instance, overviewed some of the issues researchers in cyberspace should consider, including: obtaining permissions (or not); deciding if material is more like a textual transcript or more like a recorded conversation; deciding if material is public or private; determining if, where, and to what material the doctrine of fair use applies; using technology to "lurk" or disguise one's true self or to announce one's presence; and choosing to seek IRB approval (or not). Gurak and Silker also acknowledged that the Web is such a relatively new area of research that "technical communication scholars should begin a serious conversation about the methodological issues of conducting research in cyberspace" (p. 245). Gurak continued the conversation in an article co-authored with Ann Hill Duin (2004), where they examined the impact of the Internet and digital technologies on teaching and research in technical communication, focusing on an extended example of how to conduct surveys online. But not only are there methodological issues to consider when researching communication in online spaces, there are ethical issues as well, a point David Clark (2004) made in his chapter in the interdisciplinary collection *Readings in Virtual Research Ethics*. Clark described the ethical dilemmas he faced when conducting a research study of a community that met face-to-face and online. He noted how his Institutional Review Board had different expectations for his online research and his face-to-face research, and he explored the approaches he took for determining if online texts were public or private.

Further, technical communication researchers have conducted studies on computer-mediated communication, usability, user-centered design, and more. Research in this realm relates to, for instance, the usability of handheld device interfaces and the ways in which users can be involved in development and testing processes for digital tools (see, for instance, Mirel, 1987). Other studies address issues of access, analyzing digital spaces for their compliance with World Wide Web Consortium (W3C) and U.S. Section 508 guidelines. Technical communication researchers study programming (e.g., database design, object-oriented interfaces) for digital spaces, issues of information architecture, questions related to digital property management and copyright, and more. For instance, Laura Gurak and Mary Lay's (2002) collection *Research in Technical Communication* provides methodological discussions and explores considerations related to the application of various methodologies.

Gurak's other work focuses on rhetorics of science and technology, and most recently relates to Internet research. Her work on research methods and ethics includes a 2003 chapter on Internet studies in the 21st century, a 2002 co-authored chapter examining trust in CMC spaces (Bailey, Gurak, & Konstan), and a 1996 chapter exploring the research data culled from cybertexts. Clay Spinuzzi's research explores communication in workplaces, focusing on people's interactions with technology and various technological artifacts (see, especially, *Tracing Genres through Organizations: A Sociocultural Approach to Information Design*, 2002b). Spinuzzi's research has been influential in its findings, and he has published on research practices in technical communication (2002a, 2005a, 2005b).

Stephen Doheny-Farina's (1992) *Rhetoric, Innovation, Technology: Case Studies of Technical Communication in Technology Transfer* provides three scenarios that, together, present an argument that the movement from technologies to products is a communication process. The book includes case studies focused on technical communicators involved in the movements of information and technology products, emphasizing the rhetorical moves made. Although the book does not explicitly explore methodological issues, it is a helpful model for similar studies.

Further discussion of research of digital texts and contexts was reported by the IText Working Group (2001), which includes Doheny-Farina, Cheryl Geisler, Charles Bazerman, Laura Gurak, Christina Haas, Johndan Johnson-Eilola, David Kaufer, Andrea Lunsford, and Carolyn Miller. They suggested a research agenda for electronic texts, arguing that

> the foundations for research agendas concerned with IText have been laid in the confluence of research activity over the past 25 years concerning the creation and reception of text: in rhetorical theory, in activity theory, in literacy studies, in genre theory, in usability research, and in workplace writing. (p. 271)

These activities and theories led the authors to pose such questions as: "How might we design institutional situations, specific workplaces, and technologies that are more amenable to fluid work flow? Under what circumstance should we preserve old patterns?" and "How are ITexts used across virtual and face-to-face situations? What tools can we provide users for reusing texts in new social situations?" (p. 282). Although the IText Working Group does not provide specific suggestions for methods to address such questions, their report raises a crucial set of research questions and directions for scholars interested in writing in digital spaces.

As we hope this brief review shows, scholars in the computers and writing field have begun and are continuing to develop a tradition of questioning and examining the ethics and methodologies for conducting digital writing research. There are, however, still many questions to be answered and many areas to be explored or to be explored in more depth.

THE NEXT STEPS IN RESEARCH METHODOLOGIES AND ETHICS FOR DIGITAL WRITING RESEARCH

Overview of Chapters

In this collection, we seek to extend the conversations begun in these other works by addressing a range of questions that focus upon a diverse range of research approaches and contexts. In the first section of the book,

Researching Digital Communities: Issues of Review, Triangulation, and Ethical Reporting, the authors explore approaches for and difficulties encountered when researching digital communities and texts. Specifically, in "Digital Spaces, Online Environments, and Human Participant Research: Interfacing with Institutional Review Boards," Will Banks and Michelle Eble analyze how the regulations governing Institutional Review Boards (IRBs) do not often address the complexities digital writing researchers face. Extrapolating from Banks' interactions with his institution's IRB (where Eble is a board member) when he sought IRB approval for a study of gay youths' blogs, Banks and Eble provide a list of issues for digital researchers to consider when seeking IRB approval for online research. As Banks and Eble point out, IRBs address ethical issues from a more narrow regulatory function, and there are obviously many other issues researchers need to consider when working with digital communities, issues that some of the other chapters in this section present.

In "Through the Eyes of Researchers, Rhetors, and Audiences: Triangulation and the Study of Digital Rhetoric," Kevin DePew argues for the importance of soliciting and including online participants' perspectives in data collection and data analysis. Using triangulation as a lens, DePew examines several digital writing studies where the researchers (whom DePew interviewed) solicited and included participants' perspectives in their reports, and he argues for researchers to pursue *rhetorical triangulation*. But, as Michelle Sidler points out in the chapter that closes this section, sometimes it is not that researchers are triangulating with too little data, but rather with too much. In "Playing Scavenger and Gazer with Scientific Discourse: Opportunities and Ethics for Online Research," Sidler reflects on her research into scientists and scientific discourse online to explore two distinct roles that Web researchers may find themselves pursuing: *scavenger* of diverse types of texts and *gazer* on online discourse. She also discusses how the hypermediated speed and volume of online information gathering serves to advantage researchers as well as to present them with new ethical questions in relation to changing definitions of "public" knowledge and in relation to the texts and persons they study.

The issues raised in the first section are continued in the second, Researching Global Citizens and Transnational Institutions, which presents three chapters focusing on international and cross-cultural research. In "Ethos and Research Positionality in Studies of Virtual Communities," Filipp Sapienza analyzes researcher and participant relations when conducting participant–observer ethnographies of online communities. Drawing from his research experience in the transnational community Virtual Russia, Sapienza focuses upon and provides examples of three overlapping and interrelated roles researchers may be called on to assume: the role of technologist, the role of participant (insider), and the role of scholar.

From Sapienza's call to analyze researcher roles when conducting cross-cultural research, the section moves to Iswari Pandey's discussion of researcher–participant relations in studies of postnational subjects. In "Researching (with) the Postnational 'Other': Ethics, Methodologies, and Qualitative Studies of Digital Literacy," Pandey argues that because of the networked global connectivity of computerized technologies, digital researchers need to recognize a deterritorialized conception of communities, kinships, and identities. Pandey presents his research into the literacy practices of South Asian gamers to illustrate why a postnational ethic is needed in research. Beatrice Smith also examines methodological and ethical issues faced by researchers working in international settings that span both online and face-to-face environments in "Researching Hybrid Literacies: Methodological Explorations of 'Ethnography' and the Practices of the *Cybertariat*." Specifically, Smith provides a technofeminist analysis of ethnography as a space from which transnational computer-based work can be studied. Smith's chapter reminds us that research practices must be malleable to span the diverse social, cultural, and technological climate of information technology work in the 21st century.

To develop more detailed understandings of how individuals interact with computerized writing technologies (in a diverse array of contexts), the chapters in the next section, Researching the Activity of Writing: Time-use Diaries, Mobile Technologies, and Video Screen Capture, discuss the ways in which digital technologies impact activity-based research. These chapters move from the application of print-based data-collection devices to technological contexts, to the application of increasingly sophisticated mobile and multimedia technologies in research. The section opens with Bill Hart-Davidson's "Studying the Mediated Action of Composing with Time-use Diaries," in which he provides an overview of time-use diaries for print-based writing and how such diaries may be adapted for use by researchers of digital contexts. Joanne Addison, in "Mobile Technologies and a Phenomenology of Literacy," describes how the use of databank watches, like other mobile technologies, may be incorporated into an experience sampling method of research, one seeking to develop more phenomenological understandings of literacy and literate practices. The last chapter in this section, Cheryl Geisler and Shaun Slattery's "Capturing the Activity of Digital Writing: Using, Analyzing, and Supplementing Video Screen Capture" presents how video screen capture programs can be used to record the second-by-second interactions of a writer's computer display, enabling researchers to study more fully writing activity in process.

From methods and methodologies for studying the activities of writing, we move in the fourth section to considerations of Researching Digital Texts and Multimodal Spaces. In "Coding Digital Texts and Multimedia," Stuart Blythe notes that although many resources exist on sorting and classifying verbal and purely textual data, digital artifacts present new challenges because they are less stable than print artifacts, alter relations between creator and audience, and can incorporate multiple media. He reviews current methods and methodologies for coding print-based texts, and he discusses how to adapt these methods for the coding of digital texts. Susan Hilligoss and Sean Williams, in "Composition Meets Visual Communication: New Research Questions," overview research approaches for studying the visual. They deploy the notion of *citizen designer* to address a set of core questions that will help us to do the research and build the theory to best equip people for analyzing and producing texts in a digital–visual world.

Moving to the contextual, Julia Romberger—in her chapter "An Ecofeminist Methodology: Studying the Ecological Dimensions of the Digital Environment"—proposes adapting feminist and ecological approaches to the study of digital writing programs. Drawing from her extensive study of corporate writers working with Microsoft Word, she presents a heuristic that includes consideration of such issues as discourse community, exchanges, evolution, corporate culture, user, audience, and investigator context. The methodology Romberger describes is applicable to a wide variety of digital environments, including the World Wide Web, which is addressed more explicitly by the next two chapters in this section. Amy Kimme Hea, in "Riding the Wave: Articulating a Critical Methodology for Web Research Practice," argues for a critical, reflexive articulation methodology, one that adapts to the mutable nature and multiple characteristics of the Web. After providing a brief overview of articulation theory, she shows the usefulness of articulation theory for Web researchers by analyzing one particular Web site to demonstrate an analysis that considers the Web's multiple characteristics: the Web as a social space; the Web's mutable nature; the Web as information-gathering space and data disseminator; and the Web as aural, visual, and hypertextual space. We close this section with Janice McIntire-Strasburg's chapter, "Multimedia Research: Difficult Questions with Indefinite Answers," which examines the perils and possibilities related to producing and researching multimedia. Specifically, McIntire-Strasburg explores issues of privacy, fair use, and citation strategies, closing with suggestions for how researchers might best conduct ethical and thoughtful research on multimedia writing, and also become more active in current debates related to intellectual property issues.

The final section, Researching the Research Process and Research Reports, focuses on overarching issues that span numerous aspects of digital writing research. In "Whose Research Is It, Anyway? The Challenge of Deploying Feminist Methodology in Technological Spaces," Kris Blair and Christine Tulley examine several ideological and institutional constraints that hindered their collaborative work as feminist technorhetoricians. They argue for creating feminist technological communities that work to further feminist research and to create institutional and ideological change regarding what counts as acceptable research methodologies and research ethics, particularly in relation to student/faculty research collaborations.

The issue of collaboration is also examined by Joshua Burnett, Sally Chandler, and Jacklyn Lopez in "A Report from the Digital Contact Zone: Collaborative Research and the Hybridizing of Cultural Mindsets." In this report, they present on their collaborative research project focusing on insider and outsider perspectives in video game communities. They examine how Chandler (a faculty member) and Burnett and Lopez (undergraduate students) approach not only gaming but the research of gaming quite differently. Their work points to the importance of acknowledging the different understandings and uses of technological interfaces by research participants from different cultural backgrounds and how differences in understandings and use shape not only what is studied but how it is studied.

In addition to the ideological and institutional constraints shaping their research and research approaches, digital writing researchers also face technological and legal constraints, which are explored by Lory Hawkes in the next chapter, "Impact of Invasive Web Technologies on Digital Research." Hawkes examines three particular risks to researchers: the harvesting of personal information from researchers and their participants, the dangers of aggregate digital records, and the surveillance of the U.S. government now allowed by the Patriot Act (surveillance powers that may become even broader in the years to come). Hawkes suggests a number of steps researchers should take to protect themselves, their research, and their participants.

Considerations of online publication are the focus of the next chapter by Colleen Reilly and Doug Eyman. In "Multifaceted Methods for Multimodal Texts: Alternative Approaches to Citation Analysis for Electronic Sources," Reilly and Eyman argue that traditional methods for citation analysis do not work for electronic publications. Thus, scholars who publish in online journals or who produce other digital publications (Web sites, CD-roms, etc.) are not as easily able to make the case for the impact of their work to tenure and promotion committees. Reilly and Eyman propose alternative approaches to citation analysis that will help researchers publishing in or thinking of publishing in digital contexts.

In the final chapter of this section and of the collection, "Messy Contexts: Research as Rhetorical Practice," Rebecca Rickly focuses on required graduate research seminars, arguing that these seminars serve as the primary (and often the only) explicit discussion of research methodologies and ethics that graduate students receive. She notes how these courses often do not include discussions of research in digital contexts, and she argues for a rhetorical approach for presenting and analyzing research, one that includes consideration of the impact of technology upon the sites of research and the process of research.

The Need to Continue the Conversation

We hope this collection will serve as a valuable resource for the field, mapping some current negotiations about research methodologies, technologies, and ethical issues. Such maps and discussions are crucial as we as a field leave behind old technologies; remediate emergent technologies; explore new technologies; and shift our teaching, learning, writing, and research practices in tandem with and as appropriate to these technologies. Surely, just as technologies continually evolve, so too will our understandings of appropriate ethical and methodological practices. Yet, despite the diversity of issues and topics contributors provide in this collection, there are still many questions to be asked about researching in and with digital technologies. It is our hope as editors that this collection will serve to stimulate further discussion about both established *and* emerging methodological and ethical practices that shape not only what we study, but how we study it and how we present what we have learned. Engaging in these explicit discussions is essential for our work as researchers, scholars, and teachers.

PART ONE

Researching Digital Communities

Review, Triangulation, and Ethical Reporting

1

DIGITAL SPACES, ONLINE ENVIRONMENTS, AND HUMAN PARTICIPANT RESEARCH

INTERFACING WITH INSTITUTIONAL REVIEW BOARDS

William P. Banks

Michelle F. Eble

Institutional review boards (IRBs) do not often address—and are not nec-essarily historically situated to address—the complexities digital writing researchers face. Extrapolating from our experiences serving on and inter-acting with IRBs, in this chapter we first provide a brief history and back-ground for IRBs, then raise a set of complications and complexities seeded by digital writing research. We use as an example Will's current project on gay male blog authors; through this example, we hope to demonstrate the complexities of negotiations with IRBs. We conclude by pointing toward some specific issues that digital writing researchers must negotiate and strategies that such researchers may employ to influence how IRBs func-tion and regulate our research.

INTRODUCTION

Digital technologies provide researchers with a host of opportunities to con-duct research in online environments. Whereas researchers in other disciplines may use the Internet for its convenience and ease for facilitating research, researchers in computers and writing often find themselves actually conducting or wanting to conduct their research in/on/about the digital spaces themselves. One of the complexities in conducting research in digital spaces involves the federal regulations in place to protect human participants from potential risk.[1] Institutional review boards (IRBs) at universities, colleges, medical schools, and teaching hospitals must review all human participant research to ensure that those who choose to participate in research are protected from harm and that research is conducted in an ethical manner. We hope that most researchers would proceed with their research ethically even without these regulations; nevertheless, satisfying all the requirements as determined by the federal regulations and carried out by IRBs can be difficult when applied to digital research because these networked spaces did not exist when the federal regulations were first articulated.

The guidelines and requirements pertaining to human participant research, initially written to protect human participants in biomedical and behavioral research, likewise experience a problematic transfer when applied to the humanities and certain social sciences, particularly when applied to research conducted in and on digital spaces and online environments. Further, researchers must negotiate and interact with IRBs whose members may not have experience with research conducted in online environments and whose members understand and interpret the federal regulations only as applied to biomedical and behavioral research. Although we remain hopeful that the Office of Human Research Protections (OHRP), a division of the U.S. Department of Health and Human Services (DHHS), will provide guidance to IRBs in the area of Internet research, to date they have not. As a result, most IRBs are handling these cases individually as they begin to advise researchers on conducting digital research. Many IRBs now include a statement about Internet research in their policies and procedures.[2] We have learned, however, that as researchers in an emerging discipline we must understand and educate ourselves about this process rather than waiting for IRBs to educate themselves about humanities and social science research. If more of us take the opportunity to become IRB members, then we can begin to affect change at that level as well. But for now, compliance remains a central issue, and we believe we can comply with and educate IRBs at the same time while also considering the methodologies and issues involved when using human participants in our digital research.

We recognize, of course, that scholars in composition and rhetoric have been increasingly concerned with IRB oversight and compliance and have, likewise, advocated that scholars work more closely with their local IRBs to ensure more ethical research practices. Much of that work has been done by Paul Anderson. In an early collection on ethics in research practices, for example, Anderson (1996) traced a history of IRB policy, discussed its applications to composition researchers, and highlighted areas of ambiguity for composition and rhetoric researchers. He also argued in the pages of *College Composition and Communication (CCC)* that researchers in composition and rhetoric should become more thoughtful about the relationships with their human participants in their research projects (Anderson, 1998). Likewise, in a *CCC* Interchange essay, Heidi McKee (2003) took up the advocacy that Anderson began and offered some pointed critiques of the IRB process as it applies to qualitative and participant–observer research. Although Anderson and McKee have steered us toward thinking more carefully about our research practices, our field hasn't dealt sufficiently with the issues that emerge at the intersections of digital research, ethics, and IRBs. In fact, many scholars resist IRBs, and the general discourse surrounding IRBs is often negative.

In this chapter, we attempt to address this gap and these challenges by presenting readers with some of the issues and possible solutions involved when interfacing with IRBs to conduct research in digital spaces. Awareness and understanding of the federal requirements and regulations allows researchers to present their research projects to IRBs consistent with these criteria and thus become even better advocates for their projects. Central to our chapter is a discussion of Will's current project on gay male blog authors and suggestions based on his experience interfacing with IRBs. Through the example of the gay bloggers, this chapter seeks to demonstrate the complexities of negotiations with IRBs in an actual project that can be challenging and illustrative for others working on assumed "controversial" and/or unfamiliar research. We conclude by charting some particular issues that current and emerging digital research spaces present to humanities scholars engaged in social science–inflected research projects as a heuristic for thinking through such research.

HISTORY OF THE IRB: A STUDY IN NEGOTIATION

Despite often valid critiques of IRB procedures, researchers nevertheless must deal with IRB oversight. Because most universities require faculty, students, and staff who conduct research (as defined by the federal government) to submit their research procedures to the board for review, we might be better served by using the IRB process as a heuristic for our research projects instead of merely complaining about current policy. After all, IRBs are charged with a noble and just mission: to prevent perhaps well-intentioned researchers from carrying out the sort of horrific experiments that have stained our research histories, experiments like the infamous testing that was part of the Tuskegee Syphilis Study. The history and events that led to review by IRBs point out some of the complications in getting research approved through the IRB process and may illustrate why IRBs are not merely over-reacting or being excessively zealous in the oversight of human participant research.

The current federal regulations administered by OHRP and carried out by individual IRBs on campuses throughout the nation have gone through their own set of negotiations as new situations have come under the purview of the federal government. The history of IRBs and the federal regulations that govern them illustrate the rhetorical contexts of various commissions, committees, and professional groups that have addressed new situations within research contexts to protect human participants. The National Institutes of Health (NIH) *Policy for the Protection of Human Subjects*, published in 1966, created IRBs as part of the formal system for ethical review to protect human research subjects. IRBs are required to follow two documents: the *Code of Federal Regulations, Title 45, Part 46: Protection of Human Subjects*, which outlines the various regulations pertaining to protection of human beings in research projects, and the *Belmont Report*, which summarizes the ethical principles that should be considered while conducting research (Amdur & Bankert, 2002).

These documents have been in existence only since the late 1970s; however, discussion of a code of research ethics and informed consent began with the Nuremburg Code of 1947, which resulted from the war tribunals that tried WWII physicians who conducted unethical "medical experiments" on "non-German nationals, including Jews and 'asocial persons'" ("Nuremberg Code," 2002, p. 490) held in concentration camps as well as "non-Jewish Germans: tuberculosis or handicapped children; mentally ill or retarded adults; the institutionalized elderly; the unemployed poor; prostitutes; alcoholics" (Götz, Chroust, & Pross, 1994, p. xiii). The judges outlined a list of 10 principles, known as the Nuremberg Code of 1947, which should be considered in human participant research. Sadly, this code had no immediate effect on the protection of human participants. Even with the Nuremburg Code and the Declaration of Helsinki, which stated "ethical principles to provide guidance to physicians and other participants in medical research involving human subjects," questionable and unethical research was still conducted during the 1950s and 1960s (World Medical Association Declaration, 2002, p. 499). Research that involved the injection of live cancer cells into hospital patients and the Tuskegee Syphilis Study that observed the progress of syphilis in African-American patients who were not treated for the disease are just two examples of the type of problematic medical research that continued to occur even with the new regulations in place. Other studies of deception in psychological and social science research finally forced the issue into the public and eventually the governmental sphere (Faden & Beauchamp, 1986). Public outrage led to the creation of the Commission for the Protection of Human Subjects of Biomedical and Behavioral Research. The federal guidelines proposed by this Commission in 1974 were codified based on the two earlier codes that focused on medical research. This Commission also published the *Belmont Report* (1979), which officially codified the principles of research ethics that should be followed in any sort of human participant research.

The *Belmont Report* outlines and discusses three research principles researchers must account for in their projects—respect for persons, beneficence, and autonomy—and suggested applications for considering these principles in research involving human participants. Informed consent of participants, assessment of risk/benefit ratios, and fair selection of subjects represent three common measures to help ensure that researchers consider these principles. Consequently, IRBs exist to provide necessary oversight to guarantee that these ethical principles have been carefully considered by researchers. The *Code of Federal Regulations: Title 45, Part 46* (45 CFR 46), approved and implemented in 1974, was later adopted as the Common Rule in 1991 when 16 federal agencies adopted the regulations in 45 CFR 46 as the common *Federal Policy for the Protection of Human Subjects*. As a result, all research funded by a federal agency requires IRB review. Since 1991, all federally funded universities have been required to review *all* human participant research to verify that the research projects are either exempt from oversight or conducted in such a way as not to violate the stipulations mandated in the federal regulations. (See Appendix for additional resources.)

RESEARCH CONSIDERATIONS AND THE IRB

IRBs have become concerned with digital spaces precisely because research in these environments may involve interaction with the human beings who create Web sites, discussion forums, blogs, email, Instant

Messages, chat conversations, and so forth. As researchers of such spaces, then, we have to be aware of these regulations and the problematic transfer from "real life" to the "virtual" realm. Accounting for the regulations as we present our research projects to IRBs (through filling out the necessary forms) can be an important heuristic as evidenced in the digital research project discussed in the next section. In this section, we review some of the chief issues researchers need to consider and procedures they need to follow as they engage in different projects.

Researchers whose projects involve human participants are required to file for IRB review if their projects fit the regulatory definition of "research" as defined by the federal government:

> Research means a systematic investigation, including research development, testing and evaluation, designed to develop or contribute to generalizable knowledge. (45 CFR 46.102 [d])

The key to the definition is whether or not researchers plan for their research to contribute to "generalizable knowledge," which may be interpreted in a wide variety of ways. Generalizable knowledge is not defined or interpreted in the regulations, and OHRP provides no additional guidance on how IRBs might understand the phrase. The American Historical Association assumes "the term does not simply mean knowledge that lends itself to generalizations, which characterizes every form of scholarly inquiry and human communication" but rather refers to "principles of development or nature that have predictive value and can be applied to future outcomes" (Joint AHA-OAH Policy, 2004, n.p.). The AHA has lobbied the OHRP to rule that oral history projects, for example, do not contribute to "generalizable knowledge" and thus are not considered research as defined by the federal regulations and need not undergo IRB review. Nevertheless, we recommend that researchers always check with their own IRBs about the research they would like to conduct.

The second pertinent definition involves the phrase *human subjects*: "*Human subject* means a living individual about whom an investigator (whether professional or student) conducting research obtains (1) data through intervention or interaction with the individual, or (2) identifiable private information" (45 CFR 46.102 [f]). Researchers who intend to conduct a rhetorical analysis of a Web site or blog, for instance, may not need IRB approval as such a project may not meet the requirements of "research as defined by the federal regulations," and may not actually involve interaction with "human subjects." But what if the researcher decides to comment (even anonymously) on a blog? Although this is a normal and common practice for blog readers, this possibly creates an "interaction" with the writer and may move the blogger's status from *author* of a published text to *research participant* (human subject). Is this merely an issue of "participant observation" that the researcher should account for in her report, or does it constitute problematic "interaction" or "intervention?" At the same time, if the researcher "interacts" with the blog author to let him know that the researcher plans to use a particular post (or the whole blog) in a research article—merely as an instance of professional courtesy—the researcher is not necessarily "interacting" with the author in a way that would make this blogger a *research participant*. Ultimately, any research that includes human participants—even as authors—should be reviewed by the IRB so as to ensure the research and researcher(s) are protected from possible unwitting violations of the federal regulations and from possible lawsuits. Knowing the definitions and concepts of IRB oversight only improves the researcher's ability to articulate and advocate for her project; it does not give individual researchers the power to ignore IRB oversight.

Researchers should also familiarize themselves with the three types of review: exempt, expedited, and full. *Exempt review* applies to those studies that constitute minimal risk for the human subjects and fall into a particular category defined in the federal regulations. Research that is not exempt but still represents minimal risk can be reviewed by the chair of the IRB through *expedited review*. *Full review* applies to research that offers more than minimal risk and must be reviewed by all members of the IRB and voted on during a meeting. Projects that are exempt are usually declared so by IRB administrators or the IRB chair. Knowledge of the levels of review is one of the first spaces for rhetorical agency in the process, because knowledge of the levels as well as awareness of the federal regulations can aid researchers in their communication with their IRBs. At our university, researchers can email or call the IRB office to find out what level of review their research may require. In many cases, knowing what level and whether particular research might qualify as exempt will dictate which forms researchers will fill out. The forms help IRBs account for the criteria they must consider when reviewing research. Knowing this criteria and how to articulate one's research in its terms is one productive step toward successfully negotiating with IRBs.

Although most humanities research, including research in digital spaces, will be declared exempt or will be approved through expedited review, ethical researchers should always seek IRB guidance. If the researcher should prove wrong about possible violations and the research project is questioned, the researcher's university could face litigious retribution and the loss of federal funding. Likewise, any data collected in a research project that has not been reviewed and/or approved by an IRB could be confiscated and lost to the investigator, meaning the researcher cannot ever use that data in any presentations or publications.

For research to be approved by the IRB, it must be determined that certain requirements have been met and documented. For nonexempt research, IRBs make certain that the researcher minimizes risk to participants and provides a reasonable benefit-to-risk ratio. IRBs likewise require equitable participant selection, which brings up issues of recruiting participants online, because we still have a digital divide (Monroe, 2004; Selfe, 1999b). Research on digital writing environments represents a significantly different situation for IRBs to contemplate. Consider the marked differences for other research projects. A research project on the psychological effects of the fear response in humans, for example, can occur outside a digital environment even if it might be easier to recruit participants online. If such a project came before an IRB and had recruited participants only online, the IRB might respond that the selection of research participants is not equitable because a significant portion of possible participants do not have online access. Further, participants must participate in the informed consent process, and where appropriate, data collected is monitored to minimize risk and confidentiality is maintained to protect participants from risks. If any of the participants fall into vulnerable populations—children, prisoners, pregnant women, and/or other disadvantaged populations—safeguards are included to protect these individuals (45 CFR 46.111[a.1-7] [b]).

Along with the complexity of inviting research participation online is protecting data collected online. Given the data traces possible in online communication, digital researchers must be vigilant in ensuring that names and other identifying information are not kept in easily compromised digital spaces, such as Web servers. For example, although surveys collected on the campus quad may create no real trace back to participants, online surveys, which may transmit IP addresses of participants or other identifiable material, require a different level of scrutiny for IRBs. As such, digital researchers must be prepared to create research methods that account for such problematic data-collection methods.

As researchers who have interacted with different IRBs, we cannot stress enough how important it is for researchers to be aware of the make-up of their local IRBs—especially the chair or chair's representative, as this person can approve expedited research or help researchers know how to revise their applications to better articulate data-collection methods or methods for protecting human participants. Researchers should also know the federal regulations and account for the criteria being used by the IRB to assess how their research will be conducted to minimize risks to human participants. The questions asked in the forms researchers fill out address these criteria, and IRBs document that researchers have considered the criteria in the process of reviewing and approving research projects.

DIGITAL RESEARCH AND THE COMPLICATIONS OF IRB OVERSIGHT: A BRIEF CASE STUDY

So far, we have discussed some of the history and evolution of the Institutional Review Board, noting (we hope) how beneficial this board can be in preventing egregious violations of personal rights and health that have unfortunately been too much a part of research history. We also hope to have persuaded readers that the IRB process can be helpful in thinking through digital writing research projects. In this section, we turn briefly to one particular case of digital research that has engaged in human participant research and thus has needed (and sought) IRB approval. This project represents vexing issues for researchers, even as it demonstrates how interfacing with IRBs can be a productive, heuristic experience in shaping a research project.

Traditionally, humanities research has dealt with written or spoken texts rather than the individuals who write or speak them, and it still does for the most part. Consider, for example, the Toni Morrison scholar. Although she may do extensive work on Morrison's writings, most likely no one would see this as human participant research. Even if the scholar interviewed Morrison, it would be highly unlikely that the scholar would seek— or be asked to seek—IRB approval for what clearly involves interacting with a research subject. However, with the creation of digital technologies and online environments, scholars have begun conducting research within and about these digital contexts in which writing and communication occur. What changes if we substitute the research subject from Toni Morrison and her writings to a 22-year-old blog author and his posts published online? For many, the IRB issues suddenly seem less clear. Why? Is it because Morrison's fame changes her position in the research? Is it that we do not offer the blog author the same authority or agency that we offer Morrison? Or do we? IRBs have yet to articulate such distinctions.

Beyond research on individuals in cyberspaces, digital environments themselves represent interesting places. They are often referred to as "virtual," suggesting "not real," yet we can't always agree about the implications of this real-ness, nor are we clear about what constitutes public and/or private space in these environments (see Ess & Association of Internet Researchers [AoIR], 2002; Frankel & Siang, 1999). If we then try adapting federal regulations to an environment that didn't exist when these regulations were written, we have a frustrated group of diverse people trying to articulate approaches and negotiate regulations. We hope the following example demonstrates why interfacing with IRBs, rather than throwing our hands up at the far too prevalent inconsistencies and confusions, is so important to our field.

Recently, Will began an extended research project in which he observed the rhetorical practices of young (age 18–25) gay male blog authors.[3] As he began reading blogs, he quickly realized that many young gay males were exhibiting a particularly postmodern self in these spaces, a sort of persona significantly aided by the blogging technologies available to tech-savvy writers.[4] Initially, Will was content to study only the blogs themselves as rhetorical artifacts, but as these observations continued, Will realized that these writers were engaging in some rather complex literacy practices that ranged from serving as "literacy sponsors" (Brandt, 2001) to other young gay males, to interrogating pat assumptions about language, the construction of self, and the intersections of visual and verbal rhetorics to produce complex arguments about a wide variety of subjects. It became increasingly clear to Will that he would need to interview or survey these writers. But would this work require IRB oversight? Did his initial observations and readings of the blogs require oversight? Was he an ethnographer of this space? Could he be a participant–observer and comment on the blogs? This research project, violating most of the boundaries Will had learned about research in graduate school, began to frustrate him as he sought advice about what did and didn't require IRB oversight. Further, LGBT people are often considered part of a high-risk research group because of homophobia and the possibility for harm should the LGBT people be outed in the process of the research. These are the considerations that this section of our chapter explores: how this project came to be, how Will worked on/with/through IRB procedures, and, ultimately, how this project itself demonstrates the vast chasm between what we know and what we still need to articulate vis-à-vis digital research and IRB oversight.

Harm, Privacy, and "Public" Documents

Undoubtedly, the ways in which research and published scholarship might "harm" participants is a central concern to IRBs and should also be to researchers. What constitutes *harm*, however, is rather complex, particularly when our understandings of what is and isn't harmful reflect our subject positions and our interpretations of the impact of our research and actions. It is, likewise, rather easy to rationalize our research to ourselves, constructing projects in our minds as constituting virtually no harm to participants. Medical IRBs often see no problem with research practices that might cause great alarm in those of us in the humanities or social sciences, and research practices that those in gender and sexuality studies might take for granted can seem bizarre and vexing to those who do not conduct such research. Therefore, researchers must go to great lengths to articulate possible risks to human participants and must justify their interactions with participants in ways that will reduce these risks as much as possible. Ultimately, filling out an IRB protocol document is a rhetorical activity, one that requires the writer to know ahead of time the problems he/she might encounter and to explain how those possible risks are minimized by effective research methods and methodologies.

With the research project on gay male bloggers, Will initially saw no possible harm that would come to his research subjects if they participated in the project, as they were (a) at a significant distance from him and thus he could not influence them or control their behavior in any obvious way, nor could he compel their participation; (b) they were already out about their sexualities on their blogs; (c) many included their real names and pictures, and thus his research would not reveal any information about them that was not already public knowledge to anyone reading the blogs; and (d) because the online performances were ultimately not bound to biological bodies/realities, they may have been highly fictionalized performances that would be relatively untraceable to lived human subjects in such a way as to create physical or emotional harm. After consulting with Michelle, who sits on both the medical and the social sciences/humanities IRBs at his school, as well as the Research Ethics Oversight Committee, Will realized that there were possible harms that he hadn't taken into consideration, specifically:

- Would Will's published research bring attention to these bloggers by those who would not normally know about them and thus possibly create a conflict where none had existed prior to the reporting of the research in print or at conferences?
- Was the fact that these blogs were publicly available to any Web surfer significant evidence that the blogs were public and thus not private or privileged communication?

- Or does the Web constitute such a huge and populous *space* that individuals can go virtually unnoticed, as individuals in real life can, until called out by a published research report?

Further, Will also had to consider whether or not these blogs were considered *by their writers* to be private or public documents. As a training[5] module related to Internet research notes, many groups on the Internet *perceive* a particular level of privacy for their writing. For example, victims of sexual abuse may perceive their online interaction (perhaps under pseudonyms) in discussion forums to be private even though they can be found through a search engine. A significant factor in the contributions of those individuals to the forums involves their assumptions that others are not (mis)using their writings for reasons beyond self-help and/or recovery from sexual abuse. If these individuals consider their conversations on various forums as private, the researcher must also respect that privacy.[6] The blogs that Will was researching, however, *seemed* quite different to him as reader and researcher; most of these blogs had built-in commenting features as part of the blogging software, and other blogs used second-party plug-ins to enable reader comments when the blogging software itself attempted to prevent reader comments. For these writers, there was an explicit desire to develop a reading public, one that would both consume the blogs as readers and respond to their content as reviewers and commenters.[7] To Will, it seemed unlikely that any of these bloggers, who also maintained links to other gay male blogs on their own blogs, would see these blogs as anything other than public. Further solidifying this idea was the fact that so many of the writers in his research sample had responded on their blogs to harassing emails and comments they had received from homophobic readers. In fact, responding to such harassment by folding it into the center of the blog suggested to Will that the bloggers welcomed a diverse reading public, if only to engage in a counterstrike tactic.

More problematic, however, was that Will couldn't know whether the bloggers perceived themselves as writing in public or private spaces *without actually interacting with them through interviews or surveys*, interactions that would certainly require IRB approval. This decision—to move beyond just reading and critiquing the rhetorical elements of the public blogs and to interact with the bloggers in an ethnographic move to understand the blogs and bloggers through their own words—meant that Will would be affecting the research group through interaction and would need IRB approval to insure the safety and privacy of his research subjects. Because these participants were a group only online, meaning that bloggers don't necessarily exist *as such* apart from their online publications, the traditional notions of ethnography and interview may not apply.[8] IRBs would be especially concerned about issues of privacy and confidentiality, so an email interview would be a problem, as email creates a trace and copies of emails reside on servers over which neither the researcher nor the research participant have control. Although it is unlikely that these texts would ever be recovered or used by anyone other than the researcher, the possibility remains, made even more troubling in the current political climate and considering the rights the Patriot Act allows law-enforcement officials.

Will decided to use an online survey tool; PhpESP, the survey tool, is an open-source, server-resident piece of software that Will could create and customize his surveys with. Built into the software platform is a welcome page that contextualizes the research and allows the researcher to supply an email address for participants to use should they choose to opt out of the project at some later date or should they wish to contact the researcher with questions, as well as a confirmation page that allows the researcher to remind participants about the goals and purposes of the research. Most important, however, is that the server-resident software allows for encryption so that data submitted by respondents is not sent back and forth across the Internet in packets that anyone could easily intercept and decode. Such encryption allows a greater degree of privacy and confidentiality to research participants, key concerns of IRBs in an age of digital research practices. Likewise, because Will is one of the server administrators, he can delete the survey and results from the server at the completion of the project, further minimizing the risk that this data would be hacked by those outside the research project. These options for online technologies have been important for Will because he couldn't assume that the IRB would know them, even if they might engage in digital research. Will needed to be able to articulate the security measures in a rhetorical move to assuage the IRB's possible concerns. In this way, digital researchers in our field may already be well-suited to make arguments to their local IRBs in ways that would help these boards better understand research in digital environments.

Protection and Reflection in Online Research

At this stage in the research project, many issues have become more clear in Will's mind. For one, digital space itself is highly complex, and different spaces may require different kinds of IRB oversight. Returning to the issue of participant privacy and confidentiality, a key concern is whether it is possible to do text-based research on blogs and maintain any degree of privacy for the writer. For Will to publish his scholarship and quote from any of the bloggers would ultimately make it simple to find said blogger; a reader could select a unique phrase from the quote and enter it into a search engine. What purpose would it then serve to create pseudonyms for the bloggers to demonstrate what we might traditionally call "Respect for Persons?" Because a researcher collecting data from students in a first-year composition course may be the only one with access to students' papers, quoting, using pseudonyms, and changing other minor data (locations, proper names, etc.) might truly function to protect the student–participant from being harmed. But when those same students publish their texts online as part of the course requirement, the same level of protection for the individual research subject can no longer be guaranteed. Will's project doesn't involve students, and that's a major difference, but it does suggest how quickly our traditional, face-to-face research, when moved into a digital space, can create some problems for the researcher. Will has realized that for the initial phase of his research project—the rhetorical analysis of the blogs themselves—participants cannot really be protected in any traditional sense; to do so would mean preventing the scholarship from being published at all. In the second phase, however—surveys and interviews with the bloggers—the bloggers might say something under the auspices of confidentiality, something they might *never* publish on their blogs. This part of the project clearly requires both IRB oversight and ethical research practices on Will's part (e.g., not linking any survey responses to the rhetorical analyses of the blog texts that might link survey participants to particular bloggers). Digital researchers must be ever vigilant in their reflective practice, thinking through possible harms to participants but also selecting carefully among the research methods that *are* and *are not* possible in digital environments.

CHARTING THE COMPLEXITY OF DIGITAL RESEARCH

We believe that Will's project demonstrates some of the complexities that researchers in digital environments must face. Before we conclude, we'd like briefly to mention three different Web-publishing environments and how hard it can be for researchers and IRBs alike to determine whether investigations of these spaces will require IRB oversight to further articulate the complexities of interfacing digital research with local IRBs. Although the casual Web surfer may make few, if any, distinctions among Web pages, blogs, and content management systems (CMS), those of us conducting research in these spaces quickly realize how different these genres are, so much so that we will not seek to answer the questions we raise here; instead, we encourage readers to think through these problems as they may apply to their own research projects.

Consider the traditional, single- or multi-authored static Web page. How does the researcher decide if using Web pages as part of a project constitutes human participant research? After all, we've cited an article from an online newspaper in this chapter, as well as the online version of the federal regulations. Did we need permission? Informed consent from the authors? How are these Web pages significantly different from Web pages constructed by a 23-year-old car enthusiast? A counter-cultural music group that promotes its creative work online? If we're researching the masculinist rhetorics of car fanaticism, would we need IRB approval to use that first hypothetical Web site? At what point does our use of the site involve interaction or intervention? Would it ever? These questions may seem obvious to some, but we can assure readers that they have not been adequately answered by IRBs around the country in ways that can guide researchers; as a result, we might find ourselves having to articulate a position on these types of research sites to garner IRB approval for our research.

Ultimately, digital researchers might ask, "What does it mean to *publish* in cyberspace?" Does a 13-year-old's blog constitute a *published* document that's available without going through the IRB process? Would the researcher have needed IRB approval to interview Toni Morrison? What about the 22-year-old blogger? Because most blogs invite comments from readers, can a researcher join that throng without violation of federal and IRB policies? And at what point does reading blogs with a researcher's eye turn into "systematic investigation" as defined by the federal regulations? Because most blogs contain long lists of similar blogs read by the blogger, would following these links to gain additional research participants violate the principle of equitable subject selection? Or is it simply the most obvious method for subject selection in an amorphous realm like cyberspace? If a Web page or a blog can be considered a "publication," the investigation of which doesn't constitute human participant research necessarily, what do we do with CMS platforms? If these portals are part of an educational setting and the investigation involves "instructional strategies" or "comparison among instructional techniques" (45 CFR 46.101.b1), the Common Rule would suggest that such research may be exempt from considering all the criteria for full IRB review. A common current use for CMS platforms outside the classroom, however, involves open-source initiatives like Drupal and other types of software available at Web sites such as Sourceforge and OpenCMS, where software developers and users can collaborate on the further development of software and its documentation. If a researcher in technical and professional communication were to investigate the collaborative process for creating documentation on an open-source software project, would the researcher need to get IRB approval and informed consent from all the users involved with the CMS? At what point would interaction or intervention play a role in this research project? Could a researcher start the project merely observing and then seek IRB approval if he/she decided to interview or survey the collaborators?

CONCLUSION

We purposely do not attempt to answer the questions posed in this short chapter, but offer them to suggest to readers how complicated the process of protecting human participants can be for researchers and for IRBs. Because IRB members may have no extensive research experience in electronic environments, researchers in and of these spaces simply cannot leave all issues of oversight to IRBs to interpret—that significant rhetorical and epistemological work must be carried out as well by the researchers who understand these venues best.

Ultimately, we have recognized through our work with IRBs that the federal regulations, though exacting at times in their detail, are only guidelines that are invariably interpreted at different institutions in different ways. Although this fact may frustrate some researchers who would enjoy the presumed stability of more universal interpretations, we recognize as rhetorical scholars that these differences can provide us with productive spaces to argue carefully for our research, which has the benefit of helping us to understand our work in ways that will help us write our research reports for publication and distribution to larger audiences both within and outside our field. Because "risk" is a subjective concept, and because federal regulations require that benefits of the research should at least equal or offset possible risks, much social sciences research has already been in a problematic space vis-à-vis these regulations, as a large percentage of our research, even with human subjects, doesn't demonstrate clear benefits to research participants or to the larger society in ways that those in medical and laboratory sciences might understand the concept of benefit. Research in the humanities and social sciences already requires us to think rhetorically about risk and benefit and to make arguments about the social value of our work. As we move increasingly into digital environments for research, these arguments will become increasingly important to refine and articulate. We hope that researchers in our discipline will make the ethical choice to engage with their IRBs rather than to avoid or resist them, or to assume that their research doesn't necessarily require IRB approval or oversight. It seems clear to us that we and our research participants all stand to benefit by making this process an open and collaborative one.

NOTES

1. Throughout this chapter, we use the term *participant* instead of the biomedical and regulatory term *subject* and prefer the use of human participant research rather than human subject research for a whole host of reasons that would take another chapter to delineate. In short, however, we refer to people who take part in digital writing research as participants rather than as subjects because we believe that doing so allows these participants a certain degree of agency that is stripped away by making them subjects. In our minds, whereas subjects are acted upon, often unwittingly, participants make choices about their participation.

2. University of Texas at Austin, University of Chicago, University of Georgia, and the Research Foundation at the City University of New York all include guidelines for conducting research using the Internet or studying the Internet (see the Appendix for a list of URLs for these Web sites). Additionally, Duke University offered continuing education to its investigators in 2005, addressing using the Internet as a research tool and studying Internet communications.

3. Will had originally intended to include bloggers aged 15–17 because he had been impressed with the amount of non-school-based writing this group was doing on blogs. The Child Online Privacy Protection Act of 1998 protects the online privacy of children under the age of 13, and came about due to the number of Web sites asking children for personal information and identification (e.g., birth date, street address). As for children above the age of 13, federal regulations require that researchers obtain parental consent when studying minors, a requirement made more complicated for online research, especially research about sexual orientation. Will realized that if bloggers were not out to their parents, requiring parental consent might cause harm in its potential to out them. Although Will could have tried to make a case to the IRB that parental consent should be waived in this case, the concern for underage participants discouraged Will from including this group in his early research.

4. Similar observations have been made recently in Jonathan Alexander's (2005) book *Digital Youth: Emerging Literacies and the World Wide Web*. See also Alexander's (2002) earlier essay, "Ravers on the Web: Resistance, Multidimensionality, and Writing (about) Youth Cultures."

5. The Institutional Review Board of East Carolina University now requires all researchers whose projects involve human subjects to complete a series of online modules titled "Course in the Protection of Human Research Subjects." These modules are provided by CITI (http://www.citiprogram.org), which stands for Collaborative IRB Training Initiative, an initiative co-founded in March 2000 by Karen Hansen and Paul Braunschweiger as part of a joint venture between the University of Miami and the Fred Hutchinson Cancer Research Center.

6. Some forums have even gone so far as to post disclaimers on their gateway pages instructing researchers to "stay out"; participants on these sites have decided that observational research doesn't keep with the purpose of the forum and, in fact, inhibits honest discussion. These individuals see their Web-based discussion forums as private, thus compelling researchers to likewise respect their position.

7. Daniel Weintraub (2004) recognized that the blogosphere has "evolve[ed] into a self-correcting culture. Anyone making a claim is expected to link to supporting evidence, when available. And when readers have a voice, if not a blog of their own, a blogger who strays from the facts will be slapped down in a nanosecond, either by his own ideological allies or the opposition. Besides, bloggers know that the road to big readership lies in being reliable and credible" (n.p.). This "self-correcting" function that has emerged in blogs suggests that readers aren't merely saying "yes" to content, but are actively critiquing content, refining what's online through rhetorical moves similar to academic peer review.

8. See, for example, Katie Ward's (1999) "Cyber-Ethnography and the Emergence of the Virtually New Community," which argues for a reconfiguring of traditional notions of ethnography to account for the particularities of network-based *space*. The fact that traditional research methods are being modified for digital research further complicates applications for IRB approval. In such spaces, even the methods that qualitatively oriented IRBs have fought for, as valid research practices, are changing and thus must be rearticulated and redefended as valid methods.

APPENDIX

Institutional Review Boards (with Internet Research Guidance)

University of Texas at Austin
http://www.utexas.edu/research/rsc/humanresearch/special_top
ics/internet_research.php

University of Chicago
http://humansubjects.uchicago.edu/sbsirb/manual/special_rese
arch.shtml

University of Georgia
http://www.ovpr.uga.edu/hso/guidelist.html#section13

Research Foundation City University New York (CUNY)
http://www.rfcuny.org/ResCompliance/inetresearch.html

Federal Regulations

*The Code of Federal Regulations, Title 45 Public Welfare, Part 46
Protection of Human Subjects*. Department of Health and Human
Services, Office of Human Research Protections. November 13,
1991
http://www.hhs.gov/ohrp/humansubjects/guidance/45cfr46.htm

Office for Human Research Protections (OHRP)
http://www.hhs.gov/ohrp/

Basic Protections for Human Subjects
http://www.hhs.gov/ohrp/humansubjects/guidance/basics.htm

Office for Human Research Protections (OHRP). (2004). *Human
Subject Regulations Decision Charts*.
http://www.hhs.gov/ohrp/humansubjects/guidance/decision-
charts.htm

§46.111 Criteria for IRB approval of research.
http://www.hhs.gov/ohrp/humansubjects/guidance/45cfr46.htm
#46.111

§46.101(b) Exempt Categories
http://www.hhs.gov/ohrp/humansubjects/guidance/45cfr46.htm
#46.101

Expedited Categories
http://www.hhs.gov/ohrp/humansubjects/guidance/expedited98.htm

Institutional Review Board Resources

Protecting Human Research Subjects: Institutional Review Board Guidebook
http://www.hhs.gov/ohrp/irb/irb_guidebook.htm

Office of Human Research Protection (OHRP) Policy Guidance
http://www.hhs.gov/ohrp/policy/index.html

Association for the Accreditation of Human Research Protection Programs, Inc. (AAHRPP)
http://www.aahrpp.org/

The Institutional Review Board—Discussion and News Forum (IRB Forum)
http://www.irbforum.org/

IRB: Ethics & Human Research
http://www.thehastingscenter.org/publications/irb/irb.asp

The Hastings Center Report
http://www.thehastingscenter.org/publications/hcr/hcr.asp

Research Ethics/Historical Documents

Nuremberg Code. (1949)
http://www.hhs.gov/ohrp/references/nurcode.htm

World Medical Association. (1964, amended 2004). *Declaration of Helsinki.*
http://www.wma.net/e/policy/b3.htm

Belmont Report: Ethical Principles and Guidelines for the Protection of Human Subjects of Research. The National Commission for the Protection of Human Subjects of Biomedical and Behavioral Research. (1979, April 18).
http://www.hhs.gov/ohrp/humansubjects/guidance/belmont.htm

Informed Consent Document Resources

§46.116 General requirements for informed consent
http://www.hhs.gov/ohrp/humansubjects/guidance/45cfr46.htm#46.110

§46.117 Documentation of informed consent
http://www.hhs.gov/ohrp/humansubjects/guidance/45cfr46.htm#46.110

Informed Consent Tips
http://www.hhs.gov/ohrp/humansubjects/guidance/ictips.htm

Informed Consent Checklist—Basic and Additional Elements
http://www.hhs.gov/ohrp/humansubjects/assurance/consentckls.htm

2

THROUGH THE EYES OF RESEARCHERS, RHETORS, AND AUDIENCES

TRIANGULATING DATA FROM THE DIGITAL WRITING SITUATION

Kevin Eric DePew

In this chapter, I explore the ways in which adopting a single research method may limit some digital writing studies and propose a triangulation method as a potential remedy. By reviewing four published articles and presenting information gained from interviews with the article authors, I argue why triangulation is an appropriate methodological process for studying multiple features of a rhetorical situation.

INTRODUCTION

Digital rhetoricians, in their pursuit to understand how computer technologies shape the art and the resulting artifacts of communication, have been examining the technologically influenced strategies that rhetors generate and adopt to produce discourse. Historically, research on digital writing

49

focused on the programs composition scholars were creating to facilitate the writing process (Hawisher, LeBlanc, Moran, & Selfe, 1996). More recently, research has shifted to the Internet, where we not only generate discourse *with* the technology (e.g., using word-processing and spreadsheet programs), we communicate *through* the technology (e.g., communicating synchronously and asynchronously with various audience through email, instant messaging, and courseware). As the site of communication shifts, we have had to modify how we understand, and therefore study, the rhetorical situation. Online digital writing technologies have prompted us to ask (and sometimes revisit) questions about the discourse we produce, such as how writing technologies have not only shaped the texts that we compose, but the way we understand discourse, locate the rhetor's subjectivity, and evaluate the relevance of the rhetor to the text.

To answer these questions and others, digital rhetoricians have researched the effects of online sites in many contexts—the academy, the workplace, and the public sphere. For example, many researchers—such as Kristine Blair (1998), Marilyn Cooper (1999), Cooper and Cynthia Selfe (1990), Lester Faigley (1992), Donna LeCourt (1998), Alison Regan (1993), Susan Romano (1993, 1999), and Albert Rouzie (2001)—have studied how students interact with each other using computer-mediated communication (CMC) technologies that facilitate synchronous and/or asynchronous discussion. Others—such as Lynn Cherney (1995), Julian Dibbell (1998), Beth Kolko (1995), Lisa Nakamura (2002), and Lindsey Van Gelder (1996)—have investigated how rhetors communicate through CMC technologies in socially regulated spaces, such as email lists and MOOs. In these studies, researchers theorize and retheorize how digital writers respond to specific CMC situations. Methodologically, all of these researchers analyze textual transcripts of the rhetorical situation as a primary method to support their arguments. Although some of these researchers supplement these analyses with anecdotal narratives, most researchers primarily use transcripts to illustrate how digital writers rhetorically respond to and within various online spaces. Some scholars pull transcripts from their own experiences, such as classes taught or virtual experiences they had; others draw their evidence from archives or the scholarship that others have written, such as Cooper's re-analysis of Faigley's class transcripts. This data thus facilitates how the researcher understands rhetorical interaction in online spaces.

Among these studies of online communication forums are, however, notable exceptions in which the researchers supplemented the textual analysis with other data, including interviews with participants. Many researchers have asked students to write about their online experiences; they then supplemented their readings of the digital texts with the students' commentary. The reporters, Dibbell (1998) and Van Gelder (1996), distin-guish themselves from other scholars by using journalistic strategies to paint a detailed picture of two infamous online experiences—respectively, a cybersexual violation and a false online persona that became disturbingly real. To describe how certain digital writers behaved indecently and unethi-cally, these researchers tried to supplement samples of the actual online event with the rhetors' intentions and the audiences' responses. Heidi McKee's (2002) study of the rhetoric of flaming in an online discussion forum constructed a more detailed picture of the rhetorical situation; McKee conducted in-depth interviews with the most vocal participants (as rhetors and as audience) in a cross-cultural exchange on race and affirmative action. As I will illustrate in more detail later, the data collected from these inter-views challenged commonly accepted truths held by digital writing scholars.

The Web has also provided rhetoricians sensory-rich sites for studying digital combinations of verbal, visual, and aural discourse. We have arguably seen Web authors adopting more asynchronous CMC strategies to facilitate interactivity between the audience, the site, and other sites. Like CMC studies, textual analysis has been the dominant research method for studying Web pages. Studies such as Hawisher and Sullivan's (1999) exam-ination of women's visual representation in commercial, institutional, and personal Web pages; Stephen Knadler's (2001) analysis of female, African-American students' Web pages; Tara McPherson's (2000) investigation of neo-confederate sites; Greg Wickliff and Kathi Yancey's (2001) review of the problems honor students had grasping visual arguments; and Anne Wysocki's study (2001) of the infrastructure adopted for two museum's vir-tual tours focus on various features—texts, visuals, links, design—of stu-dent-authored and professional digital texts. Yet in all these studies, despite the different research foci, the rhetoric of the various sites are presented and analyzed from one perspective—the scholars' interpretations of the texts. Just as with discussion forums, however, researchers are employing other approaches to analyzing Web sites. Scott DeWitt (1997) varied from this methodological strategy, as I will detail later, by asking LGBT Web authors to give him a tour of their Web sites. In another variation of textu-al analysis, Pamela Takayoshi collaborated with two young women Web users to explain how a young, female audience responds to the Web, espe-cially grrrl sites (Takayoshi, Huot, & Huot, 1998). Similarly, LeCourt and Luann Barnes (1999) worked together to analyze the strategies Barnes adopted in creating a feminist Web space and the exigencies she negotiat-ed in constructing a multivocal text. In another thread of digital study, pro-fessional writing scholars understand that the composition of a successful digital text requires front-end usability research with the target audience.

Whereas some scholars, such as Clay Spinuzzi (2001), analyze an artifact's effectiveness (how well it was usability tested prior to release) after it has been produced, other scholars, such as Jeffrey Grabill (2003), examine the process of doing this research.

The studies I have mentioned—as well as many other studies about digital writing practices—not only contribute to our understanding of the rhetorical impact of digital writing technologies, but they also help to further the conversation about this impact by setting methodological precedent for future inquiries. Yet, as my brief review demonstrates, this precedent is predominantly exemplified by textual analysis methods, or studies in which digital rhetoric researchers closely read or theoretically interpret tangible and/or digital texts generated with/through digital writing technologies (e.g., emails, transcripts from synchronous discussions, Web pages).[1] From these textual readings we experience the connections that scholars are making between rhetoric and technology, literacy, and power (i.e., how social hierarchies get disrupted and perpetuated by digital writing). But, as rhetoricians, we should be examining more features of the communicative situation rather than merely an artifact it produces. What else can we learn about digital rhetoric when we also study the rhetor's intentions? The audiences' response to the text? How local contexts shape this interaction?

I believe that incorporating these other features of the rhetorical situation into methodological design—as DeWitt (1997), LeCourt and Barnes (1999), McKee (2002), Takayoshi et al. (1999), and others have—can enrich research findings. In essence, I am advocating that digital rhetoric researchers adopt strategies framed by the communicative triangle—the rhetor, the audience, the digital text or discourse, and the contexts. By designing such methodological strategies, researchers insert communicative participants into the process, which gives researchers the opportunity to see both the complex nature of the research site and apertures in the field's tropes.

In this chapter, I explain triangulation strategies and argue why this methodological process is conducive and desirable for studying multiple features of a rhetorical situation, especially for digital writing studies. To illustrate this argument, I will closely analyze four digital writing studies, as they were reported in respective articles: McKee (2002), Rouzie (2001), DeWitt (1997), and Grabill (2003). My reading of these texts is discussed alongside each researcher's explanation of her or his own methodological processes, as described in personal interviews. The implications of these multiperspective analyses will, I believe, support my concluding recommendations for studying digital writing.

THROUGH A TRIANGULAR LENS

Triangulation, or the use of multiple methods, is a plan of action that will raise sociologists above the personalistic biases that form single methodologies. (Denzin, 1970, p. 300)

Researchers—in spite of their field of study, methodological training, or personal background—can never be completely unbiased or objective. Factors such as field of study, methodological training, and personal background shape the decisions researchers make as they design their data collection methods and analyze the results. Sociologist Norman Denzin (1970) acknowledged that "competing definitions, attitudes, and personal values" get advanced within fields of study (p. 300). Although researchers are disciplinarily bound to adopt certain research methods, their approach to these methods may not always coincide. Therefore, Denzin believed that researchers should be more aware of their methodological decisions and make their methodologies more public.

Recognizing the inherent bias of the research process, Denzin (1970) advanced triangulation methods as a strategy for reducing deficiencies caused by personal biases. Moreover, triangulation's "complex process of playing each method off against the other," Denzin asserted, "maximizes the validity of the field efforts" (p. 310). In describing the practice of triangulation, Denzin specifically advocated a triangulation of method, investigator, theory, and data. My discussion of triangulation will focus on data and methods triangulation; data triangulation involves sampling data from multiple sources, which helps the researcher examine multiple aspects of the rhetorical situation. Closely related to data triangulation, method triangulation guides the researcher to use various methods (e.g., archival, interviews, observations, usability tests) to collect data from various sources. Denzin supported this approach because "the flaws of one method are often the strengths of another, and by combining methods, observers can achieve the best of each, while overcoming their unique deficiencies" (p. 308).

Data Triangulation and Avoidance of the God-trick

As exemplified in the pages of *Research in the Teaching of English*, Janice Lauer and William Asher's (1988) *Composition Research: Empirical Designs*, and other scholarship, rhetoric and composition researchers have worked from the methodological traditions of other disciplines and have incorporated triangulation strategies within their methodological designs. Yet, due to the nature of the field's inquiries, textual analysis has been one of the methodological cornerstones—as one of many methods used or as the only method used. In the latter case, though, researchers risk perpetuating their own personal biases: They propose an argument; support it with a theoretical framework; analyze a text or several texts through this theoretical lens; and validate their proposition. Many such studies have been enlightening and have made significant contributions to rhetorical studies and composition studies, yet they are limited by the researcher's intention to "support a proposition," rather than the pursuit to "deliberately seek negative evidence" (Denzin, 1970, p. 307). By only examining the textual artifact, researchers potentially leave aspects of the text unaddressed, such as the outcome the rhetor intended the document to create—such as a change in the audience's actions or beliefs or a good grade. Questions that remain unanswered include how the target audience (or secondary audiences) responded to the text; whether the rhetor successfully generated the intended outcomes, and why or why not; whether the text was particularly well written for the context in which it was written; and how the document might fair in a different context. These questions, combined with the questions that researchers ask of the text, complete the rhetorical triangle and allow researchers, to the best of their ability, to reconstruct how agents negotiate a rhetorical situation. Textual analysis limits researchers to informed speculation—a strategy that resonates with Donna Haraway's (1991b) notion of the "god-trick." Haraway explained the god-trick as the "only position from which objectivity could not possibly be practiced and honored." It "is the standpoint of the master, the Man, the One God, whose Eye produces, appropriates, and orders all of indifference. . . . The god-trick is self-identical, and we have mistaken that for creativity knowledge, omniscience even" (p. 193). The god-trick is proclaiming the text's *word*. The god-trick is speaking for the rhetor and the audience. The god-trick is not necessarily an act of maliciousness, manipulation, but often is the absence of methodological self-awareness.

METHOD TRIANGULATION AND AVOIDANCE OF SINGLE-VOICEDNESS

To determine how conducive triangulation methods are for digital rhetoric projects, researchers must first decide whether the online discourse under study is a textual artifact or a site of human interaction. The researcher needs to address this to position the technology within the study; different answers will evoke different methodological approaches. If researchers believe that networked computer technologies have fulfilled their potential as a virtual commons, then researchers will want to understand how this space is being used. Therefore, they may choose to adopt ethnographic approaches and observe how individuals use the space, interact in the space, and perceive the space. Even when individual researchers have theoretically defined the online discourse, they will want to acknowledge that those who produce and read this discourse may not theoretically position it the same way. If we do not bring the individuals who inhabit and visit[2] these spaces into the epistemological process, researchers become the single voice that re-creates the space for their academic peers, who may be left ignorant about how actual users articulate this space.

Julian Kilker and Sharon Kleinman (1997) argued that research of online spaces needs to be self-aware and also needs to be more cognizant of the rhetors' and audiences' contexts outside of the digital space. Drawing parallels between anthropology's methodological history and the methodological evolution of online research, Kilker and Kleinman concluded that anthropologists' post–World War II stance of critically examining their own theories and practices resonates with the shift online researchers have made to consider how "their studies can help understand and improve online interaction" (p. 75). To present an exemplary model of this research, Kilker and Kleinman praised Shelley Correll's (1995) study of a virtual lesbian café, in which Correll examined online behaviors, conducted interviews by telephone and email, and arranged a face-to-face meeting at a lesbian bar where she was able to observe real-life interactions. Kilker and Kleinman appreciated that Correll "triangulated temporally and spatially to explore the complexity of her research context" (p. 77). Moreover, they advocated using triangulation because "[m]any articles about online environments focus solely on these environments as if they were the only ones relevant to their participants' lives, which they are not, of course" (p. 79). As we know from studies about digital writing, it is impossible to separate the "meat" (the users and their lived experiences) from the "machine" (the software programs and the digitally written texts).

The methodological position of rhetorical triangulation that I advocate ideologically resonates with postcritical and feminist methodologies, such as those Sullivan and James Porter (1997), Takayoshi (2000), and Hawisher and Selfe (2002) proposed for digital rhetoric projects. In the tradition of Denzin's (1970) and Haraway's (1991) methodological theories, these scholars believe in a critical self-awareness that actively resists the god-trick. They encourage researchers to acknowledge their position in relationship to the project and to invite their participants into the epistemological process. Digital rhetoric researchers who adopt postcritical methods, as articulated by Sullivan and Porter (1997), understand that "all methodology is rhetorical, an explicit or implicit theory of human relations which guides the operation of methods" (p. 11). There is nothing natural about the researcher's position; researchers are responsible for justifying the positions that they create for themselves. As a result, the researcher becomes a visible point—a point of connection—for the overlapping communicative and methodological triangles. In addition to answering research questions, Sullivan and Porter believe that researchers are also responsible to the individuals they study. To counter the hierarchy that allows the researcher to control the participant (i.e., being the subject of the gaze, being represented in the write-up), Sullivan and Porter believe that "the researcher is required to take an ethical action to empower the researched" (p. 140). By including the agents into data collection and giving them a voice in the reporting of the data (i.e., asking them to comment on the argument, allowing them to negotiate how they are represented), researchers take a more ethical, and potentially more empowering position. Hawisher and Selfe (2002) echoed this sentiment by arguing that researchers should not usurp participants' agency; instead, researchers should feature participants' voices "in every part of the project to keep their words, and their phrasing, intact, their grammatical structures and their distinctive words choices, even the oral markers of their speech intact whenever we reported on the project" (n.p.).[3]

In the rest of this chapter, I use the methodological framework described above to closely examine CMC and Web-based studies. I draw upon my conversation with researchers about their respective projects to support and challenge these analyses, which will illustrate the exigencies and the possibilities of triangulation methods.

RESEARCH IN PRACTICE:
FOUR DIGITAL WRITING STUDIES

As Denzin (1970) argued, most researchers will not approach the same site using the same methods. Researchers are influenced, among many factors, by the immediate context, their methodological training, and a personal philosophical approach to the objects and individuals they study. Therefore, the studies that I have chosen to analyze—by McKee (2002), Rouzie (2001), DeWitt (1997), and Grabill (2003)[4]—illustrate the various decisions four digital rhetoric researchers have made to examine specific sites. In addition to describing and analyzing the studies that the researchers did, as reported in the respective publications, I have also included the perspectives on the decisions they made in designing their respective studies—evidence collected from interviews with the researchers.[5] The questions I asked were about their research strategies and how they negotiated reporting their methodology in their respective publications.

McKee: "(Mis)Communication in an Online Interracial Discussion Forum"

In "'YOUR VIEWS SHOW YOUR TRUE IGNORANCE!!!': (Mis)Communication in an Online Interracial Discussion Forum," Heidi McKee (2002) reported on her study of the rhetoric of flaming in an online discussion by students participating in the Intercollegiate E-Democracy Project (IEDP), "a teaching and learning collaborative that enables students from across the country to discuss via asynchronous posts social and political issues in the United States" (p. 412). McKee described how reading students' participation in the IEDP forums and examining the transcripts of the various forums raised questions not only about the barriers in online interracial conversations about race and racism but also about what flaming looks like and how it functions. To address these questions, McKee chose to focus on an Affirmative Action/Diversity/Multicultural forum because it generated the most incidents of flaming (23 of 185 posts), and because so little research had been conducted about online interracial communication. She further chose to interview participants because she wanted to learn how the students' reading and responding to posts—the alternation between rhetor and audience— were "influenced in large part by the cultural and societal contexts shaping each individual's experience" (p. 414). Therefore, McKee contacted the 13 most vocal participants in the forum, including those participants who composed the posts that appeared to be flames and the recipients of these posts; 11 of these students gave her permission to quote their posts and 5 (who lived within 200 miles of her) agreed to face-to-face interviews.

By asking these five students to describe their roles as rhetor and audience, McKee learned that our field's understanding of flaming did not match the rhetors' practices. Most of the black participants described their flame-like posts as emphatic rebuttals to posts from white participants that they found offensive and ignorant (such as "Some of us worked hard to be where we are, while others got in because of Affirmative Action"). The black participants believed that their contributions were educating the white participants, in spite of tone and presentation. Although the "ignorant" posts appeared as "proper," "nonconfrontational," and "academic" in style and presentation, the black audience clearly found them inflammatory and, as McKee described, "rhetorically destructive" (p. 413).

As she began analyzing specific threads from the forum for a seminar paper, McKee realized that she could not reasonably answer some of her research questions about flaming without learning about the forum participants' input: "I soon realized . . . that given the importance of authorial intent and audience reception any categorization of flaming was primarily speculative on my part and that I needed to interview participants in the thread to hear their perspectives" (personal interview). Recognizing the limitations of her own position (i.e., white, instructor, graduate student immersed in academic discourse), McKee realized that the students' perspective would cast a different light on her interpretations. Despite the prevalence of text-based analyses in similar studies, McKee chose not to do a critical discourse analysis of the forum transcript. Instead, she adopted a participant-centered methodology and positioned the student participants as the primary hermeneutical lens to address her research questions.

Although McKee portrays herself as a fortunate researcher in the published article (i.e., the students' generosity to participate at various levels, the participants' good recall a semester later), she revealed in our discussion the constraints she negotiated throughout this research process: time (i.e., collecting and compiling thread data, driving to and from face-to-face interviews, other graduate student responsibilities), finances (i.e., mailing hundreds of consent forms with postage-paid envelopes on a graduate student budget), and getting Institutional Review Board approval at 14 different campuses. Despite these methodological trials, McKee demonstrated resolve using this approach: "I was (and am for future projects) committed to such an approach, particularly because I do not think my research questions could be answered with a text-based approach (or at least not answered as thoroughly)" (personal interview).

By methodologically attempting to recreate the rhetorical situation, the students' insights prevented her from simply using their posts to reify the fields' theories about online discourse. Had McKee simply done a textual analysis, she may have concluded the black students were flaming the white students. Instead, McKee—recognizing how cultural and societal contexts inform the discursive practices of the online forum—learned from the student participants about the unacknowledged complexity of one of digital rhetoric's well-established tropes. Because she positioned the student participants at the center of her inquiry, the triangulation methods that she used, especially those that invited the participants into the epistemological process, were most appropriate for rhetorically analyzing the posts and threads in the forum.

Even with the work that she did, McKee explained in the article and in her interview that she questions whether she could have done more to represent the rhetorical situation more accurately and fairly. For example, she could have interviewed the forum participants who posted once and left. She could have also expanded the influencing discursive features by studying how the forum discussion was shaped by the different classroom contexts. (Unfortunately, it was logistically impossible for her to include classroom observations as part of her data collection because of the dispersed national network of classrooms involved in the forum.) In addition to methodological approaches, McKee acknowledged potential problems in her reporting of research and how she tried to avoid overgeneralizing from one participant's experiences and perspectives. McKee's critiques of her methods provide insight that other digital rhetoric researchers can use to design their own studies.

Rouzie: "Conversations and Carrying-on"

Albert Rouzie, on the other hand, focused his inquiry more on the discourse, rather than the individuals who produced it. Critiquing the split produced between work and play, Rouzie studied the importance of serio-ludic discourse, or "discourse that combines or alternates between serious and playful purposes" (p. 255)—a playful discourse that encourages students to adopt the roles they will assume in the future without the responsibilities inherent in these roles. He believed that incorporating CMC discussion into the composition classroom prepares students to compose serio-ludic discourse. In "Conversations and Carrying-on: Play, Conflict, and Serio-ludic Discourse in Synchronous Computer Conferencing" (2001), Rouzie argued:

> Play in synchronous conferencing can be significant in potentiating positive, critical discourse in the college composition classroom through its ability to foment and mediate conflicts that bring out political and personal concerns, negotiate power relations among participants and encourage reformation of subject positions through internally persuasive discourse that can result from carnivalesque discussions. (p. 254)

To support his argument, Rouzie examined the transcripts of online teacher-prompted student discussions. He specifically analyzed the transcripts from John Slatin's 1994 composition course, which he retrieved from the archiving system of the computer lab classrooms. Students who signed up for these courses completed the University of Texas's Computer Writing Research Lab's permission forms that gave researchers access to and permission to study their online work. Rouzie, however, noted that under current IRB regulation, these forms would not be permissible because there was no option for the students to decline participation and stay in the class; yet these consent forms were originally drafted under the assumption that all the online discourse from classes taught in the networked labs were part of the public domain.

Using theories that privilege the audience's hermeneutical experience as his foundation, Rouzie chose to apply a methodological approach known as purposeful sampling to the transcripts. With this approach, the researcher analyzes "information-rich cases" that "illuminate the research questions" (p. 260). Using purposeful sampling, the researcher "inductively develops ideas based on what she finds significant in the data and then develops a theoretical model that is used to identify examples for more detailed analysis" (p. 260). In practice, Rouzie gave the transcripts a cursory examination to determine what discourse displayed serio-ludic qualities, including being characterized by double-edged and metacognitive features. He then applied these heuristics to the specific data sample. Rouzie found justification for his single interpretation; as he explained:

> even more detailed in-depth observations cannot guarantee absolutely reliable interpretation for two reasons. One is that there is no archimedean point from which to establish the one true interpretation of dialogue. The second is that dialogue, as hermeneutical scholars perceive it, is polysemic, containing multiple levels of often contradictory meanings. (p. 295)

According to Rouzie, a researcher cannot recreate a *true* representation of the rhetorical situation; researchers can neither find the perfect position to see the true situation, nor can they ignore that the data they collect evokes multiple interpretations.

The discussions generated by Slatin's students that Rouzie analyzed demonstrated how CMC interfaces promotes serio-ludic discourse that "provokes and relieves tensions" and "consolidate[s] divisions and diffuse[s] them" (p. 284). In the discussions, students who made thoughtful contributions were met by aggressive comments (e.g., "can you get any less specific"; "You tell [him]"; "i had a lynching in mind"; pp. 262–263). Yet, these aggressive students followed their original comments with discourse meant to diffuse the situation. Immediately following the lynching comment, the aggressive student offered a contrite "just kidding."

Rouzie, in our conversations, further explained his methodological design. He emphasized that he chose not to do an ethnographic study because of the logistical difficulty he would have interviewing participants from the eight sections he studied for the overall project (see Rouzie, 2005). But more importantly, he made this decision because his research objective was to identify instances of serio-ludic discourse in the students' discussions. Although an ethnographic methodological model may have provided him with a fuller context of the discussions, he believed that including the participant element may have skewed the outcomes:

> A risk of interviewing might have been leading students to my own conclusions about their play. I also was less concerned with how students might judge their own playfulness than in presenting their playfulness as significant to my audience of instructors and scholars. Since part of the purpose of the study was to present play as a significant social and intellectual element of the writing classroom, I decided that looking at eight sections rather than one would better accomplish that. (personal interview)

Unlike McKee, Rouzie's research does not align with the triangulation strategies that I propose, nor the postcritical/feminist methodologies these strategies can support. One could even assert that Rouzie performs the methodological "god-trick" by explaining the students' rhetorical decisions for them. Yet, he contended that students' understandings of their own texts are also interpretations that are no more or less legitimate than the researchers'. McKee's and Rouzie's respective methodological design exemplify how different inquiries and different theoretical foundations prompt different methodological designs.

DeWitt: "Out There on the Web"

Web pages can be a difficult site of study, due to the complexity of gaining access to Web authors and the various audiences of the sites themselves. Yet, as Scott Lloyd DeWitt (1997) argued in his article, "Out There on the Web: Pedagogy and Identity in Face of Opposition," the task is not methodologically impossible and the results can be gratifying and enlightening. As an instructor who both incorporated Web authoring into his pedagogy and tried to help LGBT students use their writing to come out, DeWitt wanted to know how the extremely public nature of Web writing changed how individuals used discourse to be out. He chose to address this question by learning how LGBT Web authors were already composing their online identities. To develop a pool of participants, he placed an advertisement in a Columbus, Ohio, area LGBT publication that he was associated with in which he invited willing Web authors to give him a virtual tour of their Web sites. Despite some logistical problems regarding the research site location, DeWitt was taken on six virtual tours.

In essence, DeWitt's inquiry focused primarily on the writer and the writer's authorial intentions (or lack thereof). As the Web authors showed him nodes of their Web sites, DeWitt asked them a series of questions about the ethos they sought to compose: What considerations about being "out" did you make when you created your Web site? Are you easily identifiable in person on your Web site (name, address, photo, community visibility, etc.)? From these tours, we learn that three of the six participants are out on the Web. The other three chose not to come out on the Web because they feared virtual confrontation or professional consequences for themselves and their partners. One male participant justified being out on his personal Web page because he found LGBT Web sites to be more interesting than straight people's pages—an insight DeWitt could not have gained from textual analysis. Although audience, understandably, gets de-emphasized in this methodological design, DeWitt tried to elicit the participants' perspectives of and/or experiences with their audiences by asking: Are you aware of other Web sites that have been linked to your site? Are these sites friendly or hostile? Have you experienced any positive outcomes or endured any harassment connected to your Web site? These questions addressed the various ways audiences might respond to their Web sites. But the responses from the participants were limited to the positive support one participant received when she came out in Internet Relay Chat. Other participants reported no negative interaction with their audience, but many were waiting for what they perceived to be the inevitable.

Ironically, DeWitt got a glimpse at one participant's audience while he was interviewing him. This participant, David, managed separate Web sites about the Columbus LGBT scene, shar-peis, and Godzilla films, which were all linked through his home page (a place he did not expect most of his diverse audience to visit). After telling DeWitt that he had never received any negative feedback, David showed DeWitt his guest book. To their surprise they found a message from "Tennessee Jed" haranguing the LGBT population for supporting then-president Bill Clinton and acting like fools during gay pride parades. Although this data was outside of DeWitt's research design, the design he did develop allowed him to witness this response.

As DeWitt and I talked about this article, he told me that his experience with Joie, the student who comes out to him at the beginning of his article, had originally inspired him to write a work of creative nonfiction about a composition instructor's enthusiastic adoption of new technologies (as Web authoring was pedagogically new in the mid-1990s) and the implications of this pedagogical approach to LGBT students. He wanted to create a rich portrait of the overall issue, as well as raise questions and concerns. But he was advised, as a junior faculty quickly approaching a tenure review, to include a qualitative study and make the publication more "academic." He had applied for a small grant to support his research, but did not receive it. As a result, DeWitt had to develop a methodology for conducting this research that took into account his resources, which limited the data he could viably collect.

DeWitt described the research process as smooth because all of his participants were enthusiastic about participating. Furthermore, they all insisted that he use their real names in publication.[6] In spite of his participants' enthusiasm and generosity, DeWitt began to question how representative his participants were because they had not experienced any negativity from being out on the Web. He described it as one of those experiences where the data just is not producing the anticipated results. Then, during his last interview, David received the message from "Tennessee Jed." As he read this post, DeWitt described feeling conflicted: This was the data he was looking for, but he was also witnessing someone getting bashed. Although David, who was an activist about being out, was able to brush off the message, DeWitt wondered how a student who had just used this composing experience to come out would have responded. Because none of his participants had been electronically harassed, his methods prevented him from showing how the violence toward a LGBT population can extend to online discourse. Although he was constrained by his pool of participants, he was also placed in a position to rethink his assumptions. Yet, his methodological choice to do the virtual tours, incidentally, allowed him to witness the evidence he had anticipated. A textual analysis may not have given him the opportunity to experience both the questioning and re-affirmation of his assumptions.

Grabill: "Community Computing and Citizen Productivity"

In "Community Computing and Citizen Productivity" Jeffery T. Grabill (2003) described the service work that he and his students did in Mechanicsville, an urban neighborhood in the greater Atlanta area "to design with citizens the tools that meet community needs and achieve local goals" (p. 144). Before developing this community Web site, Grabill and his students first explored whether "the Mechanicsville community even wanted a Web-based tool for community development efforts" (p. 136). Once the community's desire was affirmed, Grabill established the following research questions:

- What is the current state of computer access in the community (both individually and institutionally)?
- What are the features and functions of a usable Web site that meets community needs?
- In what ways can the Web site facilitate civic and planning-related action and increase community capacity to use the information technologies? (p. 136)

To answer these questions, Grabill and the students involved in the project used focus groups, interviews, and technology profiles to do needs-assessment and conduct usability testing to inform an initial Web site design. Grabill and the students conducted questionnaires in strategically chosen locations throughout the community. Once they used this information to map the community networks that were not computer enhanced, they developed a Web site that could "lay on top of human networks" (p. 139). With a beta version of the Web site designed, they set up two usability test sites at one of the local civic meetings so that volunteers could test the site, while other residents examined it. For the usability test, Grabill and his class focused on "the language used on the Web site, the navigational structure, and the elicitation of user-supplied needs that would help shape the site's revision" (p. 141).

Although an explicit discussion of his methodology is absent from his article, Grabill, in my interview with him, argued that almost everything he writes is about methodology and that this article was "a deliberate attempt to shape a conversation in the field" (personal interview). Grabill practices what he preaches and is constantly taking what he learns from one community project and applying it to others. The nature of this project separates it from the previously discussed projects because Grabill did not see the project as *research* as much as *work*, and the article was a by-product of this work. Unlike the previous articles—specifically designed to address a problem and enlighten digital rhetoricians and writing instructors—Grabill's "research" (and subsequent publication) were the outgrowth of his work in these communities—work that he was doing because he believed in the outcomes. Grabill's work immersed him in the rhetorical situation and from this position he saw how the community functioned; how he perceived the constraints presented by this context characterized his relationship to the community: "I honestly did not see [the constraints] as constraints, if my work was to be successful with and for the people in that community, then my work needed to fit as seamlessly as possible into the practices and rhythms of the community" (personal interview). With this research approach, knowing this rhythm is knowing the rhetorical situation.

Because highlighting this rhythm emphasizes the audience, this approach restructures the communication triangle's relationship to the research methods. Instead of the researcher examining the rhetorical situation through this triangular lens, the researcher is embedded within the rhetorical situation. As the individual collecting data to develop a community-informed Web site, the researcher also adopts the role of digital rhetor. The participants for the study are the Web site's target audience. If the project is successful, according to Grabill, the community participants will eventually become digital rhetors and take ownership of the Web site. Within this methodological framework, the rhetors' intentionality should never be divorced from the target audience's needs. Although we never directly see the community audience speak in this article, we do see how their voices shaped the final product.

TEXTUAL ANALYSIS OR TRIANGULAR METHODS?

All methodology is rhetorical, an explicit or implicit theory of human relations which guides the operations of methods (Sullivan & Porter, 1997, p. 11)

This discussion of these four studies highlights Sullivan and Porter's (1997) argument—an echo of Denzin's (1970) notion that designs reflect personal bias. These studies illustrate just four of the many ways that digital rhetoric has been studied. Yet among these four studies, we have a justification for textual analysis and three different tactics for examining multiple points of the rhetorical situation. These researchers chose different strategies for including those who use the technology into the creation of knowledge—both for the sake of the field and the sake of the users. Furthermore, my discussion with these four researchers provides new information about these projects that published articles often do not entail. These often invisible features of a project—the exigencies (e.g., tenure pressure, resources, costs), the retrospective reflections, the theoretical positioning—shed light on the researchers' deliberate choices and biases.

This examination of the absences (the research designs that were not adopted) points to important questions about digital rhetoric's movement toward a mature, self-aware field of study. Therefore I ask, how else could the methodology for these four inquiries have been designed? Obviously for each of these inquiries there are dozens of ways to methodologically design these studies. But for the sake of argument, I want to explore the general approach of the textual analysis and the triangular methods that mimic the communicative triangle. If McKee (2002) had only analyzed transcripts, how would her study present flaming? How would the study position race relations in multiracial online spaces? Had she not invited participants to read her manuscript, would the white students have ever known that their seemingly rational contributions to the forum were hurtful to some participants? If DeWitt (1997) had only examined Web sites that clearly displayed LGBT identity, what would we know about the risks of being out on the Web? If Grabill (2003) and his students had simply constructed a site for Mechanicsville, would the site be useful to and used by anybody in the community?[7] How would writing classes doing service work construct the digital texts' relationship to the community? By adopting these triangulation methods, the researcher connects with those who are actually using the writing technologies. The researcher's methodological decisions emphasize that each decision has immediate consequences on others' lives, whether it is anonymous gay-bashing or developing a community Web site.

What, then, does this line of questioning say about Rouzie's textual analysis? As Rouzie argued, his inquiry was an examination of the discourse; therefore, these triangulation methods would not facilitate his inquiry. But I wonder what other insights might we learn about serio-ludic discourse if we designed a study that asked synchronous CMC discussants to explain their composition strategies for their posts, as well as their reception of others' posts? Recognizing that every inquiry and every context is different, I believe that we should try to avoid the separation of discourse from rhetorical situation, from rhetor and audience. We cannot divorce discourse from its discursive nature—from how discourse is culturally and socially produced and received.

A textual analysis is therefore useful for exploring a theory's validity. But the researcher will want to work with the producers or recipients of this discourse to prove that a theory is reliable. For example, in his scholarship, Rouzie (2001) introduced Composition Studies to serio-ludic discourse, a playful communicative strategy that appropriates and resists serious discourse. Through his textual analysis of CMC transcripts he pinpointed what serio-ludic discourse looks like and demonstrated how students can practice these discourse strategies using the writing technologies they will use when they enter the workforce. Thus, he proves that serio-ludic discourse is a valid theory. Research should not end there; other researchers should test the reliability of this theory to address inquiries such as how students of the 21st century, those who have grown up with these writing technologies, produce and respond to serio-ludic discourse; and how the evolution and remediation of writing technologies has shaped the production and reception of this discourse. As we study the results of these various inquiries, we begin to learn how reliable a theory is.

Moreover, textual analysis strategies prove to be problematic in that they eliminate or de-emphasize the human feature of digital writing. Researchers should not overlook the use of writing technologies as a negotiation between rhetors and their audiences, but also a negotiation that these rhetors and audiences have with the corporate entities and programmers who prescribe the writing technologies' code—or determine what the application can and cannot do. When we argue that the technology shapes how the writer composes, our reference is not to the technology per se, but to those who produce it. All digital rhetoric experiences are shaped by human decisions—some actors are just more visible than others. Researchers, by recognizing these visible and invisible relationships, can position themselves to learn how actual users respond to others' rhetorical and technological choices. By talking to rhetors and audiences about their rhetorical experiences with digital texts, researchers learn how these individuals see themselves in relationship to others' invisible choices. With this knowledge, researchers are in a position to propose strategies that will inform digital rhetoricians' and writing instructors' practices.

Haraway asked, "How should we be positioned in order to see, in this situation of tensions, resonances, transformations, resistances, and complicities?" (p. 195). Where we choose to see from has social, cultural, and ideological impact. Therefore, the deliberate decisions we make in answering Haraway's question align us in relation to various axes and influence the knowledge we generate. Likewise, in describing the technologies that we use to see (e.g., microscope or satellites), she argued that they "shatter our passive vision" and "show us that all eyes, including our own organic ones, are active perceptual systems, building on translations and specific ways of seeing, that is ways of life" (p. 190). Like a microscope or satellites, methodologies are technologies for seeing, and they, like all organic and prosthetic eyes, filter and construct realities and knowledge.

NOTES

1. This analysis of primary texts is distinguishable from the analysis of secondary texts, such as interview transcripts, survey results, or observation notes.
2. I would also include programmers who write the applications and those who use the applications to create various online spaces for producing discourse among these individuals, but that discussion is beyond the scope of this chapter.
3. Despite my advocacy for triangulation methods, I recognize that these strategies may not be conducive for all digital rhetoric projects. First, researchers may pose research questions in which a single method, such as textual analysis, may be sufficient. Interface analyses, such as those done by Kolko (MOOs; 2000) and Selfe and Selfe (GUIs; 1994), provide methodological and theoretical precedent for these inquiries. Second, some theoretical positions are not strongly supported by triangulation theories. A researcher who supports the postmodern death of the author (Barthes, 1972; Foucault, 1984) may argue that the text speaks for itself. Therefore, the author's intentions for a specific audience is not as relevant as the researcher's reading of the text. Third, triangulation strategies are logistically difficult to manage. The researcher often has to address multiple exigencies with limited resources.
4. My decision for choosing these four studies was based upon three factors: I wanted (a) an even mix of CMC and hypertext studies, (b) studies in which the researcher worked with human participants (i.e., the digital rhetors and audience) or could have designed a study to work with human participants, and (c) to give the writers/researchers an opportunity to speak for themselves.
5. I chose to collect interview data for my analysis for two reasons. First, I recognize that academic publications are often the product of negotiations between the researcher and the editor. Therefore, what the academic audience reads may, upon close scrutiny, raise multiple questions that could have been addressed if a researcher had more control over the publication process. For example, the researcher may have developed a more detailed explanation and justification for the methods used, cut due to word and page constraints. Second, I wanted to practice what I preach. As a scholar who advocates triangulation as framed by postcritical/feminist traditions, I should not make assumptions about the researchers' decisions; instead I wanted to give them

the opportunity to elucidate the field about the deliberate decisions they had made. These researchers were also given the opportunity to review this work and negotiate my representation of them and their scholarship before it was published.

6. DeWitt acknowledged that this practice would not get approval under current IRB regulations.

3

PLAYING SCAVENGER AND GAZER WITH SCIENTIFIC DISCOURSE

OPPORTUNITIES AND ETHICS FOR ONLINE RESEARCH

Michelle Sidler

This chapter explores two new roles faced by researchers of online discourse, particularly those who have traditionally studied print or face-to-face communication: scavenger of diverse types of texts and gazer upon online discourse. Scavengers study discourse of many types from multiple sources, both historical and (near) real-time, which often leads them into the role of gazer, objectifying and appropriating subjects' professional and personal lives. This chapter also discusses the benefits of scavenging online spaces, such as the leveling of communication channels and the hypermediate speed of online information gathering. But with these advantages come ethical questions about research methodologies, including undertheorized challenges to researcher conduct and the changing definitions of "public" knowledge. Although the examples discussed are within the rhetoric of science, many methodological and ethical questions will affect other researchers within Composition Studies. Because ethical uncertainties in online research have received little attention within Composition Studies, this chapter also introduces research models from other disciplines, particularly the social and information sciences. Scholars in these disciplines argue that we must be proactive and critical about online research and maintain a situated, engaged, care-based approach to research ethics.

INTRODUCTION

About 3 years ago, I shifted my research interests in a rather unusual way: I began studying the rhetorical impact of digital communications on the most "positivistic" and "objective" sphere of academic discourse, science. In particular, my research examines biologists who are reconceiving our understandings of genetics and the origin of life. Currently, theories of molecular biology and evolution are to some extent in flux, resulting mainly from a group of scientists developing cutting-edge conceptions of evolution at the cellular level. Previous research in the rhetoric of science has a small body of qualitative research (Baake, 2003; Berkenkotter & Huckin, 1995; Haas, 1994; Myers, 1990), but most research takes a more hermeneutic, historical approach to scientific discovery and change, analyzing established books and articles sanctioned by the review process and published in print (Campbell, 1986, 1990; Gross 1990; Gross & Keith, 1997; Prelli, 1989; Simons, 1990). My work focuses on contemporary scientists and the online communities they develop, and this work has prompted me to rethink previous methods for studying the rhetoric of science.

Instead of relying primarily on works published in academic journals and books, I apply my background in computers and writing to examine the online spaces in which these scientists communicate. Although the two subfields—that is, molecular biology and computers and writing—at first seem to have little in common, they offer a shared line of inquiry: online communities. Using a combination of methodologies—a pastiche of ethnography, case studies, and hermeneutics—I study similarities between biologists' online communities and those of cultural minorities. This research has necessitated a new methodology for the rhetoric of science, and it has exposed new ethical complexities about the study of human subjects, including scientists and other published members of the academy. I have struggled to determine how to respect research subjects in online environments as well as how to edit and appropriate their discourse for rhetorical study.

To accommodate the multiple online discourses of current scientific research, I find myself playing two distinct roles: scavenger of diverse types of texts and gazer upon online scientific discourse. This chapter explores these two roles, particularly in relation to online research, and discusses what I see to be the greatest attribute of online access: its leveling of communication channels and the hypermediate speed of online information gathering. But with these advantages come new ethical questions about research methodologies, including undertheorized challenges to researcher conduct and the changing definitions of "public" knowledge. Although my research is within the rhetoric of science, many of the methodological and ethical questions will affect other researchers within Composition Studies, as communities of many types are increasingly reliant on digital technologies for collaboration, and scholars from all disciplines are publishing in myriad different digital forms (as well as print). Although Composition Studies has just begun to examine these issues, researchers in other fields are beginning to explore the ethical ambiguity of studying online communities, and I overview that work here as well.

RESEARCHING ONLINE COMMUNITIES

Digital technologies are changing the communicative practices of scientists, especially those whose theories are considered marginal or even revolutionary. The often exclusionary hierarchy of print publishing[1] is being challenged, at least a little, by nonmainstream scientists who exploit the multiple discursive spaces of online discourse. The Web and other technologies flatten discursive spaces, making them accessible to mainstream and nonmainstream scientists alike. Increasingly, scientific discourse happens in a variety of online venues: within scientific journals published in digital formats, on corporate and institutional Web sites, and through online communities. Nowhere are these changes more evident than in my research within the biological sciences, where technologies designed to decode genomic information have facilitated both academic and industry research in a way unanticipated even 10 years ago. Once viewed as the most "naturalistic" science—full of lone researchers studying the behavior and anatomy of worms or flies in their small, secluded labs—biology is now reliant on information technology. And, with the shift from print to digital culture, cutting-edge molecular and theoretical biologists have begun to utilize online communication as a way to circumvent formal academic gateways, creating online communities of like-minded scholars. These communities allow me, as a researcher, to access previously unseen discourse among scientists (as well as information about them), promoting a scavenger-like methodology that accesses both real-time discourse among scientists online and published print accounts of their research. However, with this methodological ambiguity comes the need for flexible ethical guidelines adaptable to a variety of discursive genres.

Online Communities at the Margins

Online scientific communities allow emerging fields to build academic, political, and social power in much the same way that other online discourse communities operate. Research about online communities has a strong tradition among computers and writing scholars, often highlighting minority communities, including feminist, gay and lesbian, Native American, and other marginalized groups (Comstock & Addison, 1997; Elbe & Breault, 2002; Gerrard, 2002; Takayoshi, Huot, & Huot, 1999). Minority communities online often exploit the rhetorical tools of Web sites and other online spaces to enact change, using discursive strategies such as the appropriation and exploitation of mainstream language; the support and encouragement of alternate voices; and world-wide information-sharing, including plans that lead to real-life community gatherings and promotion of individual member's activities. These activities bring together like-minded citizens and may foster social empowerment through sophisticated rhetorical use of the Internet's immediate access and diverse publication outlets. Online communities are often "sites of literate action" (Comstock & Addison, p. 253) where minorities can cultivate social groups and organize politically, increasing their power through discourse. They are also places where the invisible can be rendered visible, such as when gays and lesbian come out online (Addison & Hilligoss, 1999; Alexander & Banks, 2004).[2]

Although empowering, these scenarios also enable the public to gaze on writers' personal lives. In many ways, online scientific communities are similar to online minority communities because they also exploit the Internet to share knowledge, combine resources, and gather like-minded peoples together. Although the most prominent Web sites are those by major government, business, and academic entities, a small number of nonmainstream biologists, the "minority" who do not wholly subscribe to the dominant paradigm within biology, are promoting new theories of biology through online communication. Like minority communities, the Internet allows scientists with cutting-edge theories to locate like-minded scholars and organize publications, meetings, and other community-building activities; these activities foster research often ignored or discouraged by mainstream "normal science" (Kuhn, 1996, p. 10). Online discourse, however, also leaves open the possibility that scientists with nonmainstream views will be "outed" among their peers, seen as espousing radical—even revolutionary—scientific views, making such public discourse a professional risk. Although online scientific discourse can create spaces of empowerment, this discourse and these spaces also allow an uncomfortable gaze to fall on the traditionally exclusive and restrictive world of scientific discourse.

Public and Private Ambiguities in/on Online Communities

Rhetoricians of science must recognize the potential for public/private ambiguity in the study of contemporary scientific discourse while expanding their research methodologies to include new forms of digital communication. New methods will include scavenger techniques, plucking discourse of many types from multiple sources, both historical and (near) real-time. Researchers of online social communities have been mining hypermediate spaces (Bolter & Grusin, 1999) to uncover communities of empowerment for several years, particularly through the analysis of Web sites, but also through more direct methods, such as interviews (Comstock & Addison, 1997; McKee, 2002, 2004; Takayoshi, Huot, & Huot, 1999). As scientists increasingly rely on digital technologies for research and communication, rhetoricians of science must engage all of these discursive spaces as well, while still analyzing more traditional print sources. The fast pace of digital change affects my research into biotechnology; biological discoveries, up-to-the-minute data, and even the writings and thoughts of major biologists are immediately available through online databases, Web sites, and email. In many ways, by the time they reach press, print representations of scientific research (especially print books) embody historical records more than current science. Rather than play the role of a contemplative rhetor studying scientific discourse practices through the relatively static world of print journals and books, I find myself actively searching for information in the library, online, and even on broadcast media, creating a pastiche-like set of methodological strategies inspired both by the rhetoric of science tradition and Web-based research of online communities. Unlike the relatively stable research methodologies employed by rhetoricians of science in the print age, the research of emerging biological sciences requires a scavenger's cunning, locating multiple textual spaces and publishing venues in various academic and nonacademic contexts.

Not all of the most innovative and influential work in the sciences is found in the traditionally sanctioned spaces of "real world" research communities, either. Internet technologies allow scientists to communicate with other researchers across the globe, so qualitative studies of local communities must also take into account outside collaborators who may be virtually rather than physically present. Scientists are collaborating extensively in the "smooth spaces" of online nomadic discourse (Deleuze & Guattari, 1987), presenting a new discursive format for knowledge production and sharing: the Web itself is becoming a "docuverse" (Nelson, 1982) of primary research, much of which is publicly available through various Web sites and databases. Like scientists themselves, researchers who study the rhetoric of science must undergo a shift in methodology; we must seek out virtual, digital laboratories and networked, hypertextual meeting rooms. Along with Gilles Deleuze and Felix Guattari's (1987) nomad, my methodology of scavenging is inspired by Donna Haraway's (1991b) mythology of the cyborg: an animal/human, modern/postmodern hybrid that exploits "transgressed boundaries, potent fusions, and dangerous possibilities which progressive people might explore as one part of needed political work" (p. 155). Uncovering the rhetoric and epistemic of 21st-century biology, for me, means a pastiche-like, politicized approach that rejects modernist notions of absolute publishing boundaries by drawing on a range of discourses. Scavenging uncovers multiple types of texts, from both print and digital contexts, to uncover the ways small communities of scientists are subverting mainstream science and enacting local/global paradigm change. Again inspired by Haraway's cyborg, my scavenging methodology is often "unfaithful" (p. 152) to the traditions of academic publishing, mapping new textual territories and expanding the canon of "scientific discourse" to include online communications.

With our increasing access to online scientific discourse, though, comes a need for a new methodology of research that melds practices from several areas of rhetoric and composition research, including rhetorical studies, computer-mediated communication, and classroom-based composition research as well as those in other areas of computer science and the social sciences. Scavengers of 21st-century scientific research must employ textual analysis like those of 20th-century rhetoricians while approaching texts from a digital ethnographer's perspective as well. Because the Internet facilitates situated, multilayered discourse, researchers have access to records and real-time evidence of scientific information-sharing and knowledge-building. An ethics of scavenging, then, must take into account the situatedness of qualitative ethnographic studies (Sullivan, 1996) as well as hermeneutics. Online communication facilitates a record of—and meeting place for—communities of scientists at work daily, communicating new information and ideas at a speed much faster than print. Although scavenging involves the distanced analytical practices of print texts like that of hermeneutic studies of science, it also personalizes the writing subjects of a given study, requiring respect for scientists as research subjects and a situated approach to their online texts. The combination of these two methodologies opens a gateway both to established scientific discourse (such as that available in online journals) and to private and academic undercurrents of science-culture, a world much more difficult to encounter in the age of print. But, the combination also leads to unforeseen ethical and legal quandaries: scavenging online can reveal too much information about communities of scientists, and even their individual personal lives.

SCAVENGING ALONG A FINE LINE: DETERMINING PUBLIC AND PRIVATE DISCOURSE

Scavenging led me to one of the most rhetorically aware scientific "documents" I've ever encountered: the Web site of the Associazione Italiana di Biologia Teorica (the Italian Association of Theoretical Biology, ABT).[3] Because of its mixture of textual genres, styles, and communications, the ABT Web site is an interesting example of the potential confusion between "published" research and personal information. ABT is also the type of resource found not through traditional research channels, but through word of mouth, random media reports, email and email lists, blog entries, and extensive Internet searches—in other words, scavenging. It serves as a hybrid space of both community-building and professional advancement, making visible the kind of theoretical science that would have been invisible in previous scientific eras.

ABT is an organization of theoretical biologists who are attempting to expand and revise current biological paradigms of life, both among Italian scientists and other scientists around the world. Their Web site serves as an organizational bulletin board of upcoming events and a venue for publicizing related research. ABT includes links to relevant online journals, societies, conferences, and papers, making it both a storehouse for "published" scientific texts and a meeting place for its online community. Among its links to important books is Marcello Barbieri's (2003) *The Organic Codes: An Introduction to Semantic Biology*. In fact, a major function of the site is to publicize Barbieri's theory of organic codes because his work has been more or less ignored in the larger biological community over the past 25 years. To further promote that goal, the site includes a series of emails written to Barbieri by other well-known theorists and scientists, including such notables as Noam Chomsky and Richard Strohman. The emails are responses to a promotional copy of the book sent by Barbieri and indicate the recipients' interest in Barbieri's theory as well as potential critiques of it. In addition, the emails often acknowledge the exclusionary practices of normal scientific discourse and encourage a revision of the dominant paradigm governing biological codes, making this Web site a valuable artifact about conflicting scientific paradigms. As a researcher of scientific rhetoric, I want to pounce on this resource like I would when finding a ground-breaking article in an academic journal, analyzing its scientific significance and extrapolating its discursive functions. But, generically, many aspects of this Web site, especially the email correspondences, are not like published books or journal articles—the information has not been vetted through traditional academic processes such as peer review, and the discourse is much shorter, more surface-level, and more informal.

According to James Porter (1998), email correspondence should be treated as private correspondence and requires at least the writer's permission for use in public discourse. In turn, the ABT Web site does include the disclaimer that "email messages are regarded as private letters and are not published without permission" (n.p.). These materials occupy a poorly defined space between the personal and the public, particularly that of the fine line between published discourse and private discourse. In effect, it is much like the appropriation of student texts in composition classes; though we may get permission to use those texts, we must be wary of the rights of students and the protection of their privacy. In the case of the ABT Web site, the original authors of the emails have apparently waived their right to privacy by consenting to the emails' publication, but the extent to which those emails can be used in other public texts and research studies is uncertain.

Porter (1998) also lamented the current uncertainty about ownership of online discourse; he noted that materials "published" in digital spaces have no exact standards from which to draw: "Because there are no clearly established legal precedents specifically for cyberwriting, the old print precedents apply, however inappropriate they may be" (p. 118). Email, in particular, falls in a gray area between the protected privacy of postal mail and the rights to ownership by both writers and receivers. Porter's advice for semi-private correspondence was to "ask the author" (p. 119); those who wish to discuss and cite materials (or link to other online materials) that may or may not be private should obtain permission. In the case of the ABT site, the organization has already obtained and expressed partial permissions, making the emails more public. In this case, it seems, authorial permission has been granted and further permissions are probably not necessary. However, in preparing this chapter, I still felt it necessary to contact the ABT Web administrator and gain permission.[4] As science researchers scavenge online sites and analyze online writing, similar online texts will continue to raise ethical concerns.

The most valuable aspect of the ABT Web site is the direct insight it provides into the contentious discourse of theoretical biology, presenting a diversity of viewpoints not evident in most published works and thus flattening the textual hierarchies and exclusionary mechanisms of print. However, with the flattening of textual space comes a confusion about the appropriation of such research; old categories of "published works" no longer apply. As a field, we must redefine research categories, particularly those that designate "published" texts and unpublished works as well as those that separate academic, public, and personal discursive spaces. If we pursue the dream of scavenging through fluid online spaces, strict ethical lines will be difficult to draw, requiring situation-specific decisions about the accurate and responsible use of research. Scavenging through online territories entails more than transversing the land—it exposes researchers to unforeseen knowledge and promotes their inadvertent gazing.

Online Research and the Gaze: Negotiating the Academic and the Personal

Moving from legal concerns about privacy and permissions to ethical considerations of research subjects' private lives reveals another series of complications. Theoretically, scavenging for online texts involves nomadic practices that seek "active transversal or encounter rather than objectification" (Moulthrop, 1994, p. 301). But the use of such encounters in one's own publications cannot avoid elements of objectification. The activity of writing necessarily creates a stoppage of the researcher's cyber-movement and a reconstruction of others' texts. Because online scientific research has elements of community-building and facilitates the study of writing-in-process, any methodology of online scientific research must share the concerns of other qualitative research. In fact, online scientific research, like that of research about other online communities, blurs the rather firm lines often assumed between "*text-based* studies" and "*person-based* research" (Anderson, 1998, p. 63, emphasis his).[5] Although online research is text-based, it is often representative of persons in the process of writing, supplying information similar to that of classroom research. Online "published" texts also exist in an immediate hyperspace that allows both knowledge of scientific research and intimate exposure to scientists as living subjects. These conditions mirror those of person-based studies, where researchers grapple with "issues of hegemony and appropriation in relation to the subjects" of study (Blakeslee, Cole, & Conefrey, 1996, pp. 135–136). Researchers must negotiate the role of observer (gazing upon their subjects as objects) with the role of ethical researcher (collaborating with research subjects) to produce responsible, mutually respective results.

But, online environments do not supply the immediate physical conditions of person-based research, and, paradoxically, they allow more surveillance through networked connectivity. Studying the works of scientists online allows access not just to their academic and professional lives, but also to private information about their personal lives (information that may or may not be revealed by research subjects in person-based research). For example, I routinely perform online searches about the scientists I am studying, looking for information about their current research, their place of employment, and their publications. This practice is relatively common, I would assume, among researchers of many fields; it is another way to evaluate the credibility of authors and texts. However, a routine search may turn up more than the public credentials of a given scientist—it may uncover information outside the public domain of academic credentials and publications.

Such was the case of Andrew Wilkie, the Nuffield Professor of Pathology at Oxford University. Recently, I prepared a conference presentation about scientific disagreements concerning genetic determinism. I planned to cite an article by Wilkie (2001) that discussed the predictive power of genetic tests; the article clearly explained valuable scientific evidence about genetic testing, making it indispensable to my argument. However, I was unfamiliar with Wilkie's research, and the biographical information in the article was sparse. So, I performed an Internet search to determine his credibility, his special field of biology, his other research projects, and so on—the kind of information any researcher should know before citing a scientific source. Within seconds, I ascertained that Wilkie was indeed a prominent scientist with an endowed chair at Oxford, but I also discovered that he was suspended without pay for 2 months in 2003 for discrimination. According to accounts (Henry, 2003; University of Oxford, 2003), Wilkie rejected an application for a research assistantship position from an Israeli student, Amit Duvshani, sending him a politically charged and potentially discriminatory email. The case became public when Duvshani distributed and published Wilkie's email on the Web, and university officials were obliged to take disciplinary action against the scientist, suspending him without pay and requiring him to undergo training in equal opportunities hiring.

The complexities of this situation are multiple and obvious: I performed the background search simply to verify Wilkie's academic credentials, but the search led me to consider the author's personal ethics and politics as part of my evaluation. Furthermore, because Wilkie's article was a prominent aspect of my conference presentation, I had to decide whether to disclose this information to the audience who most likely was unaware of the author's history. To leave Wilkie's controversy unstated was to mislead the audience at least to some extent about his credibility, but to mention this situation might infringe on his privacy (although the story was published briefly in several newspapers and journals including the *New York Times*, Schemo, 2003; and the *Chronicle of Higher Education*, Lin-Lui & Watzman, 2003, few scholars outside of Britain would be familiar with Wilkie's story). Furthermore, the parameters of the case had little or nothing to do with the subject of Wilkie's research, genetics, and pathology.

Research in the age of print did not so easily facilitate such an intrusive gaze upon scholars, making this situation somewhat new and unique. Although some scholars' lives have become the subject of ongoing controversy, those situations are relatively rare and fairly well-known and documented. So, I was left with little guidance in deciding whether a scholar's unrelated politics should impact an evaluation of his academic credibility. Without the Internet, I would not have stumbled on this private information; Internet research put me in the role of online gazer, objectifying and appropriating not just Wilkie's research but also his personal history. Indeed, by discussing it in this chapter, I further Wilkie's appropriation in an effort to highlight these concerns. In person-based research, such information would most likely be ignored and even suppressed in respect of the writer, who most likely would not give permission for its public release.[6]

In the end, I decided to forego mentioning Wilkie's personal history in my presentation; his refusal to consider an Israeli applicant may affect one's opinion of his political action, but it does not affect his report of science. Furthermore, I chose to act in a way similar to what Porter (1998) called an "ethic of caring" (p. 119), a feminist methodology that calls on researchers to not only respect the subjects we study but care for them as well (Durst & Stanforth, 1996; Noddings, 1984, 1999). Because researchers care about the subjects we study, we must accept "the carer's responsibility to follow through" (Nodding, 1999) by caring for the welfare of others, protecting them as individuals while (admittedly) appropriating their discourse through analysis, presentation, and publication. Michelle Comstock and Joanne Addison (1997) recognized the danger of studying online communities of gays and lesbians who might be further marginalized by published studies of their lives; they enacted an ethics of caring by securing permissions from, and entering into dialogue with, many of the online community's leaders and participants.

This ethic of caring should also pertain to a researcher's audience; we should question the validity and respectfulness with which we deliver information to other individuals. The same ethic is shared implicitly by the editors and contributors of the collection *Ethics and Representation in Qualitative Studies of Literacy* (Mortensen & Kirsch, 1996), who show that qualitative research is fraught with similar dilemmas and who call for a negotiated, self-reflective approach to person-based research. Like empirical methodologies, online research tools imbue scholars with much access to—and responsibility for—their subjects. But, unlike qualitative research discussed in the collection, my work, and other studies of online communities, must employ this ethic of caring in an even more complex context: the Internet. This powerful concern needs to be addressed through formal ethical guidelines and legal practices—but, given the ambiguous state of such guidelines in the digital age, researchers must currently proceed with a situated, self-determined, and care-based ethics of our own.

TOWARD AN ETHICS OF SCAVENGING AND GAZING

As researchers who pursue scavenger and gazing methodologies, we need to be conscious and pro-active in addressing an ethics for the postmodern digital age. Unfortunately, ethical uncertainties in online research have received little attention within Composition Studies, so we must first look outside the discipline for ethical models in other areas, particularly the social and information sciences. Scholars in these disciplines have been discussing the legal and ethical guidelines of online research for several years (Bakardjieva & Feenberg, 2001; Berry, 2004; Cavanagh, 1999; Ess, 2001).[7] Their findings echo my experiences: established guidelines only partially or ambiguously provide parameters for Internet research ethics. Most significantly, two issues arise about the classification of research materials: the difference between public and private communications in online spaces and the difference between the study of online texts and the study of human subjects online. Moreover, the distinction between these two issues is often confusing, particularly when applied to online discourse.

When I first began researching online communities of scientists, I considered their work to be texts or artifacts: they should be gazed upon, analyzed, and dutifully cited like other published texts—they were not communities with whom I should engage. However, as the personal implications of those texts came to the surface, I realized that online "texts" often invoke and enable online communities of scholars—some constituting private interactions and some constituting public performance. Charles Ess and the Association of Internet Researcher's AoIR Ethics Working Committee (2002) approved a series of recommendations about Internet research, including the designation of human subjects, in November 2002. They defined the distinction as such: "*Are participants in this environment best understood as 'subjects' (in the senses common in human subjects research in medicine and the social sciences)—or as authors whose texts/artifacts are intended as public?*" (italics theirs, p. 7). Allison Cavanagh (1999) argued that the distinction between these states is vital to determining researchers' ethical obligations, but the answer to this question is often context-specific, prompting researchers to make their own ethical and legal decisions. First, a researcher must decide if the online discourse is a text rather than an interactive communication. To be a "text" like any other published work, the discourse should imply significant separation and autonomy from its producer. If a work is deemed to be a "text," then the researcher should follow intellectual property guidelines, disregarding the informed consent that accompanies human subjects research.

However, if the text implies a co-presence of the "producing self" (Cavanagh, 1999), then it should be seen as an interactive community event. In other words, if the discourse implies an immediate, deep connection between its producer and its online publication, then it may be considered a private discourse. Like "real life" interaction, online interaction has the potential to be either public or private, depending on the culture and implications of that community; in particular, the subject or type of community and its relative remoteness within cyberspace become significant factors. Cavanagh argued that individual researchers must make their own distinctions about these differences: "Only an engagement with the frameworks of meaning and relevance of the individual communities as revealed through the forms of interaction can yield an understanding of these issues" (n.p.). The researcher's decision is situational and based in a deep knowledge of the community's intentions, requiring significant engagement with, knowledge of, and caring for the community members. If it is deemed to be a public interaction, then informed consent is not necessary, but it is necessary if the producer of online discourse seems to have an expectation of privacy. Although only "private discourses" legally require consent, many online researchers (Bakardjieva & Feenberg, 2001; Cavanagh, 1999; White, 2001) tend to feel that an engaged, reciprocal relationship between the researcher and the producers of discourse is the most effective and ethical method. Such engagement requires an adventuresome, nomadic spirit and a willingness to situate ethics in discrete contexts for particular places and times, constantly scavenging for new ethical models and socially responsible methodologies.

In her discussion of humanistic research and online discourse, Michelle White (2001) argued that this situation is a particularly complex one for scholars in history, art, and English. Much of our work depends on the public nature of discourse, the ways that texts produce (and are produced by) not just authors but also cultures, making the notion of private discourse in the cultural space of the Internet even more problematic. She contended that Internet representations of people as "human subjects" are particularly unreliable, given the often fictional ways that users represent themselves and others (some users employ avatars, others fictionalize accounts of their lives, and others even stereotype entire groups of people). Humanities scholars have a long history of research about fictionalized, textualized representations, and we have a great deal to offer other disciplines about how to approach such discourse. However, with the concern about informed consent and human subjects, the close textual analysis often employed by humanists is coming under scrutiny in online research. White argued for increased cross-disciplinary research that exploits the Internet's capacity for multiple discursive types and devises multidimensional methodologies—a pastiche of approaches to online research that again implies Haraway's cyborg, disloyal to tradition and open to hybridization.

HYBRID RESEARCH AND SCIENTIFIC DISCOURSE: SOME CONCLUSIONS

The realm of scientific discourse makes these issues even more complex; science is traditionally seen as a field removed from most human subjects, with a basis in the rational, empirical world of fact and structured by the belief in detached observation. The hermeneutic branch of the rhetoric of science has more or less followed the same methodology—performing close analyses of scientific artifacts—while the qualitative study branch has been able to rely on established human subjects guidelines. Reconciling these two approaches into a more nuanced, subjective, and individual approach to Internet research will be necessary. Like much digital communication, online scientific discourse is exploding clear-cut lines, creating a pastiche of methodologies and ethical responsibilities. All researchers of online communities, but especially those in the rhetoric of science, will have to adopt a scavenger approach—not just to research methodologies, but also to their accompanying ethics.

This future will be particularly uncomfortable, both for the researchers of scientific discourse—which moves back and forth between scientific texts—and scientists themselves. In the 21st century, information technology will increasingly personalize the lives of all scientists, thrusting their personal lives into the public realm. As scientists become more "human," visible, and accessible, we need flexible humanistic guidelines that care for them as contentious, political subjects. With the rise of world-wide collaboration and the speed of online publication, any systematic, top-down approach that gazes upon scientific discourse will be increasingly problematic. Moreover, rhetoricians of science will have the responsibility to treat scientists as more than scientific-discursive objects; we must be open to viewing them in an ongoing collaborative context while recognizing and respecting them as individuals. Through publicly accessible multimedia spaces, scientists are opening the doors to cutting-edge research and collectively producing new knowledge in a more collaborative and socially conscious manner than ever before. And, these types of collaboration are common in all areas of contemporary social and academic life. Future researchers who study online communities of all types will be faced with pastiches of text–human discourses and legal and ethical uncertainties. As compositionists, researchers, and rhetoricians, we must equip ourselves with a multimedia-savvy skill set and a situationally reflective ethical awareness.

NOTES

1. Although he does not discuss publication practices to much extent, in the postscript to his *Structure of Scientific Revolutions* (originally written in 1969), Kuhn (1996) briefly mentioned research methodologies necessary for deciphering scientific communities and bemoaned researcher lack of access to nonmainstream scientific discourse: "For . . . major groupings, community membership

is readily established except at the fringes. . . . It is only at [that] next lower level that empirical problems emerge" (pp. 177–178). Because communities are the basis of scientific paradigms, Kuhn insisted that rhetorical studies of scientific knowledge production must begin by locating both mainstream and nonmainstream communities. In the age of print, nonmainstream groups often shared information through smaller conferences, shared print manuscripts, and, especially, private correspondences and cross-referenced citation lists, making this discourse difficult to access.

2. Certainly, however, scholars have challenged the often utopic rhetoric of empowerment through online discourse; see, for instance, Addison and Hilligoss (1999), Grabill (1998), Regan (1993), and Romano (1993).

3. I located the ABT site through a series of scavenging practices. First, I learned about the theoretical work of Carl Woese through a newspaper article recommended by a friend. Then, I emailed Woese, whereupon he recommended Barbieri's (2003) book. I performed a Web search on Barbieri, eventually finding the ABT site. These events unfolded within 24 hours, and it took 2 weeks before Barbieri's print book arrived in the mail—a fine example of hypermediate research in the digital age.

4. Obtaining permission to cite the ABT Web site is another great example of the flattening of research hierarchies. Upon emailing ABT, I discovered that Barbieri is the legal owner of the Web site, and through this process, I have initiated a correspondence with him about his organic code theory of biology. Again, without the Internet, such communication would have taken months or years to establish, if at all.

5. The CCCC Executive Committee (2004) recently implied this same division in a recent report. The Committee offers no guidance about online texts, except for its discussion of unpublished written works: "In their publications, presentations, and other research reports, composition specialists quote, paraphrase, or otherwise report unpublished written statements only with the author's written permission" (p. 782). Again, because of their indeterminate status, this statement may or may not apply to texts published online.

6. Porter (1998) also cautioned that asking for permission could be fatal in cases where a writer will be critiquing the work of the person to whom they ask permission. Obviously, it would have been inappropriate, and even hostile, for me to ask Wilkie's permission to tell this story.

7. The *Internet Research Ethics* site, introduced and edited by Charles Ess (2001), is a collection of several presentations from the 2001 Computer Ethics: Philosophical Enquiries conference, including Bassett and O'Riordan (2001), Elgesem (2001), Walther (2001), and White (2001).

PART TWO

*Researching
Global Citizens
and Transnational
Institutions*

4

ETHOS AND RESEARCH POSITIONALITY IN STUDIES OF VIRTUAL COMMUNITIES

Filipp Sapienza

When investigating computer-mediated discourse, researchers often use distanced data-gathering methods such as conducting controlled laboratory experiments or downloading content. Although distanced methods preserve some objectivity, scholars have criticized them because they often sever analysis from actual discursive context. To challenge methods that sever analysis from actual discursive context, I propose a methodological approach that views all interactions on computer-mediated groups, including those of the researcher, as rhetorical interactions. Drawing from my participation and research in a Russian virtual transnational community, I discuss the ways a researcher, like the other members of an online group, acquires a rhetorical ethos within a virtual community. I propose three inter-animating dimensions that researchers should consider regarding their online ethos: an ethos as a technologist, an ethos as a culturally competent member of the community, and an ethos as a scholar–expert on virtual communities. I close by reflecting upon the implications of my research for others studying virtual communities.

INTRODUCTION

When investigating the nature of computer-mediated groups, researchers often strive for credibility by using distanced data-gathering methods. Early studies of computer-mediated communication groups reported on controlled experiments, survey methods, and snapshot techniques (Mitra, 1998), in which posts were collected from an archive and coded (e.g., Herring, 1996). Although these methods preserve some measure of objectivity, scholars have criticized them because they often sever analysis from actual discursive context. As Luciano Paccagnella (1997) put it, the text logs that comprise the main source for snapshot analysis lack both the "dynamic dimension of turn taking," the "collective mood surrounding the messages," and the context of the "actual experiences of individual participants" (n.p.). To provide this context, researchers have added participatory and ethnographic methods (e.g., Alexander, 1997; Blair, 1998; Conway, 1995; Craig, Harris, & Smith, 1998; Hawisher & Sullivan, 1998; Smith, 2004; Regan, 1993). By doing so, they have also introduced the issue of research positionality (Allen, 1996)—that is, the specific relationship a researcher has within the group studied. Researchers are then compelled to explain how that positionality is integrated into the analysis of the group. Although the issue of positionality has come under investigation in the social sciences, it has received less attention in rhetoric and communication. Initially, scholars held that it was possible to maintain an objective distance from the group when using some participatory research methods. However, this belief has been criticized by virtue of its logical empiricist assumptions; what has displaced it is a movement toward "interpretive flexibility" (Paccagnella, 1997, n.p.). This framework assumes that the "outsider self never stands outside [of the group under study] . . . but in a definite relation with the Other of the study" (Abu-Lughod, 1991, p. 141). In the field of technical communication and composition, researchers have recognized this positionality (e.g., Herndl, 1991; Herrington, 1993; Kirsch & Ritchie, 1995; Spinuzzi, 2000). Facts garnered in participatory designs are not "independent of observers" but are "always the result of a situated perspective" (Paccagnella, 1997, n.p.).

Members' discussions about who they are, what they believe, and what they do are produced from negotiations of the technological logistics of discussion boards, chat rooms, electronic photo galleries, and other dimensions of the group (e.g., Braine, 2001; Cubbison, 1999; Strenski, 1995; Sujo de Montes, Oran, & Willis, 2002; Ware, 2004; Yuan, 2003).

Face-to-face interactions have an abundance of socialization strategies (talk, gestures, appearance, and so forth) that may be analyzed individually or contextually. Researchers and actual inhabitants of face-to-face groups may intentionally opt for different interaction channels and use them in ways to change their visibility. By contrast (and with the possible exception of high-end audio and visual platforms), most rhetorical acts online take place in text or static graphic format. For this reason, online groups are sometimes called "cues-reduced" settings (Lea, O'Shea, Fung, & Spears, 1992). In a cues-reduced environment, both researchers and participants have limited channels at their disposal for communication; both must interact with text and through interfaces. All interactions on computer-mediated groups, including those of the researcher, are *rhetorical* interactions. The flexible positionality of the researcher acquires not only a scholarly but rhetorical presence within the virtual group. Thus, the act of research is not a distanced act but rather an embedded rhetorical act.

As such, it becomes possible to discuss the ways that the researcher, like the members of the group, acquires a rhetorical *ethos* within the virtual community (Howard, 1997; Porter, 1998). By ethos, I refer to the credibility of a speaker as defined through choices made, typically within a specific speech context. Ethos has historically held both an individual and communal meaning. According to Michael Halloran (1982),

> the most concrete meaning given for the term [ethos] in the Greek lexicon is "a habitual gathering place," and I suspect that it is upon this image of people gathering together in a public place, sharing experiences and ideas, that its meaning as character rests. To have ethos is to manifest the virtues most valued by the culture to and for which one speaks. . . . (p. 60)

In this chapter, I suggest that researchers investigating the rhetorical nature of virtual communities think about their positionality in terms of ethos. Put differently, ethos not only applies to how participants construct rhetorical identities online, but also to researchers as well. A researcher's ethos consists of multilayered roles that intersect and inform one another: participant, observer, helper, and so forth. This ethos both defies and embraces certain conventions and expectations of locality, culture, and research position in unexpected ways, and as such is framed by postmodern principles and global digital spaces (Hawisher & Selfe, 2000). The purpose of this chapter therefore is to offer an example of how this ethos appears with respect to the researcher and within researcher–participant interactions.

My example is drawn from my experiences as a participant–researcher of the group Virtual Russia (www.virtualrussia.net). Virtual Russia has existed in one form or another since 1996. Initially, the group was called Little Russia in San Antonio, Texas, and had two foci: First, discussions revolved around matters important to Russian transnationals and immigrants, including foreign students at U.S. universities, guest workers, and Russian emigres; second, discussions focused on cultural conflicts between Russians and Americans. The group began only 4 years after the end of the Soviet Union and was one of the first to bring Russians and non-Russians (mostly Americans) together in an unmoderated rhetorical space. My initial interest in the group grew out of my experience living in Moscow and St. Petersburg in 1995 and 1996. When I returned to the United States, I sought ways to stay connected to Russian culture and to continue to learn the language. As a graduate student with a background in computing needing to fulfill a thesis requirement, I decided to study the rhetorical conventions of Russian communities on the Internet. Thus, in addition to my scholarly role, I occupied the position of someone who might potentially be a member of the site even had I not been doing the research. I am not of Russian heritage, but I do have some facility with the Russian language and probably know more about Russian culture than many Americans. In that sense, part of my rhetorical ethos was similar to the other participants in that I shared many markers of social status with other Virtual Russians. What therefore became clear almost immediately is that my rhetorical investigation was shaped by my prior experiences and identities as a computing professional, student, and person interested in Russian culture. In that sense, in no way could I truly enter the group as an outsider. Given that reality, my best option was to develop a research positionality that acknowledged and utilized a rhetorical ethos that both informed my research agenda and allowed me to participate in the group. This ethos came to have three distinct yet interanimating dimensions: my ethos as a technologist, my ethos as a culturally competent virtual Russian, and my ethos as a scholar–expert on virtual communities. In the rest of the chapter, I outline how the formation, negotiation, and integration of these different roles affected my research positionality and the research community itself. I close by reflecting upon the implications of my research for others studying virtual communities.

VIRTUAL RUSSIA

Virtual Russia has roots in an older Web site, Little Russia, which in 1995 was one of few Web sites focused on Russian culture and immigration. In the fall of 1998, Little Russia drew 500,000 visits per month. The site featured cultural resources including font collections, a photography exhibit, and a music archive of Russian songs that attracted more than one-third of all site visits. The discussion board acquired 1,000 new posts per month. Initial discussions were dominated by requests from Russian speakers in America to meet one another, Americans with interests in Russian culture, and American men looking for Russian brides. But over time, participants discussed more in-depth matters such as Russia's relationship with America and the difficulties of adapting to different cultures. From 1997 to 1998, a small contingent of frequent participants tried to manage an inflammatory debate about Russian and American society by offering various monitoring policies. A few individuals started taking greater responsibility for the maintenance of the Web site, a role that had previously been reserved for one Web administrator.

In the spring of 1998, participants formed a collective self-portrait gallery they called the "Little Russia Duma." A visitor could obtain information about participants by clicking a display of thumb-nailed portraits. Through an online form, each person submitted brief biographical information including city of residence; online contact information; favorite foods, artists, books, colors, and tastes; and responses to the questions, "What would you do if you had three wishes?" and "Name a person you would like to be stranded on a desert island with." Posts increased substantially after the Duma formed. In August 1998, someone posted material to Little Russia that the Web administrator found offensive. This act produced a controversy about censorship and board conduct that resulted in the dismantling of the Duma and banishment of its members. This banished group then created Virtual Russia, assigning control over to two new Web administrators and migrating the Duma there.

Little Russia and Virtual Russia consisted mainly of Russian immigrants, transnationals of Russian heritage, and Americans with an interest in Russian culture. Of 57 responses to an electronic survey I conducted in 1999, 37% of Little Russians indicated birth in America and 40% indicated birth in the former Soviet Union. The numbers shifted slightly on Virtual Russia: 45% from America and 34% from the former Soviet Union; 10 of 33 living in the United States indicated that they emigrated from Russia. I asked visitors what drew them to the group initially and to similar groups on the Internet. Of 61 responses, 18 indicated a desire for current news about events in Russia; 11 came for the musical or cultural archives; 7 came out of interest in the culture; 5 came to research their ancestry and make contact with others and discuss politics on the discussion boards; 4 came out of "homesickness"; and the remaining indicated a variety of purposes including commerce, computers, travel information, immigration information, Russian-American information, speaking Russian, and "other."

MY TECHNOLOGIST ETHOS

When Virtual Russia split off from Little Russia, I was not a participant within the community, and it was my preference to remain a nonmember. My interest in Virtual Russia was primarily scholarly and cultural, a position that I initially (and erroneously) felt would best be maintained outside of the group. Although this position may have been possible to maintain on other computer-mediated communities, it was not the case in Virtual Russia. When Virtual Russia began, it had only two members actively administering the site. The new Web administrators requested assistance to develop the new site, but most members lacked the technological knowledge to meet these requests. Online, communal maintenance requires specialized skills not available to everyone (e.g., the ability to navigate servers, write code, and troubleshoot technical problems). I was a nonmember with a technological background, and this presented me with a difficult choice. If I remained an uninvolved outside researcher, the two new Web administrators might not receive the help they needed, and the group might lose its server access and cease to exist. Potentially, this choice might not have affected my academic objectives. My research could have simply focused on the rise and fall of a transnational virtual community and the factors that precipitated its fate. My research, and the resulting thesis project, would have been completed and the topic might have gained worthwhile scholarly interest in its own right. However, I did not make this decision; for reasons that I will discuss more fully below, I decided to make my assistance part of the research itself. Although my interest was still primarily scholarly, my entry into the group happened by way of technology, and I began developing portions of the site. At first, my contributions were relatively timid and consisted mostly of fact-finding missions, but over time I was inexorably pulled into more substantive projects. It became clear that my technologist ethos gave me greater access to and identity within the group.

My specific contributions came to include the construction of a photo gallery of attractions in Russia, a Russian Language Guide I called "*Uchebnik russkogo iazyka*," a user photo Web site, a new portal page, and a chat room. I also assisted the Web administrators with the administration of the server software. In spite of my technologist ethos, I made certain to tell people that my interest in the group was academic. From time to time I shared research that I had found about other Russian virtual groups. But this scholarly information did not seem sufficiently large enough to overcome the perception among group members that I was primarily a technological resource. Between 1998 and 2002, I traveled to New York, New Jersey, and Toronto to discuss and/or train members on technological tasks. On two occasions, the hosting company for Virtual Russia went out of business or changed their operations in such a way as to endanger the future of the community. When this happened in October 2001, I was asked to take complete technological control of the Web site by hosting it on a Linux server I administer, an arrangement that persisted until late Fall 2005.

Although my ethos as technologist initially seemed to be my dominant interaction in the group, it did in fact assist my research in unexpected ways. The technological access contributed key insights by clarifying the integrity of group statistics, demographics, and usage patterns. I was able to ascertain the exact number of messages posted during different periods of time to help determine popular topics and discursive trends. More recently, I have found the access to be not only beneficial to my research but also a vehicle through which both my technical skills and research can aid the group. In Fall 2004, for instance, Virtual Russia had a sudden influx of new members from Moscow. None of these new members participated in discussions. A few had linked gambling sites to their nickname listing on the membership resource, a utility that logs and manages participant user names and other identifying characteristics. It was clear that these new members were using the resource to circumvent protocols banning marketing and promotion on the Virtual Russia discussion forums. By adding links to their membership profiles, these members were promoting products and services without actually joining discussions in the virtual community. A Web search showed that these individuals were exploiting other discussion forum software for exactly this purpose. Inspecting access log data to information supplied on the membership resource showed that most of the new members were probably not real people but *bots* (also known as *agents*): small programs with some artificial intelligence programming that mimic human behaviors. Marketers are increasingly using bots to transmit solicitations. The group felt that these "members" were a threat to the purpose and identity of Virtual Russia, so with my help, steps were taken to remove these bots. This event demonstrated the unforeseen ways that both a technologist and technological infrastructure can impact the cultural and communal nature of the group (for another example, see Dibbell, 1993). On Virtual Russia, my correcting the problem also restored and/or shaped the communal identity of the group.

These types of undercurrents reflect a rhetorical underground that creates a counter-politics to events on the official site. The technological access gave me a more robust and complete rhetorical vision of how exactly these sorts of formations operate. Access to the technological skeleton of this site also sensitized me to the impact that a user interface has on the communal ethos of a virtual space. As scholars of rhetoric and communication, we may be too focused on textual comments and tend to disregard interface issues (Selfe & Selfe, 1994). My research shows that certain colors, images, navigational elements, tools, and other interactive characteristics are common among Russian Web sites (Sapienza, 2001). It became important to study these characteristics before applying changes to the site. When designing the portal pages for Virtual Russia, we chose colors and typographic elements common to other Russian sites. When Virtual Russia moved to the server I administer, we included a technology that embeds syndicated content from other Russian sites. Thus, the Virtual Russia interface not only contains elements that reflect its transnational identity and that links users to intertextual and diverse content, but also incorporates diverse content into the same sphere. As such, the Web site not only gains its transnational identity via intertextuality but also via sublation of diverse messages.

Although it may seem tempting to take autonomous control over the direction and appearance of a virtual community if one has the technical access, I found that a skeletal perspective of the virtual community actually made me *more* sensitive to meeting the particular wishes of members. When Virtual Russia moved to my server, we were fortunate to gain access to more sophisticated discussion forum software. Unfortunately, this application was difficult to use in part because it differed from users' experience on other Russian sites. When members complained about the difficulty of adapting to the new software, we developed templates to make the utility simpler to use. These templates were easier in part because they mimicked the behaviors of forums on other Russian sites. This experience underscored the fact that usability is fundamentally a communication issue as much as it is a technical matter. One can thus talk about an ethos of usability, for example. Moreover, the question of usability on Virtual Russia has a marked transnational aspect. Much of the current emphasis on culture and technology is based on intercultural paradigms that treat interacting cultures as discrete entities. A growing number of researchers are arguing against binary models of intercultural interaction, calling for greater focus on the overlaps and borders of different groups (Cooks, 2001; Kapoor, 2000) and challenging narratives of difference "mapped by clear cut and confident distinctions" (Shome & Hegde, 2002, p. 176). Transnational communities are inherently multi-sided: members define their membership and self-perceptions between two or more sites (Levitt, 2001; see also Fleckenstein, 2005; Rose, 2004; Thatcher, 2005).

Members of Virtual Russia developed communal identities as members of many different Russian transnational sites, and they based their usability sensibilities on this multi-sited experience. In addition, many of the members are of mixed Russian heritage or have tenuous connections to Russian culture itself. In that respect, members construct an ethos primarily through interaction with globalized communication technology rather than something essentially connected to an indigenous space. Usability becomes a set of issues linked to and embedded within a network of navigational, interactional interfaces and behaviors between and among mediated communities. It therefore becomes difficult to isolate the expression of technological ethos from communicative identities, an issue more fully explained in the next section.

MY VIRTUAL RUSSIAN ETHOS

Although my technological ethos significantly increased my visibility in Virtual Russia, it was equally as important to establish cultural ethos to gain credibility within the online community. To demonstrate cultural competence, I had to show knowledge of and interest in the Russian language and customs, and then use that knowledge in some technological way. The following chat session (from November 1998) exemplifies how I used this connection between technology and culture in an attempt to gain credibility. Here I (*skazki-pushkina*, literally "stories of Pushkin"; also the name of a popular Russian candy bar) engaged in a discussion with two other users (Devochka and Yorik) who used humor, geography, the Russian language, and technology to test my ethos (note that items in [square brackets] are my added translations):

< skazki-pushkina > privet devochka/hello

< Devochka > Privet, skazka o ribake I ribke! :-) [hello, tale of the fisherman and fish]

< Devochka > Skazki, are you American or Russian?

< Yorik > US . . . shpion [American . . . spy]

< skazki-pushkina > american . . . a ti? Russkaya yes?

< Devochka > russkaya! :-) [Russian]

< Devochka > what did you do in Russia?

< skazki-pushkina > I lived in Moscow for 6 months, studied at library and learned some Russian

< Yorik > yay!

< Yorik > where in moscow?

< skazki-pushkina > I lived about 20 minute walk from Metro Novyie Cheremush. Orange line.

< Yorik > heh

< Yorik > buroughs . . .

< Yorik > hey skazka . . . do you have Real Player?

< skazki-pushkina > yes, I have real player

< Yorik > go to http://www.middlebury.edu/ ~ gferguso/links.html

< skazki-pushkina > yorik: go to www.octet.com, there are links to Russian Radio there.

The inquiries about my time in Moscow and where I lived demonstrate how Yorik and Devochka used geography to evaluate my credibility. In this respect, they deploy a rhetorical device that Ann Kingsolver (1992) called "placing," a strategy in which people discursively position themselves as insiders or outsiders of particular networks and situations based on where they are from or going to. For Kingsolver, "placing" is not merely a form of "ontological housekeeping," but rather, an important practice of negotiating identity and authority by shaping "a common network or work setting in which individuals can share an identity, a status, or an argument" (p. 130). Although Virtual Russia is an electronic realm, the importance of having traveled to Russia meant something to the members in this chat session and served to enhance my cultural ethos.

Another way this ethos was evaluated was through using the Russian language. In the beginning of the chat, Devochka immediately responds to me in Russian. In effect, the use of Russian serves as a kind of password permitting a certain kind of further interaction to occur. Finally, a test of my cultural credibility came about through the query about online radio and the exchange of links that demonstrated my technological literacy. The prevalence of Russian language Internet radio when this chat occurred was still infrequent, hence, any knowledge about it was unusual and most likely would be in the possession of only the most technologically savvy Russian natives. Shortly after this interaction occurred, the chat room host (Devochka) gave me channel operator status in the chat room. This status gives a participant the most power in a chat room, including the power to define how chat members can and cannot interact, remove people who act rudely, and even transform the chat room interface.

This chat session marked my transition from having an ethos as merely a technologist to having an ethos with a Russian cultural aspect. More importantly, however, it showed group members that I, or rather, *skazki pushkina*, was a member with a somewhat unique combination of Russian cultural–technological competence within the virtual community. A few days after this chat session, the Web administrator of Virtual Russia invited me to join the Virtual Russia Duma. In my questionnaire, I mentioned Lermontov's *Geroi Nashevo Vremeni* (*Hero of our Time*) as a favorite book, and I submitted a photo and entered my nickname *skazki pushkina*. I continued with this name because, as I mentioned, it means "stories of Pushkin" and because I wanted to show that I knew something more about Russia than most people. At the same time, I would not have considered myself a Russian expert. I did not want to pick a name that might be offensive. I felt that hardly anything could be offensive about a candy bar named after a children's story. In addition to these reasons, I also hoped that Russians would recognize that at the time, the candy was only available in Russia itself. People responded to me in Russian with statements like "*a prichem tut Skazki Pushkina?*" (and why are you Skazki Pushkina?) and "*Privet skazka o rybake I rybki!*" ("Hello tale of the fisherman and fish," a children's story by Pushkin). When some American students of Russian later thought it just meant "stories of Pushkin," I changed it to *belka* (squirrel) after the image of a squirrel on the candy wrapper itself. I figured that only people who had access to the candy would make the intended association because this wrapper can only be found within Russia itself. After changing my name, several participants spoke directly with me in Russian and/or assumed I was from Russia.

In developing my virtual Russian ethos as *skazki pushkina/belka*, I gambled that I could maintain a unique cultural–technological ethos that might indeed be higher than it actually should be if people met me face-to-face. This bit of fictionalizing did not trouble me because nearly every identity online is somewhat fictional. In that sense, the credibility of virtual ethos is markedly different than how it is evaluated in real life. According to Marshall Alcorn (1994), the traditional notion of ethos rests within three situated fields: (a) the speaker's location within a secular and divine order; (b) the speaker's situated-ness in place; and (c) the speaker's "singularity." The pseudonymous nature of virtual communities complicates these conventions (Faigley, 1992; Fleckenstein, 2005; Pagnucci & Mauriello, 1999). What replaces the notion of a singular speaker is net presence, often achieved not through demonstrating stability but by creativity and role playing. Indeed, the most credible characters on MOOs and MUDs are usually not the ones who are stable over time but rather characters who are able to move around and transform their virtual identities rapidly in response to rhetorical exigencies. Although such transformations are often restricted to theatrical and ritualistic frames in real life, they form the fabric of socializing in online communities.

MY SCHOLARLY ETHOS

Having worked toward building a technological and cultural ethos, I last took on the task of nurturing a more visible scholarly ethos. Although research was my first purpose, it turned out to be the last and in some ways least important role in the group. The only way I could address my scholarly interests was by gaining access to important community data hidden from public view and only available to certain insiders. Early in my research project, I tried probing the group for questions about its identity and mission, and my inquiries received only one response. Furthermore, of the three ethos, the scholarly component was the most controversial and contested. At roughly the same time I was probing the group, a sociology student clumsily posted an assignment on totalitarianism to the message board. Evidently her instructor told the student to start a fight to determine "group leaders." People directed much criticism toward her and academic studies, saying that she ruined her experiment, that the group was not a laboratory, and that people concerned with such studies are unemployable "victims of Democracy and western bureaucracy." Because of this act, I encountered a pre-existing climate hostile and mistrustful of academic researchers.

To meet my research objectives, I realized that I might need to first cultivate trust in the cultural and technological manner that I described earlier, and then hope that I could leverage that ethos to build scholarly credibility. As I indicated, my initial plan was to do this timidly, gradually, and in a way that my impact on the group would be minimal. At first, I only offered limited technological support without participation in group discussions. This level of interaction did not improve my scholarly ethos nor did it prove satisfactory to group members. As indicated in the chat excerpt above, people wanted to probe and place me, and I was asked to join the Duma rather than remain an outsider. In addition, the group was very sensitive about being watched. I realized over time that I had to respond to inquiries about my research role with honesty, and even that sometimes did not prove satisfactory. In response to this honesty one respondent joked, "So, you are using us for experiments? :-)" What I also did not anticipate was that crises threatening the group put me in a position of greater involvement. I did not have much time to ponder all of the consequences and implications. Instead, I found myself inexorably being drawn into greater involvement to assist the group. I am left to conclude that members seeing my response to these situations perceived that my motivations were sincere, as it was only after I had established an ethos as technologist and culturally competent Virtual Russian that I was able to begin interviewing members and gain access to important information.

Although many factors accounted for my decision to pursue greater involvement, perhaps the most significant was my understanding of how Russian people perceive relationships and the high value they place on interpersonal trust and friendship. Research studies suggest that Russian immigrant communities mistrust officials and bureaucracies (Gerber, 1986; Markowitz, 1995). This mistrust is retained once immigrants come to the United States and often causes considerable difficulties with U.S. bureaucratic organizations. This suspicion of authority is a cultural difference from the American preference to invest faith in the judicial and other authoritative systems. However, Russian and East European groups generally mistrust the abstract legalistic rhetoric of the American justice system and instead prefer communication styles that are concrete and experienced on a personal level. Russian interpersonal communication validates information received and emphasizes an active and responsible participation in change (Mided, 2000). This less abstract, personal touch undoubtedly accounts for how the Russian people have historically survived in a politically tumultuous and unresponsive society (Ries, 1997). Recent events suggest that the same attitudes prevail in Russia even today. The mistrust of official discourse and preference for more interpersonal communal values was also evident through the high number of messages providing assistance on Russian transnational sites.

In a recent study of a Russian-abroad Web Ring, half of the sites conveyed advice about resolving disputes with Americans, obtaining insurance and emergency medical assistance, child rearing, and other practical matters, and 80% included discussion forums and/or chat rooms that often featured interpersonal exchange of advice and viewpoints from experiences living in Russia and elsewhere (Sapienza, 2001). A content analysis of some of the posts makes clearer that members of Virtual Russia shared these mistrustful attitudes toward authority figures:

> My baby got his four vacsination shots yesterday. It made him very upset last night. He got high temperature, he vomited and cried a lot so we had hard time carring him on our arms all the evening. And he bothered our friendly American neighbors so the police broke into at 12 AM and investegated us. Why don't they tell in America who called. I would not say hello to that people anymore.

> These "friendly" neighbors are heartless bastards that do not care about anything except their piece! Of course they can justify their action saying that they thought that somebody was beating on the child but more likely they were just bothered beyond their tolerance level and they called the police to stop this poor child from interfering with their piece! We had the same problem here. It was not about a child crying and it was 10.00 a.m. so we were not in the quiet hours time but the situation was as bad as described by K——. . . . My husband is trying to explain to me that a policeman is a friend here and that I should not over-react when a policeman comes. I do not know about that! In Russia militia comes when there is a real problem!

The attitudes of group members toward authority and potential site surveillance greatly impacted how I would nurture my scholarly ethos within the group and also how the group would manage difficulties with participants. The most visible articulation of these attitudes occurred when members responded to abusive posters by invoking Russian ideas of friendship and communality.

Shortly after Virtual Russia began, a handful of people posted attacks on specific members and made insensitive political and religious remarks, forcing some members to leave in protest. I was included in several off-board discussions (via the messaging program ICQ) about how to handle these abusive members and develop responses to them. A sharp rift emerged between members who favored greater openness and informality and others who wanted policies including censorship and banishment. The solutions were sometimes contextualized with strong cultural implications. As one member remarked, "I explained why I was against banning. In Russia nobody was allowed to criticize bosses and Secretaries of the Communist Party. This way we had bad people running our country for a long time. I believe that the only true judgment is free people's mind and actions based on it." Not only did this discussion involve deliberation over pragmatics, it also incorporated some articulation of the meaning of being a Virtual Russian. As another participant remarked, "VR was born from the ashes of Banishment and censorship, and it goes against everything that you have strived so hard to create. . . . it is a step in the wrong direction for us."

The question confronting the community therefore concerned what kind of communal ethos Virtual Russia wanted to cultivate to protect independent speech and a modicum of politeness and respect. To do this, members introduced what they believed to be a very Russian idea of friendship. This idea initially received attention through a somewhat humorous response to a debate stating, "*rebyata, davayte zhit' druzhno.*" The statement literally means "guys, let's live as friends" and it originates from a hugely popular Soviet TV cartoon from the 1970s called "Kot Leopold" (Leopold the Cat). The cartoon told a story of a good-natured cat who was continuously attacked by two mice. The cat's line addressed to the mice after each mischievous attack was "*rebyata, davayte zhit' druzhno.*" In the context of Virtual Russia, the statement seems to acknowledge the cartoon-like manner of virtual communities that happen to be populated by nicknames and other media creations. The quote suggests that Virtual Russians could adopt a chimerical view of friendship that is both culturally significant in terms of communal ethos yet recognizes the ephemerality of the virtual medium. Conversely, the person who cited the quote may have been using the heated debates online to refer back to how arguments occur within Russia itself. This cultural history of friendship was explained by one member who wrote that in Russia, "a successful friendship means that you can share a couple bottles of wine, argue yourself blue in the face, maybe even beat the shit out of each other, and the next day, you shake hands and thank each other for the wonderful time."

These debates marked the only time when I was asked to use my scholarly expertise to aid the group. A desire was expressed to form a group history and motto and that by so doing, this might focus discussions away from heated arguments, or at the very least, provide a sensible explanation for why they occur. Some that were suggested included, "Virtual Russia: speak your mind, if you dare" and "Virtual Russia: it does not matter whether you are Russian or not; you've found a truly transnational community." I suggested the word "transnational," as I meant to indicate that the group was globalizing a unique and localized mixture of Russian identity, but the Web administrator, who was a Russian emigre, understood the term differently. For him, the term reflected an existing multicultural group of friends sharing an interest in Russian culture who occasionally get into bad arguments yet still remain together. My interpretation of the debates about censorship in the community is that at that particular juncture, members of Virtual Russia needed to view me through a different communicative script more amenable to interpersonal possibilities than that of an outside researcher. In other words, they no longer preferred to think of me as a disinterested scholar and they were willing to speak with me about the debates shaping their community.

Russian speakers in particular are hesitant to give out information to strangers, given the troubled political history of their country of origin. The ethos of interpersonal relationships is the main vehicle by which people nurture trust. Many people in Russia would rather trust a friend than a psychologist or priest. I used the ethos of *skazki pushkina* to form and nourish friendships. In a way, I separated me-the-researcher from the actual interacting character, *skazki pushkina*. It was *skazki pushkina* who marshaled together the three different roles of scholar, technologist, and virtual Russian to participate more fully in the emerging communal ethos of transnational friendship. In the end, the scholarly ethos itself was derived from an avatar.

CONCLUSION AND RECOMMENDATIONS

In this chapter, I have explained how three interanimating roles in a transnational virtual community gave shape to my scholarly position as a participant–researcher. These dimensions included my ethos as a technologist, my ethos as a culturally competent virtual Russian, and my ethos as a scholar on virtual communities. I have tried to show that whether one likes it or not, a researcher will acquire an ethos among the group studied in a participatory design. I would like to close by offering a few suggestions and recommendations for others planning to conduct participant research of virtual communities.

1. Be honest about your research motives. Doing research in transnational online communities inevitably implicates one into a kind of flexible and between-culture or transcultural identity. Researchers should strive to be honest about their research objectives. Even though sharing my objectives led to some sharp remarks and may have created some problems, I nonetheless urge any researcher to maintain that policy and adopt ways of gaining confidence and trust. Researchers should not mislead a group into thinking that they are not doing research, or that the group is not under scholarly surveillance. Although researchers may adopt other valuable roles, they should be very clear that the main purpose for being in the group is to do research. When asked, a researcher should not provide misleading statements about the nature of the research. Being honest does not mean that one explicitly spells out the ramifications, methodology, data, and objectives of a study. Being honest does mean, however, giving the group a straightforward and basic sense as to the nature of the research, why it is important, and, if necessary, what impacts and risks the research might have on community members. Besides being an ethical course of action, it is also, of course, part of the consent procedures required by most Institutional Review Boards when researching human subjects (see Banks and Eble, this collection).

2. *Treat private transmissions with confidentiality.* For private transmissions through ICQ messaging and email, I always asked for written permission before quoting. Public transmissions on the discussion forums present a more complicated matter. Most members of Virtual Russia understood that posts to the discussion forums were available for anyone to read. As such, I did not feel that it was necessary to seek permission to quote the public posts. However, there may exist situations where group members do not see their publicly posted comments as quotable without permission. The perception may have to do with ideological beliefs or with the infrastructure of the site. For example, if the group requires registration procedures that prevent global viewing of posts, that may be a good enough cause to view the group as private. I recommend that researchers try to ascertain the attitudes about this issue on the group before making a decision, and that researchers check with their Institutional Review Boards.

3. *Learn the language and social customs of the other cultures and integrate them in a constructive way into the research design.* If the development of a credible research position involves other roles, knowledge of the customs of a group is strongly advised. People of a different culture are much more willing to trust outsiders if they demonstrate some competence with their own language and familiarity with indigenous values. For example, it was pretty clear from my experience that the nature of credibility mingled with Russian ideas of friendship. Other cultures may have differing views of friendship and trust and therefore may be more or less reluctant to

embrace a researcher as part of a group. These sorts of matters must be understood and negotiated.

4. If called on to help, do it. If researchers find that the scholarly role makes them uniquely qualified to assist the group, they should do it. Although it is argued that staying out of certain situations *is* the ethical goal of research, this advice does not necessarily hold true in naturalistic designs that involve a rhetorical basis. There is a growing trend in rhetoric and communication toward research-as-praxis (Bleich, 1993; Cushman, 1998: Mailloux, 1988). Creating civility and fostering humane communication is a central goal of the current program in which I teach and conduct my research, and meeting this goal means taking initiative on behalf of others in a proactive way. Communication theorists and digital writing scholars have a special obligation to use the methods and results of scholarly inquiry in such a way as to benefit the communities they study.

Digital spaces—like the Virtual Russia community—allow us a window into online transnationality. Research on and in these sorts of spaces is crucial if we are to better understand how different people write, communicate, and assert identity in virtual spaces that span cultures, geographic distances, and languages. Such research, however, requires that we rethink the ways in which we adopt participant roles and establish complex, multifaceted ethos.

5

RESEARCHING (WITH) THE POSTNATIONAL "OTHER"

ETHICS, METHODOLOGIES, AND QUALITATIVE STUDIES OF DIGITAL LITERACY

Iswari P. Pandey

In a world marked by increasing globalization, constant travel and reloca-tion, and computer networks spanning cultural and geopolitical borders, we need to look at sites of literacy learning that are emerging or underrep-resented and also examine potential problems related to research at such sites. This chapter is about the limits and possibilities of researching digi-tal literacy practices through the lens of a postnational perspective. It pres-ents knowing and meaning—and writing—as complex yet provisional transactions in the ever-shifting digital domains of the increasingly tech-nology-mediated, post-positivist world. I contend that although digital environments allow for global, postnational literacy practices, only an ethics of location can help us understand the multiple ways that literacy practices and practitioners are imbricated in power relationships across networks and in the digital terrain. In this chapter, I first explore postna-tionality to situate a study I conducted and use the study to explore and illustrate some of the complexities involved with digital writing research and postnational subjects.

INTRODUCTION

> If the project of Imperialism is violently to put together the episteme that will "mean" (for others) and "know" (for the self) the colonial subject as history's nearly-selved other, the example of these deletions indicate explicitly what is always implicit: that meaning/knowledge intersects power. (Spivak, 1999, p. 215)

This chapter is about the limits and possibility of researching digital literacy practices through the lens of a postnational perspective. It is also about the possibility of knowing and meaning as complex yet provisional transactions in the ever-shifting digital domains of the increasingly technology-mediated, post-positivist world. I contend that although digital environments allow for global, postnational literacy practices, only an ethics of location can help us understand the multiple ways that literacy practices and practitioners are imbricated in power relationships across networks and in the digital terrain.

I raise the issue of "possibility" in qualitative research for a few reasons. First, ethnography and case studies have been conventionally used to study certain people's cultural practices in a given setting, where the researcher acts as a (participant–)observer in the course of the study. In common critical parlance, qualitative research is noted for multivocality and rich narrative; however, in the words of James Clifford (1992), this tendency has "privileged relations of dwelling over travel" (p. 99).[1] In this sense, traditional ethnography has rarely spotlighted travelers or cultural practices of travel. Clifford's observation about the status of anthropological research until the 1990s is also true to today's writing research. Much of the scant research in literacy and writing with participants who have traveled across geocultural borders today involves non-native English-speaking students in Anglo-American contexts in which these traveling subjects are constructed against their native Anglo-American counterparts in certain predictable ways. Such studies typically examine patterns of errors (e.g., stylistic, grammatical, organizational), citation practices in academic writing, or instances of first language (and cultural) interference in second-language products (Bloch, 2001; Pecorari, 2003; Silva, 1997). Even studies involving non-native English-speaking individuals in digital environments reproduce these similar ideological underpinnings, overlooking the complex ways in which these individuals negotiate new literacies alongside their existing ones in a variety of sites and contexts. In a world marked by increasing globalization, constant travel and relocation, and computer networks spanning conventional cultural and geopolitical borders, we need to look at sites of literacy learning that are emerging or underrepresented and also examine potential problems related to research at such sites. More specifically, studying the digital literacy practices of participants I would call postnational subjects presents a set of unique opportunities and challenges.

POSTNATIONAL SUBJECTIVITY

Before I discuss some of the ethical and methodological issues of conducting digital literacy research with postnational subjects, however, I want to frame my discussion with two discourses connected to digital literacy and the reality of postnational subjectivity today. The increased movement of people due to new transport and communication technologies has generated a discourse of diaspora and migrancy. This discourse—in various versions of globalization and postcolonial studies—highlights the realities of travel and migrancy and how they impinge upon our lives in the contemporary world. It also undercuts the conventional wisdom of nation-state in more geographical or territorial terms and forces us to redefine national and cultural identities in terms of what Benedict Anderson (1991) defined as "imagined community": an imagined cultural space of like-minded members.

The second discourse, which concerns computing technologies and the Internet, is crucial to digital literacy and is also intricately tied to the first, especially in that the Web literally breaks down the geographical borders of nation-states. The deterritorialization of nation-states through travels and migration, computing technologies including the Internet, and diffusion of cultural signs under the weight of globalization make today's subjects in general—and those who have experienced transnational migration in particular—truly postnational at the beginning of the 21st century. Their nationalities are present in passports, languages, and so on, but those signs also converge, conflict, and evolve into new signs as newer markers in terms of relocation, ethnicity, citizenship, screen names, and the like replace older ones from previous locations. Therefore, researching with postnational subjects, especially on topics as amorphous as literacy, can be both exciting and challenging. Exciting, because studies of postnational literacy practices may point to potentially new uses of, and even new meanings for, certain literacy acts. Researching with them, however, can also be challenging because postnational status complicates location and identity. It requires the researcher to be sensitive to multiple locations of identity such as class, culture, gender, nationality, language, race/caste/ethnicity, and so forth, and how these identity variables impinge on the relationship that will produce, and will be produced by, the study. Even as attention to these issues is valuable to a work involving any subjects, postnational participants bring with them subjectivities at least doubly marked in these categories. Moreover, although they are simultaneously affiliated to these locations of identity, those identity variables do not carry the same value or meaning. That is, they are differently related to different social and cultural settings. For example, a member of the ruling bourgeoisie in his or her native country is more than likely used to an identity as one with little experience of being Other. When the same person immigrates to a new place, he or she is suddenly marked as Other. Digital technologies make transnational literacies possible by enabling such individuals to overcome the limitations of physical boundaries and simultaneously connect to some or all of those locations. Therefore, digital literacies carry a special premium for these subjects, for they may facilitate postnational subjects' movement across cultural and geographical borders.

The digital, however, is also politically aligned, for each location carries a different status and cultural capital owing to colonial and imperial intervention. The literacies that digital, networked spaces afford complicate research approaches in more than one way. Learning and knowing (about) those literacies are implicated in an uneven distribution of power. To understand the interplay of the personal (learning/practicing) and the larger context in which that individual practice is understood and valued, researchers have recently started paying attention to the way individuals are positioned in what is called "cultural ecology" (Selfe & Hawisher, 2004; Romberger, this collection). Cultural ecology shapes and is shaped by individual practices, and the postnational condition greatly widens the scope of this ecology. Cultural ecology also complicates the way we understand individual subjectivity in qualitative research in ways that can potentially challenge the learner/knower binary. Attending to issues of power and representation in qualitative studies of literacy, scholars such as Ellen Cushman (1996), Gesa Kirsch (1999), Peter Mortensen and Kirsch (1996), and Patricia Sullivan (1996) have argued that qualitative research should be not just *about* subjects but, and primarily, *for* them. Although executing this call is worthwhile, transferring the techniques of traditional qualitative research to literacy studies in digital environments is fraught with difficulties, as the new, dynamic, global, and digital sites of study pose different opportunities and challenges.

To examine the opportunities and challenges of conducting digital research about and with postnational subjects, I first interrogate the idea of postnationality more fully. I then briefly reflect on a study I conducted in a digital environment, and, finally, propose an ethics for conducting and understanding digital writing research involving postnational subjects.

SITUATING THE POSTNATIONAL OTHER

Postcolonial scholars such as Partha Chatterjee (1993) have identified a hegemonically homogenizing "subject-centered rationality" (p. xi) in Western historical discourse that disqualifies the local as "fragmentary" in the interest of the putative universal. According to Chatterjee, post-Enlightenment modernity promoted a "subject-centered rationality" that:

> claims for itself a singular universality by asserting its epistemic privi-lege over all other local, plural, and often incommensurable knowl-edges; it proclaims its own unity and homogeneity by declaring all other subjectivities as inadequate, fragmentary, and subordinate; it declares for the rational subject an epistemic as well as moral sover-eignty that is meant to be self-determined, unconditioned, and self-transparent. (p. xi)

Such a predisposition to hold "self-evident" the "sovereignty" of dominant subject positions in terms of race, gender, culture, and nation-state could be challenged by studies devoted to marginal, plural subjects involved in acts of knowledge construction. In other words, qualitative studies can make a gesture toward democratizing and validating plural human subjec-tivities, their worldviews, and knowledges hitherto subordinated by the hegemonic universal subject. Historically speaking, if modernist positivist tendencies reestablished the centrality of universal subjectivity, the politi-cal implication of postmodernist questioning renders representation virtu-ally impossible. Although the political consequences of post-Enlightenment modernity and postmodern distrust of meaning and meaningful social transformation at least bear a resemblance to each other, a reconceptual-ization of human agency along lines of postcolonial theories offers a new way of looking at qualitative studies and postnational subjects. Such a position enables us to construct discursive space by rendering visible the cracks in the grand narratives of dominant subject positions and by directing focus to the historical rootedness of ethnic, gender, or national identity roles.

Researchers can examine digital environments not as free and decontexualized, but as space where traditional power hierarchies collapse and yet are retained. It is in this space that we can navigate even the most stringent of borders and create alternative communities. Yet aspects of the space itself often severely limit the extent of that possibility. As Cynthia Selfe and Richard Selfe (1994) have pointed out, and as subsequent studies have demonstrated, digital spaces are also sites where different forms of oppression are reproduced: sexism (e.g., Brady Aschauer, 1999; Brail, 1996; Haas, Tulley, & Blair, 2002; Rickly, 1999; Sullivan, 1997), racism (e.g., Bomberger, 2004; McConaghy & Snyder, 2000; McKee, 2002), colonialism (Hawisher & Selfe, 2000; Selfe & Selfe, 1994), and homophobia (DeWitt, 1997; Peters & Swanson, 2004; Woodland, 1999). Similarly, even as digital space allows artists, gamers, and writers to reach across national borders to collaborate, it also risks reducing complex lives into usernames and electronic signals. Insofar as the reach beyond geopolitical borders is concerned, both digital technology and postnational subjects share a common fate: They both are often seen as somehow decontextualized, exempt from the problem of here and now.

Postnational is a term often applied to subjects marked as foreign or transnational, but by using the term, I do not want to suggest that only such-and-such people have an aura exotic enough to elude identity categories. Just as no two research participants are identical, no subject can be treated as representative of a culture, social group, or nation. Therefore, by pointing out the unique post-/transnational condition of individual lives, I do not mean to suggest that other fairly less nomadic subjects are generalizable. Nor do I think that only those individuals who have traveled across geopolitical borders qualify as traveling subjects. Travel is a constant metaphor in today's life. In a world marked by increasing globalization and mass mediation, our daily lives intersect at multiple crossovers, and it is imperative for researchers to consider how travels across various fronts (e.g., media, family, community, culture, politics) are conditioned by one's literacy practices. Christopher Keller (2004) argued that qualitative studies of composition have mostly fixed on classroom research and failed to take into account students' travels across various socially constructed identity locations. To understand the subtle impacts of these travels in students' writing and literacy development, Keller recommended that we develop a multisited ethnographic model of research that examines more than students' "naturalized" identity as students. In this sense, all subjects are travelers, and travel is not limited to transnational experience. However, what I want to suggest by highlighting the transnational experience of research participants are the potential overlaps, slippages, and conflicts in the digital literacy practices of postnational subjects. The condition of postnationality is neither fully above and beyond nation-ness nor exclusively within it.

I deploy the term postnational not to suggest any false, teleological movement somehow beyond or after any problematics of nation-ness where subjects would be in a position to go about their identity-construction business freely, unfettered from geopolitical anchoring, or be liberated from the burden of history. Instead, the term makes it possible to imagine an alternative conception of communities, kinships, and conflicts through deterritorialized modes of contact. Although modern transport and communications technologies enable transnational movements of people and produce new possibilities of communities across geographical borders, these communities are not "pure" or exclusive. Moreover, the condition of postnationality enables affiliations of people to transcend imagined communities, allowing hybrid and diasporic modes of cultural forms and identification (Bhabha, 1994). The "hybrid" in these deterritorialized transnational spaces produces the cultural disjunctures that constitute, in the words of Arjun Appadurai (1996), contemporary "globalscapes" where different identities overlap, conflict, and transform. This condition of postnationality brings to the fore a need to redefine identity in ways similar to postcolonial theorists, who propose an identity politics that rejects the fictive categories of ethnic, class, and national subjectivities or subjecthood.[2] Before we become too euphoric about the possibility of such transformations in digital spaces, however, we also need to remember that the popular understanding of identity remains stuck on exclusive categories of race, gender, ethnicity, and nationness. The condition of postnationality today, then, is that of an in-betweenness or what Homi Bhabha called "almost, not quite," for these individuals belong to more than a singular edifice of nation, culturally or politically, and can belong to multiple locations without having been an insider anywhere. In short, I use the term postnational to point to the porous and conflictual nature of an individual's relationship to culture and nationness in a technology-rich, mass-mediated world.

ISSUES IN REPRESENTING
THE (POSTNATIONAL) OTHER

Scholars in composition research have called for reciprocal, collaborative, and mutually enriching relationships between researchers and subjects. Recognizing the seminal role of research subjects, they have also called for making research beneficial for those subjects/others. The researcher, according to Newkirk (1996), has the ethical responsibility to work with subjects to identify and rectify problem areas and to value participants' interpretations of research findings. Similarly, Sullivan (1996) argued, "if the other is the enabling condition of ethnographic research . . . then an ethnography must be both an adequate account of the literate practices of others and accountable to those others" (p. 98). To make such studies accountable, Kirsch (1999) called on researchers for "opening up the research agenda to subjects, listening to their stories, and allowing them to actively participate, as much as possible, in the design, development, and reporting of research" (p. 257) to make the research process and product ethical and beneficial to researcher and subject.

These calls, and I mention just a small sample, constitute a growing awareness in writing research to make qualitative research more ethical and accountable. However, just as there are no two identical subjects, there is no single methodological approach that fits all research subjects or settings. After all, research is always already an interested project initiated by someone for specific academic, professional, financial, or similar investments. Even as we consider the possibility of collaboration after subjects are recruited, it is possible that there are conflicts of motives and expectations. Moreover, the deeper the cultural and political differences between researcher and subjects, the lesser the chances of mutual reciprocity in goals and outcomes. My experience researching digital literacies indicates that the objectives of researcher and subject may not only *not be* mutually beneficial but may also be mutually contradictory to a certain extent. Institutional affiliation of researcher and postnationality of research participants add to an already complex process.

To illustrate more specifically the issues researchers of digital literacies need to consider in relation to fluid postnational subjects, I discuss a study on gaming and literacy I conducted in the spring of 2004 (Pandey, Pandey, & Shreshtha, in press). I then illustrate more specifically the issues researchers may encounter when researching and representing the digital literacy practices of postnational subjects.

GAMING AND DIGITAL
LITERACY PRACTICES

Some Promises and Perils of Online Research

My study was based on the current understanding of literacy as purposeful acts embedded in larger cultural, political, and economic contexts (Barton & Hamilton, 1998; Brandt, 1995; Gee, 1992, 2003; Selfe & Hawisher, 2004; Street, 1984, 1993). Brandt stated that literacy learning is highly contextualized, develops in nonacademic settings, and is often re-appropriated for divergent uses. James Paul Gee (2003) described videogaming as an alternative but powerful site of literacy learning. As Gee argued, gaming provides more effective literacy and learning environments than do schools:

> better theories of learning are embedded in the video games many children in elementary and high school play than in the schools they attend. Furthermore, the theory of learning in good video games fits better with the modern, high-tech global world today's children and teenagers live in than do the theories (and practices) of learning they see in school. (p. 7)

I wanted to explore gamers' literacy development in a cultural context, understand how individuals learn specialized knowledges and literacies in gaming environments, and examine how these literacies converge and conflict with formal literacies taught and learned at schools in transnational contexts. I studied these issues with two South Asian gamers, who were also beginning their graduate studies at two Midwestern universities. As my effort to enlist participants through a digital forum was not successful, I enlisted participants by means of personal contact. A recent acquaintance of mine (Laxman) happened to be an avid gamer, who agreed to participate and who also introduced me to another gamer (Angish). Educated in Nepal and India, both were exposed to electronic media early in their learning; played games extensively; and were highly proficient in using digital media for personal, educational, and professional purposes. Although both were technically Nepali citizens with interest in their native cultures, they were also exposed to Anglo-American culture since early childhood in their English-language schools. Both spoke four languages, considered English as their "almost" first language, and thought they were more than the citizens of any one country. As a native of Nepal like them, only older, and a graduate student, I was confident of a good collaboration with them. I also counted on my academic interest in gaming as a good match to their engagement in gaming. I hoped our seemingly common background and citizenship would help me understand and interpret the ways my research participants played and interpreted the games in relation to their experience with other kinds of literacy learning.

I emailed Laxman and Angish a set of questions to respond to at their convenience, and return as an email attachment. The responses I got were brief, perhaps because of the timing of the study, which was in the last few weeks of a busy semester for both, and also because of the demanding nature of a long list of questions. Although interviewing them via email allowed me to ask questions repeatedly without having to arrange a specific time and location, the brevity of answers made me long for a face-to-face interview in which I would also have access to various gestures and body language to understand their responses more fully and prod them further when relevant. As I learned later, their brief answers were very significant, sometimes even like standard position statements, the strategic depth of which I had failed to understand. Between the two, Angish was more direct but equally precise. My failure to interpret his responses, even though I thought I possessed an insider's knowledge of their cultural ecology, meant that I needed to constantly work on my assumptions and not take any background knowledge for granted. I read their responses for multiple meanings, contextualized them, and looked for patterns in the data: Their digital literacies were largely affected by the cultural ecology of the country—gaming had positively enhanced their reading and writing abilities and increased their understanding of life and learning in the United States, as well as their understanding of a capitalistic corporate culture they needed to know as business students. However, there were also obvious class differences between the two, from the schools they attended, their family background, and the expectations of digital literacy and future goals. This was also reflected in the kind of games they played or the different rationale they had for playing. After I crafted the first draft of the report on the research, I emailed it to them for their opinion, and I also requested them to revise the text in any way they liked. However, neither one would add or alter a single word except one or two factual details.

Reflections and Reinterpretations, Representation and Accountability

As I undertook the study, I thought that I had a sound methodology for a digital literacy research project. I wanted to make the research process collaborative and mutually enriching. I was mindful of what scholars in writing research had suggested about developing a collaborative methodology for qualitative research. Following Cynthia Selfe and Gail Hawisher (2004), I offered participants what I thought at the time was an opportunity to co-author the study (as I will discuss below, I am now not so certain about that "co-authorship"). Selfe and Hawisher argued, and also demonstrated in practice, that co-authorship could be a "viable, practical, and ethical resolution" (p. 13) to problems of representation and accountability. I appreciated the opportunity co-authorship would give me to resolve issues of representation. However, the brief responses I received, as well as little enthusiasm about co-authoring on the part of my participants, meant that the study was not as collaborative as the term co-author might imply. When I mailed the first draft with three names as authors—after all of us initially agreed to co-author the study—one of the participants immediately emailed back to say that he was pleasantly surprised to see his name as an author but added, "I don't need to be [a] named author. Please don't mind." "Don't need to be" was crucial to understanding whether he was declining to co-author, which I thought he meant the first time I read it. I even told the project editor that one participant had declined to co-author, but when I mulled over the note one more time, I wondered if he was being extremely polite. Only when I explicitly told him that my offer was genuine and he deserved the ownership and credit as an author—unless he really did not want to be named—he accepted. Later conversations revealed that he had initially had problems understanding some of the more polite professors and mentors because "they would sometimes make me feel like they are asking me to choose or there is an option. They do that even if they actually mean a command kind of thing." He also related an instance in which a professor had read a paper and emailed him suggesting that: "would you like to revise it in such and such a way . . . and if you decide to, consider so and so." He did not revise it, because the assignment did not require multiple drafts, and, as he put it, "the professor also said how he enjoyed the paper, blah blah blah." He realized the real meaning of such effusive comments as soon as he received a grade with a note "not revised." The experience made him extremely cautious, and he did not want to make the same mistake with me.

In hindsight, this misreading of responses to my offer to co-author also indicated another slippage typical to studies involving postnational participants. I see two things happening here: one at the level of manifest language and another at the level of conscious goals. As mentioned in the opening part of this chapter, postnational subjects bring with them a complex history of what counts as appropriate with regard to a range of choices and this range gets reflected in their language use. This participant, whose response to co-authorship I misread, was never involved in any study before (except surveys) and was not aware of co-authoring as a practice. On top of that, he was trying to suggest, as our subsequent conversations revealed, that if I were offering the opportunity only to appear generous, he wanted me "not [to] worry about it."

The postnational condition of research participants often leads them to produce hybridized cultural and linguistic signs that, when taken or interpreted without an understanding of accompanying context, may be easily misunderstood. I had read the response as a direct one, as is valued in the mainstream American communicative context. Other moments of similar slippage owing to language use concerned yes/no response patterns in English, which varies from most other language systems. My participants came from Nepal and Nepali was their native language, in which a "yes" response to a negative question affirms negation, unlike in standardized English in which it would challenge the question and the speaker's assumption about what is being said. This was occasionally reflected in one of my participant's responses. He sometimes followed the English response pattern and in a few cases fell back to the native Nepali system, which meant that I had to look at the larger context to infer his intention and check back with him if not completely sure. As Martin Baik and Rosa Shim (1993) noted, such instances abound in cross-cultural communication because of different discourse systems and may sometimes interfere in the process of communication itself.

It may be argued that in a face-to-face situation, there would be other ways to gauge the extent of acceptance or refusal, as we would have access to the semiotics of gestures and body language to aid in understanding words more correctly. When we have to rely on the signs transmitted through digital media alone, we have to be more cautious about the intent of any message and the cultural–rhetorical roots behind the signs to make up for the absence of other resources available to us in a one-on-one, face-to-face interview. I do not, however, mean that research in or using nondigital media is immune to any misunderstandings or misinterpretations. Rather, it is important to be mindful that digital environments do not resolve the potential to reproduce the limitations of cultural, linguistic, and ideological systems.

If language use marked by hybrid cultural practices may be one cause of misunderstanding the postnational subject in digital contexts, another source of misunderstanding, perhaps a more potent one, might be potential conflicts of interest between the researcher and the postnational other.

Perhaps the participant who was not interested in co-authorship chose to decline because co-authoring a study on gaming as digital literacy might not be of much value in his field of study. The conflict, then, was between what he was led to see as legitimate intellectual work, such as the statistically verifiable empirical studies in business and management, compared to the ostensibly story-telling type of knowledge production I was offering him. Although I valued this work because digital literacy is emerging as important intellectual work in my field of composition and literacy studies, he may have thought that it did not count as such in his own field of study or prospective career. Further, they were requested as research participants through a mutual friend and they did not set the research agenda. Moreover, they decided to participate perhaps because they could not say no. As Newkirk (1996) suggests, inviting subjects to participate already carries some force. Although the subject signs a consent form acknowledging voluntary participation, it does not necessarily mean that the subject always feels a real freedom not to, especially when the two are in some kind of culturally or institutionally valued relationship (cultural/national affiliation, teacher–student relation, etc.). In our case, too, all three of us had the cultural residue of being non-western: all three came from a culture characterized as one in which seniors both in age and qualifications command respect from their juniors. It could be possible that my participants didn't want to disappoint me by refusing to collaborate in the study. When I raised this issue recently with them, one of them said that was perhaps a cause initially. Besides, although I imagined myself being on the same level as my participants, they didn't see me as such. My institutional affiliation, my IRB approval papers, and my status as a PhD student had constructed a halo of power visible to them but not to me.

In this way, although this study on digital literacy practices was impacted by factors such as cultural backgrounds and evolving relationships, responses to gaming and to the study tools (e.g., the questionnaire) were also conditioned by factors external to that environment, creating other opportunities for slippages and misunderstandings. Some of the questions I asked participants assumed a more western, American bias toward what constitutes standard educational practice. For example, when I asked them about their childhood experiences with flash cards used by their teachers to help them to learn vocabulary and how to read, both did not know what I was talking about, because flash cards had not been available or used in their schools or homes. Instead, they interpreted the question by associating it with card playing, which was reviled as a form of gambling by their parents and teachers. Similarly, to a question asking if violent games made the gamer more aggressive, as a large body of commentary holding gaming accountable for violence has, Laxman's initial response was "I love peace." When I asked that he elaborate on it later, he explained how close and loving a family he came from. It was only much later that I realized he was challenging the question itself and strategically presenting his persona in contrast to the implied meaning of the question. At first, however, I took it only to mean that he was being defensive (which he perhaps was), evasive, or even not cooperative. It took a while to realize that I was not on the same page as he was, and it led to a substantial revision in the essay resulting from the research later. He had heard the usual complaints about gaming and its tendency to promote violence, but for him it made no sense; nor did my question mean much. More importantly, both my participants thought that the various games they played were preparing them to participate in the fast pace of American life. They also considered reading and writing in terms of how these activities would help them in professional competition rather than anything else. Such literacy practices and motivations obviously lie beneath the radar of conventional literacy research interested in surface-level language production.

Conflicting understandings of collaboration also contributed to some early confusion. For me, collaboration would mean that subjects positively respond to participate in the study and answer questions, offer new comments or thoughts where and when they considered relevant during the (email) interviews, review draft interpretations, add their thoughts where they disagreed, and, when offered, hopefully agree to co-author. However, this is not what my participants had in mind. Even as they agreed to participate in the study, co-authoring and right to interpretation were less important to them than enlisting help of a perceived expert on some of the writing tasks they needed help with, such as editing their personal statements, resumes, and so on, which would carry "real" value. I had initially resorted to what Ellen Cushman (1998) termed "missionary activism" in offering collaboration on my terms, not theirs. Katrina Powell and Pamela Takayoshi (2003) articulated such potential conflicts of goals, as they interrogated the meaning of collaboration when researchers invite their subjects "to accept a role we have created for them in a study we have shaped" (p. 398). Powell and Takayoshi proposed that

> if we want authentic reciprocity, research participants should be allowed to construct roles for themselves and us in the same way we construct roles for them. Further, we should be willing to adopt the roles created for us at least some of the time, and we need to understand that these roles might sometimes fall outside our concerns as

researchers (i.e., our research questions, our data collection processes, and goals). (p. 398)

Although Powell and Takayoshi's call is worthwhile for research with any subjects, what lies "outside our concerns as researchers" with postnational subjects might sometimes lie literally outside national boundaries. Five months after he had gone missing from email contact and since agreeing to participate in the project, Akhtar (name changed) emailed me from New Delhi in August 2004. He had traveled home to India to attend to urgent family business, but was denied a visa to re-enter the United States because he was changing his status from student to worker and the process was not yet complete. He could reach me via email and could have resumed his role in the project, but he was not interested. Understandably, I was on the other side of the fence now and wished I could help him to negotiate the U.S. bureaucratic border, ever-tightening in the post–9/11 world. In a research project with South Asian immigrants, participants have told me stories that resemble Akhtar's, only more painfully. Despite being politically as American as any other citizen, they were initially led to believe that I was an intelligence officer checking up on them. This demonstrates that in spite of an insider's status in terms of nationality and citizenship, race, language, and postnationality, continue to mark them as the other. Meanwhile, thanks to their digital literacy and communication technologies, these Pakistani-borns participate in the "imagined community" of fellow members from around the globe.

Researching postnational participants in digital environments is thus fraught with problems. From attracting research participants, to understanding and interpreting their responses, to representing them in the final research product is not easy. Even as I am writing this chapter, I am concerned about how I am representing Angish and Laxman here to readers. I am calling them at times "my participants," which is patronizing language and reflects a sense of ownership. I am *re*-presenting them in ways that suit my framing of the implications in more or less conventional forms of academic discourse. Presenting misunderstandings as "teaching" moments and drawing "wisdom" from our experiences spun for public consumption is nothing new. I admit that I may have more to say about those moments as I keep on with the business of living and learning across different cultural and geopolitical spaces—all this because I am in flux, as are my research participants. No still representation that attempts to freeze a moment and preserve it as real can be real, for the nature of life in the postnational context is such that no moment will always remain fixed—at least not for long.

IMPLICATIONS: LESSONS LEARNED

Creating Reciprocal and Collaborative Research Relationships

Because effective collaboration happens only through mutual effort, in future studies I would ask for what would be in the best interest of my participants for me to do, both within and outside of the context of our research. My inquiry would precede my research questions, and I would strive for more collaborative practices. This would help me understand their perspective of collaboration and have them on board from the beginning of the research process. Instead of emailing my long list of questions once they agreed to participate in the study, I would ask them if they had any questions or observations about their gaming practices and if they wanted to address specific issues. Such an effort at the early stage of research would also help identify the role they would construct for me and allow me to take on that role more meaningfully. Conversely, if it were a role that I would not be able to take on, I could renegotiate my space and role in the research relationship. Although digital environments are supposed to represent progress for the potential to break down power hierarchies and geopolitical distances, digital spaces reproduce the same ideologies of power (Hawisher & Selfe, 1991; Selfe & Selfe, 1994) unless the subjects at both ends of the machine can fully experience equality.

Locating Postnationality

I would also be a little more alert to the postnationality of my participants; that is, I would be more aware of potential conflicts of interest between us despite assumptions about commonality I began with. This attention would mean being more explicit about what I was doing, what I wished to achieve, and what that meant in my discipline of study. Reducing chances of misunderstanding and positioning myself this way would also help participants think through the terms and motives from their disciplinary and/or personal vantage points. Similarly, I would be more careful in describing my questions, responses, and what I expected them to do pertaining to the study. Although imbued in the competitive colonial narrative of the west reinforced by gaming practices, my subjects carried some linguistic and cultural tracing of their native homes, while at the same time they were also responsive to the needs and priorities of the information society. Our points of departure for the study were not the same.

Working Toward a Postnational Ethics of Location

Digital environments allow for postnational literacies and rhetorics, practices that transcend and yet are embedded in a specific geocultural location. Such possibilities present challenges to think about ethical issues pertaining to knowledge construction about and in these networked environments. This new environment is not a definite, closed system, but is a constantly evolving one where meanings are in flux and predicated on particular situations and experiences. Because digital literacies and rhetorics about them tend to be decontextualized, the first step toward more ethical study is defining one's location as researcher. Constant cognizance of location reminds us that we are still operating with our value-laden perspectives in the seemingly neutral space of the digital. Only when we are mindful of the fact that technologies, including digital writing, are cultural artifacts entrenched with tacit assumptions about users and user identities, will we comprehend how individuals who do not fit the role of the assumed user negotiate those technologies.

However, a mere recognition of location would not take us far. Unless we interrogate that location and the values associated with it, we will not be able to understand our relationship to the (postnational) "Other." Naïve discussions of center–periphery relationships are not so innocent: after all, they collaborate in manufacturing the margin. Thus, a mere awareness of location may result in reification of location-associated stereotypes, while a robust interrogation of location would examine the researcher–participant relationship and attend to issues in their complexity. In my case, for example, I began to notice the magnitude of my power as a researcher over my participants only when I began to wonder if my role as a researcher who initiated the research, secured IRB approval, and asked them questions influenced the ways they responded in the digital environment in which the study took place. Our common cultural roots had only a little value.

CONCLUSIONS:
ATTENDING TO ISSUES OF LOCATION

One hallmark of the present era of globalization is the transnational movement of people at an unprecedented scale and the emergence of postnational subjects, who struggle to overcome their marginality in a metropoli-
tan center away from the "margin," where the center–periphery metaphor
might not be as easily understood (for these individuals might be positioned in any number of ways to the dominant culture in another geocultural location, which in turn is marginalized to the center of global monop-
oly capital). Transnational digital literacy practices represent attempts at
inscribing histories, attempts to claim agency and power and not pass as
objects of imperial or national histories. We need to recognize that the center and margin are constantly manufactured, and we help in their reproduction when we speak from and about them without problematizing
them. The research experience I have described above indicates that I was
aware of my location as well as that of my participants, but because I did
not initially interrogate that location adequately, I also misread participants' motives and responses. I was initially unaware of the differences
between my participants and me produced by the institutionalized
research practices of the U.S. academy. Therefore, understanding the participant–researcher relationship based on a clear understanding and interrogation of location is necessary to ethical inquiry in digital writing
research.

Although the process of defining and interrogating should be a conscious and ongoing process in any qualitative research, the complex nature
of today's digital environment makes such an ethics crucial because slippages occur more easily when we have the presence of a text separated
from its embodied context of origin. Bringing to the fore issues of inequity
and dealing with them enables us to understand the postnational "Other"
better. Ignoring issues of location produces mere shadows of struggling
lives. In this way, while locating oneself in more than one way is important
in research, it is all the more important in a digital environment because of
the shifting nature and global reach of its scope. After all, no one can completely escape positionality (Chiseri-Strater, 1996) or cultural/national situatedness (Fox, 1994), but one can work to understand it and read it back
into our constructions of self and other. To rephrase Gayatri Spivak's (1999)
statement in the opening, an ethics of location helps us make explicit what
remains implicit in many ways—"that meaning/knowledge intersects

power" (p. 215) and helps reflect on how the digital and the political, the national and the postnational converge to produce one another—the researcher and the researched.

NOTES

1. Although not directly a discussion of research methods or practice, see also Lisa Nakamura's (2002) extended discussion of identity tourism in digital spaces often rhetorically constructed as "raceless."
2. For more theoretical discussions of postnationality, transnationality, and post-coloniality, see Anderson (1991), Appadurai (1996), Bhabha (1992, 1994), and Habermas (1999). For an analysis of self, other, and (post)nationalism, see Delanty (1999) and Hedetoft, Ulf, and Hjort (2002).

6

RESEARCHING HYBRID LITERACIES

METHODOLOGICAL EXPLORATIONS OF ETHNOGRAPHY AND THE PRACTICES OF THE *CYBERTARIAT*[1]

Beatrice Smith

In this chapter, I examine methodological and ethical issues faced by researchers working in international, technologized, hybrid settings—that is, in settings that are both virtual and physical. Specifically, I explore some of the methodological and ethical issues related to conducting ethnographic research in outsourcing environments. First, I provide a brief overview to contextualize outsourcing before summarizing some general principles of ethnographic research. I connect the context and the methodology with descriptions of a study I have undertaken analyzing outsourcing work settings in Ghana. I conclude with some recommendations and implications about how ethnographic methodologies might be adapted to the diverse social, cultural, and technological climate of studying information technology work in the 21st century.

INTRODUCTION

The global restructuring of capital and the information technology (IT) and business process (BP) outsourcing arrangements this restructuring has engendered now mean that thousands of people around the world engage in work practices directly tied to global connectivity and the digital networks that connectivity makes possible. These workers do not only inhabit their disembodied virtual work spaces—there are physical, material places that they call "work." For us to begin to understand the literacies related to these material and immaterial work places, we need to refashion traditional research methodologies, like ethnography, to study both the physical and the virtual spaces such work places occupy.

Research in sites where workers use information and communication technologies (ICTs) presents unique opportunities and challenges for researchers working at the intersections of literacy and technologies (Appadurai, 1990; Bruce, 1999; Castells, 1996; Hawisher & Selfe, 2000; Kellner, 2000; Luke, 2000, 2003). In western industrialized societies, considerable attention has gone into exploring how ICTs are shaping the ways people work, play, and live (Facer & Furlong, 2001; Feenberg, 2002; Luke, 2000; Nixon, 2003; Selfe, 1999a; Smith, 2002). However, as Western companies cut labor costs by outsourcing process services outside the Western hemisphere, many less "industrialized" societies are experiencing changes to their ways of life and their patterns of employment. These shifts are making global connectivity a transformative dynamic in both public and private life in these societies. As a researcher with interests in work place literacies, and having been born in Ghana, I am particularly intrigued by the convergence of technological innovation, the global restructuring of capital, and the literacies that enable participation in these networks and forums.[2] Further, as a number of scholars have noted, it is becoming apparent that epistemologies developed with less fluid environments in mind may not provide adequate tools to research these converged and technologically mediated spaces (Leander, 2003; Mackey, 2003; Nixon, 2003). Recognizing the theoretical and methodological issues facing the field in relation to literacies and ICTs, Margaret Mackey (2003) pointed out that "now more than ever we need thick description of interpretive acts, thick analysis, and thick theorizing" (p. 405) to research the full range of issues associated with online literacies. Off-shore outsourcing sites create particularly rich research contexts within which a number of theoretical and methodological issues can be explored.

In this chapter, I explore some of the methodological and ethical issues related to conducting ethnographic[3] research at ICT-infused outsourcing environments. The first part of the chapter contextualizes business process and information technology outsourcing with particular attention to the literacies that these arrangements trigger. The second part summarizes the general principles and goals of ethnography while highlighting the particular theoretical questions they raise for research in what I am calling hybrid environments—environments that combine virtual and the nonvirtual spaces and their attendant practices. The third part uses my experience conducting research in Ghana as illustration of the particular issues related to ethnographic work in hybrid environments.

MATERIAL AND IMMATERIAL LABORSCAPES: A FUSION OF PRACTICES AND SPACES

Business process outsourcing has become a specialty of a number of companies as they become hubs for other companies seeking to shift process functions elsewhere. Accounts of the work of these outsourcing companies abound in the popular press as journalists seek to document the work of these companies. With this attention has come a backlash of sorts against the exportation of American jobs.[4] For many Americans, India has become synonymous with off-shore information technology and business process outsourcing. But companies are also locating these off-shore hubs in other, less-known sites. Ghana has become one such hub for a number of companies that provide clients with IT and BP solutions (other, less-known sites are Guatemala, Jamaica, Fiji, and the Dominican Republic). Work at these companies is done in virtual, fluid, and digital environments. Thus, although these outsourcing sites are physically located in Ghana, the work is done on a virtual network, and the solutions the Ghanaian employees offer enable a number of companies to tailor solutions to their American clients almost instantaneously and often with the help of other sites on this virtual web of networks. This back and forth between sites on a virtual web of hubs raises questions about the location at which a researcher studies such a work place. Methodologically, for me at least, this research process raises the question of what ethnography looks like in the hybrid environments that have become the mainstay of ICT outsourcing work. For example:

- Where is the work place located?
- By environment, do we mean the physical work place or do we mean the virtual? Could we mean both?

  ◊ What constitutes a participant–observer stance in such an environment?
  ◊ Should we shift that stance to that of an observant participant?

◊ Is that stance applicable only to what the researcher does at the physical location?

- When a researcher decides to work in such spaces does she negotiate access to one physical site and/or does she negotiate access to all? Can a researcher assume that access to one site will lead to the other sites on the network of hubs?
- Could one research such a work place without being in any of its physical spaces and if so, which site is such work studying?
- Could one use traditional ethnographic methodology in studying the physical work space even if one does not gain access to the whole web of virtual networks?
- How does a researcher protect company confidentiality in situations where identifying the country where the research takes place may be enough to lead to company identification?
- Given how controversial outsourcing itself has become, what ethical issues confront a researcher whose work might end up being a record of where jobs have migrated?

These are the questions central to my discussion in this chapter.

PRINCIPLES AND GOALS OF TRADITIONAL ETHNOGRAPHIC RESEARCH

Ethnographic methodology allows researchers to construct a comprehensive understanding of the behaviors, social interactions, values, and beliefs of a community or social group; that is, it enables the ethnographer to paint "a picture of the people" (Florio-Ruane & McVee, 2002).[5] As a research approach, it is nonlinear—it is a dynamic, recursive, and interactive–responsive approach that requires the researcher to be reflexive (Green, Dixon, & Zaharlick, 2003). Ethnography enables the researcher to understand, in some significant detail, how people think and how they develop their particular viewpoints (Bogdan & Biklen, 2003; Geertz, 1973; Heath, 1983). The principal goal of the ethnographer then is to "study, explore, and describe a group's culture" (Moss 1992, p. 155). Through the examination of ordinary daily routines, practices, and observances of communities and groups, the ethnographer works rather self-consciously to create for outsiders a native-like (emic) accessibility to the communities under study. This traditional goal of ethnography has been subject to critique as researchers have examined the ways in which such cultural descriptions provide avenues for ethnographers to gain control over "others." Ethnography was, for example, an enabler of colonialism (Erickson, 1986).[6] Thus, as Susan Florio-Ruane and Mary McVee (2002) pointed out, contemporary ethnographers still have to grapple with how they address the ever-present danger of constructing descriptions of others that freeze or stereotype their realities and in the process leave them voiceless.

Understanding what Constitutes Ethnography

A central principle that informs ethnographic work is how that work enables the construction of culture. Although anthropologists disagree on the definition of culture, James Spradley's (1980) idea that it is "the acquired knowledge people use to interpret experience and generate behavior" (p. 6) provides a good start. Echoing the same sentiments, R. P. McDermott (1976) noted that "at its best, an ethnography should account for the behavior of people by describing what it is they know that enables them to behave appropriately given the dictates of common sense in their community" (quoted in Bogdan & Biklen, 2003, p. 159). For contemporary ethnographers, culture is not seen as a static system; it is recognized that "people and things are increasingly out of place" (Clifford & Marcus, 1988, p. 6) and therefore the focus of cultural inquiry is on the "in between spaces" where people engage one another (Bhabha, 1994). One of the most often cited conceptions of culture in ethnographic work is Clifford Geertz's (1973) idea of ethnography as "thick description." Using Gilbert Ryle's example of a person blinking one eye, Geertz demonstrated the levels at which the act of blinking may be described and in the process offers an illustration of the task of ethnography:

> Between the . . . "thin description" of what the researcher (parodist, winker, twitcher . . .) is doing ("rapidly contracting his right eyelid") and the "thick description" of what he is doing ("practicing a burlesque of a friend faking a wink to deceive an innocent into thinking a conspiracy is in motion"), lies the object of ethnography: stratified hierarchy of meaning structures in terms of which twitches, winks, fake winks, parodies, rehearsals of parodies are produced, perceived, and interpreted, and without which they would not (not even the zero-form twitches, which as a cultural category are as much non-winks as winks are twitches), in fact exist, no matter what anyone did or did not do with his eyelids. (p. 7)

For Geertz, there is an interaction between culture and the meanings people make of events and practices in their communities. The ethnographer's goal is to share in the meanings that participants take for granted and to portray these to outsiders in ways that preserve the voices and realities of communities under study.

Although there are three distinct modes of ethnographic inquiry, I will limit my discussion to topic-oriented ethnography,[7] which tends to focus on one or two aspects of life in a community, or as Steven Athanases and Shirley Brice Heath (1995) described it, "slices of organizational life within complex societies" (p. 265). My work in process outsourcing focuses on uncovering and understanding the cultural context, patterns, and practices within which literacies are acquired and used in these emerging work spaces. The mode of inquiry selected in an ethnographic project affects the conduct of the research—it influences the types of data collected, how that data collection is carried out, how long data is collected, and what role the ethnographer plays in the community she is studying (Green et al., 2003; Hymes, 1974; Moss, 1992).

Ethnographers, like all researchers, work from specific theoretical orientations, and although these may not always be explicitly articulated, they inform practice nonetheless. Theoretical persuasions originating from phenomenology, cognitive theory, cultural ecology, Marxism, critical theory, cultural studies, feminism, and postmodernism have all informed the work of various ethnographers (Agar, 1994; Behar, 1993; Behar & Gordon, 1995; Carspecken, 1996; Ogbu, 1974, 1978, 1982). Whatever the theoretical orientation of the researcher, she still has to uphold open-mindedness in the evolution of the research process to preserve its reliability and credibility. Indeed, as Judith Green, Carol Dixon, and Amy Zaharlick (2003) argued, the very logic of ethnographic inquiry means that hypotheses and lines of inquiry emerge *in situ*. This is not to say that the researcher does not make certain decisions even before entering the field. Indeed, the researcher's general interests often translate into the theoretical and conceptual frame upon which concrete descriptions are fashioned. These can, in turn, help identify settings in which data may be collected. For example, my general interests in the implications of globalization for the so-called developing world, gender and access to work in developing societies, questions about access to digital technologies, and postcolonial theories provided conceptual foundations upon which I developed a project exploring the literacies of women in outsourcing.

Situating the Research Setting

Once I had mapped out a potential project (in rather broad terms), I needed to think about potential communities to study. Ghana was a strategic choice, as it provided the opportunity to work in a culture familiar to me, but one that is undergoing tremendous change. For almost 20 years, Ghana has been the "model" tutee of the International Monetary Fund and the World Bank, as its leaders follow the economic policy directives attached to aid programs from the two bodies. Democratic processes and structural adjustment policies, coupled with free enterprise philosophy, have brought about fundamental changes to traditional Ghanaian society. Ghana therefore provided a community where the patterns of globalization, gender and development, technology, and literacy could be explored.

Planning for Entry

To do their work, ethnographers need to gain entry into the communities they wish to study. Thus, a key aspect of ethnographic work is getting permission from "gatekeepers" and participants. Part of the general background work the researcher does is getting to know who the gatekeepers are in a setting so entry can be (re)negotiated. There are a number of ways to go about getting permission (see Burgess, 1984, pp. 38–50). Generally, it is advisable to know about the hierarchical structure of the community one wishes to study so that decisions about who to approach and when can be made. Preliminary inquiries can facilitate gaining information that may help with the negotiating process. In my case, using the Web and the popular press, I researched a number of outsourcing companies with establishments in Ghana and then set about locating intermediaries to collect names, roles, phone numbers, and email addresses. At one company, having the name of the site manager enabled me to call his secretary; that initial introductory phone call resulted in a meeting with the site manager. At this initial meeting, I explained what my interests were and why I had chosen that particular company. I described my research interests broadly. The site manager, though agreeable to my request, explained that he did not have the authority to grant permission. I had to clear my request with his corporate bosses in the United States. I queried the site manager about what I may need to provide the corporate office to gain entry. In these conversations, I was alert for signals about potential issues that might influence how the corporate office would respond to my request. The site manager provided me with names, email addresses, and phone numbers. Because of my conversations and contact with the local office, I now had a name and a way of introducing myself to the company's home office. After a number of conversations with a number of people at the company's corporate home office on the phone and by email, permission was granted for me to work at the Ghana site. Because the head office had agreed to a blanket-access request with the caveat that the site manager would sort out the logistics and conditions with me directly, I still had to negotiate the specific conditions of access with the local site manager.

Negotiating Researcher Role and Stance

A cardinal principle in ethnographic work relates to the role of the researcher in the community once the researcher has gained access. The paramount goal is to make the researcher's presence as undisruptive as possible within the daily routines of the community. In traditional ethnography, this role embodies the stance of participant–observer. The role the researcher is able to negotiate affects the extent of participant observation. As a participant–observer, the researcher engages in activities and observes activities, people, and situations in the community. These processes allow the researcher to experience the actions of the community as fully as possible, thereby granting the researcher something that mere observation may not provide. Yet even within traditional ethnography there have been critiques of this researcher role that merits discussion, as the critiques have implications for online research. Some researchers have noted the need to shift to an "observant participant" stance. This is because of the belief that ethnographic work needs an inherent acknowledgement that understanding and describing the lives of others is a process "mediated by our own autobiographies" (Florio-Ruane & McVee, 2002, p. 84). Because, in my view, one of the critical methodological issues with ethnographic research in hybrid environments relates to this principle, I devote more space to addressing it below.

Understanding the Field and Fieldwork in Ethnographic Research

Fieldwork is the bedrock of all traditional ethnography and is crucial to the ethnographer's capacity to construct a native (emic) perspective. Fieldwork enables researchers to enter a community to uncover what its inhabitants consider their native perspectives (Green et al., 2003, p. 213). Fieldwork involves a reflexive and interactive–responsive orientation. What Geertz (1973) described as the "thick description" of the culture under study is based upon how participants describe their community. Participant descriptions are themselves based on how members of a community make meaning and explain or interpret the social actions of their community— that is, such descriptions are based on how participants define their culture (Moss, 1992). Fieldwork and the participant–observer or observant participant stance allow the researcher to collect data by immersing herself in the community being studied. Central to the data-collection process is the conceptual and theoretical principles that orient the researcher and guide her practices. Fieldwork generates the data that will help the ethnographer explain the complex relationships in the particular community under study. Consequently, for fieldwork to be successful, the researcher needs the support and cooperation of members of the community, particularly those who hold what Zaharlick and Green (1991) termed *cultural knowledge* about the meaning of actions, events, objects and behaviors, values, beliefs, and attitudes embodied in the community. Yet, as Green et al. (2003) pointed out, cultural knowledge—like the broader culture in which it is embedded—is not static.

Fieldwork may have the following components: participant observation/observant participant, formal or informal interviews, photographs, audio and video recordings of daily routines, and gathering of physical artifacts such as written documents. Although all of these components may not be present in every study, no study uses only one method for data gathering. Using my work in Ghana as an example, my work in the field utilized the following mechanisms: participant observation/observant participant, formal and informal interviews, document and artifact gathering, audio recordings, and photographs.

Designing Research Practices

Ethnographers and other qualitative researchers work within an emergent design orientation; that is, the research design emerges *in situ*. In my case, I began fieldwork with only a general sense of what I wanted to explore. My overarching interest was to understand how ICTs were shaping the literacy practices of the many women who now work in IT and BP outsourcing. As I began fieldwork, the following questions guided my exploratory directions:

- In what ways and for what purposes do women in process out-sourcing use digital and information communications technolo-gies in their work place literacy practices?
- In what ways and for what purposes do women enact gender and culturally specific literacy practices in their online and offline work spaces?
- How are constructions of gender implicated in women's technol-ogy-mediated literacy practices within their online work commu-nities?
- How do the local and the global intersect? That is to say, what are the global economic conditions that make this arrangement pro-liferate for outsourcing companies?
- What are the current and potential future political implications of such arrangements? How are these economic and political issues perceived by Ghanaian workers?

Even then I knew full well that new lines of inquiry might emerge and orig-inal ideas might be refined, altered, or even set aside as data was collect-ed and analyzed. As I learned about the community I was immersed in, my original lines of inquiry evolved and new lines of inquiry emerged. For example, although I had originally planned to focus a lot of my attention on the virtual environment in which the women worked, the company's unease with letting me in to all areas of its network meant that I had to refocus my attention on the areas for which I had access and then figure out how to get at other areas. This shift was a direct result of what was hap-pening in the culture under study. In my general planning of the project, I had not anticipated the impact the conceptualization of the research space was going have on data collection. This emerged as I began fieldwork. The key issue was establishing parameters for what I was calling the field. At one site, for example, there were 21 semi-autonomous departments—some with as many as 200 employees and others with as few as 5 employ-ees. I could not possibly observe in all these physical spaces and do credi-ble work in them, yet I could not arbitrarily choose just any to study given my research interests. Thus, after what I came to term "the weeks of my grand tour" of the establishment, I developed a set of criteria to guide which departments to focus on. These were the:

- gender dynamics among rank-and-file employees and between employees, supervisors, and managers;
- nature and variability in the literacy practices of the departments; and

- dynamics of the interpersonal relationships among the women in particular departments.

As part of this process, I also identified three focal women and their immediate network of friends, whose practices became key elements of my explorations. All these were decisions made in the process of working at the site: They emerged *in situ*.

Early data analysis helps refine and refocus ongoing work, often opening up lines of inquiry for the researcher. Participants are asked about what they are experiencing, how they interpret their experiences, and how they structure the social world in which they live. In so doing, the research process becomes an ongoing dialogue with participants. Patterns and impressions that emerge are tested by comparing one source of data against another to eliminate competing explanations. Notes may thus be checked against informant's explanations and vice versa. This is generally called triangulation, and it is the principal process through which the ethnographer establishes reliability for the data and the interpretation rendered based on that data (see De Pew, this collection, for an extended discussion of triangulation). Ethnographic data can be analyzed and reported in a number of ways. Although by its very nature ethnographic research is qualitative, quantitative methods can be incorporated into its design and analysis. Ethnographers may use no statistical analysis, or they may use very sophisticated statistical analysis (Bogdan & Biklen, 2003; Moss, 1992).[8]

These general principles of ethnography have informed research traditions for generations, with researchers adapting the methodology for different settings and contexts. Fieldwork, for example, traditionally meant spending considerable time in the community under study. Often, though, time and other logistical constraints have led some researchers to opt for in-depth interviewing—an approach that is less time-consuming. Digital technologies and the mutations in literacy practices they have produced have caused some strains on ethnographic methodology and it is to these that I now turn.

ETHNOGRAPHY IN HYBRID ENVIRONMENTS

The nature of ethnographic inquiry in literacy studies and the ways in which that inquiry has imagined and conceptualized the spatial has, according to Kevin Leander (2003), been "powerfully shaped by" situated accounts such as Heath's (1983) place constructions of Roadville and Trackton. These accounts of "relatively boundless places" often analyze "texts, literacy events, classrooms, schools and communities" (p. 396). Although traditional ethnographic principles provided ample research tools for studying these place-bound communities and practices, these approaches may not be as useful when we shift our focus to the hybrid environments created as a result of information technology and business process outsourcing. These environments are almost always powered by digital technologies that require users to combine old and new literacy practices (Hagood, 2003). Here, traditional ethnographic methods—such as interviewing, observations, video recordings, and artifact analysis—may not account for the totality of member experiences in the physical and virtual communities under study, because researchers need to identify "ways with words" that do not isolate virtual activity from its material settings. To get the full meaning of literacy practices in outsourcing, for example, we cannot bracket virtual work from the physical social situations that shape its meaning without losing sight of issues related to, for instance, context and identity (Leander, 2003).

As a number of scholars have pointed out, traditional conceptions of the "field" have to be rethought significantly when research shifts into online environments (e.g., Bruce, 1997; Clifford, 1997). Indeed, as Helen Nixon (2003) pointed out, the argument that research on new media and online literacies needs to incorporate "thick description of interpretive acts, thick analysis and thick theorizing" (p. 410) may not be acknowledging the inadequacy of traditional methodologies for the task. Ethnographic work that targets Internet culture significantly alters the nature of fieldwork as traditionally understood, because it is possible for researcher to complete fieldwork without ever meeting participants (Bogdan & Biklen, 2003; Clifford, 1997; Marcus, 1996). The field, in this case, becomes an ever-shifting milieu. As Leander (2003) argued, we need ethnographies of online literacies that examine the "field of relations" (p. 395) among multiple locations of practice. In my case, I have had to do fieldwork in Ghana at two outsourcing sites; doing work across sites is congruent with traditional fieldwork. But this immersion in these material work places are not the only "fields" in which fieldwork is taking place and herein lies the challenge.

Ethnography and Virtual Work: Other Conceptions of "Field"

Socially situated practices of what I am calling hybrid work spaces pose some challenges because work in them is accomplished in dedicated corporate-owned spaces that owners guard judiciously. These spaces are the proprietary resources of their owners. One of my research sites, for example, had a dedicated Internet-based network enabled by ICTs and satellites that allowed its employees in Ghana to work on BP solutions and transmit their work back to the United States or to other company BP locations. Thus, in the placeless and immaterial Internet environment, employees as users-readers-and-viewers interact with the virtual from an "embodied space, a material place" (that is, the work floor; Luke, 2003, p. 402). From this space they read and process transactions, sometimes in real time. There is a materiality to these interactions that traditional ethnographic methodology can help a researcher investigate—there are real bodies working in real time (Luke, 2003). However, there is also fluidity to this work that is difficult to track. Further, given the hybrid nature of outsourcing work spaces, it is hard to figure out how to systematically participate and/or observe practices associated with ICT use when corporate owners make certain areas off limits to a researcher.

In my case, I negotiated to observe employees working in areas of their network off limits for me as a participant—in these instances, I became an observant participant and relied on focal participants to show me these places on the network that I couldn't physically get to on my own. Although this made learning how these areas of the network worked rather difficult, I could count on double checking and rechecking my impressions and understandings with different participants for clarification. I had access through the participants, but I still had to figure out ways around the following questions: How do I collect data in a network I do not have total access to and therefore cannot master myself? How do I learn how workers navigate the work network given the constraints I have in access? How do I know I have actually learned how such a network works? There were a number of occasions where my conversations with focal participants, area managers, and other personnel centered on my mapping of what and how I understood the work the women in the study did in the areas that were off-limits to me. The goal was to share my learning, to check on the accuracy of my learning, and to seek clarification from those who live the realities of working in these online spaces.

METHOD AND METHODOLOGICAL CHALLENGES

Another issue researchers confront when working in a hybrid setting is the methodological and conceptual problem of understanding practices from the community's perspective. As Robert Bogdan and Sara Biklen (2003) noted, the viewpoint the ethnographer seeks is itself a research construct, as there is a degree to which the attempt to understand someone's viewpoint distorts that experience or viewpoint. This is even more of an issue in an outsourcing setting where both management and employees are very much aware of the geopolitical implications of their work and may have competing interests at stake. As the researcher, I decided on how to deal with this issue by recognizing that the meaning people give to their experiences and the processes they use in interpreting their experiences are critical components of what those experiences are. Thus, for the ethnographer to understand practices and behaviors, she has to understand the ways and processes by which people create them. In an outsourcing environment, though no community member goes about his or her work life thinking self consciously about his or her perspective on the literacies used in their community, I had to understand their practices and behaviors in the larger context of the work environment and the larger Ghanaian context into which that work environment was embedded.

In my study in Ghana, my interest has been to understand the nature of the literacy practices women—who make up 97 % of the work force at one site and 72 % at the other—use in these settings. For my purposes, literacy denotes a "repertoire of practices for communicating and for getting things in particular social and cultural contexts" (Nixon, 2003, p. 407). To get at this, I have had to learn and develop a level of understanding of the culture of particular BP and IT outsourcing environments. Data were collected through sustained contact with the people who work in these outsourcing settings. Further, because the practices that occur in these settings are embedded in specific cultural contexts—in this case, the social contexts within which outsourcing transpires—I also had to collect data on larger Ghanaian employment patterns. Gathering information on employment patterns was one method of understanding the literacy practices of the work places. To understand the cultural context as best as possible, I had to develop a historical understanding of the setting. I analyzed the data as I gathered it by identifying patterns and relationships as they emerged from within the larger cultural context. This process of data analysis is inductive and cyclical, taking place throughout and across a study.

Being Ghanaian, I had cultural background knowledge and a general familiarity with the country and people. A July 2002 *New York Times* piece on a Ghanaian outsourcing outfit had drawn my attention to the subject (Worth, 2002). During the summer of 2003, I visited Ghana and explored the extent of the outsourcing economy. This provided the groundwork for identifying two outsourcing companies for the study. Although I had a general sense of how to approach companies to gain access to them as research sites, I knew nonetheless that having spent most of my life living elsewhere, I was going to have to do some learning to figure out how the particular outsourcing companies I wanted to study worked.

Initially, my paramount concern was to negotiate conditions of access that would not foreclose on possibilities I did not know about as I went into the field. With my rather limited knowledge about the sites at that time, I wanted to seek as vague an entry as I could negotiate while also leaving open the possibility of renegotiating access to people, places, and spaces as the research evolved. Given the nature of the settings and my interests, I had to gain access to both the physical production floors and the virtual environments in which production was carried out. Although access to the physical space was initially considered a thorny issue, it was understandably even more so along with access to the virtual environment. This is because the virtual networks were proprietary spaces for these companies and the companies needed to protect them for both legal privacy issues and for securing their operations.

The process of negotiating access at the setting mentioned earlier involved having a meeting with the human resources and marketing departments and with the local director to set up the conditions under which I would conduct research at one site. Initially, for example, the site manager wanted to make certain client-related data off limits. This would have restricted my access to the literacy practices at the site enormously. I therefore had to think of alternative ways of protecting what he wanted protected while gaining access to what I needed. I asked rather directly about his concerns and then suggested ways to address these concerns. For example, he was concerned that company and client names might be made public. He was also concerned about the effect my presence would have on employee productivity. The Institutional Review Board (IRB) approval documents from my U.S. institution and my assurance that I was committed to and ethically bound to protect confidentiality put him at ease. Finally, I shared the fact that his corporate bosses had requested that I write something about my work for the company newsletter, and this changed the tenor of our conversation. It became a case of "if they can trust her, I guess she is alright." With the site manager's permission, the director of human resources and I drafted a memo to all employees describing the research project and asking those interested to meet with me. This process yielded the participant pool.

At the other research site (a comparatively smaller outfit), gaining access was fairly straightforward. During my exploratory visit in the summer of 2003, I identified the work place as a potential research site. When I returned in early summer 2004, I emailed the managing director and asked to meet with her. At a meeting in her office, I described my interests and why I had chosen her site. Although she saw the merits of my proposal, her concern was about what the women had to gain from participating in the research process. I could not promise her anything, but I pointed out the possible policy implications of such an investigation; that is, it could help policy makers by providing information from those in the trenches of IT work. This seemed acceptable to her and she gave me a conditional approval to work at the site if I would provide her with copies of the IRB approval and consent forms. When I arrived back in the United States, I emailed the materials to her. A week after that email exchange, she approved my request to conduct research at the site. During my first visit to the site, when I began fieldwork, the managing director invited three members of her management team to meet with us. At this meeting, we discussed what I wanted to do and how they could help. An email broadcast introduced me to all employees and described my research project; it also invited interested employees to meet with me.

Understanding Identification and Researcher Stance

The extent to which a researcher identifies with a community does affect the research process. Beverly Moss (1992) discussed the complex dynamics of defining membership and isolated some of the questions ethnographers who study their own communities face. In my case, my being Ghanaian and my familiarity with the culture and some of the languages, history, and customs provided a good backdrop. I was not, however, a member of the work place communities I had elected to study. Thus, although I was not in any serious danger of assuming that my mere identification with the group meant that I had access to the information I sought, I still had to learn how to seek information about the literacy practices of these work places and I had to know what kinds of questions would yield the information I sought. I also had to figure out how to participate and observe in the community without assuming I knew it. As Moss (1992) deftly demonstrated, both community and researcher expectations also have to be addressed. Researchers who have some relationship to the community under study have to be self-conscious about how that relationship may affect judgment about what is deemed important and thereby affect how decisions about what information to value are made (Shami, 1988). There is also the other side of this dynamic: the idea that working in a community that one knows means that one can identify patterns of behavior and their meaning to the community far more quickly than outsiders. Even though the communities of interest in my case were work places with which I had no prior relationship, my understanding and history of the larger culture within which these work places were embedded meant that I had to be cognizant of the danger of drawing on previous knowledge to make decisions about the meaning and significance of behaviors and patterns in the data collected. To guard against this danger, I relied on other data sources and on the focal participants from whom I often checked and rechecked my impressions and understandings.

Negotiating Ethical Tensions in Hybrid Research Settings

Another methodological issue with ethnographic work in hybrid outsourcing settings relates to the ethical dilemmas a researcher has to confront. Some scholars have noted the new kinds of ethical responsibilities researchers assume when they research new media and communication technologies (e.g., Leander, 2003; Luke, 2003). As I drafted this chapter, for example, I agonized whether or not identifying the country where the research took place would be enough to identify the companies involved. Yet, in not identifying the country, there is the risk of distorting the significance of the meanings that accrue from practices in the work spaces studied. I had either to rethink how to situate my research sites or identify the total number of such companies and therefore confidently avoid the likelihood that country identification would be an *ipso facto* company identification. I chose the latter—I found census data on the number of outsourcing operations and on that basis made the decision to identify the country.

Ethics is again an issue when it comes to protecting the various layers of confidentiality. To gain entry to the work floor, I committed to protecting the confidentiality of the companies whose work these sites did. Given my pledge to protect the identity of the sites, I felt obligated to do all I could to deliver on that pledge. No matter what one's views on the topic might be, as an ethnographer one is obligated to participants' portrayal of the practices of their community and how they situate these in the specific cultural context of their work place. To conduct research online, the researcher should obviously have knowledge and be immersed in the online culture she seeks to investigate. Yet, in process outsourcing there is the dual level of privacy and confidentiality issues. Outsourcing outfits would rather their identity be kept confidential, and they definitely want client confidentiality upheld. Companies involved in outsourcing services do not want to be "outed." For the women who work in these environments, however, there is the hope that a researcher's work would lead to disclosures that might mean better jobs, higher wages, and better working conditions.

Because the participants were engaged in work-related practices, and because they had to document their work online to be paid, they left traces in the form of logins, clock-ins, identification numbers, and other network records. As a participant–observer/observant participant, however, there were ethical dilemmas about how to collect data that related to how employees often circumvented company directives by appropriating network capability for other uses. These illicit uses included gaming, movie watching, and cheating on time spent on tasks (Nixon, 2003). As a participant–observer/observant participant, I was often privy to these appropriations, but was never sure of how to document them without compromising data sources. Depending on how entry is negotiated, a researcher is ethically bound to collect data without compromising the sources of the data. In my case, by the time I understood the nature of illicit technology use, I had developed relationships with a number of the women so that they were no longer hiding these practices from me, though they continued to hide them from their floor supervisors. To underline my role to all parties, I took advantage of opportunities where women and managers were together to reiterate the fact that my interests were only related to the literacy practices at the work place. In addition, I made a very conscious decision not to discuss my observations of the production floor with supervisors and managers except when I needed their perspective on issues. Most of these conversations took place on the production floor. One of the ethical responsibilities that comes with my role as a researcher is to learn about what the women did—as I learned they did both that which was sanctioned by their employers as well as that which was not. As a result, I had to wrestle with both the ethical and the practical questions of how one collects such data in ethically responsible ways. (I also had to wrestle with technical difficulties, such as how to collect quality audio data in a sometimes noisy work place that at least in theory prohibits some of the evidence one seeks to collect.) In the end, I decided to document the illicit uses of network access in my field notes and then ask focal participants about these uses. This gave the women the opportunity to discuss their uses of these technologies from their standpoint.

Rethinking Researcher Stance: Women's Lives Online and Offline

Because ethnographic approaches traditionally focus on studying bounded social spaces, they are ideally suited for studying offline lives. Online lives disrupt the sense of bounded space. The coalescing of these two into what I call hybrid spaces requires rethinking the relationship between ethnography and space while simultaneously accounting for the virtual. In investigating the online lives of women at work (given the conditions of access that I had), I had to address the problem posed by my limited network access. Given this limited network access, testing knowledge through direct experience and interaction online in all spaces was just not conceivable. I therefore reframed the issue somewhat by theorizing my role as being one of seeking similar experiences as those of the women—however these experiences were mediated (Hine, 2000).

To get a better sense of the relationships between the online and offline lives of the women at these sites, I extended traditional observation beyond the work place. I met focal participants outside of work. When the women began calling me with information about practices and issues that occurred on the days I was not at their particular physical site, I knew I had been granted some level of acceptance. Even then, my approach here also highlights the difficulties of fashioning research orientations that allow one to study online and offline experiences in settings like these in a seamless manner.

For the researcher, the issue of online immersion is singularly fraught with tensions. The researcher as a participant–observer/observant participant has to learn the network and the work done on it. She has to learn the processes used to complete transactions and in the process build some credibility with those who do that work. However, given the desire of companies to keep certain aspects of their operations off-limits, there is only so much that a researcher can have access to. Thus, unlike research in some dedicated spaces such as gaming areas on the Internet, virtual work spaces cannot be accessed undercover. The researcher cannot lurk anonymously; she enters that space on record. In fact, the whole IRB process means that researchers have to be "out" at least in a general sense about what it is they seek to study (for an extended discussion of IRBs and review processes, see Banks and Eble, this collection).

Compounding research visibility are problems related to the fluidity of Internet-based research. Carmen Luke (2003), for instance, has called for analytic tools for tracking highly mobile travel across links, knowledge domains, Web pages, email routes, and so forth, to capture the flow of ideas and practices across the Internet. Although her focus is on the online lives of youth, these issues are also prevalent in the world of cyberwork. In fact, in the sites I studied, tracking these flows is a crucial practice and required the development of a certain faith in the technologies used in the work place. Online surveillance of employees was routine, but the utilization of that surveillance ranged among the different parties; for management, there was a sense that the virtual work space needed to be policed. Yet for the women, the surveillance mechanisms could be appropriated for tracking their work volume and therefore their wages. The dynamic and fluid nature of work in such a virtual network cannot be ignored. For example, there was a case where the women at one site contended that their work volume for a whole day had "disappeared" and as a result their corporate bosses had not paid them for that work. There was a back-and-forth discussion about these "disappearing" workloads while I was working in this community. Often the women would share their version of events with me; management would also share its version. In spite of these competing realities, as a researcher the very idea that work "disappears" on such a network was of theoretical interest to me. Clearly, interviews, electronic transcript analysis, and network logs alone were not going to be enough to capture the "practices of mobility and flows" (Luke, 2003, p. 402) in such a work space. On the other hand, the fact that I did not have permission to roam freely on the network meant that I could not independently investigate the entire system. A researcher's knowledge of a site is, of course, always partial and contingent upon access and what participants are willing or able to share. But when researching hybrid spaces, the physical and technological gaps of the locations being studied (if you can even say there *is* a location) may serve to emphasize the incompleteness of a researcher's knowledge.

ADAPTIVE HYBRID ETHNOGRAPHY: LESSONS FROM EXPLORATIONS IN OUTSOURCING SETTINGS

Leander (2003) noted that the "methodological issues of researching online literacies are legion" (p. 4). The issues mutate when research shifts to explorations of hybrid spaces that straddle the boundaries of the material and immaterial. It is clear that although research in such settings can adopt the logic of ethnographic inquiry, there can be no *a priori* checklist of practices to offer. Ethnography in hybrid work places takes on the particular inflections of the hybrid environment and culture that a researcher elects to study. Research in these settings calls for confronting the specific conditions of the physical and virtual spaces and work done in these spaces. Although ethnography continues to provide powerful resources for understanding the cultures of bounded spaces, virtual experiences oblige a reassessment of some of its practices.

Specifically, investigating experiential displacement with ethnographic approaches in work places that operate 24/7 raises the issue of how a researcher participates in the online and offline lives of participants. The lesson here is navigating the physical and virtual work worlds of participants through real-time observations, retrospective analyses, and snapshots of "frozen" moments that allow the researcher to analyze practices enacted at particular times. The situated account offered by this project therefore enacts explorations of the form ethnography takes when it is no longer about only physical displacement but also about largely experiential displacement. Situated accounts can enable us to develop research methodologies that do justice to the complexities that digital technologies are engendering in contemporary work places (Leander, 2003). In fact, it could be argued that the company-owned network spaces are themselves bounded social spaces and therefore are cultures in themselves even as they are also cultural artifacts. These spaces enable the creation of meanings in contexts shaped by the circumstances under which networks are used (offline) and also create the social spaces that materialize as a result of these uses (online; Hine, 2000). In my case, traditional ethnographic methods facilitated research in the material work place where Ghanaian women offered business solutions for American companies. Nonetheless, a focus on that material location alone would not have accounted for the totality of the experiences and practices of these outsourcing environments. To understand the virtual component, there was a need to broaden some of the practices of traditional ethnography as well as experiment with strategies that may have been only useful for these particular work places.

Negotiating access is tricky business in IT and BP outsourcing. Companies are fairly suspicious of the intentions of academic researchers, and it may take considerable effort on the part of the researcher to help companies and their representatives come to terms with their presence. As in all fieldwork, the beginning may be bumpy and even uncomfortable, but researchers have to accept that discomfort and work through it. For me, the first few weeks in the field were times I used to learn and understand the dynamics of work in the hybrid spaces I sought to study. As I learned, access to the physical production floor does not mean automatic access to its virtual spaces. It is therefore imperative that in discussing access, a researcher's interest in the digital environment is foregrounded. And, depending on what IT or BP work is done at a site, researchers have to be willing to learn or be trained to participate. This is because legal questions about privacy may otherwise bar a company from granting researchers access without training and/or other accommodations. Researcher stance is also affected by the conditions upon which access is provided. The very logic of IT and BP outsourcing—that is, the goal of running highly efficient and cost-effective operations in proprietary environments to maximize profits—may translate into restricting access to information or to workers because of concerns about productivity. Under such circumstances the researcher has to be creative in designing ways to get at information deemed essential to a project.

Researchers who work in IT and BP outsourcing have the added responsibility of navigating dual minefields, one of which is the public backlash in the United States against outsourcing practices. The other relates to needs and goals of the employees at outsourcing sites, such as negotiations of fair and humane working conditions. Although these issues cannot be avoided, one can elect to focus on understanding the culture of outsourcing to understand its logic and that logic's effect on those who work in it.

It is clear that conceptions of key practices in traditional ethnography—such as researcher stance, research design, fieldwork, and questions about the ethical responsibilities of researchers—have to be adapted for the specific demands of hybrid, global work places. Flexibility is crucial to navigating hybrid settings, as work within them affects notions of time, space, place, experience, and reflexivity—all principal tenets of traditional ethnography.

ACKNOWLEDGMENT

The Ghana research was funded through a fellowship from the American Association of University Women.

NOTES

1. *Cybertariat* is the term Ursula Huws (2003) coined to describe the workforce and the working conditions associated with the technology revolution in her book, *The Making of a Cybertariat: Virtual Work in a Real World.*
2. Manuel Castells (1996) identified most of Subsaharan Africa as part of the *fourth world.* For Castells, this designation underscores the processes of social and economic exclusion or marginalization that have occurred as a result of the shifts in the global economy.

3. There are a good number of accessible introductory texts on ethnography (see, for instance, Agar, 1996; Dobbert, 1984; Ellen, 1984; Hymes, 1982). My focus here is on the dimensions online work adds to this research tradition.

4. Within a span of several months in 2004, for instance, the *Wall Street Journal, The Economist, Business Week,* the *Financial Times,* and *Fortune* all published articles pointing out the benefits of outsourcing. Others—like *The New York Times* and *The New Yorker*—have written balanced exposés on the subject. In September 2004, CNN's Jim Clancy moderated a special, *The Other Side of Outsourcing: A Global Debate,* that brought workers, politicians, activists, members of the press, and business leaders from both India and the United States together. The intensity of public discomfort was evident in the swift bipartisan response to N. Gregory Mankiw's (President Bush's economic adviser) February 2004 comment that "outsourcing is just a new way of doing international trade. . . . More things are tradable than were tradable in the past and that is a good thing" (Brownfield, 2004, n.p.).

5. My discussion here is side-stepping the broader issues and critiques about what counts as ethnography; for discussions of these, see Athanases and Heath (1995), Ellen (1984), Green et al. (2003), Rist (1980).

6. Dobbert (1984) made the case that ethnography originated from accounts produced by travelers, missionaries, poets, and historians who sought to describe the "strange-seeming peoples" they came into contact with as they traveled or lived outside their own communities and countries. Erickson (1996) argued that ethnography as a methodology further expanded in the 19th century in the interest of colonial expansion, noting "another line of interest developed in the late nineteenth century in the kinds of unlettered people who lacked power and about whom little was known. These were the nonliterate peoples of the European-controlled colonial territories of Africa and Asia, which were burgeoning by the end of the 19th century" (p. 123).

7. For a detailed discussion of the three modes of ethnographic inquiry, see Hymes (1974, pp. 22–32). Hymes identified these as topic-oriented ethnography, comprehensive-oriented ethnography (which seeks to generate a complete description of a way of life), and hypothesis-oriented ethnography (which is usually the product of comprehensive and topic-oriented inquiries, because the researcher should have considerable ethnographic knowledge about the community being studied). See also Heath (1983) and Moss (1992).

8. A number of researchers have conducted ethnographic research while incorporating quantitative analysis. Jacob (1982), for example, offered suggestions and examples for combining approaches in rather accessible ways. Ethnographers often use statistical background data in their work, though they may contextualize the data to make them meaningful for their purposes. For other perspectives on combining qualitative and quantitative approaches or comparing and contrasting their uses in qualitative research see Shkedi (2004) and Berger (2000).

PART THREE

Researching the Activity of Writing

Time-use Diaries, Mobile Technologies, and Video Screen Capture

7

STUDYING THE MEDIATED ACTION OF COMPOSING WITH TIME-USE DIARIES

William Hart-Davidson

Time-use diaries are an excellent tool for studying the situated, contextual, everyday actions of writers, particularly in relation to their use of digitized writing technologies. In time-use studies, participants keep detailed records of a specific activity. Time-use diaries allow researchers a window into composing practices and provide access to information about the ongoing work and technology-mediated activities of writers. This chapter provides an overview of methods of time-use studies, addresses methodological complexities related to diary studies in relation to digital writing research, and offers advice for researchers considering employing time-use diaries.

INTRODUCTION

The term "time-use diary" or "diary study" describes a qualitative research technique wherein research participants keep detailed records of their time usage relative to a specific activity (e.g., use of computer applications during composing) or a broader domain of activity (e.g., time spent at work). Participants are asked to record details about their use of time and are given explicit instructions regarding what to record, how often to report, and how to attend to phenomena that may well be, in the context of day-to-day activity, mundane and routine behavior.

Time-use diaries have been used for some time by social scientists interested in comparative demographic trends (e.g., how much time white-collar workers in Britain spend using email compared to white-collar workers in the United States), linguists studying language acquisition, and educational researchers tracing the development of learners. More recently, diary studies have been embraced by the community of researchers interested in computer-supported cooperative work (CSCW). Diary studies have been especially attractive to those CSCW researchers who, following the work of Lucy Suchman (1987), adopt a situated action perspective or, following Yrjö Engestrom (1987), an activity theory perspective (Kuutti, 1991, 1996; Nardi, 1996; see Geisler and Slattery, this collection, for further discussion of activity theory). Researchers of digital writing have much in common with those working in CSCW, as they take work in computer-mediated environments to be the primary object of inquiry. Naturally, this means that much of what CSCW researchers examine is recognizable as "writing," defined as both action and artifact. A key benefit of diary studies for both groups of researchers is the ability to gather information about writing technologies and how they are used in the ongoing work and life activities of research participants.

The value most researchers see in diary methods lies in the ability to capture data that is otherwise very difficult to collect owing to the fact that researchers cannot be with a participant at every moment, in every location where important details of activities such as "composing" may occur. Consider a recent writing project that you completed—think of something larger and more complicated than you were able to complete in one sitting. Starting from the first time you began thinking about the project, can you account for where you were each time you worked on it? And if we change the question somewhat: Where did the invention process occur? What technologies or information resources did you use in the processes of invention? Odds are the answers to these questions involve many discrete but connected moments, each with unique circumstances and constraints and each characterized by different encounters with composing technologies.

In asking these questions, we are acknowledging the difficulty but also attending to the exciting proposition of studying writing—and the influence of various technologies on the writing process—as a phenomenon woven into people's lived experiences. After all, people invent in their car on their way to work, perhaps after hearing something interesting on the radio or seeing something along the road that triggered an idea. People compose in a variety of ways, by writing email to a colleague with an idea for a project, by preparing class notes that get re-purposed into a passage in a textbook or article, even by drawing on a whiteboard in a colleague's office. We know this intuitively, but much of this sort of activity has gone relatively unnoticed by researchers of composition. Even those interested in the ways technologies influence writing practices and the teaching of writing have not often found ways to gather information about the composing process as it unfolds in the lived experience of writers. Among the aspects of composing we know little about are fairly significant details such as the specific times and places, the combinations of technologies employed, and the types of social interactions that make composing a rich, technologically mediated, socially and culturally situated activity.

The main prohibition that has kept researchers from gathering this sort of data, I believe, is the methodological complexity of capturing it. Certainly, we understand writing to be the sort of socially and culturally rich (Flower, 1994; Gere 1987, 1997; Grabill, 2001; LeFevre, 1987; Richardson, 2002), technologically mediated (Bolter, 2001; Cushman 1998; Havelock, 1988; Hayles, 2002; Ong, 1982), and temporally and spatially distributed (Bazerman, 1988; Bazerman & Prior, 2004; Derrida, 1988; Duguid & Brown, 2002; Goody, 1986; Yates, 1993) activity described above. Our theoretical foundations tell us as much. And we've done our best to capture the details of composing by using methods that rely on recall and/or observation of key moments, sometimes controlled by the researcher and sometimes not (Emig, 1971; Flower & Hayes, 1981; Sternglass, 1997). But a blind spot remains.

COMPLEXITIES ASSOCIATED WITH CAPTURING COMPOSITION

This chapter will discuss the ways diary studies might be used to address this blind spot, helping writing researchers learn more about the distributed, collaborative, and mediated nature of composing processes. Citing examples from diary studies of composing processes conducted by the author as well as diary studies published in other fields, the chapter will address a methodological issue that researchers of writing, particularly those interested in studying the composing process, have long faced: How can we capture rich, accurate representations of a writer's composing process?

Four aspects of the composing process pose methodological problems worthy of note, but I pay particular attention here to the last one in the following list:

1. Composition unfolds in an improvisational way in response to a rhetorical situation, social and organizational setting, and immediate physical surroundings the writer finds herself within;
2. Composition can take place over relatively long periods of time and in a variety of locations;
3. Composition is typically influenced by or directly involves the efforts of many people, even when a writer is working "alone" or is perceived to be the sole author; and
4. **Composition is mediated by multiple technologies, some of which work in concert with the writer's goals and are therefore fairly seamlessly integrated into composing activity, and some of which profoundly alter or conflict with the writer's goals.**

Computers and writing researchers are not alone, fortunately, in their quest to understand the influence of technology on writing and the contexts in which people write. In fact, the effort to understand how technology use happens in a detailed way and in the environments that users inhabit rather than in usability labs or other controlled environments has influenced many researchers in the fields of human–computer interaction (HCI) and CSCW in choosing diary study approaches. As computing has become increasingly distributed in the environments that users inhabit—built into mobile devices and interconnected via wireless networks—diary studies offer a minimally obtrusive way to glimpse how users select, use, struggle, and succeed with these technologies.

These pragmatic reasons for choosing diary studies to examine technology use are further supported by a theoretical rationale, one shared by many researchers of composing. Simply stated, the rationale is that all activity is mediated. This view as it applies to writing is nicely summarized by Paul Prior (1998):

> Writing happens in moments that are richly equipped with tools (material and semiotic) and populated with others (past, present, future). When seen as situated activity, writing does not stand alone as the dis-

crete act of a writer, but emerges as a confluence of many streams of activity: reading, talking, observing, acting, making, thinking, and feeling as well as transcribing words on paper. (p. xi)

My use of the term "mediated" in this chapter is influenced by a group of theories that emphasize the way human activity and cognition can be understood within—rather than apart from—the sociohistorical conditions that humans inhabit (Bazerman & Prior, 2004; Luria, 1983; Prior & Shipka, 2002; Russell, 1997; Spinuzzi, 2003; Vygotsky, 1978, 1986; Wertsch, 1991). These theories—among them cultural–historical activity theory, distributed cognition, situated action perspective, and actor–network theory—share a key understanding of human behavior as influenced by material artifacts that are, themselves, understood to have social and cultural meaning. These theories differ in a number of ways, but perhaps the most important feature that distinguishes among them for the purpose of the present discussion is their interest in and focus on individual versus system-wide development. Unraveling all of the differences among these theories and/or placing them relative to one another along a continuum of system/individual is beyond the scope of this chapter.[1] In the interest of maintaining a focus on time-use diaries to study composing processes, I will simply say that diaries gather data from the perspective of individual participants acting as individual agents. But the accounts that emerge are more accurately understood as first-person accounts of individuals' participation in social activity. This is the case because writing involves acting within broader social and technological systems, and interacting with people, tools, and information along the way.

Individuals make diary entries when they decide to, recording their interpretation of events. And although the *what* and *when* of an entry is typically structured a great deal by prompting from the researcher, time-use diaries have much in common with the popular notion of a "diary" as a genre of self-reporting and self-reflection. A helpful way to think of the diary as a tool for data collection is to consider it a tool for dialogue between the researcher and the researched. Although the diary-keeping itself and, to a lesser degree, each entry is shaped by an explicit request from the researcher for information, the timing, the details, and the collective nature of the responses are all shaped by the participant. In the examples that follow, I discuss my attempts at constructing prompts that yield timely and helpful data without placing undue constraints on participants.

The activity window that time-use diaries can be said to provide offers a first-person view of action that is typically too complex, too spread out in time or space, too internal to an individual, or too minutely detailed for a third-person perspective to capture effectively. It is still a partial view biased toward the development of individuals within a sociocultural system. This is one reason why time-use diaries are almost always used in combination with other methods, including recall and observational methods that allow researchers to shift perspective or compare data across individual cases.

WAYS OF SEEING THE COMPOSING PROCESS

As the four descriptions of the composing process above suggest, theoretical issues pertaining to what composing *is* are very much intertwined with the methodological complexities associated with capturing information about composing processes. Even the earliest research on the composing process (e.g., Emig, 1971; Flower & Hayes, 1981) acknowledged the improvisational and distributed nature of composing, factors that led these and other researchers to stage composing "moments" for observation and explication, using methods that reveal first-person details, such as talk-aloud protocols. The nature of composing as an activity distributed in time and space—taking place over days, weeks, and years sometimes—is knowingly compromised in this sort of observational research. Researchers acknowledge that they are seeing only a piece of the action. But how do we know they are seeing (or have seen) the most important pieces? How can we adequately account for the role others play in the decisions individuals make, assuming that we take seriously the idea that writing is an inherently social activity? And how do we understand the role technologies play in the invention and composing processes?

One way of putting observational episodes into context is to use recall methods, typically interviews with writers or other participants in the composing process, in conjunction with or in place of staged scenarios. An especially compelling example of this approach was developed by Paul Prior and Jody Shipka (2002) for the express purpose of capturing the ways composing activities take place in and among other events in writers' lives. To capture the ways that "writing" happens while one is walking to work in the morning, while in the shower, during conversations with others, and with the aid of high- and low-tech artifacts, Prior and Shipka asked their participants to recall writing processes by drawing pictures of the significant events that shaped their experience. The resulting drawings are at once quite surprising and quite familiar. They show authors interacting with other people, with technologies, and even with their pets! Pets? Any cat owner chuckles when they see in these drawings familiar scenes: a furry friend, seeking attention, walks on the keyboard and strives to insert himself between the human's gaze and the computer display. For good or ill, this is part of the lived experience of composing for many people, though we seldom see it acknowledged and never see it theorized or strategized.

Recall methods such as those employed by Prior and Shipka (2002) can produce rich accounts, to be sure. But they have an inherent weakness in that they tend to include only those events that stand out as significant for writers after some time has elapsed. For those of us interested in the way composing processes are mediated by multiple technologies, this can be an especially vexing problem. Writers working fluently do not usually notice the role that technology plays in their moment-by-moment practices unless these technologies cause breakdowns. If all is going smoothly, writers see through the technology to the goals of the composing tasks in which they are engaged. Similarly, composers may not include in their list of "writing activity" the bits of conversation, emails, chats, sticky notes, or drafts that were important steps along the way to a version of their target genre. Asking writers to attend to these types of events, moreover, can disrupt and fragment the very activity we are trying to understand.

TIME-USE DIARIES AS SUPPLEMENTS TO OBSERVATIONAL AND RECALL METHODS

Diary studies can help to fill in the gaps left by participants when recalling the details of complex practice and they can help researchers to identify where observed (or observable) moments of the writing process fit into the stream of actions that constitute the broader experience of composing. Diary studies can be used to get a composer's eye view of the whole process so that researchers can select when, where, and how to get other types of views.

To illustrate, I will discuss two studies that employed time-use diaries as part of a larger methodological toolkit. The first study is one I conducted as part of a project that aimed to develop a method of visualizing writing processes in a systematic and descriptive way. The second is a study of reading, writing, and other document-use practices in a large policy organization by Abigail Sellen and Richard Harper that has produced two full-length books and numerous articles (Harper, 1998; Sellen & Harper, 2001).

My discussion of the first study will focus on practical matters, including why and how I used time-use diaries to capture information for visualizing writing processes. My focus in this study was not exclusively on the role of technology in the writing process, but the role technology played became immediately visible due to the way the time-use diaries attended, in detail, to the nature of communication events in the study. Visualizing the data from the diaries made clear just how fundamental and pervasive technologies such as email are in workplace writing. My discussion of Sellen and Harper's work will delve more deeply into the benefits diary studies hold for investigating further how specific technologies, old and new, influence work. I am convinced that we have much to learn about the way work today is mediated by writing technologies in very detailed and interesting ways that researchers in our field have yet to pay much attention to.

Using A Diary Study to "See the Project"

My experience with diary studies began because I was interested in rendering visible and intelligible the ways writers within organizations work not merely on individual written products, but on larger projects that include multiple genres; involve others in the organization; and depend on a variety of technologies for composing, viewing, and distributing information in the form of texts. My understanding of what I was attempting to capture in these visualizations was shaped a great deal by Lester Faigley (1986), who suggested that researchers who adopt a social perspective on writing "view written texts not as detached objects possessing meaning on their own, but as links in communicative chains, with their meaning emerging from their relationships to previous texts and the present context" (p. x). I did, indeed, view texts this way. Taking a further cue from Marilyn Cooper (1986; Cooper & Holtzman, 1989), who has challenged the field of writing studies to put the social view of writing frequently espoused in theory to the test in examining "ecologies of writing," I wanted to demonstrate and question the degree to which the theoretical vision of writing as a social activity matched up with writing processes that occur in organizations.

An example of what these writing process visualizations might look like was provided by B. L. Gunnarson (1997), a sociolinguist who devised a way to picture communicative processes as a series of "communication events," oral and written, ordered chronologically. Gunnarson's image, meant to demonstrate how thoroughly intertwined writing and speaking are in organizational contexts, was not based on a representation of actual events but was instead a "fictive communication chain" meant to describe the typical process as represented by one of Gunnarson's interviewees. Like the images drawn by Prior and Shipka's (2002) informants, Gunnarson's communicative chain diagram is a wonderfully fresh and yet startlingly familiar look at the writing process at the same time. I wondered: Could we make similar diagrams that represented actual writing processes?

To find out, I asked two people working in different organizational contexts to keep a record of their work on a project that, for them, was typical of their workplace writing practice (Hart-Davidson, 2002). One participant, whom I will call Teresa, was an administrative assistant and finance officer in an academic department of a university. She kept a diary recording all of the communication events associated with a routine reporting task, the compilation of a human resource allocation document commonly known as a "loading report." The report was a document prepared each quarter by all of the academic units in the school where Teresa's department was housed, and it consisted mostly of a spreadsheet with fields that contained both numerical data and text to describe and/or justify loading figures. The other participant, whom I will call Jared, was a freelance Web developer. He kept a diary recording all of the communication events associated with the negotiation of a new Web development contract for a client. Figure 7.1 represents the diary form I asked Teresa and Jared to use—a simple table embedded in a word-processing program the writers were likely to have open.

List Communication Events that Influence the Target Document			
Date & Time	Type of Event	Title or Topic	Direct/Indirect Influence?
1/15/2002	E-mail	Request from Dean to address Advisory	Direct. Explicit mention of "progress report" Board

Figure 7.1.   Teresa and Jared's Communication Event Diary Format

I asked Jared and Teresa to record all of the communication events they participated in that had some influence on the "target document" for which their project was named (for Teresa, the loading report, and for Jared, the client Web site). For each entry, they recorded the following information: date and time; the type of event it was (such as email, phone call, etc.); the title or a brief description of the event; and whether it had a direct or indirect influence on the target. Later, in response to questions from both participants, the last category was modified to be a choice among the following characterizations: project work, team coordination, technical support or process clarification, and socializing. Generally, Jared and Teresa characterized the first two categories as "on-task" and the last three were labeled "wheel spinning."

In all, Jared recorded 70 events leading up to but not including the development work for the client's Web site. Of these 70, 9 were documents prepared to be printed, 40 were email messages, 18 were face-to-face conversations, and 3 were phone conversations or conference calls. At first glance, a staggering amount of communicating—but all very routine and typical of the project-development process, according to Jared.

For her project, Teresa recorded 30 events over the course of 3 months. Because preparing the report was an ongoing responsibility for Teresa, she spread the work out over the quarter. Figure 7.2 shows the process that emerged from Teresa's diary of her project. The legend in the upper left corner explains the icons that represent the medium and give information about the genres of each event. Written events are rectangular; oral events are elliptical. Events are diagrammed in chronological order from left to right and top to bottom, with the dates presented for reference along the left side. Events are also diagrammed in two dimensions, with the "on-task" and "wheel-spinning" data point being used to determine when a new horizontal line begins in the diagram. The aim of this approach is to demonstrate how we might make sense of a complex writing project by producing visualizations that help writers to reflect on issues they care about. The example of sorting and diagramming above helps to show how on-task Teresa felt the project was by representing on-task work in the vertical dimension. Horizontal strings of events represent wheel-spinning in Teresa's estimation. As we might expect in the case of a routine reporting task such as this one, Teresa's project, although complex, proceeds very efficiently and involves very little wheel spinning.

Since my first foray into diary studies with the Teresa and Jared study—effectively a proof-of-concept project for visualizing writing projects based on real data—I have worked to refine the data-gathering method for the purpose of producing more informative visualizations of writing proj-

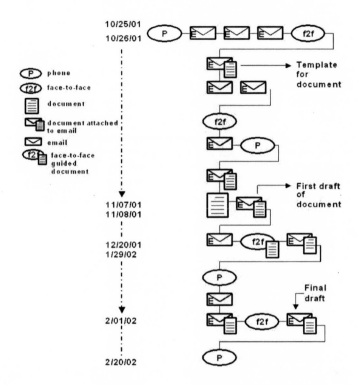

Figure 7.2   Teresa's Communication Event Diagram (Hart-Davidson, 2002)

ects (Hart-Davidson, 2003; Spinuzzi, Hart-Davidson, & Zachry, 2004). A list of considerations for using time-use diaries effectively include:

- **Diary studies capture a moment of technology use and a reflective, mediational step to participants' practice**. It is best to think of diaries not as an unobtrusive measure, but as a minimally intrusive means to facilitate dialogue between participants and the researcher. This dialogue is well-suited to studies of digital writing, because it is essentially a way to add contextual information to a stream of discursive events that are all the more rapid when they take place in online environments. Keeping the diary can also be a bit easier for participants when they look back at the records already being kept by applications they use, such as an email outbox, a list of "recent" documents in a word-processing program, or a personal information management application on a PDA. Much of our online lives is already time-indexed, but the formats for accessing these ad-hoc logs of practice do not currently function well as a resource for reflecting on practice. This is precisely what time-use diaries attempt to be.

- **Designing the diary format effectively requires up-front thinking about the ways data will be analyzed**. In the Jared and Teresa project, the categories for describing "on-task" vs. "wheel spinning" events arose from the participants' own characterization of their work. This sort of development was possible because I had already decided that my unit of analysis—a writing project—was made up of smaller units with attributes that would affect the way these were arranged, visually, when diagramming a project. The "on-task" categories, though unknown ahead of time, filled a known slot in my analytic scheme: attributes of communication events.
- **Time-use diaries require that your unit of analysis correspond well with event-based data collection**. This is common sense, but the implications are important not only for the theoretical value of the data you gather, but also for the practical considerations you need to make about how to gather (or, more precisely, how to have your participants gather) data. For example, are the events you are asking participants to log long enough in duration to be easily distinguished from one another, but short enough to be attended to as discrete events? If they are not, making diary entries will be difficult for your participants and you will get incomplete diaries back.[2]
- **Time-use diary formats must make it as easy as possible for participants to make entries**. Entries should take only a little time to make and the process of making an entry should be as seamless with the other work a user is doing as possible. Palen and Salzman (2002), studying the use patterns of mobile phone users, asked participants to make entries via voice mail. This allowed a relatively rich descriptive data set to emerge despite the challenges of documenting an inherently transient activity. In a follow-up to the Jared and Teresa study (Amponsah, 2003; Hart-Davidson 2003; Slattery, 2003), my co-researchers and I refined the diary entry method through user testing of the form itself until it was possible to make a single entry in about 90 seconds. Figure 7.3 shows the revised diary form.

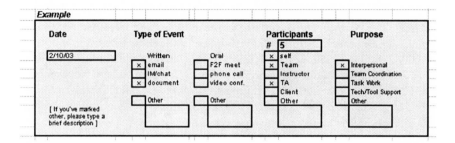

Figure 7.3. Revised Communication Event Diary Form

The changes made to the form allowed participants to check boxes instead of writing out repeated information. Because the visualization method was a bit more refined, we were able to give users constrained lists to choose from while still allowing our categories to be modified using the "other" selection.

The Role of Technology in Using Time-use Diaries to Analyze Mediated Activity

One way to describe the data that emerges from time-use diaries is plausible accounts of lived experience. A distinctive feature of these accounts is that they are told in first-person. Another, less obvious feature is that these accounts almost always include—implicitly or explicitly—clues about participants' encounters with technologies. This makes time-use diaries especially valuable as a kind of preliminary data-gathering technique for researchers interested in computers and writing. Gathering diary information about when, where, and how writers work with a given technology over the course of a project, for example, can let researchers know where to be if they want to observe a particular type of technology use scenario. In a recent study of mobile phone text messaging (SMS, or short message service), for example, Huatong Sun (2004) used a diary study to trace the contours of SMS activity for 20 participants in the United States and 20 participants in China. Each user kept a diary of SMS messages sent and received over a 4-day period that included two week days and two weekend days. Sun then used these snapshots of use patterns to identify interesting times to conduct observations of her participants' SMS activity *in situ*. These moments were chosen because they involved heavy use and because the social and physical context of use made it likely that Sun could investigate issues related to her research questions. One issue she was interested in, for example, was the way participants used SMS in workplace contexts to send messages that were primarily for the purpose of socializing or maintaining nonwork relationships. Sun was able to see this sort of activity pattern in the diary of one of her users, a retail manager, who texted to friends and family members during a typically slow sales period each morning. Sun was able to select appropriate times and places for observing what is by all accounts a tricky form of writing to see—mobile text messaging.

Diaries were used in a similar way by Abigail Sellen and Richard Harper (2001) to zero in on moments of document use at the International Monetary Fund (IMF). With ties to Xerox PARC and an associated interest in the way office technologies—especially documents and document systems—are used by knowledge workers at the IMF, Sellen and Harper used time-use diaries to map the specific ways that reading practices were or were not supported by paper documents. One question they asked was a simple one: What are all the ways that people read at the IMF? This is a great question for a diary study because it is open-ended and exploratory, and yet tied to real-world events that participants can identify and mark the temporal boundaries of. The resulting data exemplifies the basic approach to analyzing data from time-use diaries, which involves comparing actions with time spent. Consider the following list of document-use categories (see Figure 7.4) for which Sellen and Harper considered both the job role and format (paper, electronic, or some combination).

Using a stacked bar chart, Sellen and Harper (2001) were able to show quite dramatic differences in the document-use habits associated with

drafting own text	creating own data	editing own text
editing own data	revising another's text	revising another's data
collaborative authoring	collaborative data analysis	conversations
meetings	reading only	document delivery
note taking	formatting text	form filling
typing text	organizing documents	photocopying
dealing with mail	printing	searching for documents
searching for information	dealing with software	telephone activity
thinking & planning	responding to mail	language class

Figure 7.4. Example Document-use Categories (Sellen & Harper, 2001, p. 58)

economists at the IMF and those associated with other job categories such as administrative staff or management. Taken together, these views of document-mediated work formed an "activity profile" made up of trends that characterize work but are otherwise tacit or so fragmented as to be unnoticeable. Sellen and Harper were able to show, for example, that a great deal of the intellectual work done by economists is supported by the affordances of paper documents. The term *affordance* describes features of a given technology that map its use and act as implicit or explicit signals to users about the "fit" of a given technology with some goal they have. Sellen and Harper showed that the affordances of electronic document formats are also powerful, and so the activity of administrative staff workers largely consisted of transforming paper documents to electronic formats and vice versa.

Sellen and Harper (2001) did not rely exclusively on diary data in their study of the IMF. They also used ethnographic methods including participant observation and interviewing. What the diary data helped them to do, however, was to frame detailed questions related to their overall goal of understanding document use within the organization. This is perhaps the best use of diary study data when the object of study is a process like writing and the aim is to discover how people use technology to carry out writing tasks. Participant diaries can give us a snapshot of what kinds of actions happen frequently, where they occur in the relative sequence of actions that comprise a larger activity, and with what mediational resources available to actors. For example, Sellen and Harper noticed that knowledge workers (economists) at the IMF spent much more time revising and reviewing reports they and others had written than they did drafting text or data displays such as tables. On average, reviewing and revising took up 71% of their time, whereas only 29% of their time was spent on authoring. Most of the reviewing and revising (89%), moreover, occurred online, though paper was almost always used as well.

The scene Sellen and Harper (2001) described is familiar and intuitive, perhaps, to computers and writing specialists: Knowledge workers at the IMF were working collaboratively, always, to produce sections of reports that would eventually get incorporated into other documents. The desktops of the economists featured both paper documents and electronic documents on computer screens. Paper documents allowed the economists to more readily engage in the work of cross-checking, verifying, and coordinating information because the physical proximity and appearance of the paper documents could encode meaning relevant to the economists' goals. Stacks of documents, for example, could represent sections of reports awaiting revision and those already completed; dog-eared pages represented specific locations to attend to. Electronic documents could not support the document-coordination aspect of reviewing and revising quite as well, despite the ability to display multiple windows on computer screens. Sellen and Harper explained that "knowledge workers did use multiple windows on their computer screens, but this was mainly for electronic cutting and pasting, not for the back-and-forth cross-referencing of other materials during their authoring work" (p. 61).

The breakthrough here, from a computers and writing research perspective, is clear evidence that two actions identifiable as aspects of "revising"—moving text from one document to another via cut-and-paste, and cross-referencing information contained in documents that have or will have an important relationship—require fundamentally different types of mediational support. It should cause us to ask, as researchers and teachers of writing in digital environments, what other revelations like this lie in the details of the composing process? What other details of composing as mediated social activity will a method such as time-use diaries reveal?

THE TIME HAS COME: USING DIARY STUDIES TO LEARN ABOUT WRITING IN DIGITAL ENVIRONMENTS

An interesting by-product of the phenomenon of all facets of the writing process—from composing to reading—taking place in digital environments is that writing researchers now have access to very rich, time-indexed sequences of events that have the potential to tell us about people's encounters with texts. Every keystroke, every line of text that scrolls by on the screen is understood as an "event" in the digital landscape, and many different applications keep track of these events on a nanosecond scale to provide useful features such as going "back" to where we were previously in a text, "undoing" a change to a draft, or keeping a co-author's changes to a manuscript distinct from one's own. The digital writing landscape is full of stories of writing unfolding. But these stories are, at present, not terribly interesting nor are they very easy to read. Still, the rich amount of detail they hold calls out to writing researchers who want more detailed and naturalistic methods for creating accounts of writing in digital environments. Diary studies offer a way to make sense of some of this detail through the co-construction of similar event-based accounts in which researchers and participants identify the important moments, artifacts, sequences, and roles that lend context to machine-generated event records.

The possibilities for researching writing that these two types of data-collection methods promise include not only more detailed accounts of isolated composing moments, but also more expansive and longitudinal accounts of an individual or group's writing strategies, or a text's lifecycle from invention to reception in multiple contexts. If we consider "moments of contact" with a text to be the subject of a time-indexed study of the writing process, for example, we could construct fascinating accounts of how a chapter like this one came to be, how it circulated during the drafting, review, and revision stages of its life, and how it will travel to the screens and desktops of others, perhaps becoming part of other texts. A combination of a digital event log produced, say, by tagging a document with an electronic signature that acts as the textual equivalent of a radio collar could be augmented by a diary study that invited each person who came in contact with the document to log events related to reading and using it on a blog. Such a study could, perhaps, demonstrate deeper connections between the actions and decisions writers and others involved in composing a text make and those that readers and users make when they encounter it further down the timeline, helping to define the sort of higher standard for "rhetorical success" called for by Paul Danette, Davida Charney, and Aimee Kendall (2001).

The longitudinal view enabled by this sort of digital writing diary study could also help to extend the reach and value of writing instruction. Armed with more detailed longitudinal accounts of the actions and decisions required to make texts successful, researchers and writing program administrators could begin to make the case for extending writing instruction well beyond the one or two semesters most students in American universities receive. And when the collaborative and social nature of writing is demonstrated—perhaps visually as a result of diagramming data from diary event logs—similar arguments might be made to change the physical and curricular spaces in which writing is taught to better suit the way writers must coordinate with each other, with information resources, and with software and hardware tools necessary to ensure rhetorical success.

NOTES

1. See Nardi (1996) for a comparison of activity theory, distributed cognition, and situated action approaches; see Spinuzzi (2003) for examples of how the individual/system issue plays out methodologically when studying computer-mediated writing.

2. See Czerwinski, Horvitz, and Wilhite (2004) for an interesting diary study design that tackled this issue in relation to multitasking and interruption recovery in knowledge work situations.

8

MOBILE TECHNOLOGIES AND A PHENOMENOLOGY OF LITERACY

Joanne Addison

Conducting research that captures the full and robust dynamics of literacy requires direct, situated methods—methods that appropriately reflect the complexity of everyday choices, multiple writing-related tasks, and interactions with technologies. In this chapter, I explore the ways that mobile technologies can help us record, measure, and understand literacy as a lived experience. I offer hermeneutic phenomenology as a critical framework and describe experience sampling methods as a way to bridge the critical framework of our research and the practical deployment of mobile technologies in conducting research. I describe two studies that used mobile technologies, and I conclude with directions for future research.

INTRODUCTION

In *Literacy in American Lives*, Deborah Brandt (2001) stated:

> Only recently have we begun to accumulate more systematic and
> direct accounts of contemporary literacy as it has been experienced.
> Nevertheless, many current debates about literacy education and poli-
> cy continue to be based largely on indirect evidence, such as standard-
> ized tests scores or education levels or surveys of reading habits. (p. 11)

Indirect evidence can be useful in helping us construct valid inferences
when research questions or theoretical speculations are difficult or impossible to prove. But, when used as the sole or even primary source of information, indirect evidence leaves us with incomplete and often skewed versions of literacy. Instead, Brandt called for studies using direct accounts of
literacy and emphasized that the purpose of her research is to describe literacy as it has been lived within certain cultural, historical, and socioeconomic moments in time. Thus, instead of focusing on surveys or textual
analysis of participants' writing, Brandt gathered the life histories of 80
participants to "understand the vicissitudes of individual literacy development in relationship to the large-scale economic forces that set the routes
and determine the worldly worth of that literacy" (p. 18). Her phenomenological approach to literacy research provides a complex account of the
ways in which people acquire specific types of literacy as well as the socioeconomic implications of varying levels of acquisition.

In general, phenomenological research strives to describe and interpret some aspect of human experience from the point of view of those who
have lived the experience via direct evidence. As Brandt (2001) argued, it
is this type of critical interpretation that should gain more prominence in
public debates and policy-setting discussions of literacy, as the implications
of research that rely on direct evidence go far beyond what can be gleaned
from the indirect evidence of standardized tests or simple surveys. The
field of rhetoric and composition is well positioned to take a leadership role
in the design and implementation of research that contributes to systematic, contextualized accounts of literacy in ways that positively alter educational practices and policy decisions. Doing so requires the type of direct,
situated research conducted by Brandt:[1] an increase in the number of longitudinal, large-scale/multisite research projects; and the further incorpora-

tion of technologies into our repertoire of data collection and analysis strategies. In this chapter, I explore the ways that mobile technologies can help us record, measure, and understand literacy as a lived experience. I also discuss hermeneutic phenomenology as a critical framework that can guide us in the use of mobile technologies.

RESEARCH AND MOBILE TECHNOLOGIES FRAMED BY HERMENEUTIC PHENOMENOLOGY

In talking about mobile technologies, I am generally referring to those technologies we can easily carry with us throughout a day. From a research perspective, mobile technology refers to those devices researchers can employ in an effort to understand literacy as a lived experience. In other words, although it is nearly impossible to follow even a small number of research participants 24 hours a day, observing and recording all of their literacy experiences, it is possible to employ mobile technologies that research participants carry with them throughout the day for the days or weeks of the study to learn more about their daily experiences. Perhaps the most readily available mobile technology is the cell phone. A more targeted type of mobile technology is a databank watch. A databank watch is essentially a wristwatch that can be programmed to beep at a set time or throughout the day in a controlled or random pattern. When beeped, a research participant fills out a response form in relation to the activity in which she is engaged. These response forms can then be collected and analyzed and followed by in-depth interviews. (A more detailed account of this type of research technology as well as others is provided later.)

The use of any technology for research purposes must, of course, occur within a critical framework. I suggest the use of hermeneutic phenomenology in the study of situated literacy. Hermeneutic phenomenology finds its roots in the work of Martin Heidegger (1969, 1977, 1982, 1987), Hans-Georg Gadamer (1976a, 1976b, 1980, 1989), Paul Ricouer (1981), and Max van Manen (1997), among others. As a methodology, it is used to describe and critically understand the situated nature of human experience so that any phenomenon, such as literacy, is studied within the context of a person's cultural, social, and historical moment. Participants are viewed as co-creators of the world-view constructed through and within their cultural, social, and historical contexts. It is the researcher's job to describe what is transparent and what is hidden, and to identify patterns and ruptures within an individual's lived experiences and across a group's lived experiences. In *Researching Lived Experience*, van Manen identified six research activities that mark a hermeneutic phenomenological approach to research:

1. Turning to a phenomenon which seriously interests us and commits us to the world;
2. Investigating experience as we live it rather than as we conceptualize it;
3. Reflecting on the essential themes which characterize the phenomenon;
4. Describing the phenomenon through the art of writing and rewriting;
5. Maintaining a strong and oriented pedagogical relation to the phenomenon;
6. Balancing the research context by considering parts and whole. (pp. 30–31)

A full discussion of all six of these points is beyond the scope of this chapter. Instead, I focus on the ways that mobile technologies can help us get at van Manen's second and third component: "investigating experience as we live it rather than as we conceptualize it" in ways that allow us to reflect on "the essential themes which characterize the phenomenon."

Following Ricouer (1981), the project of hermeneutics is to address the meaning of and in lived experience. Researchers accomplish this by studying discourse from a situated perspective, which requires the consideration of literacy as part of the larger discourse of an individual or community. As Ricouer argued:

> what we understand first in a discourse is not another person, but a project, that is, the outline of a new being-in-the-world. Only writing, in freeing itself, not only from its author, but from the narrowness of the dialogical situation, reveals this destination of discourse as projecting a world. (p. 202)

If we view discourse as a projection of the world and writing as an artifact of discourse,[2] then understanding literacy as it is variously situated in the world requires research methods that allow us to identify and reflect upon the essential themes that characterize literacy within a specific socioeconomic moment. This is, in fact, very much what Brandt's (2001) research in *Literacy in American Lives* accomplishes. Through her research on the literacy experiences of 80 Americans ranging in age from 10 to 98 years old, she is able to reveal the worlds projected via discourse. Her book is about the worlds constructed by ordinary people during the last century, when literacy skill was treated as a commodity from economic, political, intellectual, and spiritual perspectives. In particular, her book is about the ways in which Americans inhabit literacy, creating and recreating their world as they obtain the types of literate skills required by our current historical moment.

If we view discourse—and by extension literacy—as the projection of a world, how can we materially fix[3] discourse in a way that allows for systematic investigation? Further, how can we materially fix discourse in a way that allows for the type of hermeneutic interpretation called for by educational researcher Pamela Moss (1994)? Moss, specifically, challenged researchers to consider how:

> interpretation might be warranted by criteria like a reader's extensive knowledge of the learning context; multiple and varied sources of evidence; an ethic of disciplined, collaborative inquiry that encourages challenges and revisions to initial interpretations; and the transparency of the trail of evidence leading to the interpretations, which allows users to evaluate the conclusions for themselves. . . . Inconsistency . . . does not invalidate the assessment . . . [it calls for] a more elaborate or comprehensive interpretation. (pp. 7–8)

Certainly Brandt (2001) offered one option through the use of interviews and life histories. Another option is experience sampling, a group of research methods that can employ mobile technologies to provide detailed accounts of experience from a situated perspective.

EXPERIENCE SAMPLING METHODS AND MOBILE TECHNOLOGIES

Although experience sampling methods (ESM) have existed in various forms since at least 1940, it is the work of Reed Larson and Mihaly Csikszentmihalyi, beginning in the late 1970s, that established ESM as a groundbreaking research method (see, particularly, Csikszentmihalyi & Larson, 1987; Csikszentmihalyi,

Larson, & Prescott, 1977; Freeman, Csikszentmihalyi, & Larson, 1986; Larson, 1989; Larson & Csikszentmihalyi, 1983; Larson, Csikszentmihalyi, & Freeman, 1984; Larson & Lampman-Petraitis, 1989). Varying definitions of ESM exist; for the purposes of this chapter, I refer to ESM as a research method in which participants are signaled at the occurrence of certain events or random intervals during a given time period to stop and record what they are doing and how they feel about what they are doing. For example, during an event-contingent study, participants complete response forms immediately after a particular event (e.g., peer group work) for a set period of time (e.g., 3 weeks). During a random-interval study, participants complete a response form upon being signaled to do so by some device programmed to emit signals at random intervals during a set time period (e.g., seven times a day for one week). This data can then be further illuminated through in-depth interviews, samples of written documents, and other forms of data.

The primary advantage of ESM is that it allows researchers to collect data within the context of participants' daily lives. As Robert Kubey, Larson, and Csikszentmihalyi (1996) noted: "The most obvious advantage of the ESM is that it provides a way of getting detailed data about important subjective elements of people's lives in ways that cannot always be matched by other methodologies. It is one of the tools of choice for inquiries into systematic phenomenology" (p. 100). Further, this method allows researchers to collect data synchronously; in other words, participants describe what they are doing and how they feel about what they are doing at the exact moment they are engaged in an activity. Thus, this method allows researchers to avoid some of the problems associated with methods that rely on a participant's short or long-term memory to recall and reconstruct events and reactions to an event.

As with any particular research method, ESM has its drawbacks: the methods are time- and resource-intensive, and, because they are defined by naturalistic settings, do not allow for tight control of variables. In addition, ESM studies, although they can be conducted with a smaller subject pool, are more reliable when conducted with a large number of participants. Although seeking this larger participant pool is a drawback in terms of structuring and conducting research, it is also a benefit because in using ESM, we can potentially move beyond research subjects who are easily available to us. Further, large-scale research allows us to develop smaller studies of specific populations (e.g., first-generation college students, online students, women students) that can allow for meaningful comparisons not possible if we limit ourselves to those students easily available to us.

EXPERIENCE SAMPLING METHODS: RESEARCH EXAMPLES

I am currently engaged in a multisite study of literacy development using ESM. My goal is to study the literacy development of college students across space and time (e.g., online courses, writing center tutorials, work at home, first-year composition, workplace writing) to begin developing a complex, comprehensive picture of the shape of literacy acquisition both within and beyond an academic setting—especially in relation to student engagement and outcomes. One set of participants is drawn from online business writing classes. These participants from online courses wear a databank watch preprogrammed to signal once every 2 hours at random intervals from 8:00 a.m. to 10:00 p.m. for one week. This results in a possible 50 responses from each participant (the general response rate is close to 75%). When a participant is signaled, she completes a self-report form (see Appendix) adapted from the work of Mihaly Csikszentmihalyi (Yair, 2000). If she is not involved in a reading or writing activity at the time of the signal, she simply lists what she is doing. If she is involved in a reading or writing activity at the time of the signal, she completes the self-report form, which consists primarily of a series of rating scales and open-ended questions designed to explore behavioral and intrapsychic aspects of literacy learning. This data is then entered into a statistical analysis program such as SPSS (Statistical Package for the Social Sciences) and/or HLM (Hierarchical Linear and Nonlinear Modeling). The goal is to capture literacy events during a typical week in the lives of these students. I want to know what types of literacy acts students participate in during a typical week and which school and nonschool activities they find most engaging. Once enough data has been collected to identify essential themes, the study will continue with in-depth interviews of a specific set of research participants. My hope is that a better accounting of the types of literacy events in students' lives—as well as measuring engagement levels in relation to various literacy events—will help us to develop curricula and educational policy that better meets the needs of students as citizens.

In a more narrowly focused study, I have been collecting data using ESM to measure student engagement in first-year composition classes. The setting for this strand of my research is a networked computer classroom. At this site, students in our second-semester, first-year composition course volunteer to participate during class sessions. In the networked classrooms, teachers wear databank watches preprogrammed to beep twice during their class period over the course of 2 weeks. When the watch beeps, students who have volunteered to participate click on the ESM icon on their computers. They fill out an automated form sent directly to a secure server upon completion. The goal of this research is to obtain direct accounts of student engagement with typical instructional practices in networked classrooms. Additionally, I have recently teamed with two of my colleagues to study writing center tutorials and the experiences of new teaching assistants using ESM. Ultimately we hope to provide a comprehensive, integrated account of the sites typically inhabited by rhetoric and composition faculty and their students.

ESM WITH MOBILE TECHNOLOGIES

In the examples above, we are using what I would call entry-level mobile technology—databank watches (i.e., a Casio databank 150) that participants wear during the day and that randomly signals them for a written response (students carry a booklet of response forms) in whatever situations they are engaged. The advantage to this technology is that it is a relatively cheap option for a research method that is generally time- and resource-intensive. Databank watches can be purchased for $30–$40 each and, importantly, cost little in the way of maintenance (i.e., they do not easily break, replacing batteries is inexpensive, and there are no software or programming costs). The greatest disadvantage is that each participant record must be entered into a computer program by hand, requiring a great deal of time and subject to human error.

Moving toward computerized experience sampling requires personal data assistants (PDAs). As with databank watches, PDAs can be programmed to randomly signal a participant to complete a response form; the form is then stored in the PDA. Research to date using PDAs suggests a greater response rate among participants. Human error is reduced in that computerized methods can ensure that participants complete reports as instructed and that data entered into a PDA can be transferred directly to a master computer. This direct transfer also greatly decreases the amount of time spent entering data. Although PDAs cost at least twice as much as databank watches and are far more expensive to maintain, the time saved on data entry and the reduction in human error may offset the increased cost. Those with small initial research budgets might begin with databank watches and move toward PDAs as the budget allows. There are a number of software options available for use with PDAs—both those that are free to researchers and those that are commercial products. These programs, both free-ware and commercial software, vary in terms of level of flexibility and degree of proven reliability.

One of the more recent and intriguing developments in the use of mobile technologies and ESM is the open source Context-Aware Experience Sampling Tool (CAES) developed by researchers at MIT. Although CAES is rooted in traditional ESM methods, it differs significantly in that it uses "emerging computational perception and sensing technologies to *automatically* detect events that can trigger sampling and thereby data collection" (MIT, 2003, n.p.). For example, if a researcher wanted to focus on literacy events within a specific context or set of related contexts, using GPS-determined locations, participants could be signaled to respond when in those contexts. This allows for more targeted research projects and less intrusion into the lives of research participants.[4]

Although these technologies can lead to variations in data collection, basic data-collection methods and analysis procedures remain the same. Participants complete an experience sampling form such as the example included at the end of this chapter (see Appendix) each time they are signaled to do so. They can store their responses on paper or in a digital format using a PDA or other device. These responses are then entered into a statistical analysis program such as SPSS for first-level analysis. The descriptive statistics generated provide interesting information, but the meaning of these descriptive statistics must be further explored by in-depth interviews. The interviews should be transcribed and coded and, in an effort to establish validity, a subset of the interviews should also be coded by a peer to test the strength of the categories being established. When possible, participants should be asked to comment on the meanings derived from the statistics and the coding procedure, as it is their lived experiences we are seeking to represent.

FURTHER DIRECTIONS AND COMPLICATIONS IN EXPERIENCE SAMPLING METHODS USE

There are certainly many questions that must be asked concerning the use of mobile technologies in literacy research in general, as well as the use of experience sampling methods in particular. We need to develop a critical awareness of mobile technologies and sampling methods in terms of the ways they can shape data collection and influence our ability to understand literacy as it is lived. We need to discuss the ways in which the use of mobile technologies and sampling methods both challenge and are challenged by the theoretical lenses we bring to any research project (e.g., feminism, postmodernism). Perhaps the most compelling aspects of this research that need to be explored are the opportunities for expansion and collaboration. Once a database is established, it can be added to over many years by multiple researchers working with additional groups of participants. Use of ESM not only helps researchers study literacy as a lived experience, but makes a significant contribution to establishing a history of writing and writing instruction in the 21st century and beyond.

NOTES

1. I use Brandt's study as a touchstone throughout this chapter, as it is an excellent example of the type of phenomenological research called for by many in our field. During the course of writing this chapter, Cynthia Selfe and Gail Hawisher's (2004) *Literate Lives in the Information Age* was published; this book is another example of phenomenological research.
2. Ricouer (1981) was concerned with hermeneutics and its application to the human sciences. Human science is essentially the study of peoples' actions and artifacts (e.g., writing) with the goal of understanding how people experience their world.
3. See Ricoeur (1981) for a discussion of material fixation.
4. Although the argument might be made that GPS coordinates of research participants *is* more intrusive, it can certainly be less disruptive.

APPENDIX:
EXAMPLE EXPERIENCE SAMPLING FORM

Name_____

Time_____

Date_____

At the time you were beeped, what was the MAIN thing you were doing:

__reading for pleasure

__reading for school subject_____

__reading for work

__online course lecture

__video/internet/tv presentation

__online small groups

__whole class discussion board

__individual writing for school

__individual writing for work

__group writing for school

__group writing for work

__talking individually with teacher in person

__talking individually with teacher via email

__surfing the internet (class related)

__checking email

__daydreaming

__nothing

__other reading and or writing?_____

To what, specifically, were you reading and/or writing and/or listening?

	NOT AT ALL		SOMEWHAT			NOT QUITE		VERY	
How well were you concentrating?	0	1	2	3	4	5	6	7	8	9
Was it hard to concentrate?	0	1	2	3	4	5	6	7	8	9

How self-conscious were you?	0	1	2	3	4	5	6	7	8	9
Did you feel good about yourself?	0	1	2	3	4	5	6	7	8	9
Were you in control of the situation?	0	1	2	3	4	5	6	7	8	9
Were you living up to your own expectations?	0	1	2	3	4	5	6	7	8	9
Were you living up to expectations of others?	0	1	2	3	4	5	6	7	8	9

Describe your mood as you were beeped:

Happy	0	o	•	——	•	o	0	Sad
Irritable	0	o	•	——	•	o	0	Cheerful
Strong	0	o	•	——	•	o	0	Weak
Active	0	o	•	——	•	o	0	Passive
Lonely	0	o	•	——	•	o	0	Sociable
Ashamed	0	o	•	——	•	o	0	Proud
Involved	0	o	•	——	•	o	0	Detached
Excited	0	o	•	——	•	o	0	Bored
Closed	0	o	•	——	•	o	0	Open
Clear	0	o	•	——	•	o	0	Confused
Worried	0	o	•	——	•	o	0	Relaxed
Competitive	0	o	•	——	•	o	0	Cooperative

How did you feel about the reading and/or writing in which you were engaged?

---

	low						high			
Did you feel good about yourself?	0	1	2	3	4	5	6	7	8	9
Challenges of the reading and/or writing	0	1	2	3	4	5	6	7	8	9
Your skills in this reading and/or writing	0	1	2	3	4	5	6	7	8	9
Was this reading and/or writing important to you?	0	1	2	3	4	5	6	7	8	9

Was this reading and/or writing important to others?	0	1	2	3	4	5	6	7	8	9
Were you succeeding at what you were doing?	0	1	2	3	4	5	6	7	8	9
Do you wish you had been doing something else?	0	1	2	3	4	5	6	7	8	9
Were you satisfied with how you were doing?	0	1	2	3	4	5	6	7	8	9
How important was this activity in relation to your overall goals?	0	1	2	3	4	5	6	7	8	9
What is the likelihood that this reading and/or writing will affect your thinking in relation to this subject?	0	1	2	3	4	5	6	7	8	9
What is the likelihood that this reading and/or writing will affect your actions in relation to this subject?	0	1	2	3	4	5	6	7	8	9

Any explanation you'd like to add concerning the last 3 questions above?

Other comments?

9

CAPTURING THE ACTIVITY OF DIGITAL WRITING

USING, ANALYZING, AND SUPPLEMENTING VIDEO SCREEN CAPTURE

Cheryl Geisler

Shaun Slattery

Digital writing researchers have begun to explore the potential of video screen captures, the product of screen-capture software that records users' on-screen activity as a series of screen-captured images spliced together to comprise a digital video. Video capture technologies provide a useful means of capturing a rich sense of writerly activity by producing a detailed record of digital writing processes and of the artifacts produced in a digital writing environment. Video-captured data can be analyzed based on an activity theory framework, ranging from a fine-grain analysis at the level of operation to a big-picture analysis at the level of action and activity. In this chapter, we introduce the use of video capture in the context of activity theory, illustrate how it can be used to capture the activity of digital writing, and discuss some of the complications that can arise within studies using video screen capture.

INTRODUCTION

The ability to produce, circulate, and use texts digitally has changed how writing is done. The goals of many literate practices remain the same, yet the mechanisms by which these practices are accomplished have shifted. Students still look up sources, for example, but they are more likely to pursue this goal through a search on the Web than through a physical visit to the library stacks. In the face of such shifts, the IText working group (Geisler et al.) called, in 2001, for explicit study of the way that new information technologies change the nature and activities associated with text. ITexts—the artifacts of digital writing—are, it was suggested, "at the core of the information revolution" (p. 269). Given the prominence of digital writing, it is especially important that we develop methods that help us understand computer-mediated writing with sufficient sophistication. Innovative methodologies have been developed for studying writing activities in general.[1] Nevertheless, it has, until recently, been physically and therefore methodologically difficult to record the moment-by-moment operations that comprise writing in digital environments. Fortunately, recent technological developments have brought new methods within our reach; in particular, a handful of researchers have begun to explore the potential for using video screen capture.

Video screen captures are the product of screen-capture software that records users' on-screen activity as a series of images spliced together to comprise a digital video. The software can run in the background of other activities (such as using word-processing software or a Web browser) and thus provides the potential for capturing second-by-second detail in an unobtrusive manner. Once captured, such videos can then be played back, stopped, reversed, or saved as individual still shots using the functions bundled with the screen-capture software itself. The captures can also be imported into and manipulated with a wide range of video editing tools.

Although video screen capture is familiar to practitioners of technical communication as a way to create computer tutorials, little attention has been paid to the way it can be used as a method for studying digital writing activity. Recent work suggests, however, that it can be used to illustrate a number of interesting activities related to the processes of digital writing:

- Geisler (2001, 2003), for example, used video screen capture to analyze reading and writing in a computer-based personal management system. As revealed through video screen capture, a writer moved among calendar, task list, email, and Web browser to coordinate work with others and to produce her own writing, producing a kind of *textualization of self.*

- Slattery (2003, 2005, 2006) used video screen capture to describe the way technical writers use multiple texts as they write. As caught on video screen capture, technical writers used complex routines to orchestrate the interplay among multiple texts as they worked to produce a new document—suggesting the important role *textual coordination* can play in rhetorical action.

- Jason Swarts (2004) used video screen capture to provide writers with a window of their own writing activities. Using video screen capture, apprentice writers recorded their writing activities and used them as a starting point for discussion of rhetorical choice with their workplace supervisors—extending the concept of "instant replay" to become *textual replay*, a foundation for writerly reflection-in-action.

Video screen capture has thus made visible phenomena that might otherwise have gone unnoticed in digital writing.

Video screen capture can best be understood as one of a family of process-tracing methodologies that focus on providing a record of events over time. In research on writing, the earliest use of process tracing involved the analysis of concurrent think-aloud protocols, recordings of verbalizations when participants are asked to "say whatever comes to mind" as they undertake an activity (Ericsson & Simon, 1984; Hayes & Flower, 1983). Seldom used in writing research today, think-aloud protocols are still common in usability studies (e.g., Benbunan-Fich, 2001), although they have been subject to critique (Boren & Ramey, 2000). In essence, problems with think-aloud protocols may involve both incompleteness and distortion. If consciousness during a given activity is not normally verbal, the think-aloud record may be incomplete; if participants turn their attention toward communicating with the researcher and away from the activity at hand, their activity may be distorted.

Video screen capture does not raise issues of distortion and is more closely related to a second process-tracing methodology, the event log (Lohse & Johnson, 1996; van der Aalst, Weitjer, & Maruster, 2004). Events such as mouse clicks, keystrokes, commands, and toggling between applications are automatically recorded in a log by a computing system along with other potentially useful information such as time stamps or mouse coordinates. Researchers can mine such logs either by hand or through automatic methods to determine the frequency or sequence of events of interest. Unlike think-aloud protocols, event logs are unobtrusive, but their utility can depend upon the appropriateness of the kind of event captured. In old-fashioned command-driven computing environments, for example, keystrokes were used to move through a text as well as make changes to it. In environments to which a mouse has been added as an input device, however, movement through text is achieved through the movement of the mouse rather than keystroke commands. As a result, keystroke capture, once thought a promising methodology for studying writing activity, is no longer used in studying digital writing. Video screen captures are closely related to event logs in the sense that they represent a record of computing activity, but rather than capture computing events, they capture the consequences of those events as displayed to the screen.[2]

Video screen capture can be an important process-tracing tool in understanding the complexity of digital writing activity. Our purpose in this chapter, then, is to introduce the use of video capture, illustrate how it can be used to capture the activity of digital writing, and discuss some of the complications that can arise when using video screen capture in digital writing research. Before we turn to these topics, however, in the next section, we place video capture methods in the context of activity theory.

ACTIVITY THEORY AS A FRAMEWORK FOR STUDYING DIGITAL WRITING

Increasingly, researchers of text have argued for using activity as the basis for studies of writing. Drawing on activity theory, collections and monographs studying the activity of writing have begun to appear (Bazerman & Russell, 2003; Dias, Freedman, Medway, & Paré, 1999). As described by Viktor Kaptelinin and Bonnie Nardi (1997) and by Nardi (1996), activity theory is a conceptual system that conceives of human behavior as goal driven and mediated by artifacts. There are five basic principles of activity theory, each of which describes a certain property of human behavior:

- First, human behavior is goal-oriented. We perform tasks and engage in activities not randomly or mechanically but in the service of larger goals. For example, a student undertakes a search of the Web as way of achieving her goal of receiving a good grade on a research paper.

- Second, human behavior is hierarchical. The things we do are organized as a series of nested behaviors (Kaptelinin, 1997). At the highest level are our *activities* pursued in the service of our larger goals. Activities tell us *why* we do things. Within these activities, we may undertake any number of actions to achieve those goals. Actions tell us *what* we are doing. And within these actions, we may engage in any number of operations to accomplish our actions. Operations tell us *how* we do what we do. The student researcher might enter search terms on the library Web site at the operational level to accomplish the action of finding sources, all as part of the activity of writing a research paper.[3]
- Third, human behavior is both external and internal. We do things both in the world and in our minds, and these two processes interact. For example, a student's library research is often a back-and-forth external process of coming up with search terms that, in turn, changes or adapts her internal thinking about the topic.
- Fourth, human behavior is always mediated. Tools—both physical and symbolic, both internalized and in the world—become incorporated into the way we do things in a way that inextricably knits us together with the environments in which we act. So, for example, the activity of doing a research paper becomes, for any individual, knit together with the symbolic tools (concepts of sources, authors, intellectual contribution) and the material tools (Web browsers, books, notecards) that together mediate research activity. When an individual shifts concepts (understanding, for example, credibility) or shifts tools (moving, for example, from paper-based notes to a digital bibliographic system), the entire activity shifts and is reknit within a new constellation of tools.
- Fifth and finally, human behavior develops over time. Activity is not stable over time, but rather develops in two distinct ways. At the level of the individual, activities develop as new symbolic and material tools knit and reknit us to changing environments and changing goals. At the level of culture, activities develop as new symbolic and material tools that structure and restructure the invitations an environment offers its members. For our student, then, the activity of research may develop with new digital technologies like Web searches, but—and at the same time—a whole society's understanding of the nature and use of sources may shift under the affordances of the digital age.

Through these five principles, activity theory aims to provide a framework for focusing the researcher's gaze. In addition to looking at context, it suggests that we look closely at both the tools that mediate our behavior and at the moment-by-moment activities by which they play out over time. It is important to recognize that the focus on tools and goals provides a breadth of focus beyond the purely instrumental (Herndl & Nahrwold, 2000). That is, a commitment to seeing the human being as *motivated* does not limit our view to the near-term horizon of actors' current purposes and contexts. Research can, of course, ask, "how can we make the activity we are observing easier?" or "how can we make it more efficient?" But it is also possible to ask, as Geisler (2003) did, "how did this activity come to be, and how could it be different?" Within a broad framework of research purposes, then, video capture technologies provide a useful means to capture a rich sense of writerly activity by providing a detailed record of the knitting together of mediating artifacts and the larger digital environment.

USING VIDEO CAPTURE SOFTWARE

Video capture software records writers' on-screen activity as a digital video that can be played back and analyzed or used for stimulated-recall interviews with writers. It is not unlike having a videocamera recording the writer's monitor, and the software is complete with start, stop, and pause buttons. The software is loaded on whatever computer the writers will use, be it at home or in an office, allowing them to work more naturally, using the tools and configurations they themselves have created. Once a recording session is begun, the program runs unobtrusively in the background as the writers go about their work.

We wish to avoid an overly detailed and soon-dated list of software features, many of which are developed for producing computer tutorials and not for the re-appropriation of this software as a data-collection tool. For the purposes of capturing digital writing activity, however, it is useful to focus on several features:

Output: Many video capture programs are built upon the basic functionality of image screen capture and offer the option of doing either image capture or video capture. Obviously we are talking about the second option here, though the ability to create a single image is often a useful supplement.

File Format: With video capture, some software offers only one file format; others offer a choice. The context and modes of analysis along with where and how the video files will be stored should dictate the format in which the video is generated.

Frame Rate: Many video capture programs allow users to choose the frame rate at which images are captured. The more frames per second, the higher the quality and seamlessness of the video, but the larger the file size. A researcher should experiment with various frame rates and the kind of activity being captured to find the most appropriate rate.

Input: Most video capture programs provide options regarding the screen object to be captured. For instance, you may be able to capture the entire screen, just an active window, or a specific region of the screen.

Audio: Many video capture programs allow the recording of sound during the capture session, a feature that may facilitate speak-aloud protocols. Others allow the addition of voice-over to a previously captured file. This can be useful for doing a stimulated-recall interview. Both of these options significantly increases file size, however, and will require special arrangements for storage.

Triggers: Most video capture programs can be launched from the software's window itself or through hot keys or hot key combinations. If a researcher is asking writers to launch the software themselves while they work alone, some thought must be given to establishing an easy-to-use trigger.

The record produced by the video capture software is a digital video file that can be handled like any other media file: stored, moved, opened, and viewed whenever needed. During viewing, the video may be paused, fast-forwarded and rewound, and even played slowly, depending on the media-viewing software. Video-editing software can be used that allows special viewing and editing options, including segmenting, splicing, and the addition of audio tracks, among other features.

When and how long to record depends upon the phenomenon the researcher hopes to observe. We have found it is useful to limit the recording of sessions to around one more or less discrete task. Another option is to record segments of activity at set or random times throughout the day to sample from and across a writer's work. Time-based triggers are not part of software packages we have encountered, however, and would probably require some programming to establish.

ANALYZING VIDEO CAPTURE DATA

Depending on the phenomenon of interest in the study, video-captured data can be analyzed at different scales based on an activity theory framework, ranging from a fine-grain analysis at the level of operation to a big-picture analysis at the level of action and activity. It is important to remember, however, that screen-capture software records only what is on the screen for the duration of the capture. Despite its intuitively appealing quality, the capture record can present researchers accustomed to text-based research with significant challenges in analysis.

As illustrated by Figure 9.1, the data is fundamentally a visual record. Each frame of the video capture shows what the writer was viewing at the time of the capture. Here, for example, we see a file open in Microsoft Word in the active window, viewed at 50% magnification. Behind and to the side, we see a window containing the body of an email message. Less obvious, we also see several open email indices.

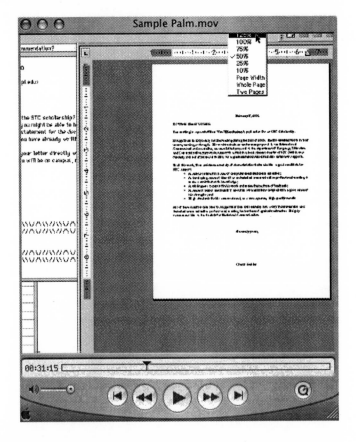

FIGURE 9.1.   Sample Frame from a Video Capture

Action in video captures is inferred from changes between frames. That is, the frame in Figure 9.1 above tells us little about what the writer is actually doing. When viewed in the context of the two subsequent frames shown in Figure 9.2, however, we can see that the writer is pulling down the magnification menu in Frame 1, selecting 100% magnification in Frame 2, and finally viewing the text 100% magnified in Frame 3. As this sequence suggests, seeing someone else's moment-by-moment process can be disorienting at first. Understanding what is happening depends on the researcher's level of familiarity with the writer's task and the software and operations they use. Viewing the recorded session several times is often necessary.

We have found it useful to analyze each video capture in a two-stage process beginning with first-order phenomena that can be directly "read" from a video-captured frame and then moving to second-order or inferred phenomena that require inferences across several frames. In the rest of this section, we describe this two-phase analytic procedure.

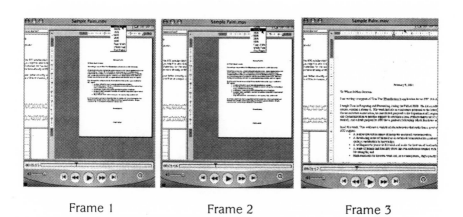

Frame 1   Frame 2   Frame 3

FIGURE 9.2. A Sequence of Three Video-Captured Frames

Identifying First-order Phenomena

First-order phenomena are features that can be more or less directly "read" from a video capture, frame by frame. They require low-level inferences and focus on the operational level. That is, first-order phenomena address the question of *how* the writer is doing what she is doing rather than higher-order questions of *what* she is doing or *why*. Figure 9.3 shows a spreadsheet record of the first-order phenomena associated with the video screen-capture frames shown earlier.

Using an activity theory framework, first-order writing phenomena can be extracted from video screen capture using the following five features:

1. The *time* at which the operation starts. Time can usually be read off the video capture from the time kept by the video player (as shown at the bottom of Figure 9.1).
2. The *artifact(s)* used, particularly the texts read and written. Some artifacts have names or titles that can be used to provide a unique name. In Figure 9.2, for example, we have used the email header "another recommendation?" to identify the email being read. File names and URLs are other ways of identifying artifacts.
3. The *operation* carried out on those artifacts. Operations name the lowest level of doing, but, as seen in Figure 9.3, this does not usually map onto each keystroke or cursor movement. Instead, operation points to the readily identifiable and usually repeated tasks writers perform. In terms of software, we might think of these as

Time	Artifact	Writer	Operation	Tool
026.59	another recommendation?	Tom	read next message	Eudora Pro
027.19			go to Word	Word
027.24	Letter for Tom	Cheryl	open document	Word

FIGURE 9.3.   Record Keeping for First-order Phenomena

low-level software functionality—opening files and moving windows, for example. But operations not associated with any specific software command that, nevertheless, indicate tasks the writer is doing—like reading a message in email—are equally important to consider.

4. The *writer* of the artifact. Although the user may be the writer of many texts being written and read, numerous additional writers come into play—email interlocutors, Web site authors, and so forth. When the writer uses the computer to communicate or work collaboratively online, the writer can be a particularly important first-order phenomenon to track. It may also be the case that the computer itself can be considered a "writer" when, for example, it displays an error message or otherwise communicates with the user.

5. The *tool* by which the operations are carried out. Writers may range across a variety of application borders—Web browsers, word–processing software, email clients, and so forth—as they work. Tool is the concept we use to track such movement. With applications that provide users with a variety of distinct functionalities, you will need to decide at what level to keep this record. In a personal management system, for example, writers may look at a calendar or a task list, two quite different environments that might, for some purposes, be best distinguished from one another. Within a calendaring program, on the other hand, users can look at a specific day, a whole week, or a full month, and a researcher may decide not to distinguish between these views as separate tools.

These five features can be used to create a first-order index of the session like that shown in Figure 9.3 and can provide the data from which second-order phenomena are inferred.

Inferring Second-order Phenomena

Second-order phenomena are inferred on the basis of first-order phenomena. They often require inferences that combine information across several frames, though they still remain relatively rooted in the video-captured data. That is, although second-order phenomena are a "matter of interpretation," the interpretations are relatively constrained. Second-order phenomena may include:

- *Duration*, which is typically calculated as the difference between the start time for a given operation and the start time for a subsequent operation. If, for instance, a given operation begins at 1 minute 30 seconds and the subsequent operation begins at 1 minute 45 seconds, the duration for the first operation is 15 seconds.
- *Actions* are the next highest level in the hierarchy of human behavior according to activity theory. They represent constellations of operations, tool, and artifact that usually show up across multiple frames. In Geisler (2003), for example, the user took three different actions when using an email program: read and reply, read and archive, read and hold. These three actions involved multiple operations and were not always carried out in exactly the same way, but always concluded with the same consequences: an email would be moved out of the inbox (or not, in the case of read and hold), and a reply would be generated and sent (or not, in the case of read and archive).
- *Breakdowns* are of theoretical interest in activity theory, because they can be the site of development as an individual struggles in the face of conflicting goals, inadequate tools, and so on. In our analyses, breakdowns occur at the level of action as users engage in unexpected sequences of operations to achieve their goals. A writer might, for example, attempt to open and refer to one document while writing another. In most cases, this action might be carried out fluently, but if the writer finds the document is not where expected or lost altogether, an entirely different sequence of operations may be carried out to complete the action or the action may be abandoned altogether.
- *Artifact ecologies* emerge once actions have been identified—collections of artifacts brought into play during a given action can be identified, some in focal awareness, some in background awareness. An electronic bibliography, for example, may always be open and in play for some writers during the writing of a literature review. Other writers may access online bibliographic databases or individual Web pages indexed by bookmarks. Such variation in artifact ecologies can be interesting second-order phenomena.
- Repeated *transitions* from one kind of artifact to another, or from one kind of operation to another, can also come under analysis as second-order phenomena.

These and other second-order phenomenon, combined with the first-order features we reviewed earlier, combine to form the essential data we have used for video capture analysis.

SUPPLEMENTING SCREEN-CAPTURE DATA

To produce a full activity theory analysis of video captured data, observed actions and operations must be supplemented with additional data that provide insight into the activities of digital writing. To know *why* a writer has employed a given sequence of actions, for instance, we need insight into her goals. Four methods, in particular, provide useful supplements to video capture data: inductive analysis, diaries, video recordings of the physical workspace, and stimulated-recall interviews.

Inductive analysis is an important supplement to video-capture data. After several viewings, it is possible to begin to produce an inductive interpretation of a recorded session. Often, clues to the motivation of the work reside within the recording itself. For example, it is easy to understand the writers were confused if we recorded them flipping back and forth between two documents several times and then drafting an email to ask a question. We might even see explicitly what they were confused about. Additionally, index data can be compared across sessions or among writers to examine, for example, how one writer performs different tasks or how different individuals accomplish the same task. It is important not to underestimate the value of induction, whether derived from prior experience with the task or from internal evidence from a recorded session, as induction can drive further data collection aimed at getting the writer's corroboration of their conscious motivation.

A second kind of useful supplementary data can come from writing diaries that writers keep for several days before and after a screen-capture session. A simple listing of each day's work, including such information as what they worked on, with whom they communicated, or what problems they encountered is a helpful data set. Used as the basis for an interview, this record can also be a helpful aid to the writer's memory and source of questions for the interviewer.

Another helpful supplement to video capture can be conventional video recording. One major limitation to video-capture data is that the researcher cannot see off-screen factors that affect on-screen work—phone calls, printed documents, conversations with colleagues, or even pauses for thinking. A video recording can provide important evidence concerning this off-screen activity. Recordings made with digital camcorders can often be downloaded directly to a computer, allowing simultaneous viewing of both the video-capture movie and the workspace movie. These combined recordings allow better interpretation of on-screen activity as well as analysis of the coordination of on- and off-screen artifacts.

The last, but most important, supplementary data-collection method is the stimulated-recall interview. After the researcher has had time to watch the recorded session several times to familiarize herself and make notes about specific questions to ask the writer, an interview conducted while the writer watches the screen-capture video can provide a rich description of the session's meaning and import. The writer, in describing what they were doing, can corroborate or counter the researcher's hunches concerning the writer's goals. For example, through interviews, Slattery learned that one writer later undid much of the work of an observed session; another interview revealed that a writer worked for 2 hours only to find a coworker had already done the same work. Most importantly from an activity theory perspective, however, is the way a stimulated-recall interview can help identify the activity structure of the session: the writer's goals, the typicality or uniqueness of operations, significant environmental conditions, and the writer's history with the tools being used.

It is important to conduct this interview as soon as possible after the session is recorded. Although writers are often able to describe even moment-by-moment decision making in surprising detail during these interviews, they begin to forget details within days. For this reason, we recommend no more than 5 days between capture session and interview. It is also important to realize the potential discomfort writers may experience seeing themselves work, especially in the presence of someone else. Careful explanation of the purpose of the research—to see how real work happens, not to see that they are "on-task"—is often enough to mitigate discomfort.

COMPLICATIONS WITH VIDEO CAPTURE

Although the use of screen-capture software provides an automated, detailed, and relatively unobtrusive method for collecting data on the activity of digital writing, the method is not without its complications. These problems include researcher access, writer surveillance, and level of detail.

Getting permission for video capture can be problematic, particularly for gaining access in workplaces where intellectual property and proprietary information may be closely guarded. Gaining access is, of course, not a new problem for naturalistic researchers (Lofland & Lofland, 1984; Patton, 2002). Often, access requires the researcher to sign a nondisclosure agreement, which has implications for how data can be used (Crumpton, 1999; Euben, 2000). Because screen-capture software records all documents and interfaces as they appear on-screen, the data set may be replete with confidential information. The need to protect such information may mean that data must be carefully protected and any data to appear in a publication must be carefully screened and identifying information changed.

Screen-capture software also creates the potential for surveillance, often an issue in digital research (White, 2002). Although writers are often aware of this surveillance, many express relief that the researcher will not be physically present while they work. Indeed, once access was negotiated, few of our participants have expressed concern with screen-capturing methods. To help writers feel comfortable, writers can be invited to start and stop their own sessions and even pause the recordings if they wish. Nevertheless, with the complex interweaving of work and life in the digital age, it is not unreasonable to assume that there may be barriers to video-recording that would extend beyond work sessions into the more personal uses of computing (see, for example, Thomas, 1996).

Finally, one theoretical complication with the analysis of video-captured data stems from lack of specificity within activity theory as to what "counts" as an operation, action, and activity (Kaptelinin, 1997). Despite extensive discussion, few models for detailed activity analysis exist. Depending on frame rate, video-captured data can yield analyses down to the keystroke level—so fine grained that it becomes impossible to tell what is going on. To illustrate, imagine a writer composing a document in a desktop-publishing program. If we begin to count each drop-down menu, button, and quick-key command as a tool and each mouse glide or keystroke as an operation, the analysis becomes unworkable. The key to solving this problem lies in the writer's consciousness; operations lie just below the level of consciousness. With suitable prodding such as that provided by a stimulated-recall interview, writers can articulate and identify behavior at the operational level.

CONCLUSION

In this chapter, we have made a case for the use of video screen capture as a method for studying the activity of digital writing. Recent advances in computer memory, file compression, and capturing tools have put the creation and analysis of video captures within the reach of many digital writing researchers. Further technological trends will make the techniques we have described here even more easy to access and use. Much effort, for example, is being given to creating systems to index and search video data. Although not within the reach of most of us, we can expect to see such video annotation systems appearing on the near horizon and greatly simplifying the analytic tasks we have described here.

What will remain constant, however, is the close match between the theoretical imperatives of an activity theory framework—with its focus on behavior, artifacts, and history—and the affordances of video screen capture. If we want to look at digital writing as activity, video screen capture, especially when supplemented in ways we have described here, can provide us with an important tool for the study of writing in the digital age.

NOTES

1. In genre studies, for example, scholars have used archival methods to uncover writing activity: Carol Berkenkotter has used archives to look at the conventions for using reported speech in psychiatry (Berkenkotter, 2002b, 2004; Ravotas & Berkenkotter, 1998); Charles Bazerman has used archival methods to study the evolution of the scientific article (1988) and the emergence of electric light (1999). Another method for studying activity, the think-aloud protocol, was pioneered by Linda Flower and John R. Hayes (1981). Cheryl Geisler (1994) later used this methodology as part of an exploration of academic literacy. Paul Prior and colleagues (Prior, 2004; Prior & Shipka, 2003) explored the use of interviews and drawings to uncover writers' activity. Graham Smart's (1999, 2003) work provides interesting examples of research that has actually shadowed writers at work.

2. Other ways of technically capturing display output exist, and more may be developing. Most promising, display signals from a computing device can be intercepted on their way to the screen and recorded as digital video. In this case, the data can be analyzed in the same way as that produced by video screen capture described here.

3. It is important to note that these levels of activity are not necessarily stable. Typing search terms is only an operation as long as it goes smoothly. If the Web site freezes, the student may employ other operations toward the action of finding sources.

PART FOUR

Researching Digital Texts and Multimodal Spaces

10

CODING DIGITAL TEXTS AND MULTIMEDIA

Stuart Blythe

Sorting, classifying, and coding data allow researchers to identify a set of artifacts, to define a unit worth analyzing within them, to create codes for classifying instances of that unit, and to extrapolate based on the results of such coding. Digital artifacts pose interesting coding-related issues because they are less stable than print artifacts, alter relations between creator and audience, and can incorporate multiple media. This chapter addresses the challenges of coding digital data by discussing the procedures and assumptions that inform many data-coding activities and by exploring ways that such activities may be adapted for digital writing research. This chapter addresses both procedures and assumptions and draws examples from a study analyzing how colleges and universities use the World Wide Web to promote campus–community partnerships.

INTRODUCTION

Many of the questions we ask about digital writing require us to look for patterns in large amounts of data. If we wanted to explore social relations on an email discussion list, to know how a group of people represents themselves on the Web, or to compare uses of written and visual communication in multimedia instructional texts, then we would need a way to sort and classify the phenomena we encountered. Let's say you were curious about how racial and ethnic diversity was being represented in the many Web sites and CD-ROMs that now supplement college-level composition texts. You could devise a way to count the number of times males and females of various races and ethnicities were depicted in these resources. Such depictions could come from gender-, ethnicity-, and race-based references in the written portions of the sites; audio spoken by a male or female voice, with a dialect that marks the speaker as a member of some group; and photos, drawings, and video that depict males or females of various races and ethnicities. You could also devise a way to classify the activities being depicted in these media. How often are different people shown writing, recreating, collaborating, or volunteering? How often are different people depicted as leaders, as followers, as effective writers, as ineffective writers, and so on? What might all this suggest regarding publishers and prevailing views of diversity? Such a study would involve numerous variables and large amounts of data. How would you handle such a quantity and range of phenomena? For that matter, how would you determine what was worth classifying?

The act of sorting and classifying can be called data coding. Coding requires researchers to identify a set of artifacts (e.g., written documents, photographs, videotaped interactions), to define a unit worth analyzing within them, to create codes for classifying instances of that unit, in many cases to test the reliability of that work, and to make these decisions and actions public. The process of coding ideally provides a way to measure the prevalence of some set of phenomena. Thus "coding schemes," as Roger Bakeman (2005) said, "can be thought of as measuring instruments just like rulers and thermometers" (p. 375). Although many resources exist on sorting and classifying verbal data,[1] digital artifacts present new challenges because they are less stable than printed artifacts, alter relations between creator and audience, and can incorporate multiple media. This chapter addresses these new challenges by discussing the procedures and assumptions that inform many data-coding activities and by exploring ways that such activities may be adapted to digital writing. Because this chapter addresses both procedures and assumptions, it is divided into two major sections: method and methodology. I have adopted this organizational pattern because how you approach any coding activity depends in part on what you want to explore and your assumptions regarding research and the epistemological status of verbal and visual language. If you already understand methods of data coding, you may want to skim the sections "Methods of Coding Data" and focus on "From Method to Methodology." If you are unfamiliar with data-coding methods, or if you seek tips for coding the variety of media presented in digital writing, begin with "Methods of Coding Data."

Writers such as Sandra Harding (1987), Gesa Kirsch and Patricia Sullivan (1992), and Sullivan and James Porter (1997) distinguished between method (procedures, techniques) and methodology (assumptions, theories). Sullivan and Porter (1997) wrote that method can be equated "with particular observational procedures or data-collection strategies and with specific data analysis techniques" (p. 11). The first portion of this chapter is focused on method because it offers an introduction to techniques of data coding and advice on adapting that method to digital artifacts. The set of strategies and techniques discussed in this chapter are used in various social scientific methods such as content, discourse, and genre analysis. Moreover, they are used in a range of disciplines, including linguistics, communication, writing studies, and psychology. These methods[2] have been used to study a wide range of phenomena, including interview transcripts, chat sessions, Web sites, banner ads, television shows, and videotaped interactions.

The second portion of the chapter is focused on methodology. As Kirsch and Sullivan (1992) stated, methodology is "the underlying theory and analysis of how research does or should proceed" (p. 2). Methodology is worth discussing because most data-coding techniques were developed within a modernist context of truth and objectivity, but have been adapted by researchers who have rejected modernist claims. Sullivan and Porter (1997) differentiated, for instance, between a modernist approach to *Theory* ("the traditional kind that claims universal authorizing status") and a more postmodern approach to *theorizing* ("local, contingent, and situated reflection and analysis that has a status as heuristic rather than as Law"; p. 102). Some who still accept modernist assumptions regarding truth and objectivity have focused on ensuring scientific rigor through objectivity, validity, and reliability when coding digital writing (see, for example, McMillan, 2000; Potter & Levinne-Donnerstein, 1999; Weare & Lin, 2000). Others have argued specifically for the value of data coding given postmodern assumptions (see, for example, Barton, 2002). In this chapter, I argue for the continuing value of data coding for *theory* rather than *Theory*; I explore this theme by discussing the epistemological status of texts and the value of data coding in critical research.

METHODS OF CODING DATA

Data coding appears in several variations, including content, discourse, genre, and rhetorical analysis. Because these variations share a core set of steps, this chapter is focused on common features rather than on differences. This overview of core steps should provide a manageable introduction to data coding and the ways it may be adapted to digital environments. Because such environments increasingly present a range of media, this chapter draws ideas and suggestions not only from writing studies, but also from fields such as psychology, communication, and journalism—all of which have a history of coding nonverbal phenomena.

Two caveats before we proceed: First, although the print medium requires me to present the following steps in one order, they are not necessarily sequential. A researcher may define a unit of analysis, for instance, before selecting a sample. Also, units of analysis and coding schemes may be revised as a project progresses. As with writing, data coding can be a recursive process. Second, the purpose of the following sections is to provide an overview of possibilities, but not to offer canned methods. As Cindy White and Jack Sargent (2005) wrote, "ready-made research solutions are rare" (p. 3); researchers must develop codes and units to fit their circumstances. I hope to aid such development by offering ideas, examples, and references to other sources. Moreover, because multimedia can present writing researchers with the challenge of coding nonverbal phenomena, I draw from various traditions (such as psychology and communication) that have well-established coding practices for such types of texts.

Defining Sets and Selecting Samples

Any research into communication requires an appropriate group of texts for study. Texts are necessary even in studies of spoken communication, where researchers must somehow record what was said before they can analyze it. To identify such a group, you should: (a) define a set of potential texts, and (b) select a sample from that set. The type of set you define depends on the kind of question you wish to ask. Paul Kei Matsuda (2002), for example, noted that most studies of identity and power in online discourse were focused on speakers of English. Because he believed that "conclusions drawn from the perspective of only one language may not be applicable to other languages," he analyzed "about 200 e-mail messages that were exchanged among the members of TESOL Link between July and September 1997" (pp. 40–41). Recently, to provide another example and one I focus on later in this chapter, I wanted to know how colleges and universities were using the World Wide Web to promote campus–community partnerships; such partnerships are often set up by colleges and universities as a way to foster civic participation, urban problem solving, and service learning (Blythe, 2004). I wanted, in part, to know whether institutions were using the Web merely to promote their services, or whether and how they were using networked computers to do community work (e.g., by constructing community databases or sponsoring online forums). The data set in this case included all campus-sponsored Web sites in the United States devoted to campus–community partnerships.

Once you have identified a set of potential texts, you need to select a sample from it. In some projects, the set you define will be small enough to allow you to code every item, which would be called *comprehensive sampling*. In other cases, however, the set you define may be too big to code in its entirety. You may have to select a sample from that set. Samples may be selected in several ways; for example:

- With *convenience sampling*, you select a set of texts because they are readily available. Although this sampling method is easier than others, it carries little credibility on its own and should not be the sole method of selection. With increased levels of access provided by the Internet, many texts are conveniently available. That was certainly the case when I studied ways that campuses were using the Internet for community outreach. Although convenience can play a role, samples should be selected through a mix of methods.
- With *criterion sampling*, you select a set of texts because they meet certain criteria, which may be defined according to such factors as textual features, author attributes, intended audience, or types of media. For example, you may want to sample texts that present a best, typical, or worst case of the phenomenon you wish to study. (How you decide what is best, typical, or worst may depend upon how others have defined the terms. In other

words, background reading is crucial to setting criteria.) Or you may want to sample texts written by students at certain types of universities, or by people who have been maintaining blogs for more than 2 years, or by female students to female instructors. Or you may want to select projects that incorporate at least three types of media (e.g., audio, text, and animation; or text, audio, and video).

- With *random sampling*, you assign a number to each element in your overall set and then use a random number generator or chart to guide the selection of elements from that set. For example, if you were studying the transcripts of student chat sessions during collaborative projects, you could assign a number to each session and then use a random number generator to select a set of sessions to code.

Because of the scope and mutability of the Web, you may need to use a variety of sampling methods. For example, in my study of campus–community partnerships, I followed the advice of Christopher Weare and Wan-Ying Lin (2000) for seeking publicly available sites on the Internet. I consulted a "collector site" (i.e., an index of campus outreach grant winners maintained by the Department of Housing and Urban Development), a search engine (Google.com), and two people involved in such partnerships. I consulted these different resources because any one method would have presented a skewed list—Google.com presents sites based on popularity, and the collector site presented only grant winners. From these resources, I was able to build a set of sites and then use a mix of criterion and convenience sampling to select my sample.

Even after a sample has been selected, digital writing presents additional challenges. One primary challenge involves defining boundaries. In print texts, boundaries are usually easier to find. We can tell where a journal article begins and ends. Boundaries are less obvious, however, when studying hypertexts such as Web sites or blogs. Which links should be followed and which ignored? One way to alleviate this conundrum is to rely on the domain name system. You may decide to look only at pages from, say, www.school.edu/class1/. You'd examine www.school.edu/class1/page 1.htm and www.school.edu/class1/page3.htm but not www.school.edu/class2/page1.htm (because the latter comes from "class 2" rather than "class 1")—unless, of course, you decide to code all pages on www.school.edu (for additional advice on sampling in networked environments, see Weare & Lin, 2000). Although this technical approach to defining a sample may be helpful, it cannot be relied upon exclusively. For example, I noticed that one campus–community outreach project I was studying presented reports and promotional information under one domain name and a community database under another. In that case, I had to decide whether to include both sites.

Another challenge for the analysis of digital writing involves the instability of many digital texts. Parts of a sample that you decide to code on one day may have been revised by the time you actually do your coding. You may want to gather your own copies of the texts you intend to code,[3] making sure to note the dates on which you made your copies. You may even want to insert your own information into downloaded and stored Web pages by using the < !.... > tag in HTML. For example:

< !....downloaded from **www.school.edu/class1/page1.htm** on **2004.10.15**.... >

This tag lets you keep notes underneath the page without affecting how the page is presented in a Web browser.

Defining a Unit of Analysis

A unit of analysis is the clearly defined phenomenon that you wish to study. Geisler (2004) called it "the level at which the phenomena of interest occurs" (p. 29). Units can range from small (such as words) to large (such as entire texts); they can be verbal, visual, aural, and even what I would call "technical," such as links in a hypertext. This section describes points along that range.

Verbal Units in Written and Spoken Language

Researchers have examined words at all levels—from small linguistic units to longer rhetorical statements. The list below, though not comprehensive, provides a sense of the range of verbal units that may be coded.[4]

- **Words, Phrases, or Clauses.** For example, you may want to code indexical words (*I*, *she*, *here*, *there*, *now*, *then*) to see how a writer orients her reader to other phenomena. Or you may want to code nouns and nominal phrases as a way to identify the metaphors people use when describing computer technology (e.g., *master*, *slave*). Or you may want to code clauses that contain modals to determine the extent to which a group communicates probability (*We might do that*), advisability (*You ought to do that*), or conditionality (*We would have done that*). Matsuda (2002), for example, looked for "social relation markers—formal verbal endings, address terms, and honorifics" (p. 46) as evidence of power relations between members of an email list with the goal of providing "a Japanese-language medium list for English teachers in Japan who pursued graduate studies in TESOL or related fields in the United States" (p. 41).

- **T-Units.** As Geisler (2004) wrote, a t-unit "consists of a principle clause and any subordinate clauses or nonclausal structures attached to or embedded in it" (p. 31). T-units are worth coding when you want to examine the kinds of moves people make in language because such units contain relationships between people or things (nominals) and actions (verbals). You may want, for instance, to count the number of times people pose questions, make assertions, or give directions. Yi Yuan (2003), for example, examined the number of times two non-native speakers of English "repaired" their statements in chat room sessions, either by "seek[ing] remedies or confirmation" from Yuan or by "offer[ing] solutions or suggestions themselves to rectify the errors" (p. 198).

- **Exchanges.** Exchanges involve the give-and-take between two or more people. For example, an exchange occurs when a writing center consultant poses a question and a student responds. If you were coding exchanges, you would apply one code to the entire exchange. In the case of email correspondence, you might apply one code to two messages, the query and the reply. Although the boundaries of exchanges are relatively easy to spot in many circumstances, they would be more elusive in a transcript from something like a MUD/MOO session with four or five participants. Because person A may respond to person C just as person B is responding to person D, a chat transcript often presents a jumble of exchanges. Coders have to determine where the exchanges occur.

- **Rhetorical Units.** A rhetorical unit is a segment that can be classified as one type of rhetorical move—a move with the same author, intended audience, and purpose. More than any other type of analytical unit, a rhetorical unit can vary in length. An entire Web page may be devoted to sharing contact information. Or an entire email message may be devoted to soliciting one type of response from a writing center consultant. Or, conversely, one type of Web page or email message may contain several moves. Susan Herring (1996), for example, studied a type of rhetorical unit called the *macrosegment,* which had such features as a coherent purpose, a consistent set of linguistic choices, and sometimes visual cues such as blank lines or indentation. By studying these units in two email list exchanges, Herring questioned the traditional assumption that women communicate for interpersonal reasons but men communicate to exchange information.

Nonverbal Units in Spoken Language

Whereas verbal units help researchers explore how meaning is conveyed through *what* is said or written, nonverbal units help us explore *how* something is communicated. Multimedia projects that incorporate significant portions of audio or video may merit the exploration of nonverbal features. If your interest focuses on multimedia projects with audio, you may want to learn how others have coded spoken language. Speakers can convey meaning using a range of gestures and nonverbal features such as loudness (amplitude), pitch (frequency), and rate of speech (often measured as syllables per minute). Consider, for example, how changes in pitch can add variety to the sentence *Were you there last night?* The meaning would change if the speaker changed pitch for various words in the sentence. Emphasis on the word *you* (Were *you* there last night?) would suggest that the speaker knew when an event had happened but wondered whether another person had attended; emphasis on the word *night* (Were you there last *night?*) would suggest that the speaker was uncertain when an event happened. Such nonverbal features of speech have been shown to have social significance because they reinforce expressions of emotion, attachment, and social influence (see Buller & Jones, 2005; Carrère & Gottman, 2005; for a brief history of the measurement of nonverbal features of speech as well as information on software that can be used to aid such coding, see Tusing, 2005). Physical phenomena such as gestures and facial expressions constitute another form of nonverbal communication. If your interest focuses on multimedia that contains significant amounts of video depicting people, then you might draw from psychology to code the behaviors depicted. For example, the Specific Affect Coding System (SPAFF) "is a gestalt system of observation that integrates non-verbal and physical cues, voice tone, and speech content to identify specific affects" (Jones et al., 2005, p. 164). This system has been used to code interpersonal behaviors such as touching, physical distance, body orientation, gazing, nodding, smiling, and furrowing of the eyebrows (for an extended list of codes for such behaviors, see Guerrero, 2005, pp. 225–230). Another approach to examining such phenomena is tie-sign typology. As Walid Afifi and Michelle Johnson (2005) explained, tie-signs are "actions that provide evidence of a personal relationship" (p. 189). Such evidence includes handshakes, arm links, kissing, and various types of embraces.

Coding Visuals

In the previous two sections, I distinguished between verbal *(what)* and nonverbal *(how)* units of written and spoken language. A similar distinction can be made regarding the coding of visuals such as photographs, drawings, and animation. In this section, you will find advice on coding the content of an image, on *what* appears there; in the next, you'll find advice on coding the way an image is constructed, on *how* it was designed to present content. When it comes to coding what is portrayed in a visual, researchers have created units to help them isolate and count the appearance of certain types of images. For example, Ken Smith and Cindy Price (2005) developed a coding scheme that let them study the ways members of different races were depicted in photojournalism. They created codes to identify the race of the people in the photos (black, white, and other) and the subject matter (e.g., politics, education, sports, religion). Then they examined photographs in 500 "general circulation nondaily newspapers in the United States" (p. 131). Their coding scheme let them explore whether blacks are represented fairly in nondaily newspapers.[5]

As Smith and Price's (2005) study illustrates, codes can be developed to identify visual phenomena that carry social meaning—phenomena such as skin color, clothing, artifacts, setting, and so forth. Researchers who wish to develop a set of culturally significant codes might want to explore the work of Sandra Moriarty and Lisa Rohe (2005) who wrote about "cultural palettes" in advertising. A cultural palette is "a set of culturally sensitive symbols and colors, as well as other graphic elements such as layouts and artistic styles, that may reflect cultural nuances" (p. 119). For example, an appropriate cultural palette for Korean students may include symbols (tiger, dragon, bamboo, but not cat, cowbird, snake) and colors (white, blue, green, but not purple, pink, black). Although the cultural palette concept was developed to aid advertisers, it could be adapted for coding. That is, one could code for types of colors, types of symbols, and types of activities that appear in a set of multimedia projects.

Coding and Aesthetics

In addition to coding what is depicted in multimedia, there are ways to code how visual elements are constructed. Aesthetics theory may provide a set of concepts to aid such an examination. As Herbert Zettl (2005) wrote, "media aesthetics examines five basic aesthetic image elements that provide the aesthetic *materia*—the raw material—of television, film, and computer-generated images" (p. 366). Those elements are:

- **Light and color.** Consider whether light is directionless (coming from no particular source and casting no shadows) or highly directional (coming from an obvious source and casting shadows). If the light is highly directional, you could code the location of the source. Does the light come from above, below, to the left? Or you might code the amount of light (brightness versus darkness). When it comes to color, remember that colors are associated with certain feelings and meanings. (See Moriarty & Rohe, 2005, whose work was discussed in the previous section.)
- **Two-dimensional space.** Examine the way multimedia designers use aspect ratio (the relation between picture width and height) and screen size. Are designers trying to reproduce the feel of a movie, book, television show? You might develop a code for the way designers frame certain elements within that space. Zettl (2005) wrote about *vectors*, which he described as "forces with a direction and magnitude (relative strength)" (p. 372). Graphic vectors are created by a collection of elements in an image; index vectors "are created by somebody or something pointing unquestionably in a specific direction" (p. 372). What kinds of dominant lines are created in an image? Is a person looking directly at the camera or to the right or left?
- **Three-dimensional space.** Examine whether images are presented up close (as with a zoom lens) or further away (as with a wide-angle lens). You might examine whether a drawing or photograph is intended to present detail or a sense of intimacy and intensity, or whether the visual is intended to present a panorama or a group shot that loses individual detail. For example, Robert Tiemens (2005) coded the number of times that four major networks used wide-angle, medium, close-up, and extreme close-up shots of Jesse Jackson's speech at the 1988 Democratic national convention. Tiemens wanted to code these

shots because the way an image is framed "directs the viewer's attention to the speaker or to pertinent details of the event" (p. 394). A close-up draws attention to the speaker while a wide-angle shot commands less attention.

- **Time–motion.** If you were coding multimedia that included animation or video, code for changes over time. For example, is the video live or edited after-the-fact? If the video was edited after-the-fact, or if you were looking at animation, then you might code how one sequence transitions into another. Such codes could be drawn from film and television studies. You might code for cuts, dissolves, zooming in or out, or panning (see Tiemens, 2005, p. 190). For other types of codes relating to time–motion, see the section below on coding transitions.
- **Sound.** Code types of sounds (e.g., sounds from nature versus sounds from urban spaces, upbeat music versus sad music). You might also code the relationship between what one hears and what one sees or reads. For example, does the background music in a multimedia piece reinforce or juxtapose with the words in the piece?

Just as nonverbal cues can affect the reception of verbal data, so can media elements affect perception. Such elements, argued Zettl (2005), "are primarily responsible for providing the all-important background against which we tend to interpret all the literal aspects of the event" (p. 366).

Coding Links

If you are studying hypertext, you may want to examine ways that transitions and cohesion are created through links. For example, you might use the "hyperphoric grammar" developed by David Norton, Beverly Zimmerman, and Neil Lindeman (1999). Relying on the work of M. A. K. Halliday and Ruqaiya Hasan (1976), Norton et al. developed a classification scheme that described whether links were sequential (*chronophora*), referential in relation to a starting point or location (*primaphora,* such as a link back to a home page), nonsequential (*paraphora*), or related to a computer action (*compuphora,* such as an email link; they offer a helpful table that summarizes and illustrates types of links; see p. 187). If you were studying multimedia and narrative, you might adapt Scott McCloud's (1994) typology of transitions between panels in comic strips. McCloud identifies six types of transitions: With *moment-to-moment transitions,* very little time has elapsed between each panel. A blink may be represented in two panels. In the first a girl may have her eyes open, and in the second she may have them shut. With *action-to-action transitions*, more time has elapsed between each panel. One panel may depict a pitcher pitching a ball, and another may depict a batter hitting it. With *subject-to-subject trans*itions a sequence of panels "stay[s] within a scene or idea" (p. 71). One panel may show a runner crossing a finish line, and another may show a hand stopping a stopwatch. *Scene-to-scene transitions* represent significant shifts in time and space. This may include a shift from one city to another or from action outside a building to action inside. *Aspect-to-aspect transitions* ignore time to show "different aspects of a place, idea or mood" (p. 72). A sequence of panels may, for instance, show different views of the same room in the same instance of time. Finally, *non-sequitur transitions* present a sequence of panels with no clear relationship of time, place, or idea.

Coding for Manifest or Latent Content

The range of units described in the previous set of sections can be split into two subsets: *manifest* units and *latent* units. Manifest units are observable phenomena in a text. Such codes are typically lexical or syntactic, such as words, phrases, clauses, and t-units (Grant-Davie, 1992). Consequently, manifest content is relatively easy to spot and can be measured quantitatively. You could even use the search function in word-processing software or a Web browser to find words and phrases. Latent content, on the other hand, "shifts the focus to the meaning underlying the elements on the surface of a message" (Potter & Levine-Donnerstein, 1999, p. 259). Researchers who examine latent content look either for the purposes to which language is put or for the schema that such language evokes in readers (a measure of reader response). Rhetorical units are examples of units of latent content because they require the coder to make an interpretation, to infer purpose, and to decide when purpose or audience has shifted. To code for latent content requires a "sensitivity to context," and an ability to understand the purpose, audience, and other factors that motivate any statement (Huckin, 2004, p. 15). For example, I examined latent content in the studies of campus–community partnerships. I had to infer the purpose that faculty and staff had for creating content for their Web sites. Were writers advertising their services, providing raw data or analysis, or promoting online collaboration? Such judgments cannot always be made easily, as is illustrated in the next section.

Creating a Set of Codes

As was mentioned previously, data coding is more recursive than linear. Consequently, when and how a set of codes is defined varies from study to study. Some researchers come to a project with a set of codes in mind. They may have defined a set for themselves, or they may have adopted an existing set. Milena Collot and Nancy Belmore (1996) adopted an existing set, for example, when they studied "electronic language." For them, the unit they studied was the word, which they coded grammatically—nouns, prepositions, pronouns, adjectives (that is, they searched for manifest content). Using the codes from Douglas Biber's (1988) multidimensional-multifeature model, Collot and Belmore were able not only to identify significant features of language used by visitors to electronic bulletin board systems but also to compare that language to other types, such as speech or print. The advantage of this approach was that it enabled comparisons: Collot and Belmore could use the same "ruler" to measure language produced in various print and digital settings, which allowed them to argue that the language they encountered online was different from other kinds of language.

Rather than define codes ahead of time, some researchers let codes emerge through a preliminary reading of the material they intend to code. This is a method advocated by Huckin (1992) and described by Barton (2002). Barton described how she pursued a hunch that inexperienced writers use evidentials differently from their experienced counterparts. As Barton wrote, "evidentials are a form of metadiscourse used to express attitudes toward knowledge (e.g., *probably, generally, certainly*)" (p. 25; author's emphasis). As a teacher as well as researcher, Barton believed that the way students used evidentials was significantly different from the way experienced writers used them. Her codes emerged from an initial reading of the types of texts she wanted to study; then she devised a method for studying student texts more formally (Barton offers an illuminating reflection on her methods on pp. 36–38).

Just as Barton (2002) described, I learned that a set of codes can emerge from an initial reading of a potential corpus. When I wanted to study the use of Web sites to promote campus–community partnerships, I began with two tasks: I read about ideals for networked computers and civic participation, and I reviewed sample sites. From my reading, I found general consensus regarding ways that networked computers could be used to empower citizens and improve government service, such as creating new forums for deliberation and improving access to elected officials and information. I also began to notice that the few sites I knew of shared many features with civic Web sites. I reasoned that if campuses were also trying to empower citizens through community outreach, then they should be using networked computers in ways similar to the ideals I was reading about. I defined my own set of codes (based on readings about the ideals of civic computing) and then sampled sites (see the earlier section on defining sets and selecting samples). By defining my own set of codes, I hoped to explore the extent to which campus uses of networked computers met or deviated from ideals expressed in the literature.

Whatever method you choose for defining a set of codes, you need to address several issues. First, all codes in a set must be defined at the same level. That is, the codes should identify the same type of unit. You may decide to code words or exchanges, for example, but not both simultaneously within the same set. You can, of course, code a larger rhetorical unit and then words within that unit. But you would do so with two different sets of codes—a two-tier coding system. You could, for instance, count the numbers of evidentials used in certain rhetorical units. This would require you to develop a set of codes for evidentials and another for rhetorical units. Second, make your codes as discrete as possible. Some researchers claim that you should not be able to apply two codes to the same unit. As Weare and Lin (2000) put it, the codes must be "comprehensive and mutually exclusive" (p. 284). Other researchers understand that this goal is more an ideal than a realistic objective—it can be especially difficult to meet when coding for latent content. Let's say you were coding statements made by citizens and experts during an online national forum on air quality sponsored by the United States Environmental Protection Agency. Let's say also that you had created codes to identify the ways people characterize an environmental problem. For example, some may characterize a problem as an issue of justice. If a person writes, "It is no accident when a landfill is built in a community of economically poor minorities," you might code it *justice*. Or they may characterize a problem as one of public health. If a person writes, "If the EPA does not enforce air quality standards during construction of this landfill, asthma rates will increase," you might code it *health*. Or they may characterize a problem as an environmental issue. If a person writes, "The failure of the EPA to enforce air quality standards during landfill construction will damage our environment," you might code it *environment*. The challenge of coding for latent content is most clearly illustrated in the statement coded *environment*. What does the person mean by *our environment*? The person may mean the environment (nature) in general, or she may be referring to the neighborhood where she lives, in which case she may be thinking more about economic or public health issues than environmental issues. So, should the statement be coded as a public health characterization or as an environmental characterization? In such a case, you must look at the context to understand what the person might mean. Or you may need to define a new code (say, *unclear* or *multiple*) to show places where you know that a person is characterizing the problem but the language makes the exact nature of that characterization unclear.

Coding the Data

Once you are ready to begin coding the data, do three things. First, perform at least one test run on a subset of your sample. Do this to determine whether your codes are indeed mutually exclusive—or at least approach that ideal. Also ask yourself whether you are encountering interesting phenomena that the codes do not cover. If you modify your codes significantly, you may even want to run a second test. Second, consider using a spreadsheet program to record your codes, as is illustrated in Table 10.1.[6] Record the name of the file in which the coded passage appears, the code you gave to that passage, the passage itself, and perhaps your comments on the passage or on why you coded it as you did. By using spreadsheet software, you can easily count codes when the time comes. (For instance, in Microsoft Excel, you can use the AutoFilter feature to display one type of code at a time.)

Third, and perhaps most important, keep a journal. Reflect on your progress and note potential problems or interesting dilemmas that arise. Note for yourself how you resolved those dilemmas. This can be especially useful when coding for latent content. In the previous section, for example, I mentioned the difficulty of coding for latent content when people use the word "environment." If you decided to give a public *health* code (rather

TABLE 10.1   Example Spreadsheet Used to Record File Name, Codes, Passages, and Comments

FILE	CODE	PASSAGE	COMMENT
1.htm	justice	As a predominately minority area, we felt that someone has to stand up against such prejudice.	Landfill proposal characterized as a form of prejudice. See Mirel (1994) on sources of outrage in risk communication.
2.htm	health	Citizens in the Midwest may soon face a serious health threat.	The writer defines the landfill as a public health issue.

than an *environment* code) to statements such as "The failure of the EPA to enforce air quality standards damages our environment" whenever they follow statements about a group of people, then you ought to note that decision.

Testing Reliability

With data coding, reliability is established by showing that different people would code a set of texts, visuals, audio, video, and so forth similarly. Reliability is usually determined by training others to code at least a subset of the phenomena (approximately 10% to 20%) that the researcher coded. The more that other coders and the researcher agree, the higher the rate of reliability. Whether you would want to test for reliability depends on at least two factors. First, it depends on whether you are coding manifest content or latent content. If you are coding manifest content and are taking a more quantitative approach, then you should be able to measure reliability. If, however, you are coding latent content and are taking a more qualitative approach, then it becomes more difficult to measure reliability because of the degree of interpretation. Second, on a practical level, whether to test for reliability also depends on the audience for your research. As McMillan (2000) noted, "an important requirement for any social-science based research is that it be carried out in such a way that its results can be verified by other investigators" (p. 88). Many readers will expect evidence of interrater reliability, especially readers of journals that publish more traditional forms of social scientific research. Other readers, however, don't expect an account of reliability. In the journal *Computers and Composition*, for example, you'll regularly find studies that involved data coding but seldom find reports of interrater reliability. One way to assure adequate reliability is to conduct pre- and post-tests. After you test codes initially yourself, but before you code your entire sample, ask one or two raters to test the codes as well. Use their feedback to help you refine your codes. Once you have coded your entire sample, ask the raters to code another subset of that sample. Use the post-test as the basis for measuring reliability.

Simple agreement can be measured by dividing the number of agreements between two coders by the number of coding decisions they made. For example, if you and your rater coded 20 items in one text, and if the two of you agreed on 17 of them, then you would divide 17 by 20. Your simple agreement would be 85%. Although useful as a basic measure, such agreement does not account for chance. It is possible, of course, that two people agreed on some percentage of coded units simply by accident. You can minimize the effects of chance by using Cohen's Kappa; Geisler (2004) described this formula (see pp. 79–84) as did Janice Lauer and William Asher (1988, see pp. 261–263). Cohen's Kappa can be calculated by hand or automatically by using a calculator designed for the purpose. When I calculated reliability for my study of campus–community partnership Web sites, I used a convenient online calculator.

As you plan to test your coding, remember that some types of digital writing are modified regularly, especially Web pages. You may want to archive a set of Web pages to be coded, thus ensuring that other coders see the same set of pages. In my study of campus–community partnerships, for example, I burned a CD of Web pages for each coder. Remember, also, that many hypertexts are designed to be explored in numerous ways. Give your raters instructions on how to work through the pages. If you are saving an archive of pages, you could rename each file to indicate the order in which they should be read (e.g., 01.htm, 02.htm, 03.htm). Ask raters to read each file in order and to ignore links within any page. Such a precaution will save you time because, with any luck, your sequence of codes and your rater's sequence of codes will appear in about the same order. You won't have to spend time sorting your rater's sequence so that you can compare it to yours.

Analyzing Results

Essentially, analysis involves finding patterns and interesting anomalies in the coded data. To some extent, analysis may be an intuitive process based upon a researcher's ability to find interesting trends in the data. It can be approached, however, from a more quantitative point of view. Geisler (2004), in *Analyzing Streams of Language: Twelve Steps to the Systematic Coding of Text, Talk, and Other Verbal Data*, devoted several chapters to ways of detecting patterns, including frequency (which measures how often each code was used) and distribution (which measures the degree to which codes appeared in one setting or another). When I analyzed campus–community Web sites, for example, I was struck by how often Web resources were used either to make an institution's reports available or to promote an institution. (With one institution that I coded, 83% of the units were devoted to promotion through such texts as testimonials, descriptions of staff, and descriptions of past programs.) I based my analysis, in other words, on frequency. I was struck by the focus on sharing reports (essentially a one-way form of communication) and promoting institutions, because those moves were preferred so heavily over other communicative acts, such as online collaboration and dialogue. What I was seeing differed significantly from ideals that I held regarding the use of networked computers for campus–community collaboration.

FROM METHOD TO METHODOLOGY

You may well ask whether data coding merits the effort—merits all that defining of codes and units and all that sorting, counting, and analysis. What might it enable that other methods might not? Wouldn't a simple "close reading" of texts be enough? As with most issues, the best answer is that *it depends*. It depends on your assumptions regarding the epistemological status of texts, on whether the method can support a commitment to others in research projects, and on whether you view research as reflective practice.

Data Coding and the Epistemological Status of Texts

Whether data coding is worth your time depends in part on what you assume about texts and what we may learn from them. I believe that texts in general, and digital texts in particular, are worth analyzing because they reveal important characteristics of culture and human behavior. Their study can also help students work more reflectively with digital media. Some postmodern critics would say that texts cannot be studied as sites "of determinable meaning from which concrete, systematic cultural expectations can appropriately emerge" (Thomas, 1994, n.p.). If texts are indeterminate, then any inference stemming from them is merely the product of interpretation; the results of data coding tells us more about the person doing the coding than about the texts being coded. Although I grant that texts are open to interpretation, I reject the argument that most texts are indeterminate to a degree that renders data coding useless. As with most philosophical issues, truth lies somewhere in the middle. Consider a simple set of directions: With a few well-worded phrases (e.g., "turn left at the light and proceed for 1 mile"), most people can find a place they've not visited before. Or consider written policy: Texts that contain criteria (e.g., "students must have at least a 3.0 GPA to be eligible to interview on campus") can have a profound effect on social patterns. A passage may indeed be interpreted in several ways, but it usually cannot be interpreted in *any* way (unless perhaps we're talking about something like Surrealist poetry). Data coding is not random interpretation disguised as social science.

But, some might say that data coding allows only indirect, inferential evidence of culture and human behavior. It would thus be better to study such behavior directly. We should interview participants and observe group meetings, for example, rather than code Web sites for evidence of how digital writing is used in campus–community partnerships. I accept the argument that other forms of observation and analysis are important. Huckin (2004) rightly claimed that data coding (he was writing specifically about content analysis) should be combined with "more sophisticated forms of discourse analysis" (p. 13). However, I am skeptical of the argument that observation of human behavior is more direct and therefore less susceptible to interpretation. As Thomas (1994) argued, all behaviors essentially create "texts" that must be interpreted (n.p.). If I want to study the assumptions that go into the development of campus–community partnerships, I could observe and interview a group of people as they develop such a partnership. I could videotape meetings to record gestures, tone of voice, facial features, and other variables. Still, I would have to interpret those moves. I would be left, in other words, with a new set of texts to be interpreted.

Rather than privilege the use of interviews and observations as somehow more honest, direct, or unfiltered than forms of text analysis, we should acknowledge what each method of data gathering is likely to reveal. In the study of digital writing, data coding can tell us about how the Internet and multimedia are being used, about how group and individual identities are constituted and maintained online, about people's attitudes toward the new media, and more. Data coding, in other words, helps us answer many *who* and *what* questions, such as *Who is participating in this group? What are they saying?* For instance, we can explore the personal and professional identities some professional women and men create in part through the photographs and drawings they include on their home pages (Hawisher & Sullivan, 1999; Hess, 2002). Data coding is also uniquely qualified to address questions of *how much?* Sometimes it simply helps to know how often something occurs. How often, for example, do Japanese teachers of English use social relation markers to indicate hierarchical or egalitarian power relations (Matsuda, 2002)? How often are blacks presented photographically in positive or negative social activities (Smith & Price, 2005)?

When we analyze texts, we analyze products. What we cannot analyze are processes. In other words, data coding may help us explain *what* is presented in texts, and *how often*, but it does not help us understand *why* the texts look like they do. As Berkenkotter (2002a) pointed out, textual analysis has "been criticized as being too narrow and reductive... as it tends to focus on textual phenomenon per se, and not to attend to context" (p. 49). That would be true if a researcher were to rely on data coding alone. However, textual analytic methods can be combined with others, such as interviews and participant observation, to provide such context.

Data Coding and Commitment to Others

Because data coding focuses on patterns and trends in texts rather than on individuals, it is fair to ask whether the method has any place within critical research. Sullivan and Porter (1997) assumed that critical research begins and ends with a commitment to research participants, which is its "ultimate aim" (pp. ix–x). This commitment led Sullivan and Porter to define overlapping goals for critical research:

- *Respect difference.* Sullivan and Porter argued that researchers must recognize differences between groups and individuals, and they must avoid research practices that ignore those differences. Moreover, researchers also should not "instrumentalize" people— that is, should not use others for their own ends, such as publication.
- *Care for others.* Sullivan and Porter argued that researchers "should not proceed primarily out of a motivation to discover new knowledge, but rather should be motivated by a commitment to the participants, a concern for their welfare" (p. 113). This care should be based not on some universal commitment but on a local commitment to the people with whom a researcher works.
- *Promote access to rhetorical procedures enabling justice.* "Justice is realizable," wrote Sullivan and Porter, "only when people have access to the mechanisms of policy and decisionmaking" (p. 115). People should have the ability to influence situations that affect them, including research situations. Research participants should have "a say in determining their status within research projects" (p. 118).
- *Liberate the oppressed through empowerment of participants.* With this goal, Sullivan and Porter rejected the notion that a researcher is some sort of powerful liberator. Rather, they pointed out that

"researchers and participants" should enjoy "a reciprocal relationship" in which participants as well as "our research communities" benefit from research (p. 124). Participants should have a
say in how research is presented, and they should be able to use
the results of that research in ways that suit them.

Given that critical research begins with a commitment to others, its focus
is directed toward action rather than observation. Critical research is about
working with others in order to improve real conditions. When applied to
digital writing, critical research obliges researchers to "pay attention to
users in context" (Sullivan & Porter, p. 107). Data coding, however, does not
even require a research participant. What role, if any, might the method
play if a commitment to others is a cornerstone to methodology?

If commitment to others forms the core of your methodology, you may
simply have to acknowledge that data coding may be most vulnerable to
critique. Coding offers no direct support for research participants; however, it may in some situations contribute to the ethical treatment of research
participants, and it could be a form of research in which participants themselves could engage. For example, if I were working with a group of local
environmental activists to try to help them create a Web site and database,
then I would want to describe for them how others have created such
resources (or, even better, they may ask me to help them create their own
data-coding study). I would want to reveal patterns to help them more fully
articulate their own approach to the problem. Or consider the value of data
coding for participants in Heidi McKee's (2002) study of the dynamics of
interracial electronic communication. If participants could see patterns in
the ways they talk about race, in the assumptions revealed by their post-
ings, could such self-awareness improve interracial communication in that
group? Or, what if the students completed a data-coding exercise documenting interracial communication in another public forum? Could the
knowledge gathered from such a study help students as they began their
own forum? Although data coding may not have the direct interpersonal
appeal of, say, participant observation, it could be used as a lens to help
participants see how others communicate or as a mirror to reveal for participants their own patterns of communication.

Data Coding and Reflection

Although data coding may offer only indirect commitment to others, it may
have its greatest value as a form of reflective practice. Sullivan and Porter

(1997) argued that critical researchers should recognize "the rhetorical nature of research activity" (p. ix). They should

> recognize that such issues as the posing of research questions, the framing of a research study, and the choice of methods are discursive activities. Because they are discursive, researchers must keep themselves alert to those elements in their practices that adopt positions or attitudes or actions without reflection. (p. 16)

The need for reflection always exists because method influences results. As Grant-Davie (1992) wrote, "what researchers find in the data is influenced by what they look for" (p. 273); I would say results are also influenced by *how* they look. We know, moreover, that researchers must devise and revise methods as they go. Few would argue that researchers should pick a pre-existing method and follow it lock step. Researchers should interrogate their own work; if a researcher must analyze a set of texts, then data coding actually provides a mechanism for reflecting on such analysis.

Conceiving of research as a journey from theoretical assumption to observation to analysis, Titscher, Meyer, Wodak, and Vetter (2000) wrote:

> If one proceeds systematically wrong turnings are avoidable. Methodical procedure can, like Ariadne's thread, guarantee the researcher a safe route back. By giving them experience along the way, methodical procedure may also assist those investigators who look over their shoulders and see their starting point differently, even deciding not to go back what to find other more interesting starting points. No matter how the investigative journey may turn out, methodical procedure will make it easier to report findings and to compile reports of experience. (p. 6)

Data coding is most valuable, in my view, because it asks researchers to create a record of decisions made during a project. Researchers must record their method for finding texts (which is especially important in studies of the Web where no comprehensive index exists to aid selection); their rationale for choosing texts they find; and the concepts they used to analyze words, visuals, audio, video, and links. With this record, a researcher can reflect more fully on decisions made along the way.

Coding is also valuable because the record a researcher makes is then available for others as they examine the basis for a researcher's analysis. As Thomas (1994) wrote, methods of data coding (such as content analysis) are not "objective" in the sense that they present a "socially uncontaminated" path to Truth. Rather,

> what makes content analysis "objective" is that, as much as possible,
> the researcher is obliged to make public the bases for the sampling and
> analytic choices. Most important, the content analyst's culminating
> interpretations are tied to these revealed procedures. (n.p.)

Granted, Barton (2002) reminded us that the methods sections in which
our research process is revealed are often kept short and vague, that sometimes they are even contradictory. Despite the limitations of some methods
sections, data coding remains valuable, not because it confers a kind of
social scientific legitimacy, but because it enables the kind of complete disclosure and reflection that Sullivan and Porter (1997) advocated.

CONCLUSION

Data coding presents researchers with a trade-off. As Grant-Davie (1992)
noted, researchers "sacrifice detail" when they code, but "they do so in
order to translate the data into more abstract forms, forms that can reveal
patterns that would be lost in the mass and complexity of uncoded data"
(p. 284). Data coding is about finding patterns, about seeing big pictures in
large amounts of data. In the search for large-scale trends, though, individuals can get lost. The key to data coding, then, is knowing what it will
reveal and conceal, and to combine it with other methods in order to create a more complete picture.

NOTES

1. Resources on coding verbal data include Barton (2002, 2004), Berkenkotter
   (2002a), Grant-Davie (1992), Huckin (1992, 2004), Titscher, Meyer, Wodak, and
   Vetter (2000), see especially Geisler (2004).
2. Although I could have focused on one approach, such as content analysis, I have
   chosen instead to focus on data coding—on the steps that such social scientific methods share. As Titscher et al. (2000) argued, the boundaries between
   methods such as content or discourse analysis blur to the point of near unintel-
   ligibility. I do not mean to criticize when I describe the difficulty of distinguish-
   ing one form of text analysis from another. I believe, however, that the method
   of selecting a corpus, coding data, and revealing one's method can be discussed
   in general.

3. To gather your own copies for coding is considered fair use, but you should destroy the copies once you have completed the project. If you publish your work and decide to quote extensively from a copy, especially if you want to include a screen capture, then most likely you will need permission from the copyright holder.
4. For a more comprehensive list of such units, see chapter 3 in Geisler (2004).
5. Smith and Price (2005) found that blacks were significantly underrepresented compared to whites in nondailies but that when blacks were depicted, it was in much more positive ways than in daily papers.
6. Several software packages have been developed to support data coding, including Atlas, Ethnograph, Hyperresearch, and NVIVO. I have used Microsoft Excel to code data because I'm already familiar with it and I already own it. That is, it presents no learning curve and costs me nothing extra.

11

COMPOSITION MEETS VISUAL COMMUNICATION

NEW RESEARCH QUESTIONS

Susan Hilligoss

Sean Williams

Digital technology is one of the catalysts for the increasing turn to the visual in the teaching and research of writing. In this chapter, we overview research approaches that have been used for studying the visual. We deploy the notion of citizen designer *to illustrate the need for writers well equipped to analyze and craft visuals in today's world of multimodal, multimedia writing. Figuring out how best to impart these skills must become a significant part of composition research; we thus address a set of core questions that will help us to do the research and build the theory to best equip citizen designers in a digital visual world.*

INTRODUCTION

Digital technology, chiefly but not exclusively the Web, has played multiple roles in making images and visual displays both ubiquitous and manipulable, fueling the explosion of interest in the visual in Composition Studies and other fields. Any examination of the visual now means the "digital visual." In fact, much of the work in composition that addresses the production and consumption of visual texts—whether pedagogical practice, professional guidance, or scholarship—is often subsumed under the headings of "technology," "new media," "digital rhetoric," or "digital literacy." The interaction of multimedia genres has scholars coining terms such as *remediation* (Bolter & Grusin, 1999) and, following the New London School theorists, electronically mediated *multiliteracies* or *multimodal literacies* (Cope & Kalantzis, 2000; Kress & van Leeuwen, 2001). One prominent scholarly fusion of the visual and digital is the 2001 double issue of *Computers and Composition* on the topic of digital literacy, which, according to guest editor Carolyn Handa, began as an issue on "*visual* literacy and *visual* rhetoric" (p. 2). Another is the 2003 collection, *Eloquent Images: Word and Image in the Age of New Media*, in which the editors—Mary Hocks and Michelle Kendrick—claimed that new media and the visual are inextricably intertwined; they reasserted the arguments of Jay David Bolter and others that electronic media theories and practices bring rhetorical and cultural scholars to new understandings of the historically "dynamic" relationships between verbal and visual texts.

To acknowledge composition's enlarged mission and emphasis on the visual, we propose to call today's new digital communicator the *citizen designer*. We have chosen citizen designer to avoid making assumptions about what the communication specialist or design professional would do, to encompass multiple literacies without privileging a single type, and to emphasize composition's goal to educate nonspecialists to produce and interpret cultural texts critically and ethically. This term, citizen designer, evolves from an understanding put forth in a collection of essays edited by graphic artists Steven Heller and Veronique Vienne (2003) in *Citizen Designer: Perspectives on Design Responsibility*. The collection offers articles and interviews that together argue for designers to "be good citizens and participate in the shaping of our government and society" (p. 2). More importantly, the editors argue in their introduction that when teaching, "we must stop inadvertently training our students to ignore their convictions and be passive economic servants. Instead, we must help them to clarify their personal values and to give them the tools to recognize when it is appropriate to act on them" (p. 8).

In other words, students as citizen designers must have the ability to analyze, to respond critically, and to produce visuals in a variety of genres. Figuring out how best to impart these skills must become a significant part of composition research. Because composition as a discipline has historically been eclectic and inclusive in its analytical practices, and because our research covers a wide variety of contexts—from first-year composition classrooms to writing across the disciplines, from community-based literacies to workplace communication—compositionists are uniquely placed to study digital visual practices and their intersections with civic discourse. Scholars of composition have also shown, by their turn toward inquiries into the visual, that thoughtful, methodical research is now important for the discipline. The question is, then, what should that research be?

What the digital visual revolution has done for writing studies, then, is drop into the lap of compositionists a new expectation for imparting a much larger set of literacies, preparing people who can, like architects or designers or technical communicators, work equally well in multiple media to express themselves and ethically critique others as part of their professional and civic responsibility. These concerns inform our discussion of composition research into the digital visual. In what follows, we suggest some possible research questions that compositionists could address to help build an understanding in the field of visual rhetoric and how it interacts with the historical concerns of composition. Specifically, we propose characteristics of research that recognize the dynamic interaction of visual rhetoric and citizen designers, providing exemplar cases for the questions we pose and showing how these exemplar studies suggest a direction for future research in digital visual communication.

DIGITAL VISUAL RESEARCH

In the sections that follow, we address a set of core questions that allow us to draw upon previous work and to chart future directions in digital visual writing research:

- How can we best build theory to guide digital visual research?
- How can we best address the verbal/visual binary through digital visual research?
- What is the role of ethics in digital visual communication and research?
- What genres has digital visual research overlooked, and how might we research them?
- How can we equip citizen designers to construct ethical and appropriate visuals?

- What do we know and what do we need to know about digital visual research across cultures?

We address these complex, multifaceted questions and offer a variety of methods and tools for the ways in which research can continue to address these questions. We close this chapter with a set of conclusions and implications for future work.

How Can We Best Build Theory to Guide Digital Visual Research?

We see the project of theory in digital visual studies as the development of a rich set of concepts by which to (a) understand visual experiences; (b) connect those concepts with other more established theories in composition and rhetoric; and (c) expand our understanding of all visually represented communication, including writing. The theoretical questions we pose here attempt, where possible, to connect established theories in composition and rhetoric with an understanding of the visual and verbal and their complex interplay, while at the same time suggesting the limits of rhetorical and composition theory in comprehending visual experiences. In short, we argue, following W. J. T. Mitchell's (1994) *Picture Theory*, that studying visual communication from a theoretical perspective, if it is to be a rich endeavor, *must* avoid reductionism and simple answers. Understanding visual experiences requires a range of theoretical and disciplinary approaches. As Mitchell put it:

> Whatever the pictorial turn is, then, it should be clear that it is not a return to naïve mimesis, copy or correspondence theories of representation, or a renewed metaphysics of pictorial "presence": it is rather a postlinguistic, postsemiotic rediscovery of the picture as a complex interplay between visuality, apparatus, institutions, discourse, bodies, and figurality. It is the realization that spectatorship (the look, the gaze, the glance, the practices of observation, surveillance, and visual pleasure) may be as deep a problem as various forms of reading (decipherment, decoding, interpretation, etc.) and that visual experience or "visual literacy" might not be fully explicable on the model of textuality. (p. 16)

Mapping the concepts of rhetoric or argument (among other "textual" theories) onto visual experiences may leave much to be desired in the power and scope of explication. Mitchell recognized that visual experiences must be approached flexibly and multiply, from a wide set of theoretical approaches, among them rhetoric, critical theory, new media, media studies, information design, film studies, cultural studies, art and art history, graphic design, perceptual psychology and neuroscience, anthropology, and, as David Blakesley (2004) has said, "a host of other disciplinary areas" (p. 112).

As Mitchell's (1994) words imply, for those engaged with the visual, it is not enough to apply accepted and emerging methods in isolation from each other. Therefore, we have tried in what follows to examine some of the larger theoretical questions in visual studies that evolve from the transdisciplinary nature of studying digital visual texts. We also outline some potential methodologies for answering those questions by drawing on methods familiar to those of us in writing, rhetoric, and composition scholarship.

One of the key issues in visual studies is how theory can offer sufficient scaffolding to support meaningful research methodologies in historical and empirical study for compositionists (and others). Theory provides schemas to frame research questions and provide sets of categories—and for empirical research, preferably comprehensive and mutually exclusive categories. From the perspective of composition, rhetoric, and even professional communication, visual studies is still searching for powerful, flexible, yet internally clear and cohesive schemas to energize research. By powerful, we mean potentially able to explain many types of visual phenomena; by flexible, we mean potentially able to generate nuanced interpretations of the visual and eventually generate visual concepts beyond the preconceived schematic categories. By clear and cohesive, we mean potentially able to distinguish clearly among visual phenomena in conceptual terms.

A number of investigators have approached the issue of what particular theories, such as rhetoric and in particular argumentation theory, can contribute to the study of visuals and how the study of visuals taxes, stretches, and eludes those theories. For example, David Birdsell and Leo Groarke (1996) addressed where rhetoric and other theories of textuality map, and do not map, onto visual experiences by pointedly debunking the idea that visuals cannot argue by applying formal argumentative analysis to visuals. Specifically, they made three claims to counter prevailing wisdom about the inability of visuals to argue: (a) visuals, even though they might be ambiguous, are no less so than words and, in fact, can quite effectively demonstrate premises and conclusions; (b) just as it would not make sense to extract single words of an argument from their context as complete propositions, it makes no sense to extract a single visual from a visual, verbal, or cultural context; (c) conventionalized representations (stereotypes almost) argue about the nature of the object represented rather than trying to resemble the object. What we see in Birdsell and Groarke's account, then, is theoretical research that demonstrates that visual argument can and does exist based upon its correlation to verbal argument.

Perhaps a better example of theoretical research that stretches our understanding of the visual based upon verbal argument is J. Anthony Blair's (1996) "The Possibility and Actuality of Visual Arguments." Blair described the necessary requirements for a visual to be regarded as argument: "Enough information has to be provided visually to permit an unambiguous verbal reconstruction of the propositions expressed, so that, combining that with contextual information, it is possible to reconstruct a plausible premise and conclusion combination" (p. 357). In other words, a visual argument must have a propositional structure with a debatable claim and proof for the claim, and be available for clear verbal restatement. Building on this theory, Blair analyzed magazine ads, television commercials, and political cartoons, and concluded, finally, that although propositional (i.e., rational) visual argument is possible, it is not very common. Instead, he argued, most visual argument is nonpropositional and relies on identification and manipulation.

From these two exemplars, we can gain insight into one research approach for investigating the theoretical implications of visual communication. Specifically, both of the studies cited above rely heavily on formalistic analysis of argumentative structure (that an argument must have a premise and a conclusion) to demonstrate if, in fact, visual argument can occur. Both articles initially establish their analytical framework based upon accepted notions of what constitutes verbal argument, and then both articles apply those concepts to a series of visuals to demonstrate that visuals can argue. This method of extending accepted analytical frameworks proves both productive for these scholars as well as problematic because sometimes the framework applies, and sometimes it does not. As a result, one potentially fruitful area of theoretical study would be to investigate which accepted analytical methods can, in fact, be applied to the visual.

Finally, some schemas adapted from verbal, and particularly linguistic, scholarship have such promise that they might be called "metatheories" of the visual. Thus we have seen conceptual schemes for visuals in terms that suggest such coherence, such as Gunther Kress and Theo van Leeuwen's (1996) notion of a visual grammar, presented in *Reading Images: The Grammar of Visual Design*, and more recently in *Multimodal Discourse* (2001). Kress and van Leeuwen outlined their project in the opening pages of *Reading Images* this way:

> We see representation as a process in which the makers of signs . . .
> seek to make a representation of some object or entity, whether phys-
> ical or semiotic, and in which their interest in the object, at the point
> of making representation, is a complex one, arising out of the cultural,
> social and psychological history of the sign-maker, and focused on by
> the specific context in which the sign is produced. (p. 6)

In other words, their project, drawing on work in social semiotics and discourse analysis, is to construct an abstract grammar of visual design that
can describe any visual. The categories for analysis derive from a specific
cultural situation comprised largely, they argued, of linguistic conventions.
The concepts are relevant for all visual constructions although the way concepts or categories are employed varies based upon the context in which
the visual was created. So, for example, every visual has a top and bottom
and a left and right. In Western cultures, top is privileged as "ideal" and
bottom is subordinated as "real." Likewise, the left of a visual is "known"
information and the right-side information is "new" information. These val-
uations of top, bottom, left, and right might change from culture to culture,
but the abstract structure remains: Every visual has a top, bottom, left, and
right that can be analyzed based upon the conventions derived primarily
from verbal, written language of the local context of the visual.

Kress and van Leeuwen's (1996) visual grammar has many more
abstract categories than we can discuss here—indeed the 250 pages of
Reading Images outlines a complex grammar of visuals equivalent, for
example, to M. A. K. Halliday and Ruqaiya Hassan's (1976) linguistic grammar presented in *Cohesion in English*. However, their project, and one that
could inform future research in digital visual scholarship, is to demonstrate
that abstract structures can be identified in every visual and that those
structures carry value statements based upon local context. Scholarship in
this vein would adapt principles of linguistic grammars and rhetorical structures such as the classical *topoi* to visuals to ascertain the equivalency—or
disruption—among existing linguistic or rhetorical concepts and the construction of visuals. These studies would begin with descriptive analysis of
a visual: Is the visual from a high or low angle? Is the visual frontal or
oblique? Is the visual close in or far away? They could then apply a social
semiotic view to those descriptions to demonstrate how the construction
of the visual, by reifying or extending by analogy a linguistic grammar or
common *topoi*, reflects the values present in a particular cultural milieu.

Likewise, the great success and influence of visual cultural studies suggests that this theoretical approach could inform the construction of
metatheories of the digital visual. Specifically, cultural studies should be

scrutinized for its strengths and weaknesses because broadly speaking, cultural studies approaches have proven both conceptually powerful and flexible, and generally also avoid simplistic divisions of verbal and visual. Yet in spite of its ideological critique of elite artistic genres, visual cultural studies as taught in composition tends to focus on what we would call near-canonical genres, such as photographs, paintings, and fine art; ads, posters, and marketing campaigns; film and television; political cartoons; and cultural spaces like museums. From the perspective of composition and its goals, these genres reinforce normative assumptions about specialist production and consumer reception of cultural texts, often through mass media. In other words, visual cultural studies is less a critical method than a normative approach. Either students' visual texts are ignored (as when students respond to visual texts simply as writing prompts, as Diana George, 2002, pointed out) or their visual texts are explicitly or implicitly evaluated against the productions of specialists.

There is a gap that composition researchers can fill here, in at least two ways. First, there is a project of examining the usual subjects of visual cultural studies in light of composition's goals to educate a citizenry to produce as well as critique visuals in the culture. Researchers could examine how visual cultural studies (among other approaches) is taught in writing classrooms and composition researchers could apply cultural studies approaches to genres generally that are overlooked by mainstream cultural studies and are also more likely to support the goals of composition. For example, composition scholars could examine visual and hybrid visual/verbal genres produced by nonspecialists for private or public goals and audiences such as altered books, scrapbooks, personal Web sites, or home videos. Many of these genres engage the digital. Together, these theoretical questions push us as researchers to imagine and investigate ways that we can investigate writers as citizen designers. If we agree that one purpose of writing research is to equip a citizenry with the literacy skills necessary to actively participate in shaping our social context, it is clear that understanding formal characteristics of visuals and visual arguments should be key to that project.

How Can We Best Address the Verbal/
Visual Binary Through Digital Visual Research?

One of the most deeply rooted and potentially problematic "writerly" views of visual communication is that the visual does something different than the verbal does. Words equal reason and visuals equal emotion, this line of thinking often goes. Words are precise and images are ambiguous.

Adhering to this perspective is actually only a shorthand way of preserving conservative values that allow a disciplinary center to hold—rhetoric, composition, graphic design, art history—because it creates inquiry that says, in some ways, "this is us; that is them." It inscribes a binary that allows those inside the field to have a comfortable vision about what it is that "we" do. What we, and others, propose is to fundamentally reframe this foundational assumption to examine how the visual and verbal are the same. We seek to explore the conceptual shift or shifts theorists interested in the visual can apply to blur, dissolve, or otherwise re-view the binary. Over time, these multiple moves can change the theoretical frame that all researchers apply, inserting an assumption of similarity into the field where once there was an assumption of disparity. Where once there was verbal versus visual, we might say, now there is just "composition"—a word itself bursting with implications.

Theorists are looking in several directions to establish these moves. David Blakesley and Collin Brooke (2001) have addressed the verbal/visual binary in its largest sense:

> How does the visual communicate meaning? Or, putting it another way, how do we *interpret* the visual world? Do we interpret words any differently than we do visual images? If so, what's the difference? And what's rhetorical about this process? To address these questions, we need sustained study of the integrative function of the human mind as it sees, perceives, interprets, and otherwise reacts to the visual world, drawing from works like Stephen Pinker's *The Language Instinct: How the Mind Creates Language* (2000) and *How the Mind Works* (1999) and, earlier, R. L. Gregory's *The Intelligent Eye* (1970) or *Eye and Brain* (1966; 1997). (n.p.)

Blakesley and Brooke called for a renewed alliance between rhetoric and linguistics, and between rhetoric and brain science. Because brain science has been reconceiving many of the mind's activities that involve the visual, the verbal, and the emotional, there seems to be much that theorists of rhetoric and composition can ponder, question, redirect, and integrate into their thinking. One example of this approach comes from Anne Wysocki's (2001) work theorizing the integration of the visual and verbal through analysis of two CD-roms. Wysocki found that two different texts with relatively similar verbal content but different visual compositions present the user/reader with strikingly different conclusions. In other words, by investigating how the visual impacts the verbal and verbal impacts the visual, Wysocki showed us how "the word/image distinction—with its supporting architectures of content separated from form, writing from the visual, information from design—loses its distinction" (p. 138). In other words, the visual, far from being an adjunct to the verbal expression, instead merges with it to form a coherent argument or perspective on the topic being discussed. In Wysocki's terms, if we fail to recognize the integration, ultimately we "remain unable to see or explain" the theme or emotion presented in a piece of communication (p. 140).

This closely echoes research discussed by usability specialist Donald Norman (2004), who argued in *Emotional Design: Why We Love (Or Hate) Everyday Things* that cognitive science has shown that we respond to every object or design on three levels: the visceral, the behavioral, and the reflective. According to this perspective, each object or design has an emotional and affective dimension that informs our reflective or conscious interpretation and we cannot divorce the levels. Words cannot be held separate from designs and designs cannot be held separate from words as something applied "after the fact" because the very meaning of the object or visual resides exactly in the interplay and interrelationships of its construction. If compositionists were to follow Wysocki's and Norman's lead, research could focus on the rhetorical and multilayered aspects of design and creation, investigations that might strip verbal content of its visual texture or perhaps alter a visual texture to assess the persuasive impact that integration has on an audience. Indeed, Norman discussed such studies in *Emotional Design* to demonstrate that removing a layer of visual texture significantly reduces the effectiveness of experiences.

A corollary strategy that theorists have employed and that would be of productive use for researchers is to turn away from the binary altogether and to reconceptualize what Blakesley and Brooke (2001), following Stephen Bernhardt (1993), called "the point of encounter" at the interface (n.p.). The confluence of interest in the digital and the visual has been fruitful in this regard. For example, Hocks and Kendrick (2003) explored the persistence of word/image, visual culture/print culture, linear/hypermediated, and other new media binaries as "purification narratives." They critiqued several touchstones of visual theory, including Mitchell's pictorial turn, for "either reducing images to a verbal grammar in which one can become literate . . . or idealizing images as unique, holistic truths" (p. 5). They called for recognizing "the true hybridity of new media, and all older media" through more nuanced scholarship and more reflective, theorized practice (p. 4).

Perhaps the best recent example of this approach comes from Jay David Bolter and Richard Grusin (1999) in their important work, *Remediation*. Along with other books—like Stephen Johnson's (1997)

Interface Culture, Brenda Laurel's (1991) *Computers as Theatre,* and Janet Murray's (1997) *Hamlet on the Holodeck—Remediation* shows that all new media adopts and reshapes older media that in turn reshape the older media that in turn reshape the new media, and so on: "hypermedia applications are always explicit acts of remediation: they import earlier media into a digital space in order to critique and refashion them" (p. 53). As Bolter and Grusin acknowledged, their approach to media resonates with poststructural literary theory where there is nothing prior to representation, so "every act of mediation is dependent upon another, indeed many other acts of mediation, and is therefore remediation" (p. 56). A research program that engages digital visual texts as acts of remediation, showing how the visual frames the verbal, which frames the visual in an endless cycle of simulation clearly breaks down the verbal/visual binary. To accomplish this sort of research we would read texts against one another, much as we often do with films and books in our classes. We would investigate the resonances of one text that metaphorically constructs one appearing subsequently (and consequently) in time to demonstrate that the progression of texts is not acontextual. This research would draw heavily on composition's concern with socially situated communication, showing how all communication derives from specific social and cultural forces and then in a very important turn, how the present writing we do likewise contributes to the shaping of our social-cultural contexts.

Undertaking a program that actively ignores the supposed visual/verbal binary and instead focuses on the ways writing engages with the ways our culture is constructed by texts around us is essential to building citizen designers. In fact, the activist approach that such a research agenda promotes can have significant impact, as history has proved:

> During World War II, visual communications convinced people to buy bonds and travel America and motivated women to take jobs outside the home. A single photograph of Jeffrey Miller lying on the concrete pavement of Kent State helped Americans to realize the divisive effect the Vietnam War was having on American Society. (McCarron, 2003, p. 46)

If we research and show the impact of verbal/visual texts and how both remediate the other, we can question our notion that somehow verbal texts are superior or prior to the visual. Likewise, we can show that the combination of forms add up to more than the sum of the parts because the complexity inherent in multimodal messages carries a dimension—when combined—that neither alone possesses.

What is the Role of Ethics in Digital
Visual Communication and Research?

In composition, perhaps because of its origins in classical rhetoric, combined with its responsibility for creating an educated and literate citizenry,
the role of the ethical subject has always been a source of much attention.
Visual ethics, then, would seem to be a natural source of research for compositionists interested not only in the *effective* crafting of messages but also
in the *responsible* crafting of messages. In the age of digital visual communication, addressing the ways that visuals can be manipulated becomes
extremely important, not only because visuals are easy to alter but also
because our culture possesses a "resemblance equals reality" mindset
(Baudrillard, 1994, p. 17).

Interestingly, the project of reframing the verbal/visual binary is directly related to the project of reframing the ethical discussion of the digital
visual. Blakesley and Brooke (2001) briefly addressed the visual's relationship to belief and asked "What difference [does] it makes for rhetoric that
we only see what we already believe, or that we only know what we
already believe, or that we only believe what we already see?" (n.p.). The
current posture of rhetoric (and composition) toward emotional response
or identification involving the visual has at its core the verbal/visual binary,
with the visual—represented chiefly by mass media images—being cast on
the same side of the binary as manipulation, "emotional highjacking," and
irrationality (Barry, 1997, p. 18). The exigency to understand and counter
the effects of mass culture is compelling; however, precisely because the
research of mass communication and the theorizing of mass culture is so
persuasive, we suggest that compositionists focused on the experiences of
the citizen designer should complicate mass media stances on ethics and
the visual. It will take innovative, thoughtful theorizing and investigating to
negotiate the dangers of traditional alignment (e.g., mass media images as
deterministic; the powerlessness of viewers in the face of mass media),
with the goal of developing new examinations of the ethics of digitally
mediated visuals.

Two model studies come from technical communication. First, in their
article, "Cruel Pies: The Inhumanity of Technical Illustrations," Sam Dragga
and Dan Voss (2001) questioned the ethics of minimalist design in charts
and graphs, which draw largely on the precepts set out by Edward Tufte.
Similarly, Ben Barton and Marthalee Barton (1993) critiqued the construction of maps as potentially unethical because they exclude and privilege
certain populations. More specifically, both articles ask whether or not min-

imalist design is "cruel" because it strips away the human aspect of what is being represented, for example, in statistics about home fires and smoking in bed (Dragga & Voss, 2001, p. 271), or because it misrepresents nonuniform shape and distances of the London Underground (Barton & Barton, 1993, pp. 65–68). Each article argues instead that overly rationalized and abstracted minimalist designs should be replaced by humanized visuals that require us to recognize that sensitivity to human conditions is at least as important as the accurate display of data. Both pieces study some famous examples of "cruel" illustrations. Both pieces also present alternative designs that humanize the diagrams, for example, adopting a palimpsest approach to mapmaking that displays on the map the decisions made in its construction.

As a field, composition has been concerned both with efficacy and responsibility in verbal communication at least since the 1970s and through its rhetorical heritage all the way back to antiquity. The same concerns can inform the study of digital visual communications where writing researchers begin to ask about craft and affect. We should interrogate "neutral" and "informational" visuals for the ethics of presentation. This is exactly the role of the citizen designer Michael Schmidt (2003) described: "Only through an enhanced understanding of the mechanisms that control and utilize graphic design and graphic designers can we hope to change the course [of unethical design]. Debate will be the key; more of us need to come to the table" (p. 119). In short, by creating a dialogue about what visuals leave out, what they privilege, and how they do these things, we can begin building in composition a sense of the citizen designer who is able to recognize when alternative possibilities are available and then argue both visually and verbally about the importance of alternative representations.

What Genres has Digital Visual Research Overlooked, and How Might We Research Them?

Three decades ago, historical and rhetorical studies in composition were reinvigorated by opening investigation to the wide array of artifacts of individual literacy—journals, diaries, letters, lists, annotations—and to the complex cognitive and social interactions between reading and writing surrounding those artifacts. Just as important, this new area of research reaffirmed the ethical obligation of writing scholars to the writers they study (whether in classroom, community, or workplace settings), by recognizing and valuing a wider spectrum of genres that writers knew and used in their lives. We suggest that Composition Studies return to that wider notion of inquiry as part of its unique contribution to visual studies. The historical moment generates a host of questions that compositionists are in a unique position to investigate, especially in collaboration with other specialists interested in the visual. Composition is the locus of the citizen, nonspecialist writer, and the personal communicator, or—as we have termed it—the citizen designer. The scope of those texts has expanded to the visual, via the Web, digital cameras, email, and cell phones. However, because the visual has not been an area of inquiry in traditional reading or writing research, there are many basic questions to answer, questions that the methods of writing research can address. Framed with a sophisticated understanding of visual perception and visual culture, empirical research has the potential to reconceive our assumptions about almost every aspect of creating visuals and displays.

What visual genres—digital and nondigital—have been widely available to ordinary persons in our culture and in other cultures? What archives or resources are available? What formal features do these genres exhibit and how do they relate to the visual conventions of published, more prestigious genres? What are the circumstances of creation and reception? How do our current concepts and theories (not only of the visual, but of social organization, as in activity theory) illuminate these artifacts, their creators, and the conditions of creations and reception? Conversely, how do these genres and their development inspire debate about and change in our concepts? Recent projects in technical communication offer some illustrations. Lee Brasseur (2003) investigated the social construction of several genres of data graphics in her book, *Visualizing Technical Information: A Cultural Critique*, and more recently she has begun to explore the social construction of medical visualizations, as presented, for example, in her article "Florence Nightingale's Visual Rhetoric in the Rose Diagrams" (2005). Similarly, in *Shaping Information: The Rhetoric of Visual Conventions*, Charles Kostelnick and Michael Hassett (2003) examined one genre, the statistical atlas, diachronically over 400 years to explore how it shapes and was shaped by the prevailing cultural norms and how those norms evolved over time.

Altered for composition, this technical communication model can be carried into studies of nonprofessional writing as well to examine the production and reception of private and personal digital visual composition, much like composition turned to the personal in the 1970s. There is a solid tradition in composition scholarship of examining private or personal writing; that is, writing for purposes outside the workplace or marketplace. All types of personal compositions, historical and contemporary, are suitable subjects for research, including drawings in diaries, scrapbooks, altered books, home videos, digital photographs, maps, cheat sheets for videogame play, personal Web pages, and so on.

Through examining these types of noncanonical texts, we'll be able to understand better what Julie Baugnet (2003) saw as the weaving of design and community. Specifically, Baugnet pointed to the importance of personal conviction and employing conviction, and how the citizen designer employs skill in a personal cause. Personal causes are just that—personal—and to help forge a culture of citizen designers, it is important to demonstrate to students that their convictions not only matter, but more importantly that those convictions as they are manifest in their digital visual creations are worthy of evaluation because those creations can change the world (or a small part of it anyway). As Baugnet argued, students now face more than ever difficult decisions about when to act and how to act, and "as educators, we can help them prepare" (p. 98). Part of the preparation is our willingness to engage authentically with the texts that students create. If we can examine student texts in the context of their production and reception and demonstrate that those texts are both products of a situation and have an impact on the situation—as Brasseur did with medical texts or Kostelnick did with statistical displays—we'll move one step closer to painting a picture of the citizen designer.

How Can We Equip Citizen Designers to Construct Ethical and Appropriate Visuals?

With visual composition, researchers are faced with the same rich opportunities that existed from the late 1960s through the early 1980s, the prolific period of research into the writing process and writing practices generally. Young people arrive in writing classrooms and are assigned Web pages, portfolios with visual elements, and oral presentations with slideshow support. They are expected to use digital photography and design "effective" pages. How do students approach these tasks? What images and genres have been influential in students' experiences before and during college—videos, digital photography, video and Internet gaming, graphic novels, scrapbooking? How do students conceive of these practices and genres? How do they relate them to technology and other media? What has been the educated person's engagement in visual creation and viewing, and how does the citizen designer use these materials to accomplish certain civic rhetoric goals? Composition research has a unique role that may be informed by, but not constrained to, the strategies of professional designers and graphic specialists. For example, in her introductory graphic design textbook, *Design for Communication: Conceptual Graphic Design Basics*, Elizabeth Resnick (2003) outlined the professional graphic design process:

1. define the problem and establish your objectives;
2. do the research;
3. develop your ideas by brainstorming;
4. analyze your ideas in terms of the project objectives; and
5. implement the final. (pp. 19–20)

Composition researchers should find this pattern fairly familiar because it is very similar to the process that writing research uncovered in the 1970s and 1980s (although it has classical roots, of course, in Aristotle). So the question for the researcher is simply this: What process do nonspecialist students, designing visuals for a composition class, employ? The methods for investigating this question and its implication already exist in composition, in fact, and have a venerable history. Take, for example, Janice Hays' (1983) edited collection on process research, *The Writer's Mind: Writing as a Mode of Thinking*, in which essays like Lee Odell's foundational "Written Products and the Writing Process" appeared. Or what, for instance, could research into the digital visual adapt from Stephen Witte's (1987) important article "Pre-Text and Composing," in which he argued the "pre-text represents, in effect, the writer's attempt to instantiate abstract plans and goals in linguistic form" (p. 397). What if we substituted "linguistic" for "visual?" And finally, going back even farther to 1970, what can we learn and adapt from Richard Young, Alton Becker, and Kenneth Pike's *Rhetoric: Discovery and Change*, in which they analyzed and attempted to demonstrate the writing process? These are but three examples of empirical research in the composing process (there are scores more articles and certainly dozens of books) that compositionists could adapt from our research tradition to inform new inquiry.

As we set out to equip citizen designers, these questions of process seem fundamental because at the center of these types of empirical inquiries lies the students' compositions themselves. As we've learned from the expressivist tradition in composition, students have a right to their own texts, and this line of inquiry ascribes appropriate value to those student texts. But if we follow the expressivist tradition and combine it with process research, innumerable questions arise because students create and manipulate still and moving images, work with font faces and page design, and compose and interpret visual presentations inside and outside of school. We know very little about what occurs in composing contexts outside of school—visual or otherwise—and arguably this is where the citizen designer has the most impact as they design posters for clubs, or political flyers for local groups, or participate in public art projects.

What Do We Know and What Do We Need to Know about Digital Visual Research Across Cultures?

Another empirical question that accompanies the digital visual is that of "contact zones" of visual representations from many cultures and subcultures. We have begun to see visually savvy writing textbooks—such as *Picturing Texts* (Faigley, George, Palchik, & Selfe, 2003) and *Seeing and Writing* (McQuade & McQuade, 2005)—offer digital visual assignments involving the creation of one's own visual representations and the analysis of those of others. These assignments suggest a variety of empirical studies, including action research within classroom projects. Armed with theories about culture, the diversity of writing classrooms, and, again, reframings of the verbal/visual binary, composition researchers can undertake much in the area of digital visual contact zones. Students arrive in the writing classroom having engaged in many kinds of visual creation and representation. We think that cross-cultural collaborations that examine how citizen designers in different cultural contexts approach similar assignments would be of particular interest.

Research from professional and technical communication can again point the way for us here. For example, Kaushiki Maitra and Dixie Goswami (1995) investigated cross-cultural visual communication, asking the question: "How would American readers/document designers respond to a translated document that reflects the assumptions and preferences of another culture?" (p. 199). The basic finding is that Americans were disappointed because Japanese authors had different criteria for a "successful" document than their American readers did. Much more research into cross-cultural visual communication has occurred since Maitra and Goswami's important article, but the point of these studies is usually the same (and obvious): different people have different expectations about visual design.

Adapting this now well-established principle to composition research, what can we learn from students in the "contact zones" of our classrooms where races and genders and different socioeconomic backgrounds meet? How do students attempt—or not attempt—to create visuals that expressly move across the contact zone? How can visual design teach students audience analysis and awareness? These are important questions for the citizen designer to understand because our world is smaller than it ever has been as a result of global networks and digital communication. A citizen designer needs to understand that differences exist, and that expressing values and viewpoints can alienate or include. Placing students in situations where they design documents for cross-cultural audiences, whether those are audiences separated by an ocean or by income, seems fundamental. Empirical investigations can help us not only understand how cross-cultural visual negotiations occur, but also how we can improve and subsequently implement those cross-cultural encounters into our classrooms to make the idea of designing for a diverse population very real.

THE IMPLICATIONS OF DIGITAL VISUAL RESEARCH

As we have seen, compositionists already engage in a variety of inquiries involving the digital visual. However, they do not need only to reproduce what is happening elsewhere, but can and should take methods of inquiry and sites of investigation from the composition repertoire and re-envision those in light of the digital visual. As researchers of this large and often confusing, cross-disciplinary subject, we all are obligated to learn more, question deeply, and engage in inquiry responsibly. We have sketched a daunting research agenda; we foresee that, if the digital visual is taken seriously in composition studies, future scholars and teachers will need a different kind of preparation, preparation that we can only suggest pieces of here, and the ability to move among and apply these disparate modes of inquiry to the study of new citizen designer constructions of the world.

Ultimately, we think, a view toward the citizen designer can guide future research into the digital visual. Composition, through its rhetorical tradition, has a long and venerable history of teaching students how to actively participate in shaping their worlds. The research questions we raise here are all guided by the belief that the nonspecialist designer/communicator/writer is the richest locus of inquiry for compositionists. Indeed, many of our questions aim to discover ways to better empower the citizen designer to interrogate, to create, and to compare the digital visual forms that populate our noisy and media-saturated lives. These questions are a start—only a start—for what we think should characterize the next generation of composition research because it is not enough to study "writing" anymore, as so many have said in the last few years. It is now time for us to move forward with our research agenda and build an understanding of the ways that our discipline can shift—perhaps return—to its classical roots and re-imagine students as participants in our society by learning about ways that these students are already, and can become even better, citizen designers through a richly theorized understanding of the digital visual.

12

AN ECOFEMINIST METHODOLOGY

STUDYING THE ECOLOGICAL DIMENSIONS OF THE DIGITAL ENVIRONMENT

Julia E. Romberger

A digital writing technology constitutes a rhetorical environment loaded with discursive expectations and ideologies that impact a writer's work. An ecofeminist methodology provides a lens for examining the ecology of this environment—dynamics of history, influences from discourse communities invested in the development of the technology, and exchanges of conventions from other technologies. Within an ecofeminist methodology, the science of ecology is useful as an acknowledged metaphor that provides a set of terms— evolution, influence, and exchange—to help trace the shape of a rhetorical ecology. I demonstrate the framework in a data-collection tool specifically designed to investigate software interfaces. I apply it to Microsoft Word and draw conclusions from the resulting data about discursive expectations placed upon users.

INTRODUCTION

Understanding writing technologies is necessarily important to our understanding of writing processes. A digital writing technology—be it an HTML-authoring program such as Macromedia Dreamweaver, a standard word-processing package such as Microsoft Word, or a slideshow application such as OpenOffice's Impress—with its varying capacities for editing, revising, design, and so on, influences a writer's processes. One of our tasks as scholars is to develop the framework for inquiries that do precisely what Cynthia Selfe (1999a) called for: to investigate the rhetoric of the multiple electronic writing spaces in which students and professionals compose. There is much work still to be done to understand what literacies technologies require, where the political aspects of these literacies find their roots, and how those roots might affect users who do not constitute a monolithic constituency. An ecofeminist methodology can help make these aspects evident through locating the origins of discursive expectations by tracing the rhetorical construction of a digital writing environment.

The agenda of an ecofeminist methodology is to "reorient technology toward humanity" through critical inquiry, education, and change (Conley, 1997, p. 96). The evolution of a writing technology under inquiry can and should be historicized and contextualized, and its relationship to other technologies that impact it should be described. The methodology I present in this chapter creates a heuristic for tracing the ecology of the development of a writing technology as a context with and within which a writer composes. In particular, I focus on a specific section of the writing context—the interface, an aspect that has become increasing more complex and ideologically fraught as technologies progress.

An ecofeminist methodology, in short, must be aware of context and its complexity—the ecology of the situation. It is this emphasis on the influence of environment upon subjects in an ecological ebb and flow and how these relationships are articulated that separates it from other feminist methodologies. It takes into account histories of the larger social milieu and remains aware of the context of the researcher and the system of values brought in by framing an inquiry in a specific theory and discipline. Additionally, an ecofeminist methodology works against oppressive discourses and toward empowering users to make informed decisions about a technology. It advocates critical awareness of technology and its use for those subjugated to ideologies with which they might not have fully engaged on a critical level or that they had no say in implementing as determiners of their context.

In this chapter, I discuss the value of an ecofeminist methodology for exploring the rhetorical ecology of a digital writing technology. After an introduction to some of the basic concepts of ecofeminism and its concerns with technology, I describe an ecofeminist heuristic and discuss other theories that share perspectives and agendas with ecofeminism. I give an example of a data-collection tool based upon these connections and then conclude with a short discussion that includes an application of this methodological tool.

ECOFEMINISM AND TECHNOLOGY

Ecofeminists such as Val Plumwood (1993), Noël Sturgeon (1997), and Karen Warren (1997, 2000) have argued that there is a close relationship between the dynamic development of subjectivity and the environment in which a subject is positioned—an ecology of mutually influential articulations. The positions of subject and environment allow for various oppressions of both subject and environment through ideologies and technologies.

Ecofeminists believe that the Western reification of the inherent good of progress and technology supports value articulations that allow technologies to be implemented without consideration of local environmental and social needs. Ecofeminism contends that the social constructions used to justify the projects of "man's civilization" include oppressive rhetoric that relegates nature, women, and others subject to Western man and his science (Merchant, 1980; Plumwood, 1993; Sturgeon, 1997). Ecofeminism demonstrates an interest in ethical inquiry into technologies and technologies' impacts upon users and the assumptions of those who create and implement the technologies (see Buege, 1997; Bradley, 1997; Curtain, 1997; Potiguara, 1997; Warren, 2000). Ecofeminism can bring a useful perspective to the implementation of technology by fostering connective perspectives between local context and larger technological issues. Joseph Loer (1997) wrote about such a case in "Ecofeminism in Kenya: A Chemical Engineer's Perspective." He claimed that an ecofeminist perspective could have kept a water delivery system he assisted in developing from failing because the Western male engineers failed to taken into account the culture of the Kenyan community in which the project was situated. Within this community, despite the men's role as thinkers and doers, the women were more likely to see the need for and implement maintenance, but because of the need to complete the project and the fact that the male voices overwhelmed the female voices, the social changes necessary to make the project sustainable were never argued for. Loer acknowledged that a narrow scientific perspective can obscure the more complex picture of technology *in situ*. This is where ecofeminism's emphasis on "seeing connections across disciplines and to our everyday lives—which only a local voice can do—and acknowledging them as legitimate [are] all the more important" (Loer, 1997, p. 285).

Ecofeminism advocates the development and integration of technology in a manner aware of and adaptive to the social and material specificities of local context. To date, though, ecofeminist inquiries into technology and its impact have taken the form of anecdotal or historical discussion of events. Ecofeminist theorists and researchers have a series of ethical concerns to guide research practice, but they have yet to develop a methodological tool for inquiry into the implications of any form of technology upon users, subjectivity, or the environment.[1] I use Karen Warren's (2000) ethics as a set of guiding principles for conducting rhetorical analysis. An ecofeminist theory–based methodology is useful to investigations of the rhetorical structure of a digital writing technology. Ecofeminism focuses on the ecology of the environment, on the space in which the technology is used, on users, and on the relationships between various technological attributes and affordances. Although the methodology I describe shares similarities with systems theory,[2] it differs in some significant ways. Perhaps the most important difference is that a methodology grounded in ecofeminist theory is overtly political. It identifies the agenda of the researcher and the socially bounded dissonance that creates the moment of inquiry. Systems theory tends toward an objective approach to research (see, for example, the discussions of cybernetics and the work of Norbert Wiener in Hayles' 1999 *How We Became Posthuman* and systems theory in Holland's 1975 *Adaptation in Natural and Artificial Systems*).

ECOFEMINIST ETHICS FOR METHODOLOGICAL GUIDELINES

Ecofeminism explores the intersection of feminist theory, technology, and local contexts/local peoples; this is the place that ecofeminism locates its theoretical, political, and ethical praxis. Warren (2000) developed an ethics that is comprised of several guiding principles and that makes critical gender analysis part of its methodology. Additionally, an ecofeminist methodology does nothing to promote social domination by way of sexism, racism, classism, naturism, or any other oppressive "ism." Third, and most importantly, ecofeminist methodology is contextual—it sees ecofeminist discourse and practices coming from both individual voices with individual histories and situations and from larger social histories and situations within a pluralist understanding of what constitutes a context for action. This is a move away from absolutist values, principles, and epistemologies. Fourth, an ecofeminist methodology makes genuine effort to be aware of diverse perspectives; ecofeminist methodology presumes and promotes difference. Warren rejected the "abstract individual" with the understanding that it is impossible to develop a gender-free or gender-neutral subject position. I include an additional principle, which recognizes the impact of material environmental conditions upon participants and takes into account the articulations of those conditions by agents whose opinions and knowledge affect participants and context. This principle also acknowledges how rhetorics affect the environmental condition for those who inhabit the environment.

Investigators who practice research grounded in ecofeminist ethics and methodology need to acknowledge the body of literature by ecofeminist philosophers such as Haraway (1991b, 1997), Merchant (1980), Plumwood (1993), and Sturgeon (1997), which emphasizes rhetorical connections between articulations of nature and the "nature" of others that justify oppressions. Because of the ongoing emphasis on these connections and their impact upon the construction of subjectivity, ecofeminist research should always recognize how these rhetorics impact the context and subjects being researched as well as how the rhetorics of the investigator's own discipline and agenda impact research.

In keeping with situated knowledges, an ecofeminist methodology does not make claims to objectivity and lack of bias. Ecofeminist methodology also deliberately makes a place for underrepresented and unnoticed values and epistemologies within its scope. Ecofeminist approaches rethink the modernist project of reason "typically defined in terms of mental faculties that permit one to entertain abstract, objective principles" (Warren, 2000, p. 101) and perspectives that allow researchers to decide on courses of action not grounded in context-specific consideration of issues.

Many of the guidelines for conducting ethical research identified by ecofeminism fit with the ethics of inquiry for studying writing with computers identified by Patricia Sullivan and James Porter (1997). These authors articulated an ethical inquiry as being aware of "the ways roles are constituted and reconstituted for individuals" (p. 103) and not divorced from the political implications and ramifications of both the situation of the inquiry as well as the reported outcome of research data. The aims of critical research that they identify include "respect for difference," "care for others," promotion of access to technology, and "liberation of the oppressed through empowerment of participants" (Sullivan & Porter, 1997, p. 110).

Additionally, feminist composition methodology is in agreement with many of ecofeminism's ethics and concerns. Practitioners of feminist methodology in Composition Studies believe that gender significantly impacts the composing process and are concerned that Composition Studies has not dealt adequately either with patriarchal structures that students bring to the classroom or that are embedded in the differing relationships men and women have to social institutions and how those relationships influence various discursive acts (Sullivan, 1992). In the academy, men have for the most part determined how knowledge is made, organized, expressed, and valued. Ecofeminist scholarship, like more common feminist methodologies, also works toward interrogating and, with application to discussions of composing practices, seeks to change the dominant paradigms at work within the discourse communities operative in academic, corporate, and social communicative practices. An ecofeminist methodology can provide strategies for discussing the rhetorical ecologies that shape the context of the writing situation.

AN EXAMPLE OF ECOFEMINIST-GUIDED DATA COLLECTION

An ecofeminist methodology, then, acknowledges investigator agendas while examining the exchange of rhetorical and social influences over the course of time on the development of a digital environment and how this situates users. Figure 12.1 provides a heuristic that can help trace a digital writing technology's rhetorical ecology. This heuristic is drawn from ecofeminism and the complementary theoretical threads of ecology, rhetorical studies, and feminist and postmodern historiography. To demonstrate further the potential shape of an ecofeminist-guided rhetorical analysis of a digital ecology, I discuss a data-collection tool based on this heuristic that allows for a rhetorical construction and analysis of, for instance, the graphical user interface of Microsoft Word across its various versions. I use the data to discuss the rhetorical ecology of the interface as it emerges over time and to draw conclusions about the expectations of users who write with/within the technology.

The Descriptors in Figure 12.1 (1, 2, and 3) attempt to pin down the function and representations used for the particular aspect of the digital writing technology so that they might be interrogated. These categories circumscribe the aspects of the ecology to be examined.

DESCRIPTORS

1. Location: What is the location of the item or aspect being examined (e.g., menus, toolbars)?
2. Aspect: What individual items or aspects are under consideration?
3. Description: What does the item or aspect look like? How does it function? How many clicks does it take to find?

EXCHANGES

4. Exchanges: What are the relationships with other programs, hardware, and the operating system? What icons, terminology, and functions are exchanged with or adopted from other software programs, hardware, or operating systems?

EVOLUTIONS

5. Evolution: Is this item or aspect new? How has the new version changed it? Does it do more? Has it shifted location or terminology?

INFLUENCES

6. Influences I (Discourse Community): What knowledge of rhetorical practices are assumed in the item or aspect?
7. Influences II (Corporate Culture): What does corporate culture or technology development culture say about the history or design of the item or aspect?
8. User: Who is the audience for the technology? What rhetorical assumptions are made about users? What dualisms is it privileging? Who constitutes the human presence in the technology?
9. Investigator Context: What is the relationship of the technology to the researcher's context as academic, teacher, etc.? What impact might the researcher's experience and agenda have on the data?

FIGURE 12.1.   A Heuristic for Feminist-guided Rhetorical Analysis of a Digital Ecology

The Exchanges and Evolutions (4 and 5) arise from the science of ecology, explained further in the next section. These categories are designed to collect information about ideologies embedded in the digital context and how they have shifted over time to accommodate the changing rhetorical situation of the developers. These items also work toward developing a sense of how the technology has developed in relation to other technologies associated with it and within the greater technological infrastructure.

To understand the ecology, it is imperative to understand how relationships operate within the ecosystem. The ways in which the tasks and rhetorical articulations within technologies inform each other's developments demonstrates a value system.

The most basic research questions the above categories seek to answer are why a rhetorically constituted ecology has the structure it does, and by what process it came to be in this condition. In doing this, the data-collection heuristic seeks to uncover data concerning the expectations of who the users are or are expected to become. The Influences items (6, 7, 8, and 9) help discover the value systems and ideologies in place that determine the environmental conditions, which ecofeminism sees as important to understanding how power systems are constructed that implement oppressive ideologies. Discourse Community and Corporate Culture (items 6 and 7) attempt to get at the rhetorical knowledge the user is expected to have. Item 9, Investigator Context, critically moves the research agenda in plain sight, as ecofeminist practices require.

Because ecofeminism lacks much methodological development aside from Warren's (2000) ethics and some work done in sociology, there are a number of fields I have drawn upon to create the heuristic presented in Table 12.1 (see pp. 262-263); they are a good fit with ecofeminism's aims, they are not unfamiliar to rhetorical studies, and they have more thorough discussions of sound methodological practices. The next few sections discuss the threads that I draw from and demonstrate how they fit within an ecofeminist research agenda.

ECOLOGY AS A CONCEPT ACROSS THE DISCIPLINES

Two problematic but highly important terms—context and ecology—have a history of use in the disciplines that study writing.[3] Key works that have developed ecology-tracing methods include Margaret Syverson's (1999) *The Wealth of Reality*, which includes an approach drawn from applied complex systems theory and psychology, and Clay Spinuzzi's (2003) *Tracing Genres through Organizations*, which uses genre theory and activity theory. The methodology I suggest here is another approach to tracing the complexities of the rhetorical situation by focusing on a digital writing technology's environment. In the following section, I work toward defining ecology and context in ways resonant with ecofeminism and the goals of ecofeminist methodologies.

Rhetorical Definitions of Ecology

A rhetorical ecology, in keeping with ecofeminist principles, is capable of seeing language and ideological relationships similar to those of the physical sciences. Such an ecology must accomplish tracing these relationships without losing sight of the human beings involved in the rhetorical construction of environment and in the use of electronic environments. I use ecology as a metaphor that operates as an analytical tool to map influences, exchanges, and evolutions of relationships, and, further, to analyze ideologies and discourse communities embedded in writing technologies. As Haraway (1997) has shown, ecosystems and cybernetic systems are close in nature and have been used to explain each other; therefore, using ecology as a concept to study digital space has precedence.

Scientific Definitions of Ecosystems and Ecology

A brief look at the science of ecology, specifically ecological methodology, yields a basic concept of what constitutes the relationships within an ecosystem. Ecological theory draws upon various feminist and postmodernist theories that can assist in illuminating a rhetorical understanding of relationships within an ecosystem. The foundational principle of ecology is that everything is connected or held in relationship to everything else; ecology is understood to be a set of "relations [that] emerge spontaneously, transforming both the context in which interaction occurs and the nature of the component parts" (Oelschlager, 1991, p. 131). A basic definition of ecology is the scientific study of the processes influencing the distribution and abundance of organisms, the interactions among organisms, and the interactions between organisms and the transformation and flux of energy and matter (Institute of Ecosystem Studies, n.d.). Ecologies are systems of resource exchanges between environment and inhabitants, mapped over time. Scientific models of ecosystems are meant to measure exchanges, influences between agents, and the evolution of these relationships. Leopoldian or foundational ecology is an important subset of ecology for the methodological purposes of this chapter because it gives a basis for the inclusion of the human element in the research process. Foundational ecology "recognizes that human beings are sentient elements in the evolutionary process and thus obligated to evaluate their action from a reflexive standpoint" (Oelschlager, p. 206).[4]

Ecological terminology demonstrates categories useful in constructing a metaphorical definition of ecology and conducting rhetorical examination. Three useful categories are *exchanges* (the dynamic physical and bio-logical interactions and sharing of resources with the environment and other inhabitants within the selected space); *influences* (local and global forces that affect the development of components); and *evolution* (histori-cal forces that shape the development of the components; Henderson, 2003; Krebs, 2001; Michener & Brunt, 2000). These categories are useful as a metaphorical tool for examining a rhetorically articulated environ-ment, but not if they are executed within scientific parameters, which tends to privilege objectivity and separateness, which ecofeminist, femi-nist, and postmodern researchers find to be unethical and problematic.

If these categories are read metaphorically and applied to the compo-nents of a digital environment, they are reconstituted as:

- *exchanges*—how hardware, software, and operating systems develop to share rhetorical resources like terminology, icons, and functions;
- *influences*—what internal and external discursive forces help guide the development of computer technology, including hard-ware and interfaces; and
- *evolution*—how the rhetoric of a digital writing technology emerges over versions.

These categories help trace the shape of digital writing ecologies. The dis-course used in technologies is heavily influenced by their origins and the primary contexts of their ongoing use, which is why examining influences and evolutions is so important. However, they are also shaped by their users, and to a degree by the agenda of the researcher.

Context and Discourse Communities

Context is critical to rhetorical analysis because "individuals . . . belong to discourse communities, they have socially influenced purposes and goals, they borrow language and ideas from other people—in short, they live and perform in some multivariegated, sociocultural *context*" (Huckin, 1992, p. 85). Discourse community here is taken to mean a sociorhetorical network formed of disciplines, groups, and societies that forms "to work towards sets of common goals" (Swales, 1990, p. 9). Language within these communi-ties is "constituted of clusters of words with meaning systems that are sus-tained by the power of experts" (Fairclough, 1989, pp. 94–95). Discourse communities presuppose a knowledge base consisting of both the specific lexis used in specialized and technical ways and the genres appropriate to communication within the community (Porter, 1992). A discourse community relies on consensus to build its expectations and boundaries, but this consensus "establishes boundaries and power relationships that include and exclude" (Porter, p. 95). These power relationships present in the discourse used by a community are embedded in conventions.

The concept of discourse community can be used as one context-development method as well as a way of acknowledging the slippage between contextual boundaries. Charles Bazerman (1994) pointed out that discourse community boundaries get jagged when examined closely, and Porter (1992) noted that discourse communities are "an unstable assemblage of faults, fissures, and heterogeneous layers, a network of intersecting systems, institutions, values, and practices" (p. 107). A discourse community "is unstable, changing, dynamic—it is a turbulent, chaotic system that nevertheless operates with some kind of regularity" (Porter, p. 107); a space wherein texts both perpetuate and, within varying limits, create meaning (Fairclough, 1989). Discourse communities can function like ecosystems: a "convenient ecological space defined by certain characteristics that set it off from abutting systems" (Porter, p. 86).

Identification of the discourse community from which an aspect of a writing technology is derived assists in understanding the assumptions made by developers about users, because membership in a discourse community contributes "first of all to the construction of what are variously referred to as 'social identities' and 'subject positions' for social 'subjects' and types of self" (Fairclough, 1992, p. 64). A discourse community can be described, investigated, and have claims made concerning its constitution. Examining discourse communities allows for context-sensitive analysis, which "relies openly on *plausible interpretation* rather than on any kind of proof . . . [because] given its ambitious scope, context-sensitive text analysis cannot possibly be a highly formalized and testable scientific endeavor" (Huckin, 1992, p. 89). Plausible analysis is pertinent to the goals of ecofeminist-based research because such research claims no pure objective stance and makes no contentions about being absolute truth.

For example, when applying the concept of discourse community to an interface, the visual, textual, and even interactive aspects are seen as being informed by assumptions concerning the users' understandings of the discourse or, for instance, the electronic environment of other software. Because assumptions are made by developers about what users understand, it becomes clear that boundaries are being set that the users must learn to negotiate, assimilate, and perhaps recreate to achieve literacy within a digital environment and to use the environment to fulfill certain composing tasks.

Feminist and Postmodern Historiography

In mapping the category of evolution in a rhetorical ecology, I draw upon the methods of feminist and postmodern historiography, both of which share an affinity with ecofeminism. Ecofeminists have displayed an interest in both the history of rhetorical construction and the history of technological impact upon specific populations in Western society. Merchant (1980) began her investigation into the rhetorical linkage of women and nature in the 1500s by examining both scientific and religious scholarship and imagery. She extended this examination through the 1700s and the scientific work of the Royal Society of London. Similarly, Plumwood (1993) used social constructivist theory to examine the verbal constructions used in the philosophy of Plato and Descartes and the epistemological connections to the justification of the oppressions of women, nature, and others.

As is seen in each of these works, ecofeminists find it important to inquire critically into the rhetoric of those who write histories. This imperative is shared as a primary tenet of postmodern and feminist historiography. Within postmodern historiography, it is understood that "the vocabulary of representation has the capacity to account not only for the details of the past but also for the way these details have been integrated within the totality of the historical narrative" (Ankersmit, 1988, p. 209). A responsible history is aware that "meaning has two components: the world and the insight that it can be represented in a certain way, that it can be seen from a certain point of view" (Ankersmit, 1988, p. 210). Hayden White (1973) noted that an historical account, using either chronicle or story, "represents the process of selection and arrangement of data from the *unprocessed historical record* in the interest of rendering that record more comprehensible to an *audience* of a particular kind" (p. 5). Essentially, for Frank Ankersmit, White, and other postmodern historiographers, constructing a history is an act mediated by rhetorical considerations and by the values and motives of the historian. The project of postmodern historiography attempts to make visible the work of the historian, the choices of historical items to be related, the language chosen to articulate these items and frame an interpretation of them, and the relationship of historian to audience. In making this visible, postmodern historiography relinquishes claim to absolute authority for representation of historical reality; rather, it allows for a plurality of reality.

The positioning of the historian in postmodern historiography that makes visible the work of the historian is also important to feminist historiography because it assists in the project of making visible "concepts of gender structure perception and the concrete and symbolic organization of all social life" (Scott, 1986, p. 1069). History prior to postmodern sensibilities used normative concepts that relied upon references to gender, even when they were not explicitly about gender. These normatives "set forth interpretations of meaning" and are "expressed in religious, educational, scientific, legal, and political doctrines and typically take the form of binary oppositions" (Scott, 1986, p. 167). Feminist and postmodern historiography have in common the need to make visible the agenda of the historian within the account developed.

Joan Scott identified (1986) gender as constructed through "culturally available symbols that evoke multiple (and often contradictory) representations" linguistic, visual, and metaphoric in nature (p. 1067). Feminist historiography realizes that to ascribe interest in controlling meanings for the sake of power to specific actors or to their positions—rather than understanding that they are discursively produced—limits the possibility for critical inquiry into structures of power. The type of historiography that postmodern and feminist scholarship in this field advocates fits into the ecofeminist agenda of critical gender analysis along with critical analysis of all attributes ascribed to an other. Ecofeminism and these forms of historiography also recognize that it is impossible to create a neutral subject position from which to do research.

ECOFEMINIST PRINCIPLES INTO PRACTICE

A Sample Ecofeminist-guided Data-collection Tool

The data-collection tool presented in Table 12.1 was designed to gather data in a manner consistent with the ecofeminist principles and methodology described above. The primary function of this tool is to collect data that can map the evolution of the ecology of a digital writing technology over its versions. By creating such a tool, the discursive practices reified through the inclusion in the rhetorical structure of a writing technology, those that drop out of the technology over time, and those that are excluded can be traced. Used in a study designed specifically to collect information from an historical series of interfaces, the tool identifies various discourse communities being drawn upon to create the rhetorical space of the interface and maps the ecology—the various interactions—over time.

TABLE 12.1 Example Methodology Worksheet Used to Collect Data on a Series of Microsoft Word Interfaces

LOCATION	ASPECT	DESCRIPTION	EXCHANGES	EVOLUTION
	Is it icon, interactivity, or text?	What does it look like? How does it function? How many clicks to find?	What cross-over is there with other programs/ interfaces?	New? Does more? Changed location?
File menu				
Edit menu				
Tools menu				
Main toolbar				
Formatting toolbar				
Collaboration tools				
Draw tools				
HTML-authoring tools				

TABLE 12.1   Example Methodology Worksheet Used to Collect Data on a Series of Microsoft Word Interfaces (continued)

INFLUENCES I (DISCOURSE COMMUNITY)	INFLUENCES II (CORPORATE CULTURE)	USERS[5]	INVESTIGATOR
What rhetorical assumptions are made?	What does corporate culture say? How is this culture embedded in or reflected by certain items?	How does this group use and learn to read the program? What parts do they use and what parts are ignored? Rhetorical assumptions about user? What dualisms are privileged?	How has the researcher approached the program? How did the researcher learn the program? What is the relationship to researcher context— as an academic, teacher, etc.? Kinds of pedagogical moments this has created?
File menu			
Edit menu			
Tools menu			
Main toolbar			
Formatting toolbar			
Collaboration tools			
Draw tools			
HTML- authoring tools			

This tool has both the larger categories of information from the heuristic given earlier across the top row; beneath these, there are more specific prompts about the types of information present in an interface. These questions are asked of each aspect of the technology under examination. By comparing the aspects across versions, a researcher can articulate how the ecology of the interface emerged.

Application of Methodology

My application of the methodological tool consisted of examining Microsoft Word for the Macintosh versions 1.0 through Office X, as well as Microsoft Word 6.0 and XP for Microsoft Windows. From within these interfaces, I chose toolbars and menus used most frequently in composition and professional writing classes based upon my experiences teaching those courses in computer-mediated classrooms. For a sense of the ideologies embedded in the interface and their historical origins, I also looked at corporate literature such as press releases, usability reports, studies done by people both within and outside of Microsoft about their software development practices, and histories of computer and software development not necessarily directly connected with Microsoft. This comprised six sets of completed data-collection tools, one for each version of the software, that became increasingly complex as the interfaces incorporated more information. The correlation of information examined rhetorically helped me to construct an ecology of relationships mapped over time and allowed me to make arguments about both the rationale for the Word interface and to discuss possible reasons students might have difficulty reading the program. Further, with a mapped ecology, I was able to suggest potential solutions to possible difficulties.

In the case of Microsoft Word, their rationale for many of their development choices was an ever-expanding customer base during the 1980s and 1990s. Increased catering to the primary customer base is evident in a series of shifts in the menu text used by Microsoft Word's developers. These shifts show a preference for the discourse of business and technology, at times over that of the academy. For example, "glossary" in Word version 1.0—a term common to academic texts—is replaced by "autotext" by version 6.0 (and it is so noted in the Help for Office X). Autotext is a far more mechanistic term, which mirrors the aspect's increased functionality of being able to efficiently insert prewritten text. In version 5.0, "annotate"—an academic term—appears as one of the first collaboration tools; it was changed to "comment" in version 6.0 (Romberger, 2004).

In addition to changes in terminology, Word eventually included the ability to insert movies in Word version 6.0, and later provided options for creating HTML versions of documents in Word 98. This mirrors the increased use by businesses of new forms of electronic media, intranets, and the Internet to distribute information. The ability to easily use functions like this and features like the picture-formatting tools that appear in later versions of Word, relies heavily upon previous experience with other programs such as Web browsers, HTML-authoring programs, and graphic-manipulation software. These types of inclusions show an increase in expectations of users to have experience with discourses associated with the workplace and other technologies. They also demonstrate an emphasis on efficiency through automation (Romberger, 2004).

These few examples, along with many others of a similar nature, demonstrate how complex a rhetorical environment the interface of a program like Microsoft Word has become. Because Microsoft requires standardization of interface design from developers who make programs to work in conjunction with the Windows operating system, Microsoft is imposing a new standard literacy for the digital writing environment—one that allows users little latitude to influence the ecology of the environment in which they have to work.

CONCLUSION

Users within electronic spaces are able to claim considerably more agency if they are aware of the rhetorical constructions impinging upon or even shaping their desired methods of approaching writing tasks. The ecofeminist methodology outlined in this chapter can be used to create a rhetorical inquiry into any digital writing technology. The notion of an ecofeminist critical inquiry into the rhetorical ecology of digital composing environments may prove to be particularly useful as scholars of digital rhetoric integrate more numerous and increasingly complex technologies into our classrooms and our scholarship. This methodology accounts for the presence of discourse community practices with their attendant ideologies and value systems. We can use the information gathered with this methodology and those like it to raise critical technology awareness of students and of usability practitioners, among others. Additionally, as the technologies become more integrated and borrow from each others' lexicons of icons, terminologies, and interactive practices, this methodology can assist us in locating overlap and understanding how discursively integrated a writing environment can be, which demonstrates that user subjectivity is constructed in multiple ways in all of these spaces.

To this end, there is much to be learned in analysis of the rhetorical ecology of a variety of writing technologies. Future studies using ecofeminist-guided methodologies should also include human subjects in data collection and examine how categories of difference such as gender and ethnicity are absent and/or present in the discourse communities used in computer technology. Additional analysis of digital writing spaces might also develop contrastive analyses between freeware/shareware and commercial programs; programs designed for children, such as The Amazing Writing Machine, Inspiration Software, or the Secret Writer's Society; those designed by digital rhetoric scholars like Daedalus Integrated Writing Environment and Norton Textra Connect; and commercially available products such as Microsoft Word and Corel WordPerfect. A particularly valuable venue for exploration would be software designed specifically for creating digital texts that integrate text, visuals, sound, and interactivity. Our analysis of software programs such as Macromedia Flash could provide fascinating insights into the blending of discourse community practices that take place when creating multimodal texts in digital space.

Tim Mayers and Kevin Swafford (1998) argued that

> the association of computer technology with business and commodification of information has always been in place and that the primary problem with computer technology in the writing classroom relates to obviating this relationship and exposing not only how the technology orders the virtual but how ideologies of technology order the "real" world in the service of various types of social and cultural control. (p. 150)

It is because of this potential harm and the particular ideologies that help create it that it is vital the field engage in examination of the rhetorical ecology of all digital composition spaces using methodologies such as the one outlined here.

NOTES

1. There are theoretical strands within ecofeminist theory that are valuable lenses through which to view technology of all types. Discussions about ecofeminist research exist in social work, which focuses strictly on the social environment's impact upon humans and does not directly touch upon issues of subjectivity and

environment, because these issues are not as relevant to the research questions typically asked in social work (Besthorn & McMillen, 2002). Discussions also exist in ethnographic and sociological research (see, especially, Warren, 2000).

2. Systems theory has multiple branches and draws from the fields of mathematics, physics, anthropology, philosophy, sociology, cognitive psychology, cybernetics, and ecology; systems theory is "the transdisciplinary study of the abstract organization of phenomena, independent of their substance, type, or spatial or temporal scale of existence. It investigates both the principles common to all complex entities, and the (usually mathematical) models which can be used to describe them" (Heylighen & Joslyn, 1995, p. 1). For the purposes of rhetorical inquiry, systems science is problematic in that the human element is often obscured or left out. Additionally, systems theory tends to ignore the political, which is also troublesome for rhetorical analysis. There is perhaps more to be gained from anthropological strands of systems theory, which focuses on "metapatterns" of concepts, described first by Gregory Bateson (1979) or from the work done on information and environment by Jeremy Campbell (1982).

3. Various methodological tools for examining ecologies are not new to writing studies. Each version, however, defines ecology quite differently. Marilyn Cooper (1986) proposed "an ecological model of writing, whose fundamental tenet is that writing is an activity through which a person is continually engaged with a variety of socially constituted systems" (p. 367). Cooper emphasized that this is not merely another term for context, rather what she has in mind is how writers interact to "form systems" and how the "characteristics of any individual writer . . . both determines and is determined by the characteristics of all the other writers and writings in the systems" that are "made and remade by writers in the act of writing" (p. 368). These systems are concrete structures that are constituted by clusters of ideas, purposes, interpersonal interactions, cultural norms, and textual forms. Since Cooper's article, there have been several studies that have created methodologies that trace ecologies (e.g., Spinuzzi, 2003; Syverson, 1999), workplace context, and how users adapt and link the changes they make to established genres.

4. Many conflicting definitions of what constitutes ecology exist beyond this fundamental conceptualization, but these conflicts are less pertinent to this discussion because the focus here is away from the scientific emphasis on biology, physics, and chemistry and rather on the metaphorical. The precision necessary for the justification of an appropriate mathematical model isn't needed. Instead, the methodology outlined here uses the metaphor of ecology at its most basic to articulate what constitutes an environment.

5. My project, because of its scope, did not end up using the "User" category, and instead collapsed this into the "Investigator" category. Essentially, the investigator was also understood to be the principle user in this research. Given more time, and perhaps with a narrow focus on the most recent versions of the program instead of beginning with Microsoft Word version 1.0, I would have included this category in my research project.

13

RIDING THE WAVE

ARTICULATING A CRITICAL METHODOLOGY
FOR WEB RESEARCH PRACTICES

Amy C. Kimme Hea

In this chapter, I describe issues related to digital writing researchers working on and through the Web. I turn to articulation theory—both a method of analysis and a political practice—as a means to examine the challenges and complexities of Web-based research. To situate an articulation theory approach, I first describe digital studies in terms of technological determinisms, and I then address four specific challenges of Web research. To help ground my discussion, I present the ways in which CollegeNET's Web site articulates the four concerns I raise: The Web as a social space; the Web's mutable nature; the Web as information-gathering space and data disseminator; and the Web as aural, visual, and hypertextual space. I frame these challenges so that we may re-articulate our Web-based research, working toward more equitable research practices that recognize that cultural practices and research methods cannot be seen as neutral or easily transportable across technological contexts.

269

INTRODUCTION

Computers and writing researchers have studied the World Wide Web to better understand its implications for identity formation, social movements, departmental and program identity, cultural impact, and pedagogical integration.[1] In fact, since 1994—a year often referenced as marking the Web's broader public accessibility—*Computers and Composition* alone has published more than 60 articles about the Web and its pedagogical potential. Less evident in our scholarly conversations, however, are considerations of critical *research* practices related to the Web. That is, although computers and writing researchers continue to question the role of the Web in our classrooms, we have not yet adequately confronted how the Web impacts the methods, topics, and interpretations of our research practices.[2] In her work on research methodology and technology, Pamela Takayoshi (2000) went so far as to assert that "many of the stories we tell in computers and composition scholarship, examples of either positive or negative experiences with technology, are told as relatively coherent renderings from the teacher's perspective" (p. 128). To continue to educate both students and instructors to be critical users, producers, and critics of technology (Hawisher & Selfe, 1991; Selfe, 1999), digital writing scholars must consider the ways in which Web technologies reformulate notions of context, roles of and relationships between researchers and participants, and even our understanding of data. Research projects that either fail to consider the influence of technical and cultural practices or attempt, as Takayoshi warned, to create seamless narratives about our research run the risk of reinscribing the very inequities we seek to disrupt.

This move toward critical, self-reflexive Web research is not without its complications. The Web's mutable nature; continued growth; and confluence of visual, aural, and hypertextual forms are difficult factors for a researcher to negotiate. Laura Gurak and Christine Silker (1997) emphasized the need to reconsider research methodology in light of these technological shifts, arguing that "researchers will need to continue evaluating their decisions against currently accepted research standards and ongoing technological change" (p. 404). I further believe that we must rethink our conceptions of research standards themselves in light of new concepts, practices, and changes in technology. Gurak and Silker addressed, for example, anonymity, reciprocity, and even data collection in new ways, but we also should attend to issues of ideology, norms, and assumptions about power and meaning in our culture. As critical technology theorists argue, such technological shifts and research constructions are situated within an ever-changing cultural milieu, and thus Web researchers must understand how cultural narratives influence their projects. Traditional categories and practices of research may or may not explicitly address the ideological issues inherent in Web research. Thus, the Web as a cultural manifestation is not merely changing the ways we understand traditional research practices in our field, but also the ways we interact with, think about, and discuss our work on the Web. Such changes should encourage us to seek equally dynamic research frameworks, ones that lend themselves to situated forms of critical inquiry. Through situated—rather than universal—research practices, the Web researcher can better attend to the cultural and technological scene of computers and writing research, striving to bring new approaches and configurations to projects in our field.

Rather than presenting readers with a discussion of traditional methods and their enactment on the Web, I want to illuminate new concerns for the Web researcher, concerns that grow out of the cultural narratives of the Web. Considering the challenges that a critical Web researcher faces, I turn to articulation theory as a means to examine the challenges and complexities of Web-based research. Articulation theory is both a method of analysis and a political practice. This nonessentialist, nonreductive theory strives to connect cultural discourses and practices to challenge inequitable power relations. My fuller discussion of articulation begins, however, with two technological determinisms: the substantive and the instrumental. Because these determinisms are so intimately connected with Web research, I want to explore the ways such determinisms maintain rather than disrupt traditional research categories. After providing a definition of articulation theory and its methodological assumptions, I address four specific challenges of Web research. To help ground my discussion, I present the ways in which CollegeNET's Web site articulates four concerns raised in this chapter: The Web as a social space; the Web's mutable nature; the Web as information-gathering space and data disseminator; and the Web as aural, visual, and hypertextual space. Without attention to the broader aspects of the Web as a medium, researchers may miss some of the significant interrelationships among the modes of the Web and across its ideological and political messages. In this work, articulation is offered, then, as one possible framework for conducting critical, situated Web research. This chapter demonstrates the applicability of articulation theory for critical Web research and generates a discussion of our methodological positions. We should be mindful of ways in which technologies, like the Web, cannot be examined outside of their cultural practices and our research methods cannot be seen as neutral or easily transportable across technological contexts.

CHALLENGING MYTHS
OF NEUTRAL TECHNOLOGY

Despite our work to attend to the complexity of writing technologies, computers and writing scholars still confront cultural tendencies that claim technology is easy, neutral, and pervasive. When technology is normalized in our research, we risk denying its historical, cultural, and material effects on our work. Critical theories of technology seek to disrupt such narratives by repositioning technologies.[3] Often-cited critical technology theorist Andrew Feenberg (1999) suggested that technology is an "ambivalent process" (p. 14)—one designed and imbued with social values. Technologies are sets of practices that carry traces of their historical development, use, and integration in our culture.

In *Questioning Technology*, Feenberg (1999) noted two impulses in the ways technology is defined: (a) the substantive view, where technology is constructed as inevitably good or bad, and technological progress is seen as inherently either helping humankind achieve its potential or enslaving us in a dehumanized culture, (b) the instrumental view, in which technology is neutral; that is, technology is merely a tool unaffected by its own social and historical context. These two determinisms forestall critical engagement and agency—technology seemingly has no ideological implications to critique, or researchers have no ability to affect change in our relationships with the technologies we employ.

These determinisms are evident in technology research—take the Web survey as one research practice. In the substantive view, we might mistakenly assume that online research can simplify data collection. Rather than addressing the underlying assumptions about Web surveys and the ways in which they position participants and researchers, we may be tempted to believe that Web surveys resolve issues of cost, speed, and distance. The instrumental view would suggest that the Web survey is a neutral research portal, and we merely need to translate our print-based survey practices into a new electronic form. These views assert the positive effects of technology and see shifts in one medium to another as merely a matter of translation.

To combat such determinisms and their consequences, Feenberg (1999) argued that we must recontextualize technology. In his view, we must consider the social aspects of technological development, and thus situate the design and function of a technology within its material, cultural, political, and historical environments. Critical technology theorists such as Feenberg, Donna Haraway, and Bruno Latour do not present a single, unified view of technology and its interrelationships. Nevertheless, they, along with most computers and writing scholars, share the belief that we must challenge inequitable constructions and representations of technology to create more equitable electronic spaces and relationships—a position that can be instantiated through a critical, situated methodology for research through and on technology.

SITUATING ARTICULATION THEORY FOR DIGITAL WRITING RESEARCH

Articulation theory is one possible framework to complicate technological determinisms in our research. To better understand articulation theory, we can start with a simple definition of *articulation* as a connection or linking of parts to form a unity. In articulation theory, however, this connecting is never permanent, but it is always contingent and multiple. Although the word articulation has Latin origins and the term *articulation theory* is suggestive of Western philosophical rationalism, Ernesto Laclau re-theorized articulation[4] as a means to posit a revived socialist politics in Latin America. In his work, Laclau (1982) argued that "classes exist at the ideological and political level in a process of articulation and not of reduction" (p. 161). Although the topics of their inquiry are far-reaching, most articulatory scholars share common commitments to revealing ideologies; examining dynamic, contingent, and multiple practices and structures; acknowledging difference as integral to understanding those practices and structures; and striving toward a set of political imperatives (Kimme Hea, 2002). I return to these common elements of articulation in my exploration of the challenges for Web research, deploying them more directly in my examination of CollegeNET's Web site.

As part of his contribution to articulation theory, noted cultural studies scholar Stuart Hall employed articulation theory as a means not only to critique certain interconnections but also to re-articulate those connections in ways that allow for political change. Hall (1985) explained re-articulation as the process by which "the dispersed conditions of practice of different social groups can be effectively drawn together in ways which make those social forces not simply a class in itself . . . but a class for itself, capable of establishing new collective projects" (p. 96). Building on Hall's work, Jennifer Daryl Slack presented technical communication scholars with a history of articulation theory in cultural studies (Slack, 1989) and used articulation to investigate "context" in the empirical work of communication scholarship (Slack, 1996). Hall and Slack offer us a way of instantiating articulation theory as a powerful method of re-conceiving cultural positions and intervening in the construction of cultural practices.

In her articulatory work, Donna Haraway merges both the political advocacy of Hall's practice of articulation and the flexible, tropic figuring of Fredric Jameson's (1991) uses of the theory. Throughout her scholarship, Haraway articulates and re-articulates conceptions of technoscience and knowledge-making practices. In our field, Johndan Johnson-Eilola (1997) applied articulation and re-articulation in his ground-breaking project on hypertext technology. Johnson-Eilola called for a critical practice of hypertext that seeks to politicize the production and consumption of meanings and to redraw the disciplinary boundaries that rationalize hegemonic constructions of it. Articulation theory is well-suited to examinations of technology because it addresses a range of cultural concerns manifest in the design, development, production, circulation, and consumption of technologies. Rather than relying on traditional research categories, articulation theory draws our attention to the Web as a cultural manifestation.

In the sections that follow, I take up the particular challenges that a Web researcher faces. In each section, I draw attention to ideologies, practices, issues of difference, and the politics of the Web as part of our research culture. To better ground this analysis, I rely on a specific Web-based example, CollegeNET's corporate Web site. CollegeNET, Inc. boasts that it is "the world's leading 'virtual plumber' for higher education Internet transactions. We provide here for your convenience over 1500 customized Internet admissions applications built for college and university programs" (CollegeNET, n.d.). Although a range of other Web sites can also be subject to articulation as a methodology for critical Web research, CollegeNET directly addresses educational practices and college admissions, issues relevant to our research community.

THE WEB AS SOCIAL AND CULTURAL SPACE

One way in which articulation theory can be used to address the Web is through a contextualized understanding of the non-neutrality of the Web as a social and cultural space. The Web must be understood as a constructed space with a range of ideologies, differences, and politics at play. The critical Web researcher must engage in the dual struggle of complicating positivistic notions of research sites and challenging the technological determinisms of electronic spaces. Shadowed by a belief in the laboratory and its ability to "control" for participant interactions and by the idea that a researcher can capture "native" experiences, we still fight against the positivist tradition where research sites often were elided through stories of control or mastery. This struggle is further complicated when the spaces we research are technological and thus mired in deterministic assumptions about the neutrality of tools.

The critical Web researcher strives to understand complex electronic spaces, seeking neither erasure nor mastery but rather consideration of the challenges that make the Web a space worthy of research. As noted spatial theorist Henri Lefebvre (1991) argued, we cannot separate spatial form and content from experience. In fact, he called such separation the "theoretical error . . . to be content to see a space without conceiving of it, without assembling details into a whole 'reality,' without apprehending contents in terms of their interrelationships within the containing forms" (p. 94). This artificial separation of space from lived experience can further exacerbate a sense of neutrality and objectivity. Such a separation of spatial form and content can undermine opportunities to research the interesting contradictions, connections, and tangential relationships developed on the Web.

CollegeNET, an electronic college admissions service, is one digital space worthy of study. Many campuses are moving their admission procedures to Web portals in hopes of targeting their recruitment efforts, increasing retention rates, and gathering data that can used to gain future students and even to solicit those future alumni for donations. These targeted marketing strategies were recently discussed in the March 2005 issue of *Campus Technology*. This magazine speaks to information technology professionals and is part of the Syllabus Media Group. Frank Tansey (2005) reported that e-recruitment initiatives allow administrators to "know preciously who is reading an e-mail, viewing a Web page, or responding to a survey, they [admissions officials] can focus their attention on those students who are most engaged by or responsive to the communications" (p. 36). The major incentive that universities have for using services like CollegeNET is its self-proclaimed ability to target admission campaigns to gain the best and brightest students. This competitive model is one touted throughout the literature on e-recruitment. Universities are willing to pay CollegeNET to host online application forms and feature information about their institutions. CollegeNET argues that it allows institutions to increase prestige by gaining top students and profits by establishing a market profile that will follow students throughout their college careers. Not surprisingly, the CollegeNET site assumes that its primary users are high school students and their parents. The site, however, also presumes that this particular user audience has physical access to Web technologies and limited cultural barriers to technology use.

CollegeNET and other such services ignore key ideological issues of electronic spaces. Edward Soja (1989), drawing upon his mentor Lefebvre, noted that all spaces exhibit tendencies of uneven development. Thus, to understand a space critically means to historicize that unevenness and actively engage in rehistoricizing and remaking space. Soja's point about space is demonstrated by early claims about the Web being able to erase gender and cultural differences. More recently, this narrative has been revived in claims that wireless systems can eliminate the "haves and have nots" and bridge the digital divide. These claims operate on the premise that Web technologies can rescue us from heterogeneity and provide us all with an electronic melting pot of positive pluralism. CollegeNET offers another example of this position with its "Wireless Triggers" product. In an embedded slideshow on its corporate Web site, CollegeNET pitches the technology to admission personnel, arguing that "when a student you have identified as a key prospect submits your online application, CollegeNET's patented technology automatically TRIGGERS a text message to your wireless device and the opportunity to personalize the transaction INSTANTLY" (CollegeNET, 2005c). Here, the college admissions officer becomes all-knowing, and the significance of the information almost pales by comparison to its speed, immediacy, and ability to transgress boundaries of place and time.

What seems particularly disturbing, however, is that this slideshow is placed far from the linking range of the CollegeNET's primary portal for students and parents, making this information *about* them—rather than *for* them—and nearly inaccessible by hypertext standards. Rather than agents of their own college choices, students are framed as commodities, and it is clear through the slideshow and its messages that not all students are equally coveted. Technology disparity, access, racism, sexism, homophobia, and a range of other cultural problematics continue to plague us despite past—and even more recent—promises of Web salvation. At first glance, it would seem that CollegeNET's slideshow all but ignores reports stating that:

> The majority of wireless Internet users are men, and they also tend to have higher incomes. While men make up only 48% of the overall Internet population, they are 72% of those who use PDAs or mobile phones to go online. Nearly 60% of those using mobile phones and

PDAs to go online have an annual household income of more than $60,000. (Digital Divide, 2002, n.p.)

In reality, the "Wireless Triggers" slideshow epitomizes the demographic information provided by the Digital Divide report, as the admissions official is a white professional male and the one symbolically empowered by his use of wireless technology. The white female student is led to believe in the responsiveness of her future college without ever necessarily knowing about the Triggers product or even deploying the same wireless technologies to track her own recruitment (see Figure 13.1). This type of disparity— which articulation theory makes significant to a Web researcher's practice—is all but lost if the Web remains innocently cloaked in technological determinism that makes it seem equally accessible.

Michel de Certeau (1988) theorized space as "composed of intersections of mobile elements . . . space occurs as the effect produced by the operations that orient it, situate it, temporalize it, and make it function in a polyvalent unity of conflictual programs or contractual proximities" (p. 117). This dynamic, contradictory sense of space is a suitable description of the Web, where pages, visitors, messages, and digital manifestations come, go, and collide in a range of experiences, effects, and exchanges. The space of the Web represents a range of power dynamics, and these shifts create opportunities for intervention and change, for rearticulating the Web in new configurations. Thus, critical Web researchers must consid-

Figure 13.1. Image Captured From CollegeNET's Wireless Triggers Slideshow

er both who is and is not participating in the social space of the Web, what constitutes participation, and what the material and cultural consequences are of participation and nonparticipation. CollegeNET helps to illuminate the types of spatial ideologies related to the Web, ones that must be contended with in our research.

THE MUTABLE NATURE OF THE WEB

Articulation theory also attends to the Web's mutable nature. Technological determinism makes change seem inevitable, unilateral, and without human agents. Even though texts and spaces never have an inherent, "fixed" meaning and despite the fact that qualitative researchers often struggle to represent change in the lives of their participants, we must directly contend with the Web's embodiment as an ever-shifting digital text. Despite the changing nature of other media, I have not found another text that literally "changes" itself with each new engagement of the reader. This means that one or two pages of a Web site are not isolated elements of a critical Web researcher's project, but rather they are consciously constructed cultural spaces informed by users and designers. Although legal briefs, archived manuscripts, or research transcripts are formed as static marks on a page, Web designers exploit hypertextual link–node structures and digital writing conventions. Thus, no single node of a Web site is ever necessarily published in its "final" version—it can be redesigned, relocated, and removed. Rather than assuming these changes are neutral, the critical Web researcher must interrogate the underlying assumptions related to such mutability. Otherwise, the Web becomes yet another means to circulate assumptions about change as always leading to greater equality and increased efficiency.

Articulation theory makes tracing change significant to uncovering social inequities and political agendas. The work of an articulatory researcher is to bring together disparate elements—texts, spaces, visuals, and other sites—to consider the broader implications of these linked elements. The Web as one such site is particularly unique because it is explicitly constructed as ever-changing. To illustrate this mutability and its potential effects, I want to briefly examine CollegeNET's starting page. CollegeNET loads one of four possible starting nodes with each visit to its Web site. CollegeNET's shifting opening page characterizes the type of change that a Web researcher must consider. CollegeNET's view of change is evident in not just its various rotating starting nodes (See Figures 13.2, 13.3, 13.4, 13.5) but also its slogan of "Go to college. Change the World" (CollegeNET, 2005a).

CollegeNET emphasizes change and customization as hallmarks of its business philosophy, one echoed by many other Web-based companies. In other words, CollegeNET could not conduct its business without change— it seeks to convince students that their education will change the world and colleges that they can change their admission practices. Claiming to be the "complete online guide to colleges, universities, graduate programs and financial aid," CollegeNET does not challenge the assumption that "complete" really means advertising its own college clients and not every university (CollegeNET, 2005a). With links to other resources available, CollegeNET still only provides information about scholarships and other

Figures 13.2, 13.3, 13.4, 13.5. Four Different Starting Nodes of CollegeNET

financial resources in its own database from its clients. Despite its claims to completeness and student empowerment, CollegeNET's strategy lends to student agency only if students select one of the predetermined client paths available to them.

We can think of CollegeNET, then, as a tropic figure—an articulation—of the dynamic aspects of the Web. This site, and many others, can seem fairly normal, even standard in interface, but presents the Web researcher with a dilemma of attending to shifting text and an ever-dynamic research context. The cycle of different starting nodes is just one example of Web change. Many Web sites incorporate welcome banners, counter windows, time/temperature updates, special offer messages based upon user account information, and other malleable features. The significance of these dynamic elements and subsequent redesigns of a Web site like CollegeNET might not seem profound to the company, but consider the consequences for those of us interested in engaging in critiques of and research on the Web. These changes can affect our understandings of Web sites and our analyses of them, and even more profoundly, using Web pages as part of our research means thinking through the Web's tendency to require new configurations and change as part of its culture. Such change requires a constant attention to power issues and the ways those are instantiated through shifting Web practices.

THE WEB AS INFORMATION DISTRIBUTOR AND DATA COLLECTOR

Another aspect of Web-based research is the range of documents that the Web distributes. Thinking of the Web not merely as HTML documents hosted by servers, we see that the Web is a confluence of technologies, hybrid media, and various genres. The Web uses the Internet to transport its material to users. These materials most often are developed in some combination of HTML, XML, VML, Dynamic HTML, Javascript, or other codes. Produced in simple text or Web-development programs, the "basic" Web page is not basic. Database-connected interfaces; animations; streaming video and audio; blogs; Wikis; Web-based email interfaces; hypermedia poetry and fiction; and downloadable PDFs, word-processing documents, and spreadsheets all represent only a fraction of the various electronic media and genres available on and through the Web. Jay David Bolter and Richard Grusin (1999) described this confluence of media as remediation, or a "formal logic by which new media refashion prior media forms" (p. 5). For many of us engaging technology, the Web is a portal, interface, and hypertext system. Critical Web researchers thus are not only confronted with questions about what constitutes the boundaries of an individual Web site, Web-based technologies, and Web media, but also with questions related to which electronic texts and genres constitute the Web.

Further issues arise when we consider wireless devices that code and package Web information through a different set of scripting languages— for instance, Wireless Markup Language (WML) and Extensible HyperText Markup Language Mobile Profile (XHTML MP). This change to smaller screens and different interface constraints leads us back to issues about the relationship of text and images and the ways information is distributed. Just as with CollegeNET's "Wireless Triggers" product, this reframing of the Web through portable devices sets an expectation of omnipresence, a position reified through discussions of 24/7 and anywhere, anytime mobile technologies.

Closely associated with the scope of information available on the Web is the range of information gathered and archived *through* the Web. From Web-based surveys to online forms, the Web can be used to collect information and data for a range of academic, corporate, and government individuals and entities. CollegeNET's admissions surveys and emails are designed to take the information a prospective student provides and use it as part of the university's own marketing campaign. CollegeNET's slideshow on "Intelligent Connections"—a term for its information collection services—notes that "you [admissions personnel] can respond instantly to student interests using customized HumanForm® technology" (CollegeNET, 2005b). This technology asks students to fill out a checklist of interests from sports to art to academics, and then the software is configured to email a reply message with preformed data about campus resources. One such form available from CollegeNET states "Meet our Coach . . . Hi, I'm Coach George, and we have a great team this year . . ." with a place to insert an image of the university's coach. Here, the student-supplied data is used as a way to recruit students and make them feel more intimately connected to an institution. The technological function of intimacy and customization are part of a market philosophy, one that masks the modes of production from students. Further, e-recruitment is translating student input back into its own production cycle. Tansey (2005) reported that campus administrators are using survey feedback to sell the campus to students; the information provided to the college is redistributed so that "prospective students and applicants can learn what their peers are saying, and make connections with them" (p. 39).

Critical Web researchers must measure "ease" of use, constructions of community, and ideologies of intimacy and customization against our responsibilities to research participants. Critical Web researchers must examine the underlying assumptions part of Web-based data collection, especially when we consider commitment to privacy and issues of participant representation. The same issues arise with mobile Web-based survey collection.[5] Explicit requests for information in the form of surveys or online forms, however, only represent some of the most obvious technologies, media, and genres deployed as collection mechanisms. Programs that chart Web usage, register Web site visits and hits, and embed intelligent agents all operate in the technological, often masked, codes of the Web. Even Javascript can "sniff" for your browser and deliver you an appropriately formatted Web page. Although I want to avoid the implication that all Web data-gathering efforts are panoptic or insidious, engagement with these concerns are necessary for a complex understanding of the role of the Web in our culture and classrooms. Critical Web researchers must consider the constructions of power propagated through these data-collection methods and their categorical systems, and we must know that deploying Web data-gathering practices in our work complicates participant anonymity, privacy, and security.

THE VISUAL, AURAL, AND HYPERTEXTUAL ELEMENTS OF THE WEB

Most often, analyses of Web pages have made the Web seem conservative in its forms. For example, analyses of Web pages tend to privilege the text of the page—the words presented there. Running a close second is an emphasis on the visual elements, primarily photos and graphics (typography is rarely acknowledged as a visual element). In the case of the former, text is often described on a page-by-page basis rather than across the site or against other sites and often with little notation of its visual qualities. In the case of the latter, visual elements seem largely to emphasize image color, size, and position. The visual aspects of the Web contribute to its multiple and seemingly boundless manifestations. In her attempt to complicate notions of visual rhetoric, Anne Wysocki (2002) argued that visual strategies are not merely a matter of persuading an audience but also a means of reinforcing certain values, habits, and structures. Cynthia Selfe and Richard Selfe (1994) affirmed this stance in their work politicizing the graphical user interface, its visual metaphors, and its structural design. Selfe and Selfe convincingly asserted that

> English teachers [and I would suggest researchers] cannot be content to understand the maps of computer interfaces as simple, uncomplicated spaces. . . . we need to map these virtual spaces as sites of "multiple and heterogeneous borders where different histories, languages, experiences, and voices intermingle amidst diverse relations of power and privilege" (Giroux 169). (p. 500)

The critical Web researcher must work against notions of the visual–spatial spaces of the Web as transparent representations of reality, and instead understand visual practices as always already co-constructive of cultural and material relationships. As noted earlier, the CollegeNET's starting page displays dramatic images that integrate well-known art (see Figure 13.4). This co-opting of Dali, Mondrian, Rivera, and Grant Wood paintings is yet another feature of the visual dynamics of the Web, where images can be repurposed, recycled, and reused to invoke a range of appeals.

The Web also constructs aural experiences, making sound another challenge for those of us invested in Web research. Although visual production and consumption has been an object of our attention, auditory elements and practices are often overlooked. Sound, in our field, is often linked to oppressive cultural forces, such as the silencing of voices of difference or hailing someone to take on a certain subject position. Conversely, we have countertropes of coming to voice and speaking out. Sound inhabits the Web, but we have little work that explores the technological, spatial, and cultural experiences of sounds. In their introduction to the *Auditory Culture Reader*, Michael Bull and Less Black (2003) emphasized that "sound and its reception are infused with cultural values" (p. 7). The critical Web researcher must not only attend to ocular experience, but also the auditory and the way auditory experience resonates in the space of the Web and affects research projects. Interestingly, sound is absent in CollegeNET's pages except for the "clicking" noise present as part of its slideshow features. But other sites do include auditory features, and the imprint of sound is one element of Web-based research that must be addressed.

Hypertextual elements of the Web also affect our research on and about the Web. Linking, coding, rewriting (as in Wikis), transversing Web pages, scanning them, bookmarking sites, and collecting pieces of information all represent Web and other new media hypertextual practices. In his arguments for the critical deployment of hypertext, Stuart Selber (1997) spoke of the historical shift from individual computer and local area network hypertexts to Web pages that transcend the boundaries of local space. This shifting of hypertext from individual computers and local networks to more mass production and consumption with the Web marked a rearticulation of hypertext practices. Recently, Johndan Johnson-Eilola and I (2003) discussed hypertext as both an artifact and a trope, claiming that "from its most conservative to its more iconoclastic enactments, hypertext set about shifting our perceptions of writing and reading" (p. 417). The Web as a hypertextual form further complicates our notions of research—asking us to attend to fragmentary aspects of information, dead links, relocated Web sites, and password-protected sites (Moulthrop, 2000). Deeplinking into a site, viewing its code, and locating new media elements make the work of a critical Web researcher more complex than citing just words or images. It makes the navigational structures and coding practices significant to the ideologies and political practices of the Web, and thus to our Web research.

CONCLUSIONS

We must not forget that the Web affects and is affected by discourses on and practices of technology, access, and a host of other issues. Articulation theory requires a researcher to bring together these discourses and practices through critically informed projects. One concern of Web research must be to understand participation through cultural assumptions about spatial relations; the mutability of the Web; the Web's distribution and collection potential; and the visual, aural, and hypertextual elements of the Web. Not so long ago, Charles Moran (1999) reminded us of digital disparity, explaining that we, as researchers, must take part in and responsibility for producing research agendas that seek to eliminate inequity and truly democratize the electronic learning spaces that we create and investigate. His compelling review of computers and writing research and his propositions for new projects in the field demonstrate the ever-present need to connect our theoretical commitments to our research practices. More recently, Jeffrey Grabill (2003) revisited issues of access, directly connecting access issues to interfaces—a spatial position. Further, Grabill argued that "people need to be taught how to use information . . . and to produce content for computer networks to be meaningful spaces" (p. 462).

Articulation theory allows a researcher to focus on the ideological and political implications of Web-based research and the ways in which the

Web is constructed as a meaningful space. Rather than conceiving of the Web as a neutral technology or an always positive one allows for more efficient research practices; critical Web researchers must re-articulate research practices against deterministic assumptions. Such assumptions ignore significant issues of Web access—physical, social, and cultural—and belie our opportunities to investigate important ideological and cultural questions. Interpretation, representation, and ethical questions concerning research continue to be key concerns for members of the field. We must not mistakenly assume that "new" technologies can simply be translated in relationship to our research projects. Articulation theory as a research methodology will allow us to situate our practices and make the technologies integral—not invisible—to the work we do as digital writing researchers.

NOTES

1. Some of these works include articles in the 2002 *Computers and Composition* special issue on Power and the Web, edited by Sibylle Gruber; see also Alexander (2002), Barrios (2004), DeWitt (1997), Gillette (1999), Haas, Tulley, and Blair (2002), Hawisher and Sullivan (1999), Heba (1997), O'Sullivan (1999), Pagnucci and Mauriello (1999), Schneider and Germann (1999), Sorapure, Inglesby, and Yatchisin (1998), Spinuzzi, Bowie, Rodgers, and Li (2003), Takayoshi, Huot, and Huot (1999), and Watkins (1996).
2. For notable contributions to Internet research as it applies to traditional research practices such as IRB approval and data collection, see Gurak and Silker (1997), Gurak (2001), Gurak and Duin (2004), and Banks and Eble (this volume); for the ways Web research is discussed in composition and rhetoric publications and our professional organizations, see Romano (1998).
3. Critical technology theory can be traced in a number of works (see Feenberg, 1991, 1995a, 1995b, 1999; Haraway, 1991, 1992, 1995, 1997; Latour, 1992, 1993).
4. I want to stress here that the bringing together of different aspects of cultural experience allows for critique and critical reconstruction. In her desire to retain articulation theory's forcefulness, Donna Haraway (1997) presented her own methodological position to "critically analyze, or 'deconstruct' only that which I love and only that in which I am deeply implicated" (p. 151). In a similar move to retain articulation theory's potential, Jennifer Daryl Slack (1996) defined articulation noting "the point is that it isn't *exactly* anything" (p. 117). The articulatory researcher is invested in the practice and consequences of her project, and must adapt research practices to fit the context of that project.

5. Much of this discussion is happening at international conferences; two presentations that address the issue are Buskirk and Steeh (2004), and Belak and Vehovar (2004). I anticipate, however, that as third-generation wireless technologies become more widely available, discussions such as these will become central in the U.S. as well.

14

MULTIMEDIA RESEARCH

DIFFICULT QUESTIONS WITH INDEFINITE ANSWERS

Janice McIntire-Strasburg

The increased integration of multiple media in digital texts affects our classrooms, our curricula, and, importantly, our research. In this chapter, I introduce some of the perils and possibilities related to producing and researching multimedia. Specifically, I explore issues of privacy, fair use, and citation strategies. I close with some implications and suggestions for how we can best conduct ethical and thoughtful research on multimedia writing, and also become more active in current debates related to intellectual property issues.

MULTIMEDIA AND DIGITAL WRITING RESEARCH

Multimedia writing (a term I prefer over *new media*) has become an important new area of research for rhetoric scholars in the last few years. Pioneers such as Jay David Bolter (2001), Bolter and Richard Grusin (1999),

Michael Joyce (1995), George Landow (1995), and Richard Lanham (1993) have led the way, mapping research paths to be explored in regard to how texts are changing shape and how such texts can best be analyzed and studied. Each advance in technology generates its own rhizomatic links of researchers, research, and researched, as Landow asserted in *Hyper/Text/ Theory*.

Another way to think about these paths and links is in terms of Bolter and Grusin's (1999) notion of remediation, through which more traditional forms of writing and newer forms interpenetrate and reciprocally affect each other. Others, like Anne Wysocki (1998), focus on the "materiality" of new media as a broader canvas from which to view the effects of digital and other new media forms on the culture at large, by taking into account the cultural, socioeconomic, and global implications such writing has on methods of communication. Wysocki, Johndan Johnson-Eilola, Cynthia Selfe, and Geoffrey Sirc (2004) argued that writing scholars are uniquely well-situated to think about and speak to new media and multimedia writing and research. Because of its medium of delivery—across networks, within databases, folded into larger media structures—multimedia writing requires researchers to reassess approaches to ideas of ownership and originality. Karla Kitalong (1998) explored these notions in a case study of whether or not "borrowing" Web page code can be considered plagiarism and called attention to the indeterminate nature of the line between borrowing code and borrowing an entire page.

Other writing scholars who work with issues of representation (although not necessarily digital representation) provide useful theoretical lenses through which we can approach the research of multimedia. Gesa Kirsch (1999), Kirsch and Patricia Sullivan (1992), Peter Mortensen and Kirsch (1996), Deborah Brandt (1990, 2001), and Anne Ruggles Gere (1987, 1993), for instance, study the implications of representation: how we as researchers represent subjects of study. Implications of this research will have a lasting impact upon and determine directions for research into how multimedia might also re-present or misrepresent the voices of the subjects researchers study and the representation of their work. Other scholars look at media itself—the rules and regulations (or lack thereof); the specialized properties of particular kinds of media—sound, text, images, streaming video, and combinations of all of these, for example; and new ways of reading and interpreting mixed media that influence and affect our research in these areas (see, for instance, Allen, 2002; DeVoss, Cushman, & Grabill, 2005; Hocks, 2003; Hocks & Kendrick, 2004; WIDE Research Center Collective, 2005; Wysocki, 2001, 2005; Wysocki & Jasken, 2004). In this chapter, I explore a variety of complications related to multimedia research, first introducing the problems multimedia poses generally, and then addressing the connection of these problems to research-related issues. Specifically, I explore issues of privacy, intellectual property, copyright, fair use, and citation strategies. As related to Internet and multimedia publishing, these issues threaten to change and complicate our ideas about scholarly publishing and the research products it generates.

Jay David Bolter (2001) christened the late 20th and early 21st century the "late age of print" (p. 150). In doing so, he invoked historical precedents: the shift from oral delivery to written communication and a similar shift from hand-written texts to the printing press. Bolter envisioned a similar revolution as new forms of multimedia, primarily those that are computer-based, began to take precedence over purely textual communication. Such a revolution will affect—in many instances has already affected—students, teachers, and researchers in rhetoric by complicating traditional methodologies in writing instruction and research. In addition to the more traditional written text, multimedia writing brings to the research setting images, sound, and streaming video, forcing those researching and writing in this medium to also consider how all of these elements can be integrated into text, and how such integration alters meaning and transmits knowledge. Writing researchers have become increasingly interested in studying multimedia texts and writers authoring in multimedia contexts; however, the relative novelty of the field and the nature of multimedia present a challenge to previously developed research methods.

THE PROBLEMS OF MULTIMEDIA RESEARCH

Issues of Privacy

Current research on writing and the teaching of writing as we currently understand and perform it uses student work as the backbone of evidence upon which many of our conclusions must stand. Thus, researchers have always borne the burden of balancing issues of student privacy and the accurate citation of case studies or statistical samplings with the informational needs of scholars within the field. Over time, researchers publishing their findings in hard-copy form developed methods and reporting strategies that reflected this difficult balancing act. Case studies typically renamed students, or assigned them numbers or letters that preserved their anonymity, relying upon the researcher's thorough record-keeping and accuracy to preserve the integrity, validity, and reliability of the study. In addition to this protective layer of anonymity, scholars have routinely obtained permission from subjects before citing their work; in large part, researchers could obtain permission because they could promise subjects that the audience for their work was limited in scope to other scholars in the field.

As more and more writing research is published on the Web in journals such as *The Writing Instructor, Computers and Composition Online,* and *Kairos: A Journal of Rhetoric, Technology, and Pedagogy,* and as search engines become increasingly more efficient, the potential audience for a particular text rises dramatically, and rethinking traditional approaches to permission and use becomes imperative. We can no longer promise research subjects *anything* about who will see and read their work. Curious Web surfers, who under other circumstances would not have access to scholarly research in this area, now have the potential to access subjects' writing and research reports at the click of a mouse button. In addition, Web archiving functions allow at least the possibility that such samples may remain on the Web indefinitely. This kind of accessibility complicates the promise implicit in traditional permissions. Writers' willingness to give a researcher consent to use their work might be different given this increased access and the increased potential for archiving. For example, for first-year college students, looking ahead 10 or 20 years, their neighbor, supervisor, spouse, or friends might still be able to access the writing they did in their first year of college writing. Many first-year writing assignments ask for (or receive unasked-for) self-disclosures that might prove embarrassing should the author's work be public and accessible; the "anonymous" nature of writing that seems to bring out self-examination and disclosure could conceivably come back to haunt students in their postcollege lives. As responsible researchers, we have an ethical obligation to protect subjects' privacy while still maintaining an active and ongoing research agenda. We also need to ensure that the consent forms we share with potential participants specify all possible publishing media, especially Web-based publication.

In some areas of digital publishing, traditional methods of disguising student names will continue to serve scholars. Quotes from textual products—email, essays, and MOO projects (in which students might choose fictitious identities)—adapt themselves well to traditional research methods. However, Web and other multimedia projects often include information within them that stymies attempts at anonymity. In teaching Web page design, for instance, we encourage students to include links to their email addresses; often such pages also include pictures of the students themselves, their families, or other images that are immediately identifiable. In essence, the very rules that govern a well-designed Web page increase the difficulties inherent in writing research citation. Although "concerns about the right to privacy have evolved and grown" (Finemel, 2003, p. 3), legal precedents have lagged significantly behind the capabilities of digital communication, and the result is considerable confusion about what information can be used, who may use it, and who ultimately controls multimedia products.

At most institutions, human subjects research is reviewed and regulated by an Institutional Review Board, and most boards require that researchers preserve participant anonymity when reporting on research (see Banks and Eble, this collection, for more on the review process). However, IRB regulations have yet to fully account for not only research in and on digital spaces, but also digital publishing, where intricately interwoven texts often comprise images, sound, and film clips, and where—in many cases—breaking down the digital text to protect anonymity damages, misrepresents, or radically alters the original text. Permission forms were likewise designed for hard-copy print texts, which begs the question of subjects' ability to give fully informed consent to research their work. To be effective in the future, consent forms must be designed to cover the intended scope of use across media. For potential participants to be able to give informed consent, researchers should routinely include language that delineates book, journal, and Web-based publications; online databases where the work might be archived; and whether, for example, their visual or textual work might be altered by multimedia applications (e.g., animated, soundtracked, incorporated into a collage).

But even as increasing levels of specificity within research methodologies attempt to close gaps in subjects' ability to give informed consent, scholars cannot anticipate or predict with any degree of reliability how such work will be used once it is released to the Web, or what possible uses it might be made to serve. Because eventual ownership of the product of research is still in question, researchers cannot promise writers that their work will not be borrowed, cut, pasted, or re-presented; they may be able to keep the promises of anonymity, but can make no promises about accurate representation. The possibility of a writer's work being taken completely out of context or used for purposes other than originally intended—and originally covered by permission—lends a degree of uncertainty that should be of concern for researchers, for such uncertainties may pose problems we are as yet unable to visualize.

"Picturing Work: Visual Projects in the Writing Classroom" provides a case in point; Virginia Kuhn (2005) used two illustrations (Figures 14.1 and 14.2) to demonstrate student work responding to an assignment that:

asked the students to uncover cultural identity groups to which they
belonged, to ascertain which of these were forced on them by society
and which were of their own making or influence. Then, they had to
think of a moment in which their various identities were at odds. For
example, if one was a Catholic but in favor of gay marriage, that would
be a tough conflict. (n.p.)

FIGURE 14.1. Student work from Kuhn
(2005); captioned in original as "Student
images created in Photoshop"

FIGURE 14.2. Student work from Kuhn
(2005); captioned in original as "Student
project entitled 'Jesus of Nazareth,
Carpenter, Healer, Savior, Sporting the
new line of GAP Carpenter Jeans.'"

A student generated his "Christ/Gap" photos by manipulating two different images and blending them. The images represented, for him, a clash between conflicting cultural imperatives. Placed into this context, the student's meaning is clear and readers understand the images within the context of course work meeting a particular goal. To use Kuhn's (and the student's) product for my purposes here, I right-clicked the images in the article, saved them to my computer's hard drive, and submitted them with this chapter. Prior to doing so, I contacted Kuhn via email, asking her to acquire permission from the individual student and to provide me with contextual information concerning her assignment and the student's interpretation of it. However, the nature of Web-based publication does not require such attention to detail. I could have downloaded these images without permission and subsequently used them for my own purposes. It would not be difficult to imagine a scenario in which someone downloaded these images and self-published a Web page using these very same images to depict the degeneration of religious reverence in college students as a direct reflection of XYZ College and its instructors. The original caption of Figure 14.2 read: "Student project entitled 'Jesus of Nazareth, Carpenter, Healer, Savior, Sporting the new line of GAP Carpenter Jeans.'" And, as Kuhn explained in her article, "the student successfully showed the unholy alliance between religion and capitalism" (Kuhn, 2005, n.p.). Without the caption and Kuhn's corresponding explanation, one can imagine how easily a student's work can be completely decontextualized and made to serve purposes far from the original intention.

Issues of Intellectual Property

Similar problems exist when we think about the issue of intellectual property—and, especially, copyright—as they apply to our research when it appears as digital writing. Digitally published material has the potential to add several layers of complexity to questions of ownership, which copyright laws have yet to adequately address. Current copyright protection extends to protect "original works of authorship fixed in any tangible medium of expression, now known or later developed, from which they can be perceived, reproduced, or otherwise communicated, either directly or with the aid of a machine or device" (Hefter & Litowitz, 1999, n.p.).

Thus, even if students have petitioned for and received permission to use copyrighted material (which extends to protect work ranging from software to songs, and from text to collages) in their educational projects, that permission does not extend to the researcher who wishes to cite from the student project. Further, acquiring copyright permission, especially for pop-ular music and film, is incredibly difficult and can take weeks if not months of research and legal wrangling to address questions including: Who is truly the copyright holder? Who can officially provide permission? Finding and asking for permission from the original proprietor can add countless hours to a conscientious researcher's workload, and can delay or limit publication of important research data and conclusions. Decisions on whether and when to petition for permission have also become more complicated. If a student has captured a Web image, then altered it to fit a particular project, is that image still the intellectual property of its original creator, or does its altered form now "belong" to the student? Copyright law states that *only the form* of intellectual property—and not ideas or content—is copy-rightable. If students have altered the meaning by altering the form, such significantly altered versions may no longer "belong" to the original cre-ator. As such, researchers need permission only from the student; but with-out a clear definition of "significant," potential work exists in limbo, and must be decided on a case-by-case basis. M. Ethan Katsh (2001) pointed to the dilemma of digitally downloadable and editable material in stating that:

> new media are revolutionizing the means of producing works and, more slowly, changing the form in which works appear. While the copying capability of new media is widely recognized, we will only slowly become aware of the proliferation of new creative, artistic and literary forms. (qtd. in Randall, 2001, pp. 267–268)

Copy-and-paste, text- and image-editing, and other software capabilities have significantly altered traditional writing and citation methods, and researchers have yet to take such methods fully into account when dealing with Web projects and publications.

Modern copyright law draws its language and conceptualization from pre-existing property laws, and often researchers follow that lead. As a con-sequence, copyright law favors the tangible (print) version of a text, empha-sizing rights to print, distribute, perform, and generate derivative works within specified time limits. Advancing computer and Web technologies have stretched this tangibility and time limit to its breaking point. Multimedia published work may *never* appear in "tangible" form as it has traditionally been defined. Web-based multimedia, electronic and ethereal in form, can be read from the computer screen, needing no printing for it to be consumed. This aspect of copyright law has impact upon our rights to our published work and its subsequent re-publication. Most print jour-nals will revert the rights pertaining to a published article to its author after a certain amount of time has passed; others will allow reprinting for a fee. As our research articles are placed within large-scale hosting databases, like EBSCO and JSTOR, the rights that belong to the author are ambiguous at best. Once published research has been placed in a large database, it is theoretically available forever; thus the hosting company has a vested interest in retaining the rights to exclusive publication, which may or may not be in the best interests of the original author.

Leslie Ellen Harris (1998) explored how such digital property might be viewed in the coming years, equating digital writing with the latest real estate boom:

> In terms of new media, I believe that the prices are low, sometimes nonexistent (that is, the content of the new media is accessible by the public for free), but we are on an upward trend. Now is the time to comprehend the economy of the twenty-first century and be prepared for it. . . . Understand the currency of the next century, and you'll be positioned to gain from it. (p. vii)

Her text applies more to for-profit Web-based writing, but its implications are still of importance to researchers as more of their work is synthesized into online databases. Although these metacollections of research offer researchers ready access to scholarly work that might have otherwise been difficult or impossible to obtain, they do not do so without a price to libraries and other subscribers—they are profiting from work produced by university professors and others who will gain nothing from the re-presentation in royalties. Databases and digital archives do not, admittedly, typically distort or otherwise alter work stored on servers. The original author's rights in this case are, however, unclear, and thus authors of academic research and publishers of academic journals will need to clarify original authors' rights—especially when we consider that, traditionally, when an author releases a manuscript for publication, the author transfers the copyright ownership to the journal, who may, in today's world, be linked to larger publishing entities who sell distribution rights to databases and archives.

Issues of Fair Use and Citation Practices

By definition, digital media encourage convergence—of audio, video, and other digital media, woven together across interfaces and networks. Technology also allows both student writers and authors of original research to capture and use images, sound, and video clips from the Web and incorporate them into unique expression. In doing so, students may, and often do, borrow and alter the work of others, thus entering a still hotly contested and undecided area of fair use rights and citation practices. How much alteration of a borrowed image must occur before that image becomes the new product of its creator? If a writer borrows a sound clip from a musical artist and uses it to enhance images and text either borrowed from elsewhere or original to the author, at what point does the recombination constitute a new product? At what point does an entire multimedia project, composed of a variety of media pieces—some original and some the work of others—become something new?

Madeleine Sorapure's (2003) "Five Principles of New Media: Or, Playing Lev Manovich" illustrates issues of fair use and citation that need clarification if we are to proceed along lines of multimedia research. Within her article, Sorapure included "Apprehensions," student Simone Polgar's submission for a course assignment. The film clip, with its sound and artwork, skirts these issues. She uses original artwork by Djuna Barnes, excerpts from Barnes's text, *Nightwood,* and a sound clip from published and copyright-protected music to create an "original" film clip of her own. I insert quotation marks around the word original, because one could argue that Polgar has actually created nothing original: Her own contribution was to juxtapose and animate the work of two other author/artists. However, one could just as easily argue that although some might consider her contribution minor—or merely technical—she has in fact created a new, different, and original form of art that transcends its component parts based upon the legal definitions of intellectual property mentioned above.

In addition to the murky issue of alteration, students may not perceive Web-based publications in the same light as traditional, text-based, copyright-protected material. Students, many of whom have grown up with the World Wide Web, often do not recognize material they gather from the information superhighway as the exclusive intellectual property of another. Traditional methods of citation and practices of fair use, created for print media, have little concrete meaning for Web sources. Which Web images, sound, and video are freely available for reproduction and which require permission from the proprietor? If a student captures an image from the Web and proceeds to alter it significantly for use in a digital project, as did Polgar, how does that alteration affect the need for permissions for Sorapure's research? How much alteration might be considered significant? Depending on how Polgar delivered her assignment, she may not have needed permission to use the text, sound clip, and images—fair use would allow her to use all three, as long as it had limited distribution and was not published outside of the course. However, Sorapure's research is readily available on the Web, and thus may require additional permissions and copyright releases. One can speculate that *Kairos*, a journal that receives no profit from its publication, should fall within the purview of fair use—it is, after all, produced for educational and intellectual means, but it is, nonetheless, readily available to the public sector, and could conceivably interfere with the profits of the original artists on some level. What rights do the original artists, the student, and the researcher retain? Assuming that permissions are obtained by both the student and the researcher, who grants permission for reproduction of the researched work—the author or the online journal?

Traditionally, teachers and researchers have routinely made "free use of educational materials by educational institutions" (Litman, 2001, p. 180), but copyright law revision has now classified "this non-commercial use . . . as 'large scale interference' with copyright holders' commercial opportunities" (p. 180). Web publication that relies upon such student work must confront the increasingly more complex possibility that evidence crucial to their research—multimedia projects in which images, sound, or film clips have been borrowed, altered, or incorporated from other proprietors—may involve them unwittingly in acts of copyright infringement. Consider the case study included as part of Karla Kitalong's (1998) article mentioned earlier. A student was assigned the task of writing a Web page as a part of his course work. He "downloaded Craig's HTML source code and made minor changes, mainly to remove direct references to Craig. Next, Dave published this copied and edited home page on the Web to fulfill [the] assignment" (p. 253). How much of this download must Dave change for his assignment to be "original?" In this instance, Craig felt that he had been plagiarized, and contacted Dave's instructor. Could Dave have initiated the same download and have escaped allegations of plagiarism if he had asked Craig's permission before, instead of after, he had done so? Did Dave fulfill the assignment parameters, which Kitalong cites as "learn to use HTML?" The original case of plagiarism aside, if Dave's instructor wishes to use that page as part of his research, should he obtain permission from Craig as the original proprietor, Dave as the adaptive compositor, or both?

Marilyn Randall (2001) placed questions of authorship within the context of postmodernism and situated it in terms of appropriation:

> Postmodern appropriative artists and the proponents of the "freedom" of electronic "information" are relatively unconcerned with "originality," or even with notions of propriety or integrity with respect to the

> use of intellectual property; they are, however, much concerned with
> the economic value of this property . . . . (p. 268)

Randall proposed that in the future, questions of ownership will take precedence over questions of authorship, and that "the propriety over intellectual products will not survive the onslaught of technology" (p. 269). Electronic
forms of publication have generated a new form and genre of art, that of
the appropriative artist, whose talent is based in technology—the ability to
capture borrowed material and reshape/re-present it in a new form and
context. The new product's ownership thus reverts to the new proprietor.
Dave's "borrowing" of code, as Kitalong (1998) described it, falls into a gray
area. In Randall's view, Dave is an appropriative artist (or may be) and Craig
would retain no rights to his page. How this view impacts a researcher's
citation is unclear. This same ambiguity reflects upon our Web-published
research. How much of Kuhn's (2005) or Sorapure's (2003) article can a
subsequent researcher borrow or redesign for use in her own work?

CONCLUSIONS

How any of these issues will eventually affect our most present concerns—
citation, fair use, and copyright as it affects our teaching and research—is
anyone's guess. Yet our function as researchers demands decisions *now*,
even though we cannot predict with any reliability what effect such decisions may have. In making our choices, circumstances force us to rely on
past—and perhaps antiquated—traditions. As educators, we rely upon the
goodwill of authors in promoting education, critique, and citation. Fair use
has traditionally covered hard-copy, print texts used for teaching purposes
within an admittedly limited scope. It has also traditionally permitted the
use of "timely" material (also with limitations of scope). The same has
often held true for appropriately cited use of such material by researchers
contributing to the available store of knowledge within a discipline, but
such traditional interpretations are subject to change as multimedia writing
gains status in the world of published research. Therefore, although
recourse to fair use may still apply to materials for use in teaching, it seems
clear that it remains insufficient for publication.

Martha Woodmansee (in Jazri, 1994) noted that "electronic technology
is playing a crucial role in promoting writing practices in which the identities of individual contributors to shared dynamic texts are de[-]empha-

sized, and their useful contributions effectively merged" (p. 2). As a direct result of these issues, Web authors—presently writing and publishing between the lines of current copyright laws—have added either copyright language or Creative Commons licensure to their texts that explicitly state the conditions under which their work may be copied and used. An endnote in Sybil Finemel's (2003) essay, for instance, noted that:

> Copyright of Library Media Connection is the property of Linworth Publishing, Inc. and its content may not be copied or e-mailed to multiple sites or posted to a listserv without the copyright holder's express written permission. However, users may print, download, or e-mail articles for individual use. (p. 3)

Such language makes clear under what condition infringement is actionable. On the Web site from which their conference presentations are linked, Sachs and Winther's (1998) noted:

> Permission is granted for reproduction of this document, in whole or in part, for only educational or non-commercial use provided the authors are duly cited and acknowledged by name. Permission is not granted for use as inclusion into any other publication intended for sale and content can not be remarketed without the author's written permission. (n.p.)

As researchers and Web publishers, the only protections we can maintain for ourselves and promise to research subjects are those that we specifically detail within the publication itself. Thus, if we want to protect research subjects' work that we include in our publications from potential misuse by others, we will need to detail that such work can only be cited for educational and noncommercial purposes, or that permission to cite research subjects' examples is expressly forbidden. In our teaching, if we want students to understand the nature of intellectual property (and want to simplify our later use of multimedia projects in our published research), we must include in their multimedia writing education the appropriate use of others' materials and the ethical imperatives that must guide appropriate use.

The path of digital publishing opens up the potential for wider audiences, extended possibilities, and swifter publication of scholarly journals at significantly lower costs, but such promise does not come without a price. Multimedia publishing requires a significant rethinking of issues of privacy, intellectual property, fair use, and citation practices in an often deceptively open environment. The original checks and balances scholars have used to protect research participants' privacy and the ethical integrity of their own research are no longer sufficient. Ethical integrity requires that participants be informed of potential Web publication of their work, and educators must realize more concretely than they have to date the implications of multimedia publication so that their rights and those of research participants can be sufficiently protected. Potential Web publishers must take the nature of multimedia into account in devising methods for protecting privacy and safeguarding writers' work. And those of us who work with technology as a major portion of our research need to become more forward thinking. To date, we have been *reacting* to technological innovation. To truly succeed, we need to take a more proactive approach to multimedia researching and publishing, and try to predict sites of potential problems before they occur.

PART FIVE

*Researching the
Research Process
and Research Reports*

15

WHOSE RESEARCH IS IT, ANYWAY?

THE CHALLENGE OF DEPLOYING FEMINIST METHODOLOGY IN TECHNOLOGICAL SPACES

Kristine Blair

Christine Tulley

In this chapter, we describe a qualitative project begun in 1999 where we applied several of the American Association of University Women's recommendations for increasing technological equity through the creation of an after-school computer group for 10 adolescent girls. Our collaborative research relationship initially evolved out of a joint desire to discover what impact the growing movements of cyberfeminism had on the literacy practices of young adolescent females, but has grown to examine a variety of ways that feminist scholars investigate and then write about technofeminist literacy practices. Here we describe the questions that have arisen consistently throughout our research project when we attempt to align feminism, technology, and methodology: What is "acceptable" research methodology? What does feminist research and dissertation advising look like? How can we use opportunities for digital writing research to redefine authorial constructs that continue to privilege single- and first-authored work? After exploring these questions and the ways that they manifest, we describe ways digital writing researchers can align themselves with theories and practices that call for increased multimedia and multivocal delivery of and access to scholarship that will foster a broader definition of research, authorship, and ownership.

INTRODUCTION

Publications by the American Association of University Women and others (AAUW, 2000; Cooper & Weaver, 2003; Kramarae, 2001) call for increased mentoring and support for girls and women in technological settings, pointing to a continued, gendered digital divide that privileges technology as male-dominated despite data that indicates that more and more women are learning, creating, and participating in digital spaces. In *Tech Savvy: Educating Girls in the New Computer Age*, AAUW noted a set of gender-related issues, including:

- Girls have clear and strong ideas about what kinds of games they would design: games that feature simulation, strategy, and interaction. These games, in fact, would appeal to a broad range of learners.
- Teacher training focuses on the technical properties of hardware; it does not emphasize educational applications or innovative uses of computing for each subject area.
- When women, who make up half the workforce, account for only 20% of those with information technology credentials, it is a clear sign that we have to make computers and technology relevant across the job market to nontraditional users.

Importantly, the organization also called for some specific remedies to these problems, including recommendations to:

- Promote gender-neutral software that engages a broad range of learners, including both boys and girls, and students who don't identify with the "computer nerd" stereotype.
- Prepare tech-savvy teachers: Professional development for teachers needs to emphasize more than the use of the computer as a productivity tool. It must give teachers enough understanding of how computer technology works and its basic concepts so that they are empowered users.
- Educate girls to be designers, not just users: Educators and parents should help girls imagine themselves early in life as designers and producers of new technology. Engage girls in "tinkering" activities that can stimulate deeper interest in technology and provide opportunities for girls to express their technological imaginations.

- Set a new standard for gender equity: The new benchmark for gender equity should emphasize computer fluency: girls' mastery of analytical skills, computer concepts, and their ability to imagine innovative uses for technology across a range of problems and subjects.

These goals mesh well with the goals of feminist technorhetoricians (e.g., Hawisher & Sullivan, 1998; Takayoshi, Huot, & Huot, 1999). Further, it is the nature of electronic, networked spaces themselves that may well mesh with feminist goals of identity, agency, and community.

We have been fortunate to collaborate on feminist teaching and research projects much like those advocated above, stemming from a qualitative project begun in 1999 where we applied several of the AAUW's recommendations for increasing technological equity through the creation of an after-school computer group for 10 adolescent girls attending Bowling Green Junior High School in Northwest Ohio. Our collaborative research relationship initially stemmed out of a joint desire to discover what impact cyberfeminism had on the literacy practices of young adolescent females, but has grown to examine a variety of ways that feminist scholars investigate and then write about technofeminist literacy practices. After collaborating together for over 6 years, we have confronted a range of issues regarding the potential for feminist methodology in researching digital spaces, and this chapter draws on our story as a way to highlight the issues and implications facing technofeminist researchers.

As a result of researching and reporting on our projects, specific questions related to the alignment of feminism, technology, and methodology repeatedly emerged no matter what specific angle we investigated, including:

- What is "acceptable" research methodology?
- What does feminist research and dissertation advising look like?
- How can we use opportunities for digital writing research to redefine authorial constructs that continue to privilege single, first-authored work?

Although we don't provide definitive answers in this chapter, we do illustrate what our collaboration experiences mean for other digital writing researchers who attempt similar research projects, and why these questions serve as useful starting points for investigation. We stress that digital writing researchers need to align themselves with theories and practices that call for increased multimedia and multivocal delivery of and access to scholarship that will inevitably foster broader definitions of research,

authorship, and ownership. As part of this process, we must simultaneously acknowledge the gender politics that continue to complicate the digital
literacy acquisition of girls and women as well as the need for continued—
but more varied—research methods and media distribution to document
such literacy practices.

NEGOTIATING THE CONFLICT BETWEEN MENTORING AND "ACCEPTABLE" RESEARCH METHODOLOGY

Part of the problem with women learning, researching, and composing
online is the question of how such activities are valued and what ethical
questions arise when women use digital spaces for academic projects.
Unlike the more traditional academic presses and their singular, print-ori-
ented, linear approach to research, electronic projects are often more fluid,
with fewer discrete boundaries. Further, we might argue that digital projects and contexts for research foster—in a way different from print-
anchored projects—the ability to create a broader sense of community and
more nuanced notions of collaboration as part of the research process.
Much of the AAUW's call relies on feminist pedagogical principles of collaboration, which are consistent with the following breakdown from Shulamit
Rheinharz's (1992) *Feminist Methods in Social Research*:

- feminist research aims to create social change;
- feminist research strives to represent human diversity;
- feminism is a perspective, not a research method; and
- feminist research frequently includes the researcher as a person.

These goals of feminist research and the research methodologies available
to feminist scholars in digital settings foster deeper collaboration among
researchers—and among researchers and subjects. More traditional definitions of research do not acknowledge either the theoretical or practical possibilities of conducting feminist research in digitally mediated spaces.

Feminist Practices of Collaboration: Complicating Research Relationships

One of our projects involved women teachers and adolescent females in
an after-school computer group in which one researcher (a faculty mem-

ber) actively and co-equally collaborated with a doctoral student on her dissertation research. Our collaboration as dissertation director and advisee began rather traditionally. As a doctoral candidate in Rhetoric and Writing at Bowling Green State University, Christine Tulley was enrolled in several of Kris Blair's doctoral seminars, including courses in rhetoric and writing research and computer-mediated writing theory and practice. Given Chris's interests in both technology and women's studies, Kris, being the only computers and writing specialist in the rhetoric and writing program, was a natural choice as a dissertation director for a project on the impact of a computer group on the technological attitudes of middle school girls (Haas, Tulley, & Blair, 2002; Tulley & Blair, 2002). Such a research project fits with the AAUW (2000) call to develop electronic forums in which girls and women can experiment with digital literacies in supportive, nonthreatening spaces. One such space is, of course, the Web, especially in light of the "cybergrrl" movement that was evolving at the time of our initial study; cybergrrl sites included Cybergrrl, Chickclick, and print resources such as Carla Sinclair's (1996) *NetChick* and Laurel Gilbert and Crystal Kyles' (1996) *Surfer Grrls*. In contrast to the views of the Web as alienating toward women, these resources affirmed the rights of girls to develop more liberating digital, networked social spaces. Chris was thus interested in the impact of these sites on adolescent girls, having spent 3 years as a middle school teacher in a Catholic school in Cleveland and having seen many gender inequities related to use of and attitudes toward computerized technologies.

Similarly, Kris Blair was looking to undertake a feminist project in which teaching girls and women to use technology fit with her emphasis on the politics of technological literacy acquisition, particularly the role of literacy narratives as a research methodology both for subverting more negative attitudes about computing on the part of less technologically savvy students and for using Web-based literacy narratives as a form of digital skill building. In this sense, despite the potential and admittedly inescapable hierarchies of our initial working relationship (i.e., advisee and faculty), there was a clear feminist goal in mind, consistent not only with Rheinharz (1992) and the AAUW, but also with Gesa Kirsch's (1999) observation that concern for women is tied to the sort of ethical consideration not typically foregrounded in objective research. Our concerns reflected educational philosophies that foreground collaboration and inclusion consistent both with Composition Studies' stance toward technological literacy acquisition (Hawisher, Selfe, Moraski, & Pearson, 2004; Selfe, 1999a) and with feminist research methodology itself. As Kirsch further noted, one way feminist researchers can write for audiences who can potentially benefit from our research is to "collaborate with participants, to ask them to help us shape the research questions we pose and interpret the data we gather, and to co-author the reports we publish" (p. xiv).

Literacy Narratives and/as Multivocal Texts

Given the political and ideological conditions that both help and hinder such feminist technological agendas within the academy, we collaborated in hopes of creating a space that would allow the 10 adolescent girls we worked with after school one day a week for 3 months a chance to share their stories through literacy narratives. We collected the Web sites we were having them create, conducted follow-up interviews, and also collected images throughout the study. Our plan was to incorporate as much of this work into the dissertation as possible in an attempt to give participants co-equal status. Yet as Kirsch (1999) cautioned, the potential for multivocal texts does not necessarily

> make explicit our values as scholars, our goals for the research we con-
> duct, and the effects we hope to achieve. . . . We need to acknowledge
> these motivations . . . in the sense that notions of "empowerment" still
> place in a position of authority the researcher or teacher who suppos-
> edly knows what it means to be empowered. (p. 85)

Still, there are several examples of multivocal texts published as a result of technological literacy research, notably Katrina Powell and Pamela Takayoshi (2003); Takayoshi, Emily Huot, and Meghan Huot (1999); and more recently Hawisher et al. (2004), where voices of researcher and sub-ject—or, in the case of Powell and Takayoshi, simultaneously co-investiga-tors as well as dissertation advisee and dissertation committee member—help to foster a postmodern representation and interpretation of research consistent with a feminist methodology.

Despite the potential of these and other texts to be inclusive and to allow both researchers and subjects to situate themselves and their moti-vations, Kirsch (1999) acknowledged the limitations of multivocal texts in helping scholars to "come to terms with interpretive responsibility" and to make an impact on readers of our research, particularly when we are con-strained by traditional genres such as the research article or the disserta-tion. Moreover, we began to discover that our own goals were as much about creating community and a digital safe haven as they were about measuring improvement of adolescent girls' attitudes toward technology or their technological skills sets (perhaps something we never really fully acknowledged to ourselves). We also discovered that despite the fact that we were an all-female dissertation committee committed to feminist methods, there were clear differences in what we considered to constitute objective, valid empirical research, ultimately limiting how Chris was able to report the study in her dissertation.

METHODOLOGICAL LIMITATIONS

Finding female participants willing to engage in a technology camp was a key concern for both researchers. We both worked on the Institutional Review Board approval process to solicit participants at the local junior high school. Chris distributed notices to female junior high students, and we recruited 10 participants, 7 of whom were friends with another faculty member's daughter, adding another layer of comfort and collaboration to our study. Myra Sadker and David Sadker (1994) noted that girls often enjoy computing in "friendship circles" and this ready-made friendship circle ensured that they would help each other to attend sessions regularly and to complete projects. The faculty member's daughter was also familiar with both of us, may have felt comfortable working with us, and thus may have conveyed that attitude to her friends. The study was limited by regional restraints, and our sample population was composed of white, middle-class junior high females, many with family members who worked at the university as faculty or staff. The girls were familiar with the university and comfortable walking to it from the junior high.

Another factor affecting the outcome of the study was the amount of technological knowledge the girls already possessed and felt comfortable using. Several participants knew how to alter graphics in Adobe Photoshop or how to insert backgrounds in Web pages. These more-experienced participants often helped each other with technical aspects when the two of us were busy working with others. The fact that a number of the girls were technologically literate helped to create a sense of shared expertise. As a result, some participants took leadership roles in the classroom, which also may have changed how the study participants viewed us as techno role models and responded to us. Because there was no grade involved, participants may have also tended to view us as co-investigators rather than teachers, and they frequently turned to their experienced peers rather than us when given the option. Clearly, they did not fit the profile of the techno-phobic adolescent female our study was intended to help.

Regardless of these methodological limitations, the goal of our research was to bring together a community of girls who wanted to use technology on their own terms, even if it meant in ways that contradicted our initial research hypotheses about the benefits of the Web for girls and women. Despite that those terms were more consistent with the value systems of white, middle-class girls who wanted to browse the Abercrombie and Fitch Web site to download pictures of blond male models, or despite the day when all of the girls went to the site hamsterdance.com just to have all the computers simultaneously play the theme song, we nonetheless were able to help this particular population become more critically aware of the possibilities and constraints of technology in self-representation and community building. As Takayoshi et al. (1999) put it, the "Web is a productive venue for girls' self expression because writing Web space is a two-fold act: It gives girls a place for self-expression while intimately involving them in the workings of technology" (p. 104), with the goal of equipping participants to be technology critics (Selfe, 1999a) as they increasingly use technology in their personal, professional, and academic lives.

Explaining their research methodology and reporting their process, Hawisher et al. (2004) contended that "we feature these women and their stories because they resonate with parts of our own stories . . . the ways in which they have learned to use and cope with technology . . . and the literacies they share with us" (p. 646). Moreover, this approach, as Hawisher and Selfe and other qualitative researchers have suggested, "will also help readers further appreciate the importance of situating technological literacy in specific cultural, material, educational, historical, and familial contexts" (p. 646). Ironically, although Chris's committee members had little problem with the inclusion of the narratives of student participants—formatted in ways similar to Hawisher et al. (2004) and also Takayoshi et al. (1999)—our own voices as researchers and collaborators were muted by a move toward a presumably more objective methodology by both the standard dissertation format and one particular committee member. Certainly, there is some rationale for this; Kirsch (1999) suggested that an overemphasis on the "authorial I" may lead to self-indulgence and the silencing of other voices. As Kirsch contended, however, it is the acknowledgement of the personal, of the narratives of researchers and subjects that leads to "new and unexpected insights, for revealing researchers' motivations . . . and for genuinely reinvigorating certain academic disciplines" (p. 77).

THE PRINT-ORIENTED, TRADITIONAL DISSERTATION AS A DISRUPTIVE FORCE TO TECHNOFEMINIST RESEARCH

The use of digital media, particularly audio and video, increases the ability to create a richer understanding of context and presentation of data. In addition to the problems with methodology, we also felt that the project could not be fully and accurately represented by a print-based format such as a dissertation. As Jude Edminster and Joe Moxley (2002) noted, "across the disciplines, the traditional print dissertation fails to acknowledge or address . . . a dramatic transformation of representational alternatives and resources that is taking place in the construction of knowledge" (p. 96). Our project would have lent itself well to representation in a digital format, where links to the girls' actual pages could be inserted in a hypertext dissertation. Because digital dissertations are not yet valued in the academy, and print-based dissertations remain the privileged format, this problem had to be handled by including screen captures of representative portions of a few participants' pages. Space limitations restricted inclusion of a participant's full Web project. And even if a full project was included, the project would have been represented in a linear fashion, rather than in a hypertextual one. Although there were limited uses at the time Chris completed her project, electronic theses and dissertation initiatives through the National Digital Library of Theses and Dissertations (NDLTD), along with the increasing number of online journals able to support new media, create new possibilities for reporting our results in ways that disrupt the hierarchies of traditional print authorship, including the presumption of objectivity that guided Chris's ability to tell our story and the stories of participants. It is increasingly vital that technofeminist researchers continually push for processes that allow for increased digital data collection, representation, and interpretation in a context where the print dissertation, article, and book continue to maintain their benchmark status.

What we discovered through the initial project of collaborative research was that despite the culmination of the print dissertation (the continued coin of the realm and often the precursor to the single-authored book), the reliance on this genre marginalized the voices and identities of female participants who represented themselves in digital form. This genre also re-inscribed teacher and student hierarchies between the dissertation director and advisee, because Chris was unable in the dissertation genre to articulate the feminist ideology and methodology driving our collaborative digital research because of the insistence by other committee members and, by association, the academy, on the traditional "methodology chapter," which was to emphasize what Chris, the dissertation writer, had done *vis-à-vis* the project. From the initial human subjects review to the final production of the dissertation, both ideology and university policy about what constitutes acceptable and ethical research methodology hindered our work as feminist technorhetoricians. Nevertheless, because our own ideology of creating feminist technological communities was and is a vital part of our research and because we assume that it is our ethical responsibility to serve as technological mentors, our agenda is consistent with Rheinharz's (1992) emphasis on social change, human diversity, feminism as "perspective," and the roles of feminist researchers as participants. We integrated all of these concerns into our initial study.

The dilemma that emerged once the study was completed and writing was underway involved how to address the fact that although the project was a collaborative effort, the dissertation had to be funneled into a single-authored work, based on results Chris, and Chris only, found in the study. Although we considered the study "ours"—meaning the two of us and the participants collectively "owned" our project—limitations on what was considered appropriate authorship silenced these voices, despite our intentions to include participants' voices through all steps of the Web site creation process as a way to provide agency through methodology. Not surprisingly, the print-based dissertation format does not lend itself to acknowledging these types of contributions other than noting these on the acknowledgements page, or perhaps in the literature review. As a result, the two portions of Chris' dissertation that were the most problematic to construct were the "methodology" and "results." Inevitably, problems stemmed from the fact that this was a feminist and technological project framed by theoretical approaches that presume a collaborative as opposed to a hierarchical model.

Because much of the study was grounded in the AAUW's findings that girls are shortchanged when it comes to technology, the main focus of the dissertation was a feminist one, and both the project and the dissertation aimed to manifest first and foremost the feminist research behind the project. One main problem of conducting feminist research occurred during the writing of the dissertation. As with any dissertation, there were committee members coming from areas that overlapped, but were not always congruent (digital studies, communication studies, women's studies, and English Education). This potential divide became particularly evident when feedback was given on the methodology and findings chapters. Although Kris (the digital studies member) and the women's studies member were often in agreement about the content, the English Education faculty member, schooled in more traditional research methods, was uncomfortable with the feminist approach and technique of the study. These problems were compounded by the fact that the subject of the dissertation was technologically focused. Although both of the other faculty members were somewhat familiar with the AAUW findings, neither faculty member had as extensive a knowledge of the current cybergrrl phenomenon, or a background in digital studies research. Kris had a unique perspective because she was familiar with both of these areas, but as a co-investigator, she had knowledge about study participants that the other two members did not. This difference in knowledge and approach complicated many of the chapter comments by committee members, as, occasionally, all three faculty members would disagree on the angle or approach the dissertation should take. Chris, feeling under pressure for a "passing" dissertation defense, had to accommodate all three agendas.

Inevitably, the problems we encountered were a direct result of our feminist approach. Because "feminism is a perspective, and not a research method" (Reinharz, 1992), it was initially difficult to label the methodology used, particularly when Chris began writing up the traditional methodology chapter. The English Education faculty member wanted to classify the research into commonly understood categories: Was our project a case study? Field research? An ethnographic study? The study served as a blend of these categories, particularly because it had elements of all three of these strategies and no one strategy was dominant, though they all could be classified as qualitative methodologies to some extent. The technological focus further complicated the discussion of how methodology should be handled because the study was also grounded in English Education with goals that are not always congruent with technological agendas. For example, the study made recommendations on why junior high teachers should incorporate cybergrrl pages into the English language arts classroom. But because the study had a larger focus on a feminist technological agenda, it seemed reductive to use an educational framework when a feminist one was more appropriate. It seemed unethical to use one approach to research but another more privileged one to actually write it up.

Both the women's studies faculty member and Kris were in agreement that a feminist research methodology best served the study and the dissertation, but the English Education faculty member still wanted revisions to reflect a more formalized qualitative study that privileged an educational methodology over a feminist one. Because this divide was partly political and partly ideological (regarding what constitutes "real research"), Chris ended up with a compromise in the methodology chapter; the dissertation as a whole reflected technofeminist research, but the methodology chapter modeled a standard educational pedagogy research project.

If the dissertation had not been limited in the scope and focus in the methodology section, the study would have been better represented by a more cohesive feminist methodology. And if we adapted Rheinharz's (1992) four goals of feminist research, the goals would have been the guiding focus points in both the study design and the reporting of findings. Because the study itself was a feminist project, we needed to measure our study based on these goals, not other methodological categories that existed for other studies in education not construed as feminist. This breakdown between the goals and practice of the study and the scholarly outcome indicates a serious gap in what is considered feminist and ethical research, while highlighting the need for discussions of projects that do not fit the standard dissertation format.

Despite the challenges and limitations we faced, the four goals of feminist methodology were met to varying extents. First, the study did aim to create social change on a small scale. Participants created Web pages that addressed what they felt were the most important aspects of their lives. These findings could be applied to larger studies in the junior high language arts classroom, which is what the dissertation ultimately concluded. However, the one concern of the English Education faculty member that Chris felt was right on target was the ultimate goal of the project. Although both of us wanted to introduce girls to cybergrrl Web pages and then have them make their own, our goals probably weren't as clearly defined as specified outcomes, something that happened in our later presentations and publications of the project results. Rather, we wanted to "see" what would happen when we created a community and a safe technological haven for girls. We speculated that an improvement of adolescent girls' attitudes toward technology or their technological skills sets were potential outcomes, but did not privilege these as major goals of the study (though the study was initially designed to study these factors). The English Education faculty member would have preferred a clearly defined goal was set (i.e., "skills 1 and 2 will translate into the English language arts classroom"). Feminist methodology allows for open-ended outcomes, particularly social change, and we felt the study created social change on a small scale, as many participants continued to work on their Web sites after the study was completed.

Although this wasn't a major goal of the study, our project did aim to some extent to represent human diversity. The first phase of our project involved introducing participants to a range of cybergrrl Web pages. Many of these Web pages featured women of color and women representing a range of technological experiences. However, as Barbara Warnick (2002) and others have noted, many women involved in Web creation are often white women of privilege, who typically don't consider women who lack technological skill or access to the means and media of publishing in digital spaces. This potential lack of skills and access is a problem that probably should have been better addressed with study participants, especially when our own participants also reflected this privileged group. However, because this study was limited by geographical boundaries, we could not resolve the diversity issue.

Finally, the study included the researchers as persons, and this was probably the most successful area of our study. We not only taught participants how to make Web sites, but served as sounding boards for music and graphic selections. We knew about the girls' favorite sites and they knew about ours, and they were on a first-name basis with us in our attempts to dissolve the traditional teacher–student/researcher–subject hierarchy. Although some may argue that this closeness tampers with research integrity, in a feminist study this is often encouraged and is ethical and necessary. Much of the work done in feminist digital studies supports this closeness as well and encourages women to serve as techno role models for each other (Sherman, 1998). Study participants saw us enjoy using technology regularly, and we were excited about their Web pages when they shared them with us at various stages in class. This specifically addresses the AAUW's findings that girls often consider technology use isolated and "geeky." Our participants experienced computer work in a collaborative, supportive environment with us as facilitators, who, for better or worse, fit the late-20s, early-30s world of white feminist cyberspaces.

WHAT CONSTITUTES DIGITAL WRITING RESEARCH? THE POTENTIAL OF STORYTELLING AS EXTENDED METHOD

Our collaboration on this chapter conforms to what Margaret Ewing, Adrienne Hyde, Judith Kaufman, Diane Montgomery, and Patricia Self (1999), along with Frigga Haug (1987), have defined as "memory work," a process in which researchers "reject the privileging of distant, impersonal knowing" (p. 113) common to objective research methodologies. In this process, narrative plays a powerful role in that the focus on discrete memories that are unresolved or in need of review allows for a stronger understanding of the outcome of a research agenda. Since the completion of Chris's dissertation in 2001, we have written and presented on this project in numerous forums—twice at the Conference on College Composition and Communication, at the Feminism(s) and Rhetoric(s) conference, and in print venues as well. Each time, our presentations have been heavily grounded in our story of the qualitative study's limitations; because of our subjects, their existing technological knowledge, and our own position as white feminist researchers, we must critique standards of reliability, validity, and ethics, particularly in subject participation.

Because of our conflicted experiences with the initial study and report of results via the print dissertation, we have a stronger sense of what makes a feminist digital writing research project effective. By its design as a single-authored work, the dissertation represented Chris and her first public contribution to the scholarly community in technofeminist research, with, by necessity, minimal acknowledgement of Kris' presence as co-investigator. Freed from the dissertation-related institutional constraints, we have collaborated many times on technofeminist research projects. Although the course has been smoother in publications such as *Computers and Composition*, where collaboration is an accepted part of digital studies work, other institutional restraints remain. For example, the problem of the "first" (and thus most privileged) author prevails. This can be a potential problem for both of us, as one of us needs prominent publications for tenure and the other one needs the same publications for a promotion. We have shared the credit for projects and alternated first author status as solutions, but we need to do this based on outside reviews of our work by our institutions, and not the perceptions of the digital studies community, as there are many research teams who publish in both multivocal and multimedia formats. Ultimately, as feminist technorhetors and researchers, we also have the ethical responsibility of modeling our feminist goals of identity, agency, and community, and using publication venues that challenge institutional structures that constrain digital research collaborations. Because we encouraged collaboration and community among the junior high girls in our initial study, it would seem to conflict with our agenda and goals that we ultimately privilege the competitive nature of academic writing in our own work, even while sharing our digital research story of the continuing limits on employing and reporting the results of feminist methodologies in technological literacy research.

Despite the recognition and promotion of multivocal and multimodal literacy practices within our discipline's published scholarship, as a research and writing community we must extend this conversation beyond the supportive group of digital writing researchers, including those featured in this collection. Indeed, the privileging of monologic dissemination of research results continues to drive the dissertation writing and publication process, in addition to the support and reward structures for tenure and promotion. For these reasons, it is important that we "act locally" within our own graduate programs and academic units, challenging traditional ideological, methodological, and technological assumptions. Although we have focused on issues of methodology and collaboration, digital data collection and representation are becoming a common component of the graduate-level research methods course, and such components undoubtedly will better help to unify technology with theoretical and methodological frameworks for collaborative knowledge-making. For Edminster and Moxley (2002),

> as scholars who have traditionally written and published exclusively in text, we do not yet . . . perceive the need to take such developments into account in preparing graduate students in the profession. But as our practices of writing continue to undergo transformation through digital media, future scholars in all disciplines will require more specific training in the use of tools that allow them to effective present their research. (p. 102)

Certainly, the infusion of digital writing research into the graduate curriculum is a necessary starting point; however, it is equally vital that we educate colleagues about the impact of technology on data collection and representation, just as we have stressed the need to educate colleagues at the undergraduate level about the role of technology in the teaching of writing. With hope, our story indicates that such buy-in cannot be taken for granted and that even the developing opportunities for electronic submission of dissertations (as Bowling Green State University is piloting) requires strong advocacy on departmental dissertation committees as well as Institutional Review Boards about the continuing need to acknowledge the limits of the print dissertation as a research genre. In this way, digital writing research has the potential to disrupt traditional methodological biases and epistemologies of authorship and ownership among committee members and, as we hope our story suggests, between a dissertation director and advisee who have sustained a collaborative technofeminist research agenda as co-equal colleagues.

16

A REPORT FROM THE DIGITAL CONTACT ZONE

COLLABORATIVE RESEARCH AND THE HYBRIDIZING OF CULTURAL MINDSETS

Jacklyn Lopez

Joshua Burnett

Sally Chandler

In this chapter, we draw upon Mary Louise Pratt's (1991) characterization of contact zone dynamics as a means to examine how collaborative researchers with different technological mindsets interact. We first describe the differences in insider and newcomer mindsets and explore how these differences affect research processes. We include as examples experiences from and data gathered during a study we conducted that initially began as research into videogaming literacies, but evolved to focus on mindset dynamics and how they affect research processes. We conclude with a review of our findings and brief suggestions for how contact zone arts can support and enrich digital writing research.

INTRODUCTION

Autoethnography, transculturation, critique, collaboration, bilingualism, mediation, parody, denunciation, imaginary dialog, vernacular expression—these are some of the literate arts of the contact zone. Miscomprehension, incomprehension, dead letters, unread master-pieces, absolute heterogeneity of meaning—these are some of the per-ils of writing in the contact zone. They all live among us today in the transnationalized metropolis of the United States and are becoming more widely visible, more pressing, and . . . more decipherable to those who once would have ignored them in defense of a stable, cen-tered sense of knowledge and reality. (Pratt, 1991, p. 255)

In "Arts of the Contact Zone," Mary Louise Pratt (1991) described how stu-dents negotiate identity and influence in "social spaces where cultures meet, clash, and grapple with each other, often in contexts of highly asym-metrical relations of power" (p. 34). For more than a decade, her character-ization of contact zone dynamics has provided a theoretical base for under-standing the interplay of personality, ethnicity, and ideology in multicultur-al classrooms. The rise of digital technology has introduced a new dimen-sion of difference to the contact zone: difference in technological mindset, where mindset refers to the assumptions, values, and beliefs that underlie practices for conceptualizing, interpreting, and representing experience.

According to literacy researchers Colin Lankshear and Michele Knobel (2003), differences in technological mindset currently correlate with gener-ation or age. Members of the Internet generation, those we might charac-terize as *insiders*, inhabit digital mindsets. Insiders came of age with the Internet and learned literacy practices associated with online spaces and digital technologies as part of their primary socialization in communica-tion. In contrast, members of the print generation are *newcomers* to digital technologies. Due, in part, to the different experiences structured by mate-rial versus online spaces, newcomers typically conceptualize knowledge, value, identity, and relationships quite differently than insiders. Differences between newcomer and insider mindsets drive negotiations of power and meaning not only in the classroom, but also in research collaborations between individuals from different generations.

Pratt's (1991) work is particularly relevant to collaborative research in digital writing because at this point in time, the mindsets of those new to digital technologies remain institutionalized—so that the majority of aca-demic approaches to administration, pedagogy, and research privilege greater familiarity with print-based literacies and thus print-based meth-ods, assumptions, and values. This causes collaborations between new-comer faculty and insider graduate students, undergraduates, and younger colleagues to play out within asymmetrical power relations. In this chapter, we draw upon Pratt's characterization of contact zone dynamics as a means to examine how collaborative research partners with different tech-nological mindsets interact; that is, we consider how different generations seek to understand, appropriate, endorse, subvert, and validate "the ideas, interests, histories, and attitudes of others" through experiments in "autoethnography, transculturation, collaboration, critique, bilingualism, mediation, parody, denunciation, imaginary dialogue, [and] vernacular expression" (p. 37).

We begin with a characterization of insider and newcomer mindsets and a short overview of the reflective, analytic methods we used to exam-ine mindset differences in our collaboration. We then discuss how contact zone arts helped us to communicate across technological differences in our study of literacy practices and videogaming. We draw from our research experiences as collaborators to illustrate how Jackie and Josh (students and insiders) and Sally (a faculty member and newcomer) recognized and learned to use arts for the digital contact zone. Examples illustrate how insiders and newcomers can recognize differences and rethink assump-tions so as to avoid frustration and misunderstanding. We conclude with a review of our findings and brief suggestions for how contact zone arts can support and enrich digital writing research.

CHARACTERIZATION OF INSIDERS AND NEWCOMERS

Lankshear and Knobel (2003) used the terms insider and newcomer "as markers for two competing mindsets. One affirms the world as the same as before, only more technologized; the other affirms the world as radical-ly different, precisely because of the operation of new technologies" (p. 32). In many ways, the terms insider and newcomer denote relationships that parallel the "emic" and "etic" relationships described by cultural anthropologists and linguists (e.g., Headland, Pike, & Harris, 1990) and by ethnographers in composition (e.g., Bishop, 1999). Within our discussion, insiders would be characterized as participating in an emic relationship to digital literacies, in that they can participate in digital spaces within a lan-guage of practice and internalized understanding. In contrast, newcomers would be characterized as standing in an etic relationship to digital spaces; their participation is mediated through a language of analysis and reflec-tion in which acts, ideas, and relationships are reflectively named and clas-sified in terms of a perspective shaped outside the spaces in which they find themselves now participating, researching, or both.

In general, researchers have identified three important classes of difference between insider and newcomer mindsets. The first characterizes different conceptions of how "place is constructed and controlled in terms of values, morals, knowledge, competence, and the like" (Lankshear & Knobel, 2003, p. 32); the second focuses on characterizations of how insiders and newcomers conceptualize thinking and knowing; and the third considers differences in how newcomers and insiders conceptualize self or identity within online spaces.

Mindset Difference and Space

Most differences between insider and newcomer mindsets derive from the contrasting experiences, consequences, and communication dynamics structured by virtual spaces. Lankshear and Knobel (2003) pointed out that virtual spaces seem "practically limitless—capable of almost infinite expansion," so that, at least in theory, there is "room for anyone and everyone to participate to the fullest extent of their interests and capabilities" (p. 58). Moreover, the products of virtual spaces are "nonphysical stuff . . . ideas, information, theories, data" (p. 53). One result of unlimited space and the surplus of products created by "anyone and everyone" is an economics where the value of (nonphysical) products increases as more and more users discover and learn how to use them. This economics is in contrast to the economics of material space, where increased supply and use means decreased value for particular products, as exemplified by the mass production of designer clothes, fast food, generic drugs, and so on. When material products become widely available, price goes down.

A second result of the ever-increasing number of virtual products (information and information systems) is a need for what Richard Lanham (1993) designated *human-attention structures*. Because virtual spaces are vast beyond measure and increasing in size by the minute, and because users are currently producing more products than any one person can find and track, there is an increasing need for structures to organize information to help users find and understand what they need. These two features of the economics of virtual spaces—the increasing value of nonphysical products as they become more familiar, and the need for human-attention structures to make valuable information accessible—drive assumptions, values, and beliefs central to insider mindsets.

Further, differences between insider preferences for learning through doing over newcomer approaches (such as reading background information or conferring with experts) derive from the fact that "new technology amplifies its powers as it is appropriated and redefined by users through doing" (Lankshear & Knobel, 2003, p. 58). As illustrated by examples from our research, insider preferences for learning through doing can place younger research partners in conflict with traditional newcomer practices of conducting research.

Features of virtual space also influence social interactions. Because more participation by more users results in more elites, the socialization of newcomers to "becoming 'insiders' to practices, as far as possible, and as quickly as possible" is a core insider value (Lankshear & Knobel, 2003, p. 68). Charles Jackson (2004), an insider who described his experiences coming of age with the Internet, invokes this value quite specifically when he stated that "everybody is learning how to do new things. Everyone was like that at one point. . . . If you like turn away everybody when they are just learning how to do something, then no one will want to do it again" (DeVoss, Hawisher, Jackson, Johansen, Moraski, & Selfe, 2004, p. 201). This core value is also central to the digital writing research community, where the importance of supporting newcomers is repeatedly cited not only as a core value, but as a feature that both attracts and keeps scholars engaged in digital writing research (Inman, 2004).

Epistemologies and Freedom

Differences in the experience of digital as opposed to material space structure different conceptions of knowledge. As a result, insiders and newcomers have very different assumptions about how knowledge is created and how it ought to be used. For example, within digital space, knowledge is dispersed and connected to processes of storage and access. Multiple individuals can participate in information creation, and processes for representing knowledge are frequently multimodal and embedded in nonlinguistic structures. In contrast, within the material world, knowledge is generally conceptualized as located within the self (as opposed to within collaborative processes) and independent of processes for storage and access. What can be known is thought of as immanent to physical space, such that it can be discovered or observed within the reality presented by the material world. Within the virtual world, reality itself is often seen as having been created, and insiders do not expect proof or verification derived from reality—rather, proof becomes irrelevant and knowledge is relative.

For example, because virtual knowledge is realized in nonmaterial spaces, it is not a property of those spaces; rather it is an outcome of the interactive, social negotiations that take place within those spaces. That is, knowledge does not manifest itself in virtual spaces in the same ways as it does in material spaces. A scientist can measure the boiling point of water in the material world, but in virtual space the properties of matter may be part of a storyline or features defined within a given space. They are not real or factual in the same way as they are in material space. As a consequence, for insiders knowledge is conceptualized as created collectively and in relationship rather than as discovered or immanent, and because communication in online spaces is not exclusively linguistic, negotiations through which knowledge is created are often multimodal and embedded within context in ways that knowledge in print spaces is typically not (Kress, 2003; Lemke, 1998).

Within insider–newcomer collaborations, insiders often find that dominant academic practices derived from newcomer epistemologies run directly counter to their values. For example, standard academic conceptions of authorship and intellectual property are often in conflict with insider conceptions of knowledge as dispersed, relative, collaborative, and emerging. The accompanying demand for freedom of access that insiders use to optimize conditions for the creation of knowledge is often alien to newcomers (Barlow, 1996). This preference for freedom does not mean that online spaces are not structured by discursive boundaries, however. Each online space has its own set of rules and conventions, and breaking rules can result in flaming, ostracism, ridicule, or even virtual execution (Barnes, 2001; Boese, 1999; Herring, 1994). As Dànielle DeVoss observed: "Chat rooms and bulletin board systems are complicated spaces where missteps or inappropriate talk can pretty much exclude you from a conversation, or make you the target of venomous textual assaults" (DeVoss et al., 2004, p. 185).

Mindset and Identity

Interactive digital spaces, such as videogames, require individuals to create virtual selves to represent their interests, actions, and ideas. Within a given virtual space, projected identities are created through the dynamic interaction of participants' complex personal identities and the rules or conditions that structure social interactions within that space. Experiences within both virtual and material worlds shape individuals' facility in creating appropriate projected identities. Feminist and linguistic analyses suggest that behavior in online spaces connects to multiple dimensions of material identities (e.g., Barnes, 2001). That is, insiders enter virtual spaces trailing features of their material identities. So although it is true that insider values emphasize relationship, socialization of newcomers, and collaboration, online relationships are built within systems of value particular to local virtual spaces and are mediated through the construction of projected identities that users (who inhabit physical bodies and have lived experience in the real world) create within those spaces. Both insiders and newcomers bring features of local, material mindsets acquired in physical space to digital spaces. How they deploy these mindsets, however, is typically and markedly different.

With respect to gaming spaces, James Gee (2003) observed that newcomer baby-boomers like himself find many of their "cherished ways of learning and thinking (e.g., being too quick to want to get to a goal without engaging in sufficient prior nonlinear exploration)" (p. 57) unrewarded, or even punished within gaming spaces. For participants in chat rooms and bulletin board systems, the ability to deduce social practices within a space and to construct an appropriate projected identity are crucial. Such abilities are acquired through experiences in online spaces that, at least at the outset, newcomers often do not have.

METHODS

We did not set out to write a paper on differences between newcomer and insider research practices. The three of us—Jackie and Josh, undergraduate students, and Sally, a baby-boomer faculty member in the English Department at Kean University—set out to document literacy practices surrounding videogaming. We began our study by collecting data using methods set forward by grounded theorists and modified by postmodern and feminist discussions that complicate subject–observer relationships, practices for data collection and analysis, and the creation of theory (Clifford & Marcus, 1988; Dey, 1999; Mortensen & Kirsch, 1996; Strauss & Corbin, 1998). From the outset, our research practice was informed by close attention to the role researchers' predispositions and perspectives play in shaping theory; we engaged in a collaborative, interactive research process.

In a typical data-collecting session on gaming practices, one of us would take notes while the others played. Sometimes we played with other online gamers, and sometimes only one person played while the rest of the group watched. Raw transcripts from data collection were proofread and supplemented with notes by the notetaker. Complete notes were then circulated among the group. We coded data on our own and in interactive group sessions. As we read through our notes together, we developed a second practice that became central to our study: the use of notes, coding, and analysis as primary data on individual research practices.

Our methods for reflective analysis of research practices drew from work by Caroline Brettell (1993), Elizabeth Chiseri-Strater (1996), Ruth Ray (1993), and Bonnie Sunnstein (1996). As it became increasingly clear that our study would center on mindset differences, we began to analyze differences within notes and coding that implied different assumptions, orientations, and values. We used primary notes and analyses, supplemented with self-authored descriptions of practices for creating notes and analyses. We used original notes and self-authored descriptions of research practices to document our different patterns for selecting information, taking notes, developing codes, and writing up analyses and findings.

PERILS OF COMMUNICATION IN THE CONTACT ZONE

Again, we did not set out to write a paper on differences between newcomer and insider research practices—we set out to study videogaming. We began with a shared belief that videogames have shaped the social and literacy practices of the digital generation in positive ways, and we hoped data on literacy practices surrounding gaming would support this position. Sally teaches technology-enriched writing courses, has made simple Web sites, and is a lurker in numerous online communities, but she will probably never be completely socialized as an insider, because "computer writing technologies are steeped in the powerful brew of prior experiences" (Sloane, 1999, p. 52). Sally's many years of exclusive socialization in the material world will probably always cast her mindset in terms of physical space and material literacies. In contrast, Jackie and Josh came of age with the Internet and move through virtual spaces as insiders.

We discovered early in our project that these generational differences caused us to have very different conceptions about the "right" way to play games. We also discovered that we had very different ideas about the "right" way to conduct research. For our first meeting, we sat in a park at a picnic table with Sally on one side and Jackie and Josh on the other. Sally had ordered books on literacy and gaming, new literacies, and qualitative methods; she expected that the group would talk about these books as a way to get started on the project. In theory, we all had agreed to read these books; in practice, Sally read the books, and Jackie and Josh *sort of* read *some* of them.

After some awkwardness, it became clear that either Sally would have to lecture on the assigned readings or we would have to take a new approach. We decided to shift focus. We began discussing gamers' practices for finding information about games. At this point, Jackie and Josh took the lead, and Sally took notes. We generated a list that included playing games alone, with friends, and online; visiting Web sites (demo, commercial, and fan sites); participating in online forums, discussion groups, and chat spaces; talking with friends (both online and in-person); and looking through gaming magazines. Not surprisingly, this list documents insider-preferred research practices—exploring and interacting within online spaces, and, whenever possible, playing an active role in negotiating and/or creating knowledge. Although Sally uses email lists and information groups and finds references online, she does not consider these practices "real" research. For example, she did not suggest that she, Jackie, and Josh play games or check gaming sites to prepare for the project. Rather, she chose scholarly works about games and qualitative methods and she took notes on her kids as they played games. The fact that she read and wrote about games rather than actually playing games reflects her background as an ethnographer and the discipline's investment in "writing culture," as well as the academy's faith in print's authority to validate knowledge; her approaches also reflect her status as a newcomer.

Because the academy remains invested in insider mindsets, newcomers often find themselves struggling to be heard and understood within academic power structures. As observed by digital writing scholar James Inman (2004), members of the computers and writing community "often write from the margins of their institutions . . . and those more senior and/or in more powerful institutional positions often have limited respect for the depth, breadth, and rigor of these community members' work" (p. 107). Digital researchers' different mindsets are often a key factor in the "more senior and/or more powerful" members of the academy's skeptical reception of digital writing research.

In practice, neither Sally nor most print-generation researchers in the postmodern age, particularly composition researchers invested in the social construction of knowledge, operate from strict adherence to newcomer epistemologies. Nor do Internet generation researchers think and learn entirely in terms of the negotiated, embedded, relational, multimodal processes described as deriving from online spaces. In practice, both insiders and newcomers selectively engage multiple aspects of both print-generation and Internet-generation assumptions, values, and beliefs. At the same time, newcomers and insiders frequently perceive and respond to experience—particularly online experience—differently.

Pratt (1991) introduced her discussion of arts that bridge contact zone power differentials through a story about a "dead letter" written by Felipe Guaman Poma de Ayala, a native of Cuzco in Peru in 1613. Poma's letter was written in a mixture of his native language and the language of the Spanish conquerors; it was addressed to his country's ruler, King Philip III of Spain. The manuscript was composed and presumably sent, but apparently it did not arrive and was eventually discovered by 20th-century scholars. In Pratt's analysis, dead letters are sent from the less powerful to the more powerful, who then choose not to receive them. In research collaborations between newcomers and insiders, dead letters may include any communication more powerful collaborators choose not to acknowledge or receive. Curiously, our first meeting in that park includes a "dead letter" (a request to read texts) sent by Sally to Jackie and Josh who, instead of "reading" this letter, actively worked to change the approaches to the research process, which suggested that Jackie and Josh were at least partly in control.

Power in our research collaboration was partially defined by the hierarchical structure of the academy: Sally as teacher and administrator, Jackie and Josh as students. Within this relationship (as in relationships between graduate advisors and graduate students, project directors and assistant researchers), power corresponds to seniority—or how far one has progressed within the system. At the same time, because contemporary patterns for communication and representation increasingly derive from and depend upon insider technological knowledge, collaborators with digital expertise often have another kind of seniority. The paradox remains that despite the academy's valuing of what technology can do, newcomer ways for knowing and communicating are frequently not respected, valued, understood, or even recognized as fundamentally different (Inman, 2004), yet newcomers' perspectives are essential for understanding emerging new literacies.

As pointed out by Marilyn Cooper (1999), in her reading of Foucault's relational definition of power within electronic environments, power is not a possession resulting from a particular position; rather individuals

> continually structure power relationships among themselves through the ways their actions impact others' actions. People cannot give others power or take it away; their actions always respond to the actions of others and in return set up a range of possibilities for other's actions. (p. 146)

This suggests that power within digital writing collaborations can be conceived in terms of relationships that, in Foucault's words, enable "a whole field of responses, reactions, results, and possible inventions may open up" (qtd. in Cooper, 1999, p.146). This conceptualization of power is in keeping with the dynamics described by Pratt (1991), and casts Jackie and Josh's refusal to read the assigned books as a dead letter.

Because Jackie and Josh did not read the assigned texts, they learned to code not the way Sally did (through reading textual directions and following instructions), but rather through engaging in an interactive group process where Sally, Jackie, and Josh developed coding methods through collaborative work with successive sets of notes. That is, Jackie and Josh's refusal to engage in the academy's traditional approaches for "getting newcomers up to speed" caused a shift in research practice from newcomer to insider methods.

Documentation of power dynamics between insiders and newcomers in which newcomers are administrators and faculty and insiders are students has generally indicated that the "'deep grammar' of school . . . institutionalizes the privileging of the newcomer/outsider mindsets" (Lankshear & Knobel, 2003, p. 33). Through imposing exactly the kinds of restrictions objected to by John Perry Barlow (1996), newcomers who teach with technology often exclude or make inoperable insider systems for valuing and making knowledge. Jackie and Josh's success at evading, talking back to, and ultimately transforming newcomer practice within our project suggests new, more promising relationships for insiders and newcomers within digital writing research collaborations. Within these new relationships, participation in contact zone arts can lead to the negotiation, hybridization, and redefinition of insider–newcomer power dynamics and the mindsets that define them.

ARTS OF THE CONTACT ZONE IN ACTION

Realizing that insiders and newcomers enter virtual spaces with different mindsets is a good start, but this realization will not necessarily make communication less problematic. Knowing that newcomers often bring (inappropriate) assumptions into online interactions (or into their analyses of digital composing) will not resolve miscommunication unless research partners know how to recognize and respond to the particular manifestations of difference that complicate their collaboration. When we documented the examples that follow, Jackie, Josh and Sally were well aware that they operated from different mindsets. We understood that Sally would resort to questions (requests for linguistic direction) rather than learning a game space by playing, and that Jackie and Josh's representations and analyses drew from embodied rather than linguistic logics. At the same time, as the following notes demonstrate, we were unclear about how such differences would play out within the digital contact zone.

Bilingualism > Digital Double Vision

In the following excerpt from Jackie's notes, Sally is playing *Oddworld: Abe's Exoddus*. She plays Abe, a Mudokan. Abe is trying to rescue his fellow Mudokans from the underworld factories where they work as slaves. Jackie's notes describe Sally's actions, mostly in terms of what she says. Jackie reports her instructions to help Sally understand how to sneak past a Slig, an overseer who keeps Mudokan workers in line. As the notes begin, Sally has been killed by the Slig for the third time.

Sally: . . . what did I do?

Jackie: You were walking normally.

Sally: I should have been sneaking?

Jackie: Yeah.

Sally: (Gets killed again.) I got out where he could see me. I have controller issues here.

Jackie: Laughs

Sally: All right. We've got to take the slug thing seriously. . . . Ah. [gets killed] I came out of the shadow too soon.

Jackie: No, you were walking normally so he heard you walking.

Sally: Oh I see.

Jackie: Get into the shadow.

//

Slig sees Abe

Jackie: Run. Get out of there! Run!

Sally: (dies) Ohhhhh. I had to get to the other screen?

Jackie: Yeah.

Sally: I thought you could just hide in the shadows. That was a fundamental misconception.

In this excerpt, Sally struggles to orient herself to an unfamiliar world. She is confused regarding multiple issues (including how to locate her "self" in the game's space). The primary issue Jackie addresses is Sally's misunderstanding of where she will be safe from the Slig. In instances where Jackie understands how Sally has misunderstood the game, her interventions are effective; however, when Sally's assumptions are invisible to Jackie—that is, when Jackie does not correctly interpret why Sally is making a mistake —communication is vexed, as when Jackie instructs Sally to run, but Sally does not understand where it is safe to run to. Because the structure of the project provided many hours where we observed one another playing games, Jackie and Josh soon became adept at identifying the particular features of the gaming spaces, including concepts and practices that Sally would interpret incorrectly. In this way, they refined the contact zone art of bilingualism (the ability to translate linguistic meanings between languages) into digital double vision: a way of seeing Sally's game play from both insider and newcomer perspectives.

For example, Sally tended to remain in her material self as she played games. She watched the action on the screen, including the actions of her character, as if they were a movie. Because of this, she did not realize her full possibilities to direct the game's action. Like Gee (2003), she played games in terms of baby-boomer assumptions about space and games. As Jackie and Josh watched, they became increasingly adept at providing appropriate verbal prompts to direct her attention to her online identity and the contextual clues which could provide information for appropriate choices about how to behave. (e.g., "Pay attention to where your character is looking"; "Listen to changes in the music"; "Look at the lighting"). As they watched the kinds of mistakes Sally made, they used digital double vision to see the gaming space as Sally saw it and to provide verbal articulations (a newcomer's preferred form for instruction) to expose and reorient her misconceptions in terms of insider practice.

Because digital spaces require different patterns for learning than print spaces, in most cases it is preferable for newcomers to learn digital spaces in terms of insider practices for in-depth, self-directed exploration. In practice, however, this will not always happen. Because of this, insider double vision will remain a necessary art for successful collaboration. Although this example illustrates Jackie and Josh's resort to digital double vision, Sally also had to learn to observe and translate what Jackie and Josh could not see as a result of their insider assumptions. For example, when Jackie analyzed data in terms of a performative narrative rather than the expected categorization and definition, digital double vision allowed Sally to see Jackie's different pattern of analysis and translate it into newcomer terms. In this way, we gained access to both newcomer and insider practices for analysis, and we were able to broaden and enrich the interpretation of our data.

Mediation > Mediated Identity

As part of our process of establishing accountability, each of us characterized and analyzed the content and form presented in our notes. We described what we selected as important, as well as identified patterns for representing those selections. As we engaged in these reflective analyses, we began to formulate descriptions of the particular forms newcomer and insider mindsets take within research processes. These analyses suggested that insider and newcomer identities influenced our patterns for taking and analyzing notes and that these patterns were not static. Our research processes seemed to evolve so that we unconsciously renegotiated our mindset investment in an ongoing way.

Initial analysis characterized Sally's notes as containing detailed descriptions of the context for play: the setting; who was playing; who walked in and out of the room; talk during game play; what took place onscreen; how players operated the controllers; players' gestures, facial expressions, attitudes; and so on. These descriptions certainly reflected Sally's training as an ethnographer, as well as her focus on the physical people playing the games; they also suggest an orientation that identifies the operation of the technology as both visible and relevant. The following notes on Josh playing *Silent Hill 2*, a survival horror game, illustrate this orientation:

> Josh: (Looking at street names on screen) Here you go. Benson, Harris, these are all names of members of a band. (Sees a zombie) I still don't have any weapons. I guess I just follow the blood stains [to find a weapon].
>
> Jackie: It's always great to follow the blood stains (pointing).
>
> Josh: I saw that (mock irritation)
>
> Jackie: No. I didn't say anything.
>
> Josh: You lifted your hand.

//

Scene with character walking into culvert watching zombie through chain link fence. Character picks up stick

Jackie: R1 to arm

Josh: And R2

Josh makes character beat zombie, walks up to gate, but can't go through goes to the end of Martin Street. There is a barricade and a dead person and an apartment key. Looks at map. There is a check mark on the map.

Jackie: (Points)

Josh: Thank you. Do you really think I would have missed the square with the big circle around it?

Jackie: Except that is not where you're supposed to go.

Josh: I told you not to tell me anything.

Although these notes document Josh's play, they also provide information about player interaction—pointing, looking irritated, making ironic comments—in terms of parenthetic comments, description of players' off-screen actions, and dialogue. We are told what Josh is looking at, what he makes his character do, and we are told how he responds to Jackie's suggestions. Although there is some confusion between references for Josh and references for Josh's character, Sally's primary interest seems to be in Josh, the real-world person playing the game.

As illustrated in the following example, Jackie and Josh's early notes were more oriented toward the game and less oriented toward player's real-world interactions. In the following example from Josh's notes, Sally plays the training sequence in *Tomb Raider 2*, and then moves on to the opening scene:

Sally continues practicing jumping from pillar to pillar using side-ways jump, occasionally missing because of being off center.

Sally: I know what's wrong. I'm not squared to it.

Sally walks up to the next obstacle, a climbing wall and footbridge.

Jackie: What was the look button? I can't remember . . . oh, there you go. Whatever you're holding is right now.

Sally: L1

Jackie: Stay holding L1 and press the directional pad

[Opening cinematic] Sally rappels from a helicopter into a rock quarry kind of area in the cinematic//

Sally: I'm sort of stuck there (shoots tiger that is prowling round near a cave)

Sally: Oh, I see . . . I can't visualize what's going on in this terrain very well.

Sally enters the cave.

Sally: It won't let me go that way, and there's the tiger. I can't get out of here.

//

Sally: Do you have any idea where I am?

Jackie: I'm trying not to help you too much. . .

In these notes, Josh's identification of player with character is more complete than in Sally's notes. When Josh describes the opening cinematic, he records Sally as rappelling into the quarry, whereas Sally documented "the character" as "walking" and "watching" and Josh as "making his character" pick up the weapons. Also, Josh's primary documentation of players is through dialogue, rather than description of real-world actions. When analyzing Sally's and Josh's notes, Jackie described Sally's as real-world oriented and Josh's as more game-oriented or character-oriented. Josh's game-oriented dialogue reports the consequences and frustrations players experience in terms of the character (designated by the player's name) and actions in the game. Also, although Josh's notes may be characterized as oriented toward the game, his orientation still manages to represent Sally's ambivalence in her identification with her on-screen character. In writing "I'm sort of stuck *there*," Josh represents Sally as creating a distance between the self who is playing the game, and the place where she is stuck—"there"—a place separate from the self; at the same time, he writes "Sally rappels into the quarry" and "enters cave," revealing his own collapse of the space that he has represented Sally as creating.

These differences in orientation and identification were subtle but significant, and they illustrate how location within a given mindset shapes not only perception and behavior within digital spaces, but also representation and analysis of those spaces. At the same time, bias accompanying mindset is neither permanent nor necessarily a drawback, especially in collaborations between newcomers and insiders. As we continued research, our note taking and analytic processes changed in light of our reflective analysis, resulting in fuller, more complex representations of gaming practices.

When appropriate, Jackie and Josh included more detailed documentation of player interactions, and Sally's representations of interactions between player and game became more deeply grounded in gaming processes and culture. Through realizing the particular features of how our notes and analyses differed, we became better able to interpret and apply the kind of information made available by each perspective. Such shifts in research practice imply a re-orientation of mindsets and an accompanying reconfiguration of identities. As the project progressed, each of us moved toward a hybridized, transculturated self, who could see in terms of increasingly acute double vision.

WRITING UP:
REPORT FROM THE DIGITAL CONTACT ZONE

Our research suggests a series of particular patterns for how researchers' different orientations from insider/newcomer mindsets affect digital writing research. First, we found that orientations within technological mindsets were grounded in power relations connected to researchers' locations within the research context. Because our project centered on insider practices within an insider space (gaming), Sally's need to understand and become fluent in insider practices drove her efforts to acquire a broader experiential base in insider practices. This tipped the balance of power in favor of insiders and may have contributed to her willingness to enter into insider assumptions, values, and beliefs. The result was that Sally acquired an increased facility with creating projected identities, and more complex, nonlinguistic patterns for conceptualizing and representing knowledge. At the same time, because our research was conducted at a university where print-based biases shape dominant discourses, and because Jackie and Josh needed to establish themselves as credible students and researchers in terms of newcomer expectations, they continually strove for increased fluency in newcomer conventions and logics for writing.

Second, and obviously, this chapter and the other pieces we have presented and papers we have written have been composed in newcomer formats. Although earlier drafts for this chapter included a more embodied, more performative style where the main points remained embedded in stories about our research experience, most of these embedded analyses were edited out in successive revisions. And, although it may be that we are simply not artful enough at writing to convey our findings without stating them outright, it is also true that audience expectations for this piece connect primarily to newcomer expectations with respect to form for research articles.

Third, we found—along with other new literacy researchers—that location within a given mindset is neither pure nor fixed (Alverman, 2002; Lankshear & Knobel, 2003; Selfe & Hawisher, 2004). Movement in mindset orientation seems to be driven by power dynamics, by ongoing experiences in digital spaces and material spaces, and conscious resort to contact zone arts. Specifically, we found that relying on contact zone arts allowed for increasing awareness of difference in mindset orientations, and as our perspectives opened, our mindsets hybridized.

Finally, we found that although newcomer exploration of insider perspectives and practices can enrich research practices, insider mastery of digital contact zone arts to negotiate newcomer blind spots remains especially important for successful collaboration in digital writing research. In his report on the state of the computers and writing community, Inman (2004) wrote that:

> resistance will play a foundational role in the way technology is seen and used. If present and future computers and writing scholars can be sensitive to and respectful of critique that will emerge, or if these scholars can offer critiques themselves that are constructive and well reasoned, then a wide range of new and carefully designed technologies important for the community should emerge. (p. 111)

Fluency in the arts of the digital contact zone can play a crucial role in constructing a sensitive and constructive critique of digital writing research. This critique can underpin both increased acceptance of work in digital writing, and more powerfully conceived digital writing research projects.

17

IMPACT OF INVASIVE WEB TECHNOLOGIES ON DIGITAL RESEARCH

Lory Hawkes

Digital researchers are at risk as they explore the Internet because their pursuit of information is no longer a private scholarly inquiry but often is the focus of surveillance. With new, invasive Web technologies, researchers' work can be jeopardized and the integrity of their relationship to research colleagues and study participants can be undermined. With online surveillance techniques, researchers' personal information can be acquired and analyzed. Compiled digital data records may be manipulated and disseminated by cyber exploiters, data providers, or the federal government without the researcher's knowledge or permission. Equally disturbing is the prospect of an aggregate record being compiled based on information about research study participants. In this chapter, I describe some of the current data-mining and surveillance technologies in use on the Internet and describe countermeasures digital writing researchers can employ to minimize risks to their work, to their research participants and associates, and to their reputations.

KNOWLEDGE AND/THROUGH COMPUTER INTERFACES

When Theodor Nelson (1982) envisioned Xanadu, he imagined it as a web of linked libraries with an open system of access. Nelson dreamed of an expansive vista of research opportunity to be freely traversed by people exploring and exploiting hypertext links. His Xanadu was a world-wide electronic archive based on the concept of hypertext presented by Vannevar Bush (1945) in his *Atlantic Monthly* article, "As We May Think." Bush wrote about a theoretical machine, the Memex. Housed in a standard-size desk with a system of pulleys and a deck of microcards with contents viewable on desktop monitors, the Memex would be a new kind of machine because it would foster a synergy of knowledge-gathering drawn from the interaction of a human who selected an initial path of information and a mechanism that could predict subsequent paths to related information. This human–machine synergy of knowledge-gathering relying on a computer interface is the very reason digital researchers now enjoy broad access to virtual archives of information. The promise of knowledge, however, comes with the grave risks related to data mining and cyber surveillance.

The first goal of this chapter is to focus on the electronic potential for harm to digital writing researchers. New and malevolent intrusive technologies can allow digital exploiters to hijack, distort, and bug the electronic transmission of data passed through networks or broadcast through wireless communication devices. These means, however, are not chiefly the practiced art of criminals, but are often part of a new enterprise of data mining and spam techniques that many corporations are now using to gain business. In an effort to know the characteristics of their customers or future customers, data-mining companies compile information from a number of sources to lure users into appealing offers so that "consumers will voluntarily trade their privacy for various enticements from merchants" (Rheingold, 2002, p. 187).

Whether these intrusions are benign marketing ploys or malignant and long-lasting digital infections that embed themselves deep in a user's machine, surveillance technologies jeopardize data-gathering processes and disrupt the mutual trust between researcher and subject or collegial exchange among colleagues. These intrusions can expose the researcher's identity, research subject information, and confidential findings to cyber exploiters. Threats related to intrusion, data mining, and identity theft are real and growing. According to the *Statistical Abstract of the United States:*

2004–2005, identity theft cases constitute 18.2% of all computer-related crimes in prosecutors' case loads.

A second goal of the chapter is to explore the ethical implications of digital surveillance by the federal government because of new requirements for reporting information. These methods have not been tested in the courts and carry the potential to harm the character of the digital researcher, the integrity and freedom of the research effort, and the alliance between researcher and librarian. Although the United States Patriot Act (HR 3162 RDS, 2001) was meant to find terrorists by allowing federal agents to trace their Internet-access patterns and gather information about them to confirm an early presumption of guilt, the process of identifying who might be a terrorist is fraught with contradictions related to personal rights and freedoms. In 2002, the Library Research Center of the University of Illinois surveyed over 900 public libraries for the year following the 9/11 attack on the World Trade Center and found that federal officials gathered information about patrons from 545 libraries (Chang, 2003). The ability of federal officials to enlist librarians as surrogate surveillance agents trivializes the long-standing scholarly alliance—based on respect and cooperation—between librarians and the research community. For digital researchers who are researching politically sensitive areas, this may result in a federal profile based on their book-selection patterns. As in the case of Project Lookout, in which the FBI compiled a list of "persons of interest" and shared this list with businesses (Chang), digital researchers who are identified as people of interest or who have names similar to people of interest may be eliminated from grant consideration or corporate funding, or screened out of publishing opportunities.

The third goal of the chapter is to suggest how digital researchers might benefit from proactive techniques to protect their work from intrusive technologies and to protect their reputations in response to the dire political complications brought about by new federal initiatives. To address the three goals articulated above, I first describe the potential for digital harm posed to digital writing researchers, and I then discuss possibilities for researchers to protect themselves, their data, their networks, and thus their research participants.

THE DIGITAL POTENTIAL FOR HARM

Digital harvesting is the act of compiling information about a particular user from single or multiple sources. By aggregating records on an individual, companies called data providers have insider knowledge about personal likes and dislikes and perhaps an indication of personal wealth based on purchase patterns and the type of computer with which a user performs online transactions. Although digital harvesting is not illegal, large commercial online entities such as AOL and Microsoft are taking initiatives to stifle a digital harvesting byproduct, spam. Spam is the electronic barrage of unwanted and unsolicited information about products or services from companies who buy information from data providers or who amass potential customer profiles with data-mining techniques. Although data providers attempt to self-regulate their industry with the Open Archives Initiative Protocol for Metadata,[1] the federal government and e-commerce entrepreneurs are perfecting the art of data aggregation to find out more about individuals.

Used for over a decade as a viable business strategy to identify new customers and retain current customers, *data mining* is the process of identifying a person and gathering personal information (financial, demographic, technological, etc.). *Data warehousing* is the process of storing the mined results in a large database for linking to other databases. Digital harvesting is not illegal, although it can lead to questionable manipulation of aggregated personal information across databases, which may be an invasion of privacy and possibly lead to identity theft.[2] One implication of digital harvesting and data mining for digital researchers is that nothing held in a computer file is safe. As long as a record is in electronic storage or open in an online session, it is subject to being nabbed or echoed on an intruder's computer and then compiled with other records. For example, suppose the digital researcher's academic affiliation, gender, computer make/model, and Internet provider are exposed during a harvesting episode. It is then possible for sophisticated programs and automated scripts to predict the approximate household income, for instance, of the researcher and to send this information on to other business partners, who would then generate a spiral of electronic mail.

SCRIPT PASSING TO ACQUIRE IDENTITY

Doing research online can mean that researchers follow associative links to other pages or that they use a search engine to create a list of relevant links. Both actions are complicated by the fact that while gaining information, they may also be exposing their own information. First, by following associative links, researchers might encounter a site that captures their move-ment by disabling their browser's back button. In this case, a simple JavaScript code erases the history of the sites visited by the researcher so that there is nothing to go back to, while another bit of script is lodged on the researcher's computer. This cookie script could be an innocent record-keeping process to log only the date of the site visit. Subsequently, this visit's time and date would be passed back to the site if the researcher returns and if the cookie produces a transmission back to the site (because the cookie has not yet expired). Cookie scripts, however, can also be writ-ten so that they pass information to multiple sites. Even more of a concern, cookie scripts can compile and pass information about the computer model and connected devices so that inferences about financial status and computing ability can be drawn. For the digital researcher, this can delay progress on a study, abruptly end Internet sessions, and disrupt navigation progress. If the cookie script captures the researcher's email address, the result may be frequent offers of products and services disguised by clever-ly written email subject lines.

As expert as researchers may be with using search engines, the process of composing a query and accessing matches may not be without risks. To gain site traffic, cyber exploiters embed descriptors under their Web pages that do not match the content of their site. So although the page may appear high in relevance on a search results list, the ranking may be artifi-cial and may be yet another attempt to capture the researcher's informa-tion. Worse still, the ruse could result in pop-up windows that trap the user by prohibiting her from stopping the quick sequence of pages that stack one on top of the other in separate browser windows. In effect, the researcher's mouse and movement is disabled as code in the initial page automatically re-routes the researcher's browser to a series of other Web sites. As the researcher is electronically handed off, cookie and spyware scripts can also dig under the researcher's computer before the transaction is complete. A surveillance spiral may begin without the researcher's knowledge.

Along with search-embedded identity-mining technologies are three kinds of directories available on the Internet. People finders are fee-based Web sites that continually scan public information sources to harvest data. Reverse directories provide a person's name and physical address in response to an email address or phone number. For a fee, credit-checking sites can provide pay histories or credit ratings (Bahadur, Chan, & Weber, 2002). The harm to the researcher comes with the long-term exposure of information; in essence, this information does not have a shelf life. It stays in cyberspace forever. For example, after a brief search in my Web design class, one of the students told me my age, two of my previous physical addresses, and my husband's occupation. This information had been compiled from surveys and free download forms I had completed over the span of a decade and was still publicly accessible, suspended in virtual time on the Internet. For researchers who may be revealing not only their identity but the identity of their research subjects and colleagues, this ability to compile data should be alarming. Crawlers—aptly named because they are software snoops that literally crawl through random data to compile records on individuals—can gather, compile, and distribute information. This information can remain suspended online in databases and across Web sites. Sophisticated databases can then match and link together names to demographic information. If a researcher's participant data is mined, the researcher has no control over how these records will be used or sold or how long they will exist as pieces of data provider information. If the researcher is a mark for handing off information through a series of mouse captures, the IP address of the researcher's computer can be fair game for other malicious forms of surveillance, which will be discussed next.

COVERT AND OVERT DIGITAL SURVEILLANCE

Identity-related mining presents one peril to digital researchers. Another way cyber exploiters have to elicit information from digital researchers is to engage in covert or overt surveillance. For covert surveillance, data miners create software programs called spiders that probe search engines to discover sites that active Internet users have visited. Because researchers are often active Internet users, spending hours working with search engines, they are an easy target or mark as these intelligent spiders count, rank, and predict from the accessed sites' metadata descriptors the type of information the researcher is pursuing. Cyber exploiters then repurpose content from a legitimate site by scrubbing that page—literally stripping away all the content and transferring the content to their own site. They then embed metadata descriptors equivalent to the descriptors encountered by the spiders on the authentic page in an effort to gain a high relevance the next time the researcher views the search engine's results page. When the researcher selects the bogus page, the electronic handoff begins again with the bogus page passing cookies or spyware to the researcher's computer, or disabling or trapping the researcher's mouse.

Surveillance becomes overt when hackers invade the researcher's computer to do harm. Many of our institutions have replaced clunky dial-up Internet access with faster, more stable, always-on Ethernet and broad-band connections. Whether through a cable connection, through a digital service line (DSL), or through a university high-speed network, researchers' computers are on and connected to the Internet for long periods of time, typically the entire time the computer is turned on, unless the user adjusts the settings to manually connect. This continual on and online state is an open window for hackers to take control of the researcher's computer.

MALWARE: VIRUSES, BUGS, AND MORE

Malware is the general term for any malicious code pushed onto a researcher's computer with harmful intent. Malware includes viruses, worms, trojan horses, logic bombs, Web bugs, backdoors, and a host of other software maladies. The best-known malware is a virus; a virus is code that can nest in a computer or computer network and can erase files or disable operating systems. According to Robert Slade, David Harley, and Urs Gattiker (2001), a virus consists of three component parts: *infection*—the way or ways in which the virus spreads; *payload*—what the virus does apart from replicate; and a *trigger*—the routine that sparks the payload. Viruses can be passed by email and by email attachments, by instant messaging systems, by downloading infected files, and by sharing files across infect-ed networks. Viruses usually have malicious intent and can immediately disrupt research productivity and collaboration by delaying or disrupting essential computer processes like copying files or using email. Viruses can destroy work saved in unprotected systems. Viruses can be passed on to others with similar effects. Worms are more volatile because they are pro-grams that recreate themselves as they are passed to other computers, thus multiplying the harm of any virus they may carry. The Love Bug or the "I love you" virus was an example of a fairly harmless worm that may have an effect on the professional esteem shared by researchers. Colleagues working on an infected machine may have unknowingly sent virus-laden files, or what appeared to be silly email transmissions.[3]

Malware can also be used to provide a backdoor—embedded code that becomes an access point to easily and repeatedly access a user's files, email archives, and passwords. Software programmers often insert back-doors into applications they design to enable them to bypass program secu-rity features and to fix an internal problem quickly. However, a backdoor can be exploited by a hacker who can use this access to commandeer the user's terminal. A backdoor can run undetected on a user's computer, allowing a hacker to access and view the researcher's screen contents simply by entering in the computer's unique Internet Protocol (IP) address. The hacker can then watch as the contents of the researcher's computer monitor mirrors on the hacker's monitor, exposing material such as research data and online transactions (Cole, 2002). Threats to researchers, their computers, and the networks on which they work are but a starting point for archives of mined, online information. Computers unguarded from data mining and hacker surveillance can spew facts, opinions, findings, and identities of the participants that can be organized, analyzed, and repurposed for distribution by large databases of data providers to be passed on indefinitely to other data providers and their partners.

FEDERAL GOVERNMENT SURVEILLANCE

Although hackers can be penalized for their exploits depending on the amount of damage they do, a new law gives the federal government the right to engage in covert and overt surveillance. In other words, although hackers can be punished by law for invading a user's computer or network, the federal government can perform surveillance on its citizens and be within the provisions of the U.S A. Patriot Act. This act was intended as a Homeland Security initiative to assist investigative arms of the federal government in quickly acting against suspected terrorists. Most of the Patriot Act's provisions have been made permanent by the *USA Patriot Improvement and Reauthorization Act of 2005*, with only a handful of the most-debated sections set to expire in 2009.[4] These provisions can be subject to interpretation by elite law enforcement groups. For example, if digital researchers visit controversial sites or unfriendly nations' sites in pursuit of an opinion or a varied perspective, they can be electronically followed by special FBI agents known as CyberCops, who are now empowered to monitor and determine the likelihood and the extent of terrorist activity of an individual based on their Internet searches and Web site access.

Because all the information that a researcher obtains (whether by email, Web searches, or chat rooms) can be accessed via electronic logs, by evoking the provisions of the Patriot Act enforcement authorities can scrutinize electronic logs supplied by the Internet service provider or other network entity. Should enforcement authorities determine a likelihood of guilt, they can flag the researcher's name and digitally harvest a lengthy record by accessing other federal databases. In becoming cyber suspects, digital researchers can experience additional airport screenings and an undeserved stigma of meriting government investigation—and all this can occur without their knowledge. Moreover, if a researcher's electronic path—either intentional or unintentional—indicates a presumption of guilt, federal authorities may seek a court order for wiretaps or financial records.

Jonathan Zittrain (2002), a Harvard law professor, characterized the kind of snooping authorized by the Patriot Act to find targets for investigation as "ubiquitous snooping" and argued that it goes against our essential American character:

> To make snooping routine, rather than a reaction to a reasonable suspicion of particular wrongdoers, is the sine qua non of a police state. It means spying on people otherwise presumed innocent, since it means spying on everyone. It is precisely the shackles the populations of the East cast aside with the fall of the Soviet Union. For good reason did the framers of our Bill of Rights circumscribe what can be collected by authorities in the first place, rather than merely limit the uses of that data. (n.p.)

According to the Electronic Frontier Foundation (2004), the sequel to the Patriot Act would have gone even further:

> USAPA II would create grave new violations of the privacy of ordinary Americans and place even more unchecked power into the hands of law enforcement and the intelligence community. We're only beginning to see the effects of USAPA and the administration has not made the case that we are safer as a result of it. (n.p.)[5]

In a recent court challenge, the American Civil Liberties Union (ACLU, 2004) argued against the surveillance provision of the Patriot Act. A federal court nullified the provision mandating that Internet service providers digitally harvest information about a flagged user in response to a National Security Letter. The importance of the unconstitutional ruling is twofold. First, it challenged the method of obtaining personal information through digital harvesting without a court order. Under the original provisions, law enforcement officials only had to identify an individual as a "probable" terrorist and receive surveillance permission from the U.S. Attorney General. Law enforcement officials did not have to inform suspects of their status, go before a court of law to prove to a judge that reasonable cause existed, or allow the "suspects" to challenge either the method of personal surveillance or the accuracy of the presumption. Second, the unconstitutional ruling indicated to lawmakers and enforcement officials that covert surveillance of individuals was not palatable and would not wash in judicial review. This unconstitutional ruling—along with early conjecture about a second Patriot Act—may have led lawmakers to reconsider their support of this type of legislation.

Although Internet service providers may experience some burden as federal digital harvesters, many librarians are livid about being forced into government service as snoops. Under the Patriot Act, librarians can now be agents in government service by revealing the pattern of reading sources of a flagged individual. Moreover, librarians can also be required to observe and compile the electronic record of Internet exploration made by a patron in the library without divulging the record-keeping to the patron (Gelsey, 2002). Protections for privacy, for freedom of speech, and against unreasonable search and seizure are not considerations in this federal mandate. In an appearance before a congressional committee, Attorney General Alberto Gonzalez said he had not used Section 215, which requires librarians to give federal officials library records but not reveal the delivery of these records to the individual under surveillance (Zetter, 2005). After its 2003 midwinter meeting, the American Library Association published a resolution on its Web site characterizing the law's provisions as an invasion of library users' privacy and a stifling of free speech. This excerpt captures the urgency of the proclamation:

> WHEREAS, the USA PATRIOT Act and other recently enacted laws, regulations, and guidelines increase the likelihood that the activities of library users, including their use of computers to browse the Web or access e-mail, may be under government surveillance without their knowledge or consent; now, therefore, be it RESOLVED, that the American Library Association opposes any use of governmental power to suppress the free and open exchange of knowledge and information or to intimidate individuals exercising free inquiry. (n.p.)

Digital researchers who engage in scholarly investigation may indeed find information in Web sites unfriendly to the United States, or they may access some unsavory or explicit evidence if they are pursuing investigations of contemporary social issues. In the exercise of academic freedom, should these researchers be considered terrorist suspects because they visit controversial sites? Do they deserve to be the target of covert and overt federal surveillance? What about the gag order on librarians? Paul T. Jaeger, Charles R. McClure, John Bertot, and John T. Snead (2004) found several important issues changing the relationship of librarians and researchers and in the nature of research itself. They predicted that researchers might be inhibited in doing library research when aware that their records might be compiled. These authors also reported that libraries have begun to destroy records or signup logs of Internet use to free themselves of record-keeping and government access to such records. Jaeger et al. also noted that the gag order prevented researchers and librarians from discussing the impact of the Patriot Act. Also, the untested status of the Act—absent of full judicial review of its tenets—means that librarians and researchers are unsure of their legal situation and rights, and this may inhibit researchers from addressing more controversial subjects, thus stifling our work and the potential implications of our work. Legal uncertainty also affects the academic institutions that sponsor researchers and may actually limit or curtail financial support for research activities.

The problem with this law is that legislators have endorsed a presumption of guilt based on some digital activities, rather than on understanding the purpose of those events in a reasonable context of the quest for knowledge. In essence, lawmakers have privileged the verity of the user interface as proof of human intention and left out any consideration of the human need and right to learn, seek multiple perspectives, and gather information. Lawmakers and federal enforcement authorities generalize that terrorism or social harm is inclusive of all those who seek a differing point of view. This law confers guilt in secret, with too few parameters. Consequently, the most insidious risk that digital researchers face is the excessive power of the federal government that can destroy their character and undermine their rights as citizens to freely pursue knowledge. Without recourse to judicial review, digital researchers can become "persons of interest." Although electronic files or logs of Internet activity are fragmented data and not physical objects traditionally covered by the Fourth Amendment (DeVries, 2003), they are nevertheless rightful possessions of the digital researcher—possessions that should be protected from unreasonable search and seizure.

PROACTIVE COUNTERMEASURES TO DIGITAL RISKS

Computer Protection

If left unaware of the intrusive nature of Web technologies, digital researchers are vulnerable. Any digital researcher who engages in exploring the Internet must have at the very least an active virus protection package. Virus protection software should be set to intercept and scan email, email attachments, and file downloads and to block scripts from being passed onto or embedded into the computer. In periods of intense Internet research, the virus definitions should be updated at least weekly to keep the anti-virus software current with the latest known malware profiles. Updating virus definitions takes just a few minutes; typically, the manufacturer provides a simple process of doing so within the software's menu system. Unprotected personal computers or computers with out-of-date virus definitions are easy prey for cyber exploiters who can ruin files or disable computer operations.

Operating system manufacturers such as Microsoft or Apple alert users to software updates that fix problems or security flaws in their software. These updates should be accepted and installed, especially for Microsoft operating systems (PCs are much more susceptible to viruses and malware than are machines running a Macintosh operating system). Because Web browsers are interfaces that enable users to see the contents of Web pages and their programming architecture may be a source of exploitation by hackers, users should set browser options to disable cookies, erase navigation histories, and eliminate temporary Internet files—all of which are roadmaps exploited by intruders. Software manufacturers also offer all-in-one packages that scan computer files, find infected files or embedded programs, and erase them. A practical approach during Internet sessions is to set Web browser options to reveal when a cookie is being passed so the researcher can decide whether to accept it. Although digital researchers can find and erase all cookie files on their computer, this action may cause delays in research and in maintenance of financial records, because university libraries and financial institutions may safely use cookies to quickly establish the authenticity of a known user.

Wireless technology in the form of personal data assistants, wireless routers, and other wireless telecommunication devices offer data for interception because they broadcast a signal for transmission to a receiver. A router attached to the researcher's computer may have a firewall to filter out intruders, but encryption schemes to broadcast data are usually not in place for personal computers and wireless routers. Calling the process "war driving," Howard Rheingold (2002) explained how a hacker armed with an antenna and a laptop can intrude into the flow of information on wireless networks. He noted an example when a specialist in computer security simply drove through downtown San Francisco and encountered 80 operating and open networks. Digital researchers who transmit data via data assistants, cell phones, or other wireless communication devices must take precautions to protect their data or to refrain from transmission until they have a more secure network connection.

Identity Protection

Digital researchers must make intelligent choices as they pursue knowledge in vast cyber archives. They must protect themselves against digital harvesters by being prudent in evaluating sites, their offers, and their hypertext links. They must protect themselves against malware by understanding the types of infection, the modes of delivery, and the countermeasures of antivirus and antispyware software that can thwart intrusions into their computer while ensuring their work continues with their identity held secure and intact.

Researchers have an obligation to conceal the identities of the research subjects and their personal information. Digital researchers must be cognizant of the harm that can befall participants and colleagues. By using a numbering scheme instead of personal identities on study records, by hiding email distribution lists, by having active virus and spyware detection programs, and by reorganizing information into several linkable repositories instead of one huge database of all records, digital researchers can discourage wholesale raids on data and thus preserve the integrity of their studies and their collegial relationships.

Personal Rights

Above all, digital researchers must be vigilant about their constitutional rights and the progress of legislation that threatens their work and their right to pursue knowledge. As of late 2005, provisions of the Patriot Act will expire without legislative extension (Whitaker, 2003). Although digital researchers cannot reverse the recent history of federal surveillance, there is much they can do to protect their rights. First, digital researchers must be aware that they are obligated to protect their work and the entrusted information of study participants. Although they may not be able to reverse legislation, they can make their legislators aware of concerns about the provisions of the Patriot Act. Because government investigations can be covert or overt, researchers should take steps to protect their computer and network environment from intrusive surveillance by the federal government— the same steps they would take to protect themselves from hackers. If their research activities have landed them on a federal list of "persons of interest," researchers should note any sudden changes in airport screenings, bank record requests, grant approval, and publication opportunity. In this uncertain world, digital researchers must keep safe their identity and their character by refusing to be unwitting victims of invasive Web technologies.

The list of perils described in this chapter are long, and pose significant risks and complications to digital writing researchers. We cannot, however, allow the risks of data mining, surveillance, or malware to intrude upon the important research that must be conducted on and through online spaces, nor can we allow it to pause our use of digital spaces to gather information and to do research. Rather, we have to accept these methods as part of the everyday context of digital spaces; we have to adopt methods to protect ourselves, our computers, our networks, and our projects; and we have to be advocates in protecting privacy, addressing surveillance, and fostering a safe network ecology.

NOTES

1. As the Web site explains, the Open Archives Harvesting Initiative is charged with specifying "a method for digital repositories (also called 'data providers') to expose metadata about their objects for harvesting by aggregators (also called 'service providers'). Metadata is exposed via 'sets,' or collections of metadata that data providers decide to make available for harvesting. Service providers harvest sets from data providers of interest, and provide search services for the resulting collections of metadata" (www.cdlib.org/inside/projects/harvesting); more information and complete documentation is available at www.openarchives.org/OAI/openarchivesprotocol.html

2. Identity theft is the premeditated act of stealing a victim's name and personal information to manipulate this data to unlawfully acquire goods, services, or financial gain and thereby make the victim liable for the cost. Although identity theft is against the law, it is often difficult to find the perpetrators, as they simply assume someone else's identity without a digital trace. Computer-related crime in prosecutorial offices show 27.4% for credit card fraud, 22.3% for bank card fraud, and 18.2% for identity theft (*Statistical Abstract of the United States: 2004–2005*, 2004, p. 203).

3. Emails infected with and generated by The Love Bug worm had subject lines that included such variants as LOVELETTER; fwd: Joke; I love you; Virus Alert; and Important! Read carefully! Once the worm embedded itself in a user's system and executed, it automatically sent out mass email messages that appeared as if they were sent by the user.

4. Most of the Patriot Act's sixteen sections, which were set to expire on December 31, 2005, have been made permanent by the *USA Patriot Improvement and*

Reauthorization Act of 2005 and the *USA Patriot Act Additional Reauthorizing Amendments Act of 2006* as of March 9, 2006. Senate-contested provisions (i.e., undisclosed search and seizure of evidence, use of National Security Letters for federal authorization rather than judicial review, mandated library compliance with profiling patrons, and Inernet surveillance and data warehousing of personal information of suspected terrorists without disclosure) remain in force with little modification at least until December 31, 2009.

5. The federal government was surprised by the leaked provisions of the Patriot Act II and by the extent of public outcry, especially from librarians. However, the promised reform bill, the Reauthorization Act, blurs the distinction between investigation and relentless pursuit. According to Jean Claude Paye (2006), the extension of the executive control at the sacrifice of personal liberties has been justified based on cultural climate following the September 11, 2001 terrorist attacks; Paye noted, "we leave the state of emergency and enter the permanent stage of exception" (p. 159).

18

MULTIFACETED METHODS FOR MULTIMODAL TEXTS

ALTERNATE APPROACHES TO CITATION ANALYSIS FOR ELECTRONIC SOURCES

Colleen A. Reilly

Douglas Eyman

Prompted by the need to assess the value and circulation of electronic scholarship, in this chapter we investigate methods for developing distributional and relational measurements of digital texts from the fields of bibliometrics and cybermetrics. First, we outline traditional methods of citation analysis and explain the problems these methods pose for assessing the impact of scholarly electronic publications. We then argue for the importance of assessing electronic publications in terms of their structure, the digital environments in which they reside, and the degree to which they violate traditional genre norms of print scholarship. A heuristic method for evaluating digital texts is presented as an example of a rhetorically based evaluation strategy that can complement more traditional quantitative assessments of the value of scholarly work and can also help researchers who publish in electronic environments to assess the impact of their texts on disciplinary conversations.

INTRODUCTION

As members of the editorial staff of a peer-reviewed electronic journal—
Kairos: A Journal of Rhetoric, Technology, and Pedagogy—we are highly
invested in persuading colleagues that electronic scholarship is as rigorous-
ly reviewed, credible, and influential as print scholarship. Working on the
staff of an electronic journal puts digital scholarship at the center of our
intellectual endeavors, and we can easily overestimate its perceived acceptance and importance as a result. However, to demonstrate the importance
of electronic scholarship to our field and to those external to it, particularly when making cases for tenure and promotion, we recognize that we
need more than anecdotal evidence of its impact on traditional scholarship
and its contributions to disciplinary knowledge making. To develop such
evidence, we embarked on a citation analysis project that involved determining the number and types of electronic sources cited from 1996–2003
in four print journals central to our field: *College Composition and
Communication*, *College English*, *Computers and Composition*, and the
Journal of Advanced Composition.[1] Although we were most concerned with
the citation of peer-reviewed articles in electronic journals, we wanted to
document other types of electronic sources used and cited. We suspected
that there might be few citations of peer-reviewed articles and that charting citations of other types of electronic publication might lend insight into
how electronic sources are selected and perceived.

We offer this chapter as a record of our research into how the influence
and impact of electronic sources, particularly scholarly sources, are and
should be assessed. Researchers invested in electronically delivered scholarly work need to develop persuasive methods for assessing the perceived
value and influence of those texts so that they can make informed decisions about how to best situate their work within larger institutional and
professional contexts and make cases for how their work is being used and
perceived by others within specific scholarly communities.

To develop a methodology for our analysis, we turned to citation analysis, which figures prominently in the scholarship of information and library
sciences. An initial search of the Web and of scholarly databases revealed
citation analysis to be a complex area of inquiry, employing a variety of
methods to assess the impact of authors, articles, and journals on the disciplinary conversations of specific fields. As many scholars of citation
analysis noted and as we soon discovered, traditional methods of citation
analysis, including bibliometric and co-citation analysis, yield largely neg-

ative results for electronic publications (Harter & Kim, 1996; Herring, 1997, 2002; Zhang, 1998). In response to these findings, our chapter outlines the traditional methods of citation analysis and explains the problems that these methods pose for assessing the impact of scholarly electronic publications. We then argue for the importance of assessing electronic publications in terms of their structure and their violations of the traditional genre norms of print scholarship. Additionally, we explain and evaluate alternate methods of citation analysis—such as cybermetric analyses—that are currently being developed to account for the disciplinary impact of electronic sources. We conclude with the assertion that to assess accurately the importance of electronic sources, we need new methods that provide a more complete picture of the use and influence of electronic scholarship in ways that account for the differences between print and digital environments.

IMPORTANCE OF CITATION AND METHODS OF CITATION ANALYSIS

Scholars use citations to connect their writing to that of others to highlight agreement with and provide justification for their ideas, point to oppositional perspectives, and demonstrate their understanding of the state of disciplinary knowledge. Much has been made of citation as a means of reflection and as an act of collaborative knowledge making, and its role in the scholarship of the sciences and social sciences is well-documented (Bazerman, 1988; Berkenkotter & Huckin, 1993, 1995; Budd, 1999; Gilbert & Mulkay, 1984; Latour & Woolgar, 1979).

To be cited—even as a negative or oppositional example—means that an article, author, or journal's work *matters*, in every sense of the word: It is part of the discipline, part of the conversation, and it is visible and needs to be acknowledged as belonging to the foundation for building new ideas. Citation, therefore, provides a measure of legitimation, and in many fields—although not yet ours—it is *the* measure of legitimation. Because we were seeking legitimation for scholarly electronic publications, specifically for peer-reviewed electronic journals, we looked to citation analysis for a method that would allow us to provide substantive evidence about the impact of electronic journals on our field of study. Although aware of some of the imperfections of citation analysis as a measure of an author's or journal's impact on scholarship (e.g., Harter, 1998), we agreed at the outset with Nancy Kaplan and Michael Nelsons' (2000) assertion that "in the absence of a more compelling metric, citation analysis remains the best commonly available indicator of usage" (p. 324).[2]

Citation analysis as a process and a field of study provides numerous means and methods for use in quantifying a record and history of citation for authors, articles, and journals. The simplest method of citation analysis is to first select a time frame and a body of citation data, and then to determine how many times an author, article, or journal has been cited by the publications indexed in the dataset within that timeframe. In most cases, citation data for this sort of bibliometric analysis is drawn from citation databases, such as Social Sciences Citation Index (SSCI), Science Citation Index (SCI), and Arts and Humanities Citation Index (AHCI)—all accessible online from Thomson's Institute for Scientific Information (ISI) database, also known as the Web of Science (Corby, 2001; Harter, 1998). To correct for variances in the length of time that journals have been in publication and to compensate for differences in the number of articles that journals publish each year, researchers use the raw data gleaned from bibliometric analyses in calculations to achieve more comparative and relevant results. One of the most important of these calculations is a journal's *impact rating*, determined by dividing the number of citations to articles published in a journal during a specified time frame by the number of articles published in the journal during that same time period (Funkhouser, 1996). Because the ISI databases—including SSCI, SCI, and AHCI—use a journal's impact rating as one factor in determining whether or not to index that journal in their databases, it is a particularly important measure of a journal's influence. As discussed below, a journal's exclusion from these central citation databases makes it difficult for that journal to garner the widespread influence that could be used to justify its inclusion. Additionally, scholars within particular fields may use impact ratings to determine which journals are most worthwhile to read consistently and to target for submission of their research.

Katherine Corby (2001) discussed the lack of coverage of journals in education by the Thomson ISI database. In her analysis, Corby discovered that ISI only indexes 27% of the 1,124 journals indexed by education-specific databases including ERIC's Current Index to Journals in Education (CIJE) and Education Abstracts. As a result, Corby surmised that many citations are missed by researchers using only the ISI database to collect citation data. As Edward Funkhouser (1996) explained, the lack of citation can have serious consequences, resulting in journals, authors, or whole fields being deemed to have low credibility. Like journals in the fields of education and communication, journals in rhetoric and composition and computers and writing may be underrepresented in the standard citation databases. Of the four journals from which we collected data regarding the citation of electronic publications—*College Composition and Communication (CCC)*, *College English*, *Computers and Composition*, and the *Journal of Advanced Composition*—only two (*CCC* and *College English*) are indexed by Thomson ISI. The lack of representation, particularly of *Computers and Composition*, makes using these databases for citation analysis related to electronic sources very difficult. Furthermore, no other citation database yet exists that covers the most significant journals in rhetoric and composition.[3]

With no citation database at our disposal, we manually gathered data regarding the citation of electronic sources from the four print journals we selected, which was a time-consuming task. To collect this information, we examined the bibliographies of all of the articles, reviews, and other sorts of texts found in the designated print journals and counted and entered into an online database the citations referencing electronic sources. Early in this process, we recognized that we were finding and would probably continue to find so few citations of electronic sources that we would likely to be unable to apply the methods of citation analysis discussed above in any meaningful way. In the end, of the more than 25,950 items cited in the four journals in question, fewer than 950 were to electronic sources and of those only 104 were to articles in peer-reviewed electronic journals. Furthermore, the impact factor for any of the electronic journals cited was negligible; for example, the electronic journal *Kairos: A Journal of Rhetoric, Technology and Pedagogy* received the most citations of peer-reviewed articles, 26, from 1996–2003, which, according to the formula listed above for calculating a journal's impact factor, would result in a demonstration of little or no impact.[4]

Not content with our negative citation results—which raised for us more questions than they answered—we began to look past traditional methods of citation analysis to explore other methods that could help us to more accurately assess the impact of peer-reviewed electronic journals on their respective disciplinary communities. In the remainder of this chapter we describe other methods of citation analysis that may prove useful for analyzing and more accurately representing the impact of scholarly electronic publications in their native environments. Additionally, we present methods we developed for examining and assessing electronic publications and determining their differences from print scholarship. We see the adaptation of citation analysis as a starting point for assessing the effectiveness of digital delivery as well as providing possibilities for tracking the circulation of disciplinary knowledge in and through electronic environments. However, we also assert that it is important for digital writing researchers to be able to represent forms of new media scholarship as distinct from traditional academic work, and the heuristic we provide for examining online texts as uniquely situated in their native digital environments is an initial method for enacting accurate representation. To assess and legitimate electronic scholarship, we need to develop methods native to that environment rather than relying on traditional methods that simply do not take into account the particular exigencies and affordances of networked digital spaces. Such methods will help researchers determine who is reading their own and others' electronic scholarship and revise how citation can be defined, enacted, and located in electronic environments so that we can make arguments about the usefulness and relevance of reading, analyzing, and publishing electronic scholarship.

CYBERMETRICS: QUANTITATIVE ANALYSIS METHODS FOR ELECTRONIC SCHOLARSHIP

Unlike bibliometric analyses of print documents, purely quantitative citation analyses of online documents are not reliable indicators of the journal's relative impact or reflective of its place in its discipline; moreover, bibliometric methods of citation analysis cannot be directly applied to online scholarship because they cannot account for the rhizomatic topologies of hypertext linking. Print citation practices operate in strictly hierarchical structures that either describe relationships between the scholarly work and other research publications or indicate the work's primary sources, with very clear motivators for each type of citation: documenting the origin of concepts, promoting the authority of the citing work, or criticizing the cited publication. Hypertext links, on the other hand, often enact less formal connections than print citations, creating relationships between a wide variety of publications, including personal home pages, subject resource guides, news publications, organizational home pages, email discussion list archives, blogs, and online bibliographies. Motivations for linking also vary widely and are often far less clear than the motivations for formal citation. Because the function and nature of print citations are not directly analogous to Web links, new infometric methodologies—based in part upon the principles and statistical formulas developed for bibliometric analyses—are being developed by researchers in the field of information science. Several terms for these new methodologies have been suggested, but the field currently appears to favor *cybermetrics* as the designation for the study of online scholarship.

Cybermetrics studies the network of links between electronic scholarly works, revealing how widely a specific electronic source is linked to other online texts, what types of texts link to specific sources, and how the source is used. Isidro Aguillo (2003) located cybermetrics at the intersections of "cybergeography" and "cyberdemography" across Internet genres (such as email, the Web, and online databases). Methods include adaptations of bibliometrics, user studies, calculations of "cyberindicators" (e.g., Web site hits, search engine rankings), assessment of Web data architecture and hyperlink topologies, and comparative search engine analyses.

Mapping Hyperlinks

One of the most common cybermetric methods, and one perhaps most analogous to traditional citation analysis, involves tracing the links that point to a particular document or Web site. Identifying these references (called "backlinks") is possible by conducting specific queries on search engines that support the *link:* function.[5] Currently, only three major search engines support backlink searches: AltaVista, AlltheWeb, and Google. AltaVista and AlltheWeb are consistent in their report of backlinks and are recommended for performing this type of cybermetric analysis; Google only displays results that pass a certain threshold using its PageRank algorithm (see Brin & Page, 1998). Additionally, both AltaVista and AlltheWeb allow the option of excluding the originating site so that links that come from within that site are not counted as backlinks (these internal links are referred to as "self-links"), whereas Google does not allow the exclusion of self-links.

We performed a search for backlinks to the online, peer-reviewed journal *Kairos: A Journal of Rhetoric, Technology, and Pedagogy* in October 2004 using the following search string—**link:english.ttu.edu**—and our search produced 10,100 backlinks in the AlltheWeb search engine, 10,200 backlinks in the AltaVista search engine, and 574 backlinks in the Google search engine (of which about 10% are self-links). Repeating this search over several weeks showed an increase in backlinks to the journal in AltaVista and AlltheWeb, whereas the results from Google remained static. The number of backlinks can provide a quantifiable measure of visibility; additionally, once the backlinks are identified, the links can be classified and the relationships they represent can be assessed. For example, we can determine which issues, sections, and articles within *Kairos* receive the greatest numbers of backlinks and also determine how the links function within the linking sites. As more researchers and scholars come to use and rely upon work available online (including database-driven access to electronic versions of print publications), situating online scholarship within a constellation of other influential online venues can help to assess the overall influence and importance of each site of scholarly endeavor. Mapping backlinks can allow us to create visual representations of these webs of influence. Furthermore, most studies conducted by infometric researchers focus on finding backlinks that connect scholarly works to one another (Harter & Ford, 2000; Lawrence & Giles, 1999). However, the classification of scholarly work is both specific and very limited; we would argue that a close reading of backlinks in terms of both relationship and function can help to show how digital projects that do not easily fit into traditional definitions of scholarship may in fact be scholarly in function and worthy of recognition. To that end, it is important to examine not only backlinks, but also to study *sitation* practices and measures of use to gain a more complete understanding of the impact of electronic sources.

Applying Sitation Practices

"Sitation" describes the relationship between sites on the Internet (Aguillo, 1996; McKiernan, 1996) as well as the activity of constructing the links that represent and enact those relationships. Whereas traditional citation analysis tracks references between peer-reviewed scholarly publications, Web links represent a wide range of relationships between both refereed scholarly works and unrefereed works that may be either scholarly or informal in nature. Thus cybermetrics has been challenged to provide methods not only for quantifying links, but also evaluating the type and quality of the relationships between linked texts. Two complementary approaches to link assessment have emerged in current research: (a) classifying links and the relationships they represent, and (b) identifying author motivation in constructing links in online works. This form of link-based connectivity provides a particularly useful mechanism for tracing relationships between works available on the Internet (such as the relationships of scholarly works and their primary sources or archival repositories of data and previously published texts to new works being published or distributed online). Sitation allows researchers, moreover, to both qualify and quantify connections, relationships, and patterns of circulation across texts, disciplinary spheres, and media forms. Drawing on and expanding the methods initially developed as cybermetrics holds promise for constructing rhetorical analyses of these relationships, as well as for developing a deeper understanding of digital delivery and circulation. The work in information sciences that has approached sitation thus far has provided only tantalizing suggestions of the power this method could offer if developed within a rhetorical framework.

Alistair Smith (2004) argued for classifying links as substantive (related to research and functioning as formal citation) and nonsubstantive (linking to further information, organizations, or other informal links) based on identifying the nature of the source page, the nature of the target page, and the reason for linking. Rather than examining only works published in online journals, Smith looked at a range of sources, including the web sites of universities, professional institutes, research institutes, electronic journals, and the Web pages of individual researchers. The most common source type in his data set was the directory or subject guide, whereas formal publications accounted for less than 10% of his sample size. Similarly, the most common target page type was the main page of an organization (indeed, most links pointed to an entry page for a larger site rather than to a specific reference point) with links to formal publications again representing only 10% of the sample size.[6]

Smith's (2004) work focused on link classification; although motivation played a role in the assessment of links as substantive or non-substantive, the primary measure of the classification schema was based on link topology. By contrast, Hak Joon Kim (1998, 2000) conducted a comprehensive study of why authors of scholarly electronic papers create hyperlinks. Kim identified many motivations for scholarly linking on the Web, and concluded that Web hyperlinking in a scholarly environment is mainly a subjective and private act (informal) rather than objective and public (formal). Mike Thelwall (2003) used inductive content analysis to examine a larger sample of university-based Web sites and identified four motivation types unique to Web sitation practices:

> The term "ownership" is coined for links acknowledging authorship or co-authorship of a resource, "social" for links with a primarily social reinforcement role, "general navigational" for those with a general information navigation function and "gratuitous" for those that serve no communication function at all. (n.p.)

The difficulty with such classification schema is that it often overlooks rhetorical motivations that do not fit established patterns of scholarly behavior. Thelwall, for instance, classified as "general navigational" any link that points to sites that might provide more detailed information or more in-depth description of background material, a move often not seen as "citable" in the strict sense of promoting knowledge making. Perhaps this sitation practice is not common in print texts simply because the medium does not provide mechanisms for making connections to related works on such a broad scale. Further, the sole indicator of academic quality in both Smith's classification scheme and Thelwall's motivation study is peer-review—thus denigrating online works not yet recognized as scholarly activity. Such a narrow focus does not take into account either the scope of information circulation on the Internet or the possibilities for new knowledge-making activities that do not meet the criteria for traditional, print-based scholarship. The very notion of "gratuitous" linking shows that some cybermetric researchers do not yet have a clear understanding of the rhizomatic and intertextual topologies of the Web—topologies that provide affordances for epistemic constructions that break with the generic conventions that guide traditional scholarly citation practices.

Certainly more research on the nature and classification of links is needed (particularly on the rhetorical practices enacted through the activity of linking); nonetheless, backlink analysis in conjunction with other measures—such as hyperlink mapping and sitation practices—is currently one of the strongest measures of influence available for analysis of online scholarship. Combined with ranked assessment (such as Web impact factors, discussed below) and retrieval analysis, researchers can produce a fairly robust account of the influence and importance of online publishing venues. This kind of accounting, moreover, can be applied to any document available on the Web, rather than being restricted, as it is with print texts, to those that have been published and circulated in paper-based form. The scope of research of digital writing is thus much wider than traditional approaches that rely on texts that have passed a minimum economic threshold for distribution.

Identifying Web Impact Factors

Peter Ingwersen (1998) proposed a calculation called the Web Impact Factor or Web-IF that measured the overall impact of a Web space by counting backlink pages over large areas of the Web, based on the bibliometric calculation of impact factors for journals; the same year Sergey Brin and Lawrence Page (1998) introduced Google's PageRank algorithm, which employs the principle that highly linked pages are likely to be useful, especially if pages linking to them are also highly linked to. Similarly, Jon Kleinberg's (1999) algorithm uses links and page text to group semantically related pages and to identify pages that link to many relevant pages ("hubs") and those linked to by relevant pages ("authorities").

Ingwersen's (1998) Web Impact Factor is determined by the ratio of the number of links made to a site to the number of pages in that site; in comparison, Google's PageRank assesses only single pages and is not concerned with the overall content of the site, only the links to and from individual pages. Google's PageRank works like this: Each page that is indexed has both inbound and outbound links. The number of inbound links is divided by the number of outbound links to produce the base ranking; the page ranks of the inbound links also factor into the ranking algorithm. So, for instance, a webliography with many outbound links (links to sources) and few inbound links would receive a very low page rank; a site with only a few outbound links but many inbound links would receive a high page rank. Pages are ranked on a 10-point scale with a higher numerical rating representing a more influential page: *Kairos: A Journal of Rhetoric, Technology, and Pedagogy* currently registers a 7 out of 10.

Thelwall (2003) suggested that iterative rating systems such as Google's PageRank may provide a better method for assessing the influence of online scholarly work, as the system theoretically accounts for quality of inlinks rather than simply quantifying the connections to and from a given site. The difficulty with adopting an iterative rating system is determining what elements will be evaluated and what kind of classification schemes the ranking will depend upon. Such a system, however, does provide a general measure of influence; thus we find it useful to consider Google's PageRank when combined with other measures that can help researchers evaluate impact and use.

Using Retrieval Analysis

In addition to traditional citation measurements, scholarly journals are often evaluated based on their circulation—the greater the number of readers, the more likely the journal can be declared influential (either directly, as through citation analysis, or indirectly). Online journals are uniquely positioned to measure circulation and use via a technique called retrieval analysis.

In their assessment of the impact of a digital library, Kaplan and Nelson (2000) suggested that citation analysis is only one important metric among many that may be used to determine the impact of a publication and offered retrieval analysis as a complementary metric:

> With the advent of DLs [digital libraries], it is now possible to measure another metric. The number of retrievals (or disseminations) a publication receives in a DL should be reported, when possible, along with its

citation data. This complementary metric would yield additional information regarding the potential impact of the publication. High retrievals
and high citations build a strong argument for a high impact publication, just as low retrievals and low citations would suggest a low impact
publication. It is perhaps discipline dependent if high retrieval/low citation is more significant than low retrieval/high citation. (p. 331)

Retrieval analysis relies primarily upon server log analysis, a procedure
that, although imperfect, provides some indication of a Web site's users in
terms of the quantity of visitors and the depth of their exploration of the
site. Essentially, whenever a user clicks a link in a Web site or types a URL
in the location bar of the browser, the browser sends a GET request to the
server where the page resides. The server will record this information in its
Web logs. The server's log file records not only the information sent with
the request, but also the date, protocol, IP address of the requester, and the
result of the request. Using retrieval analysis methods, the latest data available from server logs for *Kairos: A Journal of Rhetoric, Technology, and
Pedagogy* show an average 7,597 readers per month, which is comparable
to (or higher than) the circulation of *College English* and *College Composition
and Communication*—the two print journals in the field of rhetoric/compo-
sition indexed in the ISI citation index database.[7]

Stephen Harter (1996), however, distinguished between usage and
impact, stating that although access numbers on Web servers reflect a level
of usage, they do not assess the impact of electronic journals on the
advancement of knowledge or scholarly communication and research.
Although this is a valid critique (we can see how many visitors we have, but
we can't find out how they actually use the published works), we would
argue that greater visibility does have a significant impact on knowledge
production. Because visibility plays a role in determining which print journals will be available for traditional citation assessment through inclusion
in citation databases, it should not be dismissed as an indicator of impact
for electronic publications.

ALTERNATE METHODS FOR ASSESSING
ELECTRONIC SOURCES

As John Budd (1999) noted, what is not cited is often as interesting and significant as what is. As discussed above, soon after beginning our research

on the citation of electronic sources in significant print journals in rhetoric and composition and computers and writing, we realized that according to traditional measures of impact, electronic journals in our field registered little or no influence on print journal scholarship. Based on our initial findings, we revised and expanded the focus of our study to include a determination of why peer-reviewed articles in electronic journals did not seem to matter—in fact were largely invisible—in the citation records of prominent print journals. This absence was even more troubling and intriguing in light of the prominence of the issue of electronic publication as a subject for articles in print journals; in fact, at least 71 out of 190 articles in *Computers and Composition* from 1996–2003 related directly to electronic publication, writing for the Web, teaching Web/electronic writing, writing with multimedia, and/or using online sources for research. Despite the interest in electronic publication as a topic for print journal articles, print scholarship continues to be of central and almost exclusive importance in our field. Because print is so central, we surmised that the structural and formatting departures of electronic scholarship from the norms of print publication were responsible in part for making electronic texts undesirable as scholarship. In other words, electronic scholarship violates many of the genre norms of traditional print scholarship, posing obstacles for reading and citing it. To test this supposition, we developed a methodology for analyzing the degree to which electronic publications depart from the conventions of print in the hopes of using this analysis to provide at least a partial explanation for the absence of electronic scholarship in the reference lists of print journals. The heuristic we have developed can be utilized as a method for assessing a wide range of digital documents and situating them as falling on a continuum that represents distance from print precursors—the further a work is from a more traditional form, the more likely it is that scholarly readers may not have the appropriate apparatus for reading, understanding, or citing such work. Looking at the digital environment as an important contextual reference can help us begin to develop more specific methods for assessing and using online and new media scholarship, and for locating and surmounting barriers to its use and acceptance as scholarship.

The literature regarding genre and electronic publication, particularly in terms of the format and structural attributes of Web-based publications, provides some context for the development of our analysis. Electronic texts, as scholars note, cause problems for readers because they are structurally unfamiliar and do not conform to conventions of typical scholarly genres (Gregory, 2004). Kathleen Yancey (2004a) viewed the differences between print and electronic texts in terms of coherence: Print scholarship has a high level of coherence in most cases that conforms to long-established norms of unity, consistency, and linearity. Electronic texts also have coherence, particularly if coherence is viewed in terms of creating relationships, but they achieve coherence not through unity and simplicity but through "ordered complexity" that uses arrangement to create connections between visual and verbal elements (Yancey, 2004a, p. 95). Yancey designated two main categories of electronic publications: "print uploaded or digitally designed" (p. 91). As Yancey explained, print-uploaded texts bear a close generic relationship to print texts in terms of their structure and their means of achieving coherence:

> Regardless of the fact that they are housed in the digital environment, these texts do not participate in it, but instead are represented in the composition of print. As I have explained elsewhere, the text embodies the values we associate with print: a claim; a single arrangement; support, typically developed in an explicit and linear style; a conclusion. (pp. 90–91)

In contrast, digitally designed texts grow out of the electronic environment and challenge the traditional norms and conventions related to structure and coherence:

> because the context for digital compositions is still so new and ever emerging, these texts tend to live inside the gaps, such that the reader/reviewer/responder is a more active weaver, creating arrangement and meaning. (p. 95)

Although we agree with Yancey's classifications, we view them as somewhat too broad for our purposes, as many electronic texts fall in-between these designations. Drawing, as Yancey did, on Jay David Bolter and Richard Grusin (1999), we developed a continuum that we used to assess electronic publications in terms of their degree of departure from the conventions of print texts and the extent to which they exploit and even highlight the affordances, structure, and multimedia nature of texts native to the Web environment. Our continuum includes four designations for electronic texts: highly transparent, moderately transparent, moderately hypermediated, and highly hypermediated.

Highly Transparent Electronic Texts

For the "print uploaded" end of the continuum, we adapt Bolter and Grusin's (1999) definition of transparency: transparent electronic texts allow us to forget or see through their electronic mediation and to view the text as we expect it to be: linear, straightforward, hierarchical, and accessible, like a page from a print book or journal but delivered online. We are not challenged by the structural aspects of transparent electronic texts; our years of reading printed books and journals prepare us for reading these texts, and we can readily identify them as scholarship. Although PDF files epitomize transparent electronic texts, as they are largely pictures of print texts disseminated online, some hypertext documents can also be very transparent, such as the example from *Language Learning & Technology* shown in Figure 18.1. Despite the use of HTML to format texts in *Language Learning & Technology*, articles in this wholly electronic, peer-reviewed journal are transparent in that they use almost no hyperlinks, are completely linear, and even have page numbers, which incidentally do not correspond to screen numbers or any other Web-based demarcations. Preparing a transparent text for online dissemination involves converting it to PDF or HTML and doing little else to integrate it into the electronic environment; thus, it is relatively simple to situate these online documents at the transparent end of our continuum.

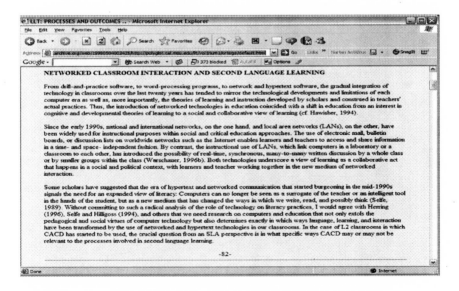

FIGURE 18.1.   Screen Shot of a Highly Transparent Article From *Language Learning & Technology* (Ortega, 1997)

Highly Hypermediated Electronic Texts

In contrast, hypermediated electronic texts, particularly those that are highly hypermediated, draw attention to their own mediation, flaunting their differences from print and defamiliarizing and challenging readers to make their own meanings—or, in Yancey's (2004a) terms, to achieve a measure of coherence—through navigating the hyperlinks, exploring interwoven graphics and text, and experiencing the multiple media, including audio and video, that comprise them. As Bolter and Grusin (1999) explained, "contemporary hypermediacy offers a heterogeneous space, in which representation is conceived of not as a window on to the world, but rather as 'windowed' itself—with windows that open on to other representations or other media. . . . In every manifestation, hypermediacy makes us aware of the medium or media" (p. 34). Highly hypermediated electronic scholarship functions in opposition to the traditional generic conventions of print scholarship, highlighting not merely its meanings but its mediation. In many cases, examples of highly hypermediated electronic texts involve interactivity—opportunities for readers to respond or significantly contribute to shaping or even adding to a text. Figure 18.2 provides an example of a highly hypermediated, peer-reviewed article from an electronic scholarly journal. As with significantly transparent works, highly hypermediated texts are relatively easy to place at the far end of the continuum.

FIGURE 18.2.   Screen Shot of a Highly Hypermediated Article from *Kairos* (Wysocki, 2002)

Moderately Transparent and Moderately Hypermediated Texts

The middle designations in our continuum are more ambiguous. Electronic publications that we consider to be moderately transparent have obvious print precursors but use some of the features facilitated by digital environments, including some links, colors, and a few graphics. Moderately transparent texts are largely linear in construction and their use of hyperlinks provides only basic navigation, such as links to connect readers to other areas of the site like the table of contents, links to email addresses, links to a few external sites that open in new windows and do not disturb the coherence of the text, and, perhaps, some internal navigational links allowing movement within the same page. In general, readers can draw on their knowledge of print texts to make sense of moderately transparent texts; such texts are presented largely as they would have been in print with the exception of some hyperlinks and the use of colors and graphics that might be cost-prohibitive for use in paper publishing. Figure 18.3 contains an example of an article from a peer-reviewed electronic journal that we designate as moderately transparent.

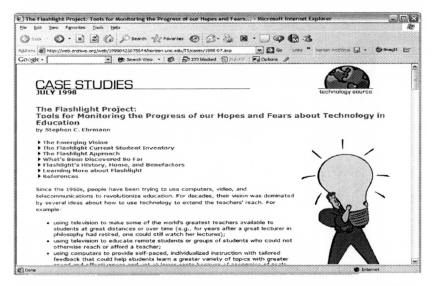

FIGURE 18.3. Screen Shot of a Moderately Transparent Article from *The Technology Source* (Ehrmann, 1998)

Finally, moderately hypermediated texts are those we found to be largely designed for the electronic environment, departing from print texts in their form or structure. These sorts of texts are designed to be read on the screen and offer the reader more options and control in terms of navigation. Moderately hypermediated texts are not necessarily complex in form and media use but may be complex in structure and require readers to understand how to read texts native to Web environments. Two different readers can possibly have very different experiences of these sorts of texts, depending on the paths that they take when navigating through them. Ease of printing also differentiates moderately hypermediated from moderately transparent texts: those that are moderately hypermediated are not easily printed nor are they fully functional if printed. They are distinguished from highly hypermediated texts by a general lack of interactivity and a relative dominance of print versus graphic elements. In moderately hypermediated articles, navigational patterns may be complex, but the navigational devices are readily apparent and visible and do not need to be discovered by the reader through play or trial and error as they often are in highly hypermediated works. An example of a moderately hypermediated article from a peer-reviewed electronic journal appears in Figure 18.4. Note the color block navigation bar at the top of the page and the chunking of the text into manageable sections that the reader can move through by clicking on the colored boxes.

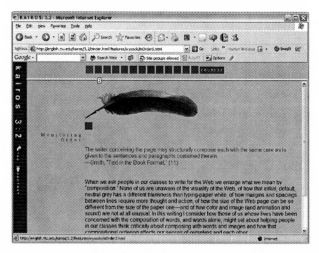

FIGURE 18.4. Screen Shot of a Moderately Hypermediated Article From *Kairos* (Wysocki, 1998)

Applying the Four-part Continuum

Using our continuum, electronic texts—most importantly peer-reviewed online scholarship—can be assessed in terms of conformity to or departure from the generic conventions of print scholarship. Through such an assessment, we can formulate possible explanations for the dearth of citations of peer-reviewed articles from electronic journals in print texts. The form of many of these sources violates generic norms, thus making them unappealing or difficult to cite. For example, when citing Wysocki's (2002) text shown in Figure 18.2 above, readers may lose track of the title because the video portion opens in a new window. Additionally, if attempting to reference specific parts of the article, scholars may have trouble describing a specific part or directing readers to a designated section because of the text's non-linear, playful navigational scheme.

Through examining all the electronic sources cited from 1996–2003 in the print journals we analyzed and placing these sources on the continuum, we found a correlation between what is cited and the text's degree of hypermediacy. From 1996–2003, 104 citations to peer-reviewed articles from electronic journals appeared in the four print journals we analyzed; of those, 45 citations were to highly transparent articles, 27 citations were to moderately transparent articles, 18 citations were to moderately hypermediated articles, 10 were to highly hypermediated articles, and 4 citations were to articles we could not assess largely because we could not recover them.

Classifying electronic texts in this manner and correlating this classification with citation data highlights the fact that although our field lauds experimentation with digital textuality in theory, it largely eschews such experiments in the practice of scholarship. Recognition of this situation is important for researchers, who we call upon to interrogate their own research practices and procedures and to broaden those practices to incorporate research using electronic texts that generically reside outside of their traditional comfort zone in terms of reading and scholarly use. Our findings are also important for researchers seeking to publish their work and have that work gain wide acceptance. Researchers who seek to build a scholarly reputation through publishing highly hypermediated scholarship, even if published in peer-reviewed electronic journals, are currently taking a risk—as our research reveals, the degree of hypermediacy of electronic texts functions as both an explanation for a lack of citation and a predictor of citation. Transparent texts are much more likely than hypermediated texts to be seen as scholarship and cited in print journals. In light of the discussion of citation methodologies above, electronic journals and the articles contained therein are not being located in citation data and are apparently not viewed as worthy of citation, particularly if they are designed to take advantage of the Web and depart from the generic conventions of print scholarship in form and function. Such evidence further supports our assertions that alternate methods of citation analysis need to be employed to assess electronic journals and articles in ways that acknowledge them as a unique scholarly genre, particularly if our field continues to advocate the development of multimodal scholarly compositions. Cybermetric analyses, such as tracking backlinks and employing sitation practices, are clearly applicable to research on the circulation of any kind of online text and may prove to be quite helpful in legitimating electronic scholarship. Such methods of determining influence—in combination with a change in research practices to include seeking scholarship outside of recognized scholarly databases (which do not index most electronic journals), and learning from and teaching others to locate, read, and use texts that do not resemble print scholarship—can help to precipitate a change in the use and acceptance of scholarship designed for and published in electronic environments.

CONCLUSION

The development of digital media has opened a space for the exploration of new forms of scholarship. Along with new possibilities and new genres comes a need for new methods of assessment, because the established methods for other media cannot appropriately be used to evaluate new scholarly works. It is important for scholars who produce digital works to be able to show that their work has influence and importance equivalent to work done in print media; without similar incentives for production (i.e., tenure and promotion), the scholarship of new media will be confined to critique published in traditional media and the possibilities for producing new media scholarship *in* new media will be diminished. Rethinking our citation practices as well as our methods of citation analysis—in other words, rethinking what counts as scholarship in our field—is the first step in reducing the divide between what our literature and pedagogy say are important and what we legitimate as significant through our citation practices.

There is much work to do in this area. The methods discussed above need to be refined, and further research on qualitative and rhetorical analysis of digital scholarship is required if we are to establish the impact and importance of online scholarly publication. Economic trends in scholarly publication continue to support the development of online publication for scholarly work, and several disciplinary associations are currently exploring the benefits of establishing electronic journals and archives not controlled by commercial entities. If we are to take advantage of the opportunity that such material and economic exigencies present, it is important that we continue to create works that take advantage of the affordances of digital media for new forms of scholarship and for greater degrees of circulation of different kinds of texts.

To these ends, there are many ways that scholars in the fields of rhetoric and composition and computers and writing—as well as editors of online publications—can help to advance the use and refinement of alternate methods of assessment for electronic publication and also make such publications, even those that are highly hypermediated, easier to cite using traditional methods. For example, in making cases for tenure and promotion, scholars who publish electronically can employ the methods outlined in this chapter to support their cases. Furthermore, employing methods to support the perception of electronic publications as equal scholarly endeavors to print publications will have more weight if supported by more studies of electronic publications using these methods described above. Scholars and editors who publish electronic texts, especially those that are highly hypermediated, need to make sure that traditional data relevant for citation are visible. For example, highly hypermediated texts should have an introductory page that includes complete citation information. Additionally, such information should be embedded somehow in the text or metadata, or linked to it, so that it can be easily located at any point in viewing the piece. Lastly, electronic journal interfaces should be revised so that complete citation information is clearly visible or at least accessible even from within the texts.

Field-wide initiatives are also needed. For instance, our field could benefit from a citation database that covers the prominent journals, including electronic journals, important to rhetoric and composition and computers and writing, and we need to attempt to have more of our journals included in other databases such as the ISI databases. Additionally, studies of the importance of electronic publication in our field need to be grounded in data rather than in anecdotal evidence or perception. For instance, discussions of multimedia composition need to account for the difficulties involved in having such texts perceived and accepted as scholarly and read in academic contexts. Finally, researchers writing about electronic publication should be ethically and intellectually bound to seek relevant scholarship that is published electronically. Failing to do so undermines electronic scholarship, and calls into question the credibility of print publications addressing electronic publication as a topic.

NOTES

1. We began our study with the broad field of composition; our next research project will look more specifically at professional and technical writing. The four journals in our initial study represent the largest number of composition-specific subscriptions.
2. We draw on *Kairos* as an example because (a) it is considered an established journal in our particular field; (b) we can best make comparisons that take into account disciplinary differences; and (c) we have access to server data not readily available from other sources. However, our use of *Kairos* should be seen as a case in point; the methods we describe here are applicable to any electronic resources (not just scholarly electronic journals).
3. Our field does have an excellent bibliographic database in Rich Haswell and Glen Blalocks' CompPile (http://comppile.tamucc.edu/); however, CompPile does not include a citation database or analysis function, and the coverage of the bibliography is from 1939–1999.
4. Of interest is the fact that of those 26 citations to *Kairos* in peer-reviewed, print journals, 20 of them were to articles published during the first 2 years of publication, 1996 and 1997, which correlates with other studies indicating that older electronic scholarship is cited most often (Kaplan & Nelson, 2000).
5. There have been, however, some concerns about the reliability of using backlinking. In a study of three search engines that support retrieval of backlinks to a given Web site, Harter and Ford (2000) found that AltaVista produced different results for the same search over very short time periods, and that although HotBot and Infoseek were more reliable, HotBot would not perform truncated searches (searches that include all of the nodes in a Web site so that each page would not have to be searched for separately), and Infoseek returned far fewer overall results than either of the other two search engines. Additionally, no search engine indexes the entire Web: Lawrence and Giles (1999) used statistical analyses to argue that search engines were indexing fewer than 50% of the extant pages on the Web. Search engines also cannot currently index "the invisible Web"—sites that are password-protected, online databases and database-driven Web sites, and sites that specifically instruct search engines not to index them through use of search-engine exclusion metadata. In the years since Harter and Ford performed their study of backlinks, however, search engines have improved both in terms of reliability and scope of indexing. Of the search engines studied by Harter and Ford, only AltaVista still provides backlink searching; it is far more reliable today than it was in 2000, now providing more consistent results.

6. The results of this study are similar to the results found by Eyman and Reilly (2004) when examining the citation of online sources in print journals in the field of rhetoric and composition.

7. From the outset, we checked each other's assessment of the degree of hyper-mediacy and other factors to be sure that we were consistently placing the same sites in the same place on the continuum. In fact, we completely cross-checked the 50 or so entries in the database as a norming exercise. Additionally, we built a cross-check field into the entry form so that we could flag particular entries for further analysis and review the initial assessments.

19

MESSY CONTEXTS

RESEARCH AS A RHETORICAL SITUATION

Rebecca Rickly

In this chapter, I argue that the required methods course for graduate students in composition and technical communication should be the location of learning not just about research methods, or how to critique them, but how to use and apply them rhetorically in increasingly complex and intricate situations, particularly in the newly technologized sites of research in which writing is being done and studied. I suggest that we—both emerging and established scholars—adopt a situated, contextualized, rhetorical approach to conducting research that might better prepare us to conduct, critique, and teach research in the digital age.

REQUIRED RESEARCH COURSES AND DIGITAL TECHNOLOGIES—WHAT A MESS!

In the spring of 2005, I conducted a pilot survey examining the required methods course in graduate programs in Composition, Rhetoric, and

Technical Communication (TC), in which 68 professors from across the United States answered questions about their experience with this course.[1] The responses were evenly divided between MA- and PhD-granting institutions, ranging from straight Composition to Composition/TC programs. Ninety percent of the respondents offered a research methods overview course, and 75% of those who participated noted that this course was required. Less then 20% of the respondents offered any other research courses in their programs. Thus, for the majority of graduate students, the overview course in research methods was the only course focusing on methods that these students would take. Most participants (85%) noted that the primary goal of the course was to provide graduate students with knowledge of and familiarity with the research methods used in our field. A slightly lower percentage of the respondents (75%) noted that another goal for the course included reading and assessing formal research in our field. Other notable goals included an opportunity to create a literature review (57%) and an opportunity to gain experience in conducting research within the confines of a course (54%).

The required research methods course, it would seem, must be vast and contain multitudes. It should prepare students to know and choose methods wisely; to design, conduct, and report on research; to read and assess existing research critically; and to conduct a literature review to precede and inform a research project. Graduate students who have taken such a course should feel comfortable in the library, in the field, and anywhere in between; they should also feel confident, in any context, determining a research problem/question, selecting and employing various methods, analyzing data gathered, and writing up the results.

Obviously, I'm overgeneralizing, but to make a point: With a few notable exceptions, the required research methods overview course is often the *only* opportunity, outside a thesis or dissertation project, that a graduate student has to learn, criticize, or apply research methods. Because of the increasingly complex subject matters and sites we deal with in our research, students need to learn—early in their graduate careers—how to situate themselves in relationship to the sites (often technological) that they study, as well as how to select methods, how to apply them, and how to analyze the data they gather. And it appears that only slightly over half of our required research methods classes are providing the opportunity for graduate students to do all of these things. As mentioned, nearly half of our required methods courses do not provide students opportunities to apply methods, focusing instead upon reading and analyzing methods. Because this collection focuses on the conduct of research in the age of digital writing technology, we must wonder whether the old ways of viewing, teaching, and learning research methods are sufficient. Has our research situation changed significantly, and with it, the research methods necessary to study digital writing? How about instruction in research methods? Should it change along with the digital contexts we now study? What should be the core of the one required research methods course that graduate students take?

It is my feeling that not enough attention is paid to the actual practice of conducting empirical research, especially in the required course, and that when attention is paid, it is often done so in a formulaic, container-like fashion. In this chapter, I argue that these typically linear, rigid methods aren't appropriate for conducting research in the newly technologized sites of research in which writing is being done/studied now. The required methods class should be the location of learning not just about research methods, or how to critique them, but how to apply them rhetorically in increasingly complex and intricate situations. I end by suggesting that we—both emerging and established scholars—adopt a situated, contextualized, rhetorical approach for the conduct of research that might better prepare us to conduct, critique, and teach research in the digital age.

COMPLEXITIES OF RESEARCH AND THE TEACHING OF RESEARCH

Research conducted today—particularly research involving complex subjects (and subjectivities) dealing with technology—demands a more thorough, comprehensive, and yet localized understanding and application of research methods. Technological contexts are not easily categorized—that is, they involve different materialities, different subjectivities, different situations. So, too, the methods we use should be less static, less rigid, and more malleable. John Law (2004), in *After Method: Mess in Social Science Research,* articulated the complexity of research sites: "Events and processes are not simply complex in the sense that they are technically difficult to grasp (thought this is certainly often the case). Rather, they are also complex because they *necessarily exceed our capacity to know them*" (p. 6). We can easily see how technology compounds the complexity of a situation involving writing, an already complex phenomenon. Early research involving technology and writing first recognized this complexity; initially, computers were seen as a boon to writers, allowing them to revise as they composed on the fly and to collaborate with those next to them in a lab or classroom setting (see, for instance, Bridwell, Nancarrow, & Ross, 1984; Halpern & Ligget, 1984; Rodrigues & Rodrigues, 1984; Schwartz, 1982; Selfe & Wahlstrom, 1989). Later, as chat programs allowed for increased collaboration and the Internet brought even more people together, early scholars heralded an era of egalitarian discourse (Cooper & Selfe, 1990). Soon, however, scholars began to question the egalitarian nature of technologized discourse, looking at race, gender, power, and other materialities in computers and writing (see, for instance, Kolko, Nakamura, & Rodman, 2000; Hawisher & Selfe, 2004; Monroe, 2004; Rickly, 1999; Sullivan & Takayoshi, in press; Wolfe, 1999). Building from these earlier critiques, we continue to acknowledge that the realities of learning, teaching, administering, keeping up, and even simply using technology in writing scenarios has grown increasingly complex.

For example, consider a relatively "simple" MOO discussion that occurs on a regular basis in the online MA and PhD Technical Communication and Rhetoric courses at Texas Tech University (TTU); several studies have examined MOO discussions,[2] so this is a site that has been researched frequently. Yet the interactions, the technology, the material conditions, and the subjectivities are all intricately interacting and are constantly in flux. In the TTU MOO discussion, the instructor often leads the discussion via an agenda, perhaps one posted on a Web page, shown via a projector in the right side of the screen, or pasted into the discussion itself. The students don't know that the instructor is also operating from Microsoft Word notes written well in advance as she cuts and pastes questions, thoughts, and points she wants to make into the discussion. She seems prepared, quick, and efficient, yet she is constantly questioning herself: How directive can/should she be? What does this act do to the "timing" of the class discussion? How will she handle tangents that inevitably arise?

Consider also that the instructor doesn't know that, during the discussion, one of the 10 students (who is also a working technical writer) is multitasking—working on a job-related deadline—one that relates to the discussion, so the student sprinkles references to it as he participates on the MOO. The student is seen by the instructor as intelligently able to apply the theoretical concepts under discussion to his real-world situation, but in fact, he is missing most of what is being discussed because of this work. The discussion is saved and posted later that evening; yet is reading a transcript the same as participating? I could continue with this scenario for the rest of this chapter, but the point is that even during this familiar, regularly scheduled, seemingly transparent graduate discussion, the complexities are such that we could never hope to know exactly what is going on: it exceeds our capacity to know, in the same way that traditional face-to-face oral discussions have done for decades—only more so.

The traditional classroom can be complex as well, as anyone who has observed teachers will know. Robert Brooke's (1987) underlife is alive and well in almost every classroom context. How do we begin to capture this complexity as we research these sites? What lenses or approaches are best? Are traditional research methods sufficient to capture the complexity when studying writing/writing scenarios? What happens when we add technology to the mix? Are traditional methods (or our understanding and/or application of them) enough, or do we need new ones? Before we can answer these questions, we need to revisit how methods are taught and understood in most research methods courses.

STATIC RESEARCH METHODS

In my pilot survey, I asked participants which books have been used in the required research methods course offered at their institutions. I supplied a list of nine common titles, and I also listed "coursepack" and "other." Over 60% of instructors surveyed required a coursepack, dominating the use of any other coherent, commonly used text. The three most common texts (ranging from 32–35% use) were, in descending order, Gesa Kirsch and Patricia Sullivan's (1992) *Methods and Methodology in Composition Research*; Janice Lauer and William Asher's (1988) *Composition Research: Empirical Designs*; and Mary Sue MacNealy's (1999) *Strategies for Empirical Research in Writing*. Texts listed as "other" ranged from social science or educational research methods texts to texts on conducting library research.

The first aspect one might notice about the most commonly used texts is that none of them were published in this century, and only one within the last 10 years. That's not to say that these texts have outlived their usefulness—far from it—but certainly the contexts we are studying have changed, in some cases significantly (for instance, the MOO discussion I describe above wasn't an instructional or technological choice—even a reality— when the first two texts were published). Only two of the books listed (both in my list and in the "other" category as noted by participants) are specifically directed at Comp/Rhet/TC and have a publication date of 2000 or more recently: Cindy Johanek's (2000) *Composing Research: A Contextualist Paradigm for Rhetoric and Composition* and Laura Gurak and Mary Lay's (2002) *Research in Technical Communication*. What allows for these top three texts to remain so popular, particularly the ones published in the late 1980s/early 1990s? The first answer might simply be that the instructors teaching the research methods course now first became acquainted with the texts as graduate students in a similar class. The books are known, they are familiar, and they are proven entities—after all, the former grad students are now professors teaching their own graduate students.

Another answer might be that the books are simply the best ones for the required research class, given the audience and subject matter. The earlier publications may well still be the best overview for a broader, Comp/Rhet/TC audience. The survey bears this hypothesis out somewhat. I asked participants to rank how useful these books had been on a scale from 1–3 (with 1 being most useful and 3 being least useful), and all three of the most commonly used books were seen as at least somewhat helpful (with scores ranging from 2.0 to 2.2). The only artifacts to score better were the coursepack (1.5) and the "other" book (selected by the instructor), which was usually not related to Comp/Rhet/TC (1.6).

Are the methods as presented in these texts sufficient grounding for research in a digital age? Sullivan and James Porter (1993) noted that the predominant view in publication is one "that sees methodology as a static and conventional set of strategies (even when 'socially constructed') for observing practices and thereby generating 'knowledge' about practice" (p. 220). Kristie Fleckenstein, Clay Spinuzzi, Rebecca Rickly, and Carole Papper (2005) also criticized the way methods are perceived in writing studies, noting that the metaphor for their representation is

> predicated on a container image, one that locks research activities into hierarchical, step-by-step, disciplinary actions and erases the situatedness of empirical knowledge. In so doing, it creates out of writing—the object of study—a phenomenon that is similarly hierarchical and decontextualized. (p. 2)

Metaphors are vital to our ability to understand complex phenomena; although they don't always portray things accurately (something we need to remember), they almost always lead to some form of understanding or meaning. Kenneth Baake (2003) discussed how metaphors help create meaning in scientific discourse. Some metaphors, he maintained, not only prove to make understanding ineffective, but actually limit understanding. Yet metaphors are vital in science—without them, not all of the various associations would be heard by other scientists. Metaphors "generate harmonics that transport meaning across terms. These force the scientists to either modify or reject the original theory so as to accommodate the harmonics" (Baake, p. 218). These metaphoric associations, or harmonics, allow for theory to develop. Dissonance, or associations that are held differently, can be part of the harmonics—yet if the dissonance becomes paramount, the metaphor breaks down and meaning becomes more and more incoherent.

The Comp/Rhet/TC research process can be understood metaphorically as well. Often portrayed as a series of steps, research is conducted according to rules, into which specifics can be inserted: epistemology, methodology, research question, research design, and methods. Similarly, each of the particular components has an accepted procedure or definition, often located in a particular discipline (ethnography as methodology comes from cultural anthropology, for example, and students who engage in ethnographic research must study texts from anthropology to learn to conduct ethnography in an appropriate fashion). Each component must be addressed logically and linearly so that the research might be seen as rigorous. Generally, graduate students are told to identify a problem and from this problem, to generate a research question. The research question should suggest methods and methodology as most appropriate to address and answer the question. The various methods will dictate tools or techniques. And guiding all of this is the researcher's undergirding epistemology. The process sounds simple enough: linear, logical, and neat. Or so it would appear.

These containers might be a bit more permeable than we first recognized, and each individual component a bit more fluid. Let us begin with Sandra Harding's (1987) distinction between method, methodology, and epistemology. A method is a specific tool or array of tools for collecting and analyzing data—a "technique for (or way of proceeding in) gathering of evidence" (p. 2). A methodology is "a theory and analysis of how research does or should proceed" (p. 3). And an epistemology is a theory of knowledge that answers questions about "who can be a 'knower' . . . what tests beliefs must pass in order to be legitimated knowledge . . . what kinds of things can be knowledge . . . and so forth" (p. 3). These distinctions are important as we look at an individual research situation and note how they are applied. But it is equally important to acknowledge that, even defined as distinctly as Harding has distinguished these terms, they nonetheless do *not* allow for neat, orderly, logical containment. Consider, for instance, ethnography, which originated from cultural anthropology as researchers devised a systematic, rigorous means of studying indigenous cultures. Ethnography as a methodology can employ a variety of techniques for gathering data, such as participant observation, interviews, surveys, and so forth. Yet it can also be a paradigm, a way of knowing. Social construction theory is based, in part, on the paradigm of understanding cultures through their social interaction, including communication. Contextual inquiry, a methodology used in the workplace, employs ethnographic techniques or focused ethnography to determine how or why a breakdown occurs in a particular situation, shifting it from methodology to method. How can ethnography be paradigm/epistemology, methodology, *and* method?

Fleckenstein et al. (2005) referred to these fluid options as "slippage: elements shifting up and down the hierarchy, up and down through the boxes" (p. 9). Law (2004) referred to them as method assemblages:

> the crafting or bundling of relations or hinterland into three parts: (a) whatever is in-here or *present*; (b) whatever is absent but is also *manifest* in its *absence*; and (c) whatever is absent but is *Other* because, while it is necessary to presence, it is not or cannot be made manifest. (p. 84)

Law believed that paradigms, the most theoretical and complex part of the hierarchical research schema (what Harding, 1987, would refer to as epistemology), are embedded in craft or skill. These method assemblages are then "entangled rather than constructed" (p. 42) and each component contains parts of itself, allowing us to see research not as an ordered, neat, linear procedure, but one that is integrated, messy, and nonhierarchical. In a sense, they are like atoms moving and creating energy on a table top that looks and feels solid. All sensory information would dictate that the table is not moving, not producing energy, yet atomic research has been able to break out of that container-like, metaphoric thinking to see the table in light of the smallest parts that constitute it.

Like the image of atomic energy given off by atoms moving at a microscopic level on a seemingly static, solid table, so our methods and our research projects are in constant movement when we apply them to localized contexts. Many of us learned methods as containers; I would like to see us re-envision these methods no longer in terms of static containers, but within ever-evolving contexts in which rhetorical applications of method are necessary.

RESEARCH PROCESSES WITH/ON/OF DYNAMIC TECHNOLOGIES

Just as metaphors surrounding research can be problematic or enlightening, so, too, the metaphors that influence our understanding of technology can determine what we see. To understand the complexity inherent in technological contexts, we might first acknowledge how we perceive technological sites, looking at them from a variety of perspectives: material, intellectual, historical, social, political, and so forth. Our relationship with/to these sites must be articulated as well. Andrew Feenberg (1991), for example, saw humans and their technologies as existing in a variety of relationships ranging from instrumentalism (systems and techniques as mere tools) to technological determinism (technology having a life of its own). Within an instrumental world view, we retain human agency, but miss opportunities to design and redesign technology when technology is seen as static and finished in relation to society. Within a technological determinist world view, we lose agency, as system evolution is predetermined. What Feenberg argued for is "deep democratization" of systems, or a balance between the neutral instrumentalist and the agency-filled determinist: a critical, user-centered stance toward the ideologically charged world of technology. A user-centered stance, however, can be difficult to articulate, in part because technology and users are constantly changing, evolving, and shifting. Identifying and communicating our relationships with complex, mutable technologies takes practice, yet it is a necessary component of the ways we study these contexts that have, do, and will continue to impact our teaching, our learning, our writing, and our knowing. As a starting place, then, acknowledging our perceptions, our relationships, and our understanding of these technological contexts helps us to be aware of the multi-faceted nature of the sites we examine. By doing so, we engage what Baake (2003) called harmonics of understanding, which help us to select and apply the best methods for understanding a situation.

Technology does not exist in a vacuum, and neither do the methods we choose to study it. Both technology and our research methods mirror and even help construct the reality we perceive. Law (2004) maintained that "methods, their rules, and even more methods' practices, not only describe but also help to produce the reality that they understand" (p. 5). As researchers, we must be perpetually aware that we are constructing a reality as we articulate our understanding of technological contexts, as well as select and apply methods, analyze data, and represent results. In describing the aims of critical research practices, Patricia Sullivan and James Porter (1997) described methodology as heuristic, and noted that "research ought to situate itself ethically and politically, especially vis-à-vis participants and aims" (p. 109). The authors note that research practices in which method becomes primary often miss important contextual aspects. Methodology, according to Sullivan and Porter, "that is portrayed as a set of immutable principles, rather than as heuristic guidelines, masks the impact

of the situation—of the practice—on the study in ways that could unconsciously reinscribe theory's dominance over practice" (p. 66). Drawing on
a range of postmodern and feminist theories and approaches, they advocated methodology as critical practice, or *praxis*, in which the notion of an
objective researcher is challenged; methodological strategies are situated
and flexible, adapting practices to meet the needs of particular situations;
and in which the researcher is self-reflexive and critical. Sullivan and Porter
saw *praxis* as "a kind of thinking that does not start with theoretical knowledge or abstract models, which are then applied to situations, but that
begins with immersion in local situations, and then uses epistemic theory
as heuristic rather than as explanatory or determining" (p. 26). Both pro-
cedural knowledge and situated action, *praxis* suggests an investment in
and understanding of local, contextualized situations.

One of few to acknowledge technological change and how it might
impact research practices, Sullivan and Porter (1997) noted that methodology as *praxis* must be "sensitive to the rhetorical situatedness of participants and technologies and that recognize themselves as a form of political and ethical action" (p. ix). However, in their desire to have us examine
critically our contexts and practices, Sullivan and Porter themselves
momentarily forget to note the shifting nature of technology and our relation to it when they declare "once oppression is identified, there can be
only one ethical stance toward it: Oppose it" (p. 122). If oppression is situated, then a particular computer interface might be seen as oppressive by
some, and it may be liberating for others—and without acknowledging a
static hierarchy of good/bad, we must be wary of labeling our contexts in
that manner. Law (2004) concurred, contending that we will need to

> unmake many of our methodological habits, including: the desire for
> certainty; the expectation that we can usually arrive at more or less sta-
> ble conclusions about the way things really are; the belief that as
> [researchers] we have special insights that allow us to see further than
> others into certain parts of social reality; and the expectations of gen-
> erality that are wrapped up in what is often called "universalism." (p. 9)

Gurak and Christine Silker (2002) also acknowledged the problematic
nature of studying complicated scenarios involving technology, noting that
"traditional research questions such as the selection of an appropriate
method, the need to obtain permission from subjects, and issues of private
versus public information become blurred in the cyberspace research site"
(pp. 230–231). The context we choose to study has a profound influence
on our research practices: our selection, application, analysis, and repre-

sentation of methods, and our choice of methodology. And technology complicates these contexts. But are traditionally conceptualized research questions and methods (i.e., as portrayed hierarchically and linearly) sufficient to capture the intricacies of technology-related contexts? Traditional academic methods of inquiry, Law (2004) maintained, don't capture the "mess, the confusion, the relative disorder" of the contexts we study, something we should try to do if we are to fairly represent these contexts. However, the acknowledgment of "mess" puts the researcher in a bind: if we do try to capture the mess, our research may appear "messy" and thus it is seen as poorly done. How can we apply the methods we know to understand some of the realities we might be missing in the messy contexts we study? Law's answer is deceptively simple:

> If the world is complex and messy, then at least some of the time we're going to have to give up on simplicities . . . if we want to think about the messes of reality at all then we're going to have to teach ourselves to think, to practice, to relate, and to know in new ways. We will need to teach ourselves to know some of the realities of the world using methods unusual to or unknown in social science. (p. 2)

Although I agree in part with Law's assertion, I would suggest that it is not only "teaching ourselves" new or unusual/re-articulated methods that will help us see, know, and represent the mess; in addition, we must revise or re-see how these methods might be adaptively applied in specific contexts, particularly technological contexts. Adapting to specific contexts falls squarely in the realm of rhetoric, so I'd like to argue that we need to see them *rhetorically*. I begin my discussion of rhetoric and research—that is, by arguing for a rhetorical application of research—by once more examining Sullivan and Porter's (1997) call for a rhetorical methodology, and then situating practice in rhetorical contexts.

RHETORICAL RESEARCH REVISITED

If technology has changed one thing, it's the site of research, or our vision of what counts as a coherent site upon which research can be done. Previously, these sites were physical spaces (labs, classrooms, companies, texts); now, however, a site of research can be a community of mutual interest spread out over the globe (see, for example, Sapienza or Smith, this collection). Most of our methodologies and methods were designed to observe and explain the former kind of site. Can they be adapted success-fully to the latter, or do we need a new sense of methodology? In *Opening Spaces*, Sullivan and Porter (1997) posited a "'rhetorical methodology' based on viewing computer writing as a situated practice" (p. 9). They described their position as rhetorical, involving local/contingent knowledge grounded in local, situated practices, and they likened the methodology used to study these contexts to rhetorical invention. Rhetoric, for them, encompasses

> three elements: ideology (assumptions about what human relations should be and about how people should use symbol systems); practice (how people actually do constitute their relations through regularized symbolic or discursive activity); and method (tactics, procedures, heuristics, or tools that people use for inquiry). (p. 10)

Like those researchers advocating action research (see, for example, Stringer, 1999), Sullivan and Porter described methodology as "an interven-ing social action and a participation in human events" (p. 13). Although the sentiments are admirable, they tend to limit how pervasively this "critical methodology" can be practiced. As noted earlier, contexts, situations, and participants change, and although ethics and social action should ultimate-ly should be part of our self-reflexive examination of a research situation, social action isn't always—nor should it be—the final goal of research.

I would like to begin with their idea, though, of linking research and rhetoric. Sullivan and Porter (1997) were among the first to associate rhet-oric with research in an admirable fashion, and I would like to recast—to update, if you will—their position. I situate the terminology used in this recasting in Harding's (1987) definitions, though any attempt to define terms brings to mind the limiting container metaphor. As noted previous-ly, a methodology—case study, for instance, a methodology which comes to us from cognitive science and is in that discipline practiced as a theory of how research should proceed—can also be used as a method, or a means of gathering evidence as a part of a larger methodology such as ethnography, for instance, or a contextual inquiry. According to Harding's definition, then, a case study can be both a method (a tool used in a larg-er ethnographic examination or a contextual inquiry) and a methodology (a theory and analysis of how research should proceed).

The slippage doesn't end there. The way any of these manifestations of case study is applied and analyzed will depend upon the researcher's epistemological stance. For instance, if the researcher defines her epistemology as social construction, in which meaning is socially created, her research will look and feel very different from someone who aligns herself with identity theory, in which each person (and her subsequent behavior) is influenced by the collection of identities associated with the various roles this person occupies. Law's (2004) concept of method assemblages makes increasing sense in increasingly complex scenarios. By locating the argument for rhetorical research in a permeable, situated definition, we can access the flexibility needed to study chaotic, changing environments. We can deal with slippage.

Rhetoric is also a slippery term, especially when we relate it to methods or methodologies. In *On Rhetoric*, Aristotle (1991) defined rhetoric as *techne*, or a body of knowledge used for a particular end. *Techne* deals with concrete ideas and circumstances (as opposed to dialectic, which deals with logical order and deals with general/philosophical questions), thus it lends itself to contextual study. The goals of rhetoric are to advance the cause of justice and truth, and to persuade. Aristotle maintained that "persuasion is clearly a sort of demonstration, since we are most fully persuaded when we consider a thing to have been demonstrated" (book 1, part 1). If rhetoric is a demonstration that persuades us, we can begin to see how research might be seen as rhetorically persuasive. Is the question appropriate, given the problem? If so, that question was persuasive. Does the method applied actually answer the question? If so, that method was persuasive. Are we convinced that the method was applied appropriately and with rigor, given the context, the question, the purpose, and constraints? If so, application was persuasive. Is the way of proceeding—the methodology—appropriate for the question, context, and methods? If so, that methodology was persuasive. Is the analysis thorough, accurate, and epistemologically consistent? If so, it was persuasive. Is the representation of the research accurate, effective, well-wrought, and appropriate? If so, it was persuasive. Therefore, if we are persuaded that all aspects of the research have been conducted, analyzed, and presented effectively for the specific question, context, and audience, the research is rhetorically sound.

Carl Herndl (1991) analyzed the rhetorical nature of the ethnography that Stephen Doheny-Farina (1989) published, noting the amount of "rhetorical work" that goes into legitimizing "through socially maintained conventions" (p. 326). Herndl noted that other studies in other contexts "might organize their descriptions around different *topoi* but they will be no less embedded in the discourse of their research community" (p. 326). The representation of research has always been somewhat formulaic (consider, for instance, the IMRAD formula—Introduction, Methods, Results, And Discussion—for publishing in the sciences/social sciences).

Researchers have some choices, depending on where the data is to be published, but they must be aware of the rhetorical situation surrounding publication. If the analysis and representation of a study must be portrayed
according to the conventions of a particular discourse community—a specific rhetorical situation—when and how should the selection of methods
and their application be affected? To answer that question, we need to
readjust our view, seeing the rhetorical situation as encompassing the conduct of research as well as its analysis and representation.

A larger perspective might be to treat rhetoric as "the faculty of observing in any given case the available means of persuasion" (Aristotle, 1991,
book 1, chapter 2) as Aristotle ultimately defined it in *On Rhetoric*. Both
rhetoric and dialectic are categorized as *organum*, or tools, which have no
subject matter of their own, yet can be applied to other subjects. If we look
back to Harding's (1987) definition of method, we note that "tool" can be
seen as "method" or part of a method. And if we are able to apply these
"tools" to other subjects, it makes sense that some slippage may occur—
thus what once was a "mere" tool may actually slip into art or *techne*, creating a body of productive knowledge that can be used for a particular end:
to understand something better, to answer a question, and so forth.
Methods, methodologies, and epistemologies are all forms of *techne* that
deal with particular, concrete situations and circumstances. *Techne* is ultimately contextual, and may be reconceived in any context so that the situation may be persuasive, just as methods, methodologies, and epistemologies may shift according to context.

"It is clear, further, that [rhetoric's] function is not simply to succeed in
persuading," Aristotle (1991) noted, "but rather to discover the means of
coming as near such success as the circumstances of each particular case
allow" (book 1, chapter 1). So, too, is it with research. A researcher must
be intimately familiar with the site, or context, of research, with persuasion
as a goal inherent in that familiarity. Given a problematic situation, a
researcher must determine a question (or series of questions), then consider the best possible way to answer that question. Data collection must be
thought through, designed carefully (considering the context and participants), and then systematically and appropriately applied. Data that has
been collected must be analyzed, then examined in light of the original
research question(s). Finally, findings must be presented in a manner that
the researcher's community will find legitimate. Ultimately, then, the goal
of research is to persuade an audience that the initial question has been
answered sufficiently—and thus research associated with a particular context becomes the available means, the tool employed to create a body of
knowledge for a particular end. And although I have articulated the process

above as somewhat linear and inflexible, I argue that knowing the context as a means of persuasion requires the researcher to consider not just a step-by-step process, but the entire rhetorical situation, context, and persuasion: the method assemblage.

Research located and conducted rhetorically is an attempt to acknowledge and account for the individual, changing complexities of research sites—particularly research sites that involve technology. And research conducted rhetorically can have structure, rigor, and validity. Most traditional methods have standard operating procedures associated with the discipline and/or the methodological tradition they come from. For instance, quasi-experimental methodology dictates that a site of study must identify controls, independent variables, and dependent variables; the groups must be as uniform as possible; and so forth. In traditional ethnographic research, the researcher must spend time identifying her background, her experiences, her belief system, and so forth as a means of negotiating researcher bias. These standard operating procedures are valuable—they offer us the opportunity for rigor, reliability, and validity. Although uniform application of these methods can theoretically lend itself toward replicability, in most technological sites, the situation is so localized and complex that replication in the strictest sense is impossible because of the inability to control variables. Acknowledging the changing, complex nature of these contexts means applying methods appropriate for the context and question, rather than for the methodological tradition. The rigor associated with these methods becomes rhetorical and contextual; that is, it draws on activities related to the application of the method, to the verification of results, or the overlay of data/perspective. Rather than rely on methodological rigor in the application, analysis, and representation of research, the rhetorical nature of the research can provide new forms of rigor, which make the research more persuasive.

Following is a list of eight procedures drawn primarily from qualitative methods that John Creswell (1998) advocated to verify results and add rigor. He encouraged researchers to include at least two of these as a means of rigor:

1. *Prolonged engagement* and *persistent observation*: Building trust with participants, learning culture, and checking for misinformation with participants.
2. *Triangulation*: Using multiple methods, sources, investigators, or perspectives.
3. *Peer review or debriefing*: Allowing for an external check on the research process.

4. *Negative case analysis*: Refining a hypothesis as inquiry advances in light of disconfirming evidence.

5. *Clarifying researcher bias*: Allowing the reader to understand the researcher's position, as well as any biases or assumptions that might impact the inquiry.

6. *Member checks*: Soliciting informants' views of the credibility of findings, interpretation, and representation.

7. *Rich, thick description*: Describing in detail the participants, setting, actions, etc. so that readers can make decisions regarding transferability.

8. *External audits*: Allowing an external consultant—an auditor—to examine both the process and product of the account to assess accuracy. (pp. 201–203)

I am advocating a localized, situated, rhetorical approach to conducting research. Sullivan and Porter (1993) argued for a similar approach, one that sees methodology not as "something we apply or select so much as something we *design out of particular situations and then argue for* in our studies" (p. 221). The discipline of Technical Communication—and, more broadly, the computers and writing community—has begun to do this. As every legitimate discipline should, it has begun to establish discipline-specific research methodologies that are rhetorically situated—that is, appropriate for the rhetorical situation under scrutiny. TC research has drawn from fields that operate in a similar manner, including human–computer interaction (HCI) studies (those concerned with design, evaluation and implementation of interactive computing systems for human use), human factors analysis (a focus dating back to the industrial revolution; the hardware version of HCI), software engineering (design, creation, usability testing, implementation, assessment, and so forth), and Scandinavian collaborative design approaches (arising from a socialist philosophy, this approach includes participants as designers of systems, software, etc.), and other associated fields. But instead of merely co-opting methods from these fields, Technical Communication has adapted them into standard user-centered design field methods: contextual inquiry, in which participant observation, interview, artifact analysis, and talk-aloud protocols can be used to identify problems and/or study problems in a particular context; participatory design, in which users and designers work together to design or redesign an artifact; and usability testing, which is the close observation of real users using real artifacts so that the usability of the artifact can be determined. These three methods have become staples in the field, both in the workplace and in more scholarly applications.[3] They have roots in ethnography, educational methodologies such as participatory action research, feminist research, and what Robert Johnson (1998) deemed user-centered design philosophies. As a group, they are locally situated—usually designed to identify and/or solve a specific contextual problem (such as designing a usable interface for a software application, or finding out where a normalized corporate process breaks down)—and the research subjects are often co-investigators.

These more specific, local, and often collaborative methodologies are a positive step toward making all research local, contextual, and meaningful when applied in a rhetorical manner. These field methods allow for a focused, problem-solving, rhetorically situated, user-centered approach to research. They are not conducive for long-term study of a culture, and replication is not a normal goal; instead, they are localized, contextualized inquiries that allow for a greater understanding of a task, a situation, a technology, a design, a system, and so forth. Although not generalizable in the traditional sense, the results of such studies are often used generally to address problems in a specific locale, system, process, community, and so on. In other words, they are appropriate for the context studied, which makes them especially beneficial to technical communicators—yet I would argue that they have value elsewhere, too, if only as models of rhetorically adapted and applied research methods.

CONCLUSIONS: WHERE DO WE BEGIN?

Because research—particularly research involving technology—is situated, messy, unpredictable, and chaotic, we need to adapt existing methods to the specific (rhetorical) situation, idea, and research question(s) being explored. This doesn't mean, however, that we simply apply methods willy nilly; we must know about research methods; we must understand the relationship between method, methodology, and epistemology. We must think rhetorically about the audience, purpose, exigency, constraints, and context surrounding the sites of our research. From this we must articulate fit or appropriateness, the specifics in application, and how the research is rigorous. Finally, we must be able to portray our analysis and results in a representation sanctioned by a particular discourse community.

Yet how can researchers learn to do this? The answer, I believe, lies in how and where we prepare students to conduct research: in our required methods overview courses, in what we require in our courses, in how we prepare students professionally, and in our textbooks. In an article overviewing the state of research in Technical Communication, Ann Blakeslee and Rachel Spilka (2004) cited that the participants in the 2000 Milwaukee Symposium[4] "bemoaned the inconsistency of what we cover and of what students learn in our research courses" (p. 81). Spilka (2005) continued this lament at the 2005 Council for Programs in Technical and Scientific Communication (CPTSC) conference in her keynote address, noting that few schools require more than one research methods course, and that course is often "inconsistent," resulting in graduate students ill-prepared to propose and conduct research. She presented her analysis of the last 3 years worth of ATTW and STC grant applications. Almost none of these, noted Spilka, were persuasive in their representations of methodology.

Although our programs are all different—Composition/Rhetoric students won't be expected to have exactly the same skills as Technical Communication/Rhetoric students—we nonetheless should be able to identify basic research skills and knowledge each graduate student should have. Given that most programs in rhetoric require at least one survey course, below I've delineated what might be taught so that students can read and conduct research rhetorically. I hope that such a list might inspire others into a dialogue regarding our teaching of research, eventually leading to model courses that achieve shared goals.

1. Early in their graduate studies, students should be **grounded in the methods used in their discipline**, as well as disciplines tangential to theirs. They should have a thorough understanding of the methods, the traditional application of these methods, and how to match method-to-question and question-to-method. A research methods book aimed toward disciplinary knowledge, such as Lauer and Asher's (1988) *Composition Research: Empirical Designs* or MacNealy's (1999) *Strategies for Empirical Research in Writing* might be appropriate vehicles—but so, too, I would argue, would be Creswell's (1998) *Qualitative Inquiry and Research Design: Choosing Among Five Traditions*.

2. Students should be taught to **read research critically**, problematizing methods, procedures, and findings. Critical analysis of reading research should be integrated into a variety of classes so the one overview course isn't overburdened. Too often, I feel, this is one of the primary goals of the required research methods

class (given the focus on coursepacks in the required research methods courses), and, as a result, I think it warrants too much time and energy, time and energy better spent learning to apply the methods they've become familiar with in a heuristic, contextual manner. Through learning to apply these methods well, students are more likely to learn how to read critically the representations of others.

3. Students should be **given the opportunity—preferably within the "safe" context of a class—to conduct actual research studies** that will mirror the larger studies they hope to do for their dissertations and for publication. The actual conduct of research should be, I believe, one of the primary goals of the required research methods class—yet my preliminary research indicates only about half those teaching research methods now actually provide students such an opportunity.

4. **Support for conducting research** should be offered frequently, throughout a graduate student's career, in the same way that support for using technology is offered: in the form of workshops, one-on-one help, and so forth. Like technology, conducting research should become comfortable and known. Once a comfort level is reached in even one area, it can translate to other areas.

5. Through familiarity with traditional research methods, as well as conducting and critiquing research, students should be **challenged to look critically at their own sites for research**, problematizing the methods they've learned, and articulating the complexities of the specific, rhetorical situation. This type of identifying and communicating doesn't come easily to everyone, and must be practiced. The required research methods course is a place for students to learn to do this type of articulation.

6. Finally, students should be able to try their hand at **adapting research methods for their particular rhetorical situation**, indicating why they have adapted the methods they have, and how they have implemented rigor in their research. A series of microstudies might be the means by which students try to adapt research methods to time, space, subject, and problem constraints. It is likely that students will fail at these microstudies by choosing a problem that is too broad or unfocused, a method not appropriate, and so forth—but often it is through failure that we learn best, especially when the failure becomes a teachable moment in the context of a class.

Students should also learn how to fill out an Institutional Review Board and other human subjects forms, as well as recognize what kinds of situations require consent, institutional approval, and so forth. Even though at most institutions student research conducted for a class (with no further publication intended) is often exempted from IRB approval, I still guide students conducting human subjects research through the process so they gain experience and have the necessary approval should they decide to publish their research. But in the confines of a semester, guiding students not only through the IRB process (if needed) and through the actual conduct of a study can seem a daunting task, and I imagine that teachers of the required methods course often feel underprepared to guide students in even a small-scale research study, and thus they choose instead to fall back on reading about and critiquing existing research. We must learn to learn ourselves and to embrace uncertainty if we want to grow as teachers (and as a discipline). Students will benefit from this experience, along with their classroom-based forays into research. The teacher's responsibility will be to see that research is conducted ethically, critically, and rhetorically; the student's responsibility will be to engage critically in the *praxis* of conducting research.

But not every program has a required research methods class. For those of us expected to conduct research without the benefit of more training, it might behoove us to consider research and technology as similar in terms of how we become proficient in them. We learn to use technology in a variety of ways: through attending workshops, through reading, through discussing it with others, through online references, and finally, through trial and error, and with practice. Eventually, our understanding of technology and our familiarity with it allows us to integrate various appropriate technologies into our everyday work. Similarly, we should think about research practices as something that we hope to integrate seamlessly and appropriately into our work. We cannot expect to do so without familiarity, practice, reflection, and feedback. Digital contexts provide us with a wealth of opportunities to conduct meaningful, exciting research; however, they also can prove to be overwhelming in their messiness. Our methods and our understanding of them needs to be able to capture the complex nature of this mess to provide helpful, positive information that will help us to understand situations, solve problems, and revise our practices. "My aim," Law (2004) wrote, "is thus to broaden method, to subvert it, but also to remake it" (p. 9). This should be our aim as well: to understand methods, subvert them, and to remake them by applying them rhetorically.

NOTES

1. This survey was intended as a pilot for a more focused survey. I sent the survey URL to the following email lists: techrhet, attw, wpa, and the consortium of graduate programs in rhetoric and composition. I asked people on the list who had taught the research methods overview to respond, and/or to pass the URL to those in their departments who had taught the research methods overview class. Sixty-eight people responded to the survey, which was live from November 2004 until March 2005.
2. See, for instance, Cynthia Haynes and Jan Rune Holmevik's *High Wired* (2001) and *MOOniversity* (2000), John Barber and Dene Grigar's (2001) *New Worlds, New Words*.
3. For an excellent overview of three field methods, see Spinuzzi (2000).
4. The goal of the 2000 Milwaukee Symposium, held at the University of Wisconsin–Milwaukee, was to identify problems of the field of Technical Communication and desirable/necessary directions for the future.

ABOUT THE AUTHORS

Joanne Addison is an associate professor and Writing Program Administrator at the University of Colorado at Denver and Health Sciences Center's Downtown Denver Campus where she teaches undergraduate and graduate courses in persuasion, empirical research, and rhetorical theory. She is co-editor of *Feminist Empirical Research: Emerging Perspectives on Qualitative and Teacher Research* (1999). Her work has been published in *Written Communication, Computers and Composition,* and *English Education* as well as in edited collections including *Don't Call it That: The Composition Practicum*; *Online Communities: Commerce, Community Action, and the Virtual University*; and *Feminist Cyberscapes: Mapping Gendered Academic Spaces*. Her current research focuses on expanding the use of experience sampling methods to intersecting literacy sites.

William P. Banks is assistant professor and Director of the First Year Writing Studio at East Carolina University. Currently, his scholarship focuses on the intersections of queer theory, performance, and digital communication technologies. Previous articles have appeared in *College English,*

Teaching English in the Two-Year College, and *Dialogue*, and his co-edited issue of *Computers and Composition*, themed "Sexualities, Technologies, and the Teaching of Writing," received the Ellen Nold Award for Distinguished Contribution to the Field of Computers and Writing.

Kristine Blair is Interim Chair of the Department of English at Bowling Green State University. Her co-authored book projects include *Feminist Cyberscapes: Mapping Gendered Academic Spaces* (1999); a monograph: *Composition: Discipline Analysis* for the National Center for Curricular Transformation for Women (1999); *Cultural Attractions/Cultural Distractions: Critical Literacy in Contemporary Contexts* (2000); and *Grammar for Language Arts Teachers* (2003). Her most recent work has appeared in *Computers and Composition*, the *Journal of Educational Technology and Society*, and the collection *Teaching Writing with Computers: An Introduction*. Currently, she serves as editor of *Computers and Composition Online* (http://www.bgsu.edu/cconline) and is co-editing a collection under contract to Hampton Press titled *Webbing Cyberfeminist Practice: Communities, Pedagogies, and Social Action*.

Stuart Blythe is an associate professor in the Department of English and Linguistics at Indiana University–Purdue University Fort Wayne, where he teaches courses in writing, multimedia, editing, and the teaching of composition. His recent work has appeared in *College Composition and Communication*, *Computers and Composition*, the *Journal of Business and Technical Communication*, and *Works and Days*.

Josh Burnett is an undergraduate student at Kean University with plans to major in Broadcast Communications. He has created and maintained several Web sites and online journals since discovering the Internet in the mid 1990s. He is also an avid video game player.

Sally Chandler is an assistant professor of English at Kean University where she teaches college composition. In addition to her work on videogaming and literacies, her research interests include the study of communication across difference, and extending ethnographic and feminist methods for collaborative research. Her work has appeared in *Feminist Teacher*, *Generations*, and *Oral History*.

Kevin Eric DePew is an assistant professor of professional writing at Old Dominion University where he teaches undergraduate and graduate courses in composition, rhetoric, electronic writing, second language writing, and writing pedagogy for grades 6–12. He has published in *Computers and Composition* and edited the special issue of *Computers and Composition*, "Second Language Writers in Digital Contexts" (22:3).

Dànielle Nicole DeVoss is an associate professor and Director of the Professional Writing Program at Michigan State University. Her research interests include computer/technological literacies; feminist interpretations of and interventions in computer technologies; philosophy of technology/technoscience; professional writing; technical communication; gender/identity play in online spaces; online representation and embodiment; and issues of rhetoric in disciplines such as nursing and medicine. DeVoss' work has most recently appeared in *Computers and Composition*; *Journal of Business and Technical Communication*; *Pedagogy: Critical Approaches to Teaching Literature, Language, Composition, and Culture*; *Moving a Mountain: Transforming the Role of Contingent Faculty in Composition Studies and Higher Education* (2001); and *Writing Center Research: Extending the Conversation* (2001). DeVoss recently co-edited a collection on behavioral interventions in cancer care: *Evidence-based Cancer Care and Prevention* (2003).

Michelle F. Eble is an assistant professor of Professional and Technical Communication in the Department of English at East Carolina University, where she teaches undergraduate and graduate courses in professional writing, publications development, electronic writing, ethical issues in professional communication, and editing. Her research on writing technologies, rhetoric, and the theory and practice of professional writing has appeared in *Computers and Composition*, *Technical Communication*, and *Technical Communication Quarterly*. She also serves on her University and Medical Center Institutional Review Boards. She is currently investigating technologies used to deliver courses and/or content online and the implications for rhetorical theory informing this digital delivery.

Douglas Eyman is co-editor of *Kairos: A Journal of Rhetoric, Technology, and Pedagogy* and is currently pursuing graduate studies in the Rhetoric & Writing Program at Michigan State University. He has served on the board of directors of the Alliance for Computers and Writing and as a member of NCTE's Instructional Technology Committee; he is currently a member of the CCCC Committee on Computers in Composition and Communication. Eyman has also served as the Web Manager for *Teaching English in the Two Year College* online and taught online courses for the Graduate Center at Marlboro College and the Community College of Southern Nevada.

Cheryl Geisler is a joint professor of Rhetoric and Composition and Information Technology as well as chair of the Department of Language, Literature, and Communication at Rensselaer Polytechnic Institute where she conducts research on writing in the context of emerging communication technologies. She is author of *Analyzing Streams of Language*, a textbook on methods for analyzing verbal data, published by Longman in 2003.

Bill Hart-Davidson is an assistant professor in the Writing, Rhetoric, and American Cultures Department at Michigan State University and a co-director of the Writing in Digital Environments (WIDE) Research Center. His research interests lie at the intersection of technical communication and human-computer interaction in such areas as digital writing, visualizing knowledge work processes, and information and user experience design. He is working on several projects that include the design and development of new software tools for writers in both workplace and community contexts.

Lory Hawkes is a senior professor at DeVry University where she teaches professional writing in the General Education department and Web design in the Computer Information Systems department. She has written essays and two books on the Internet/Web technologies, and with her co-authors Christina Murphy and Joe Law, compiled the annotated bibliography, *The Theory and Criticism of Virtual Texts* (2000). She is a member of the board of directors for the Society for Technical Communication and also a Fellow in the organization.

Susan Hilligoss is a professor of Professional Communication and Rhetoric in the English Department of Clemson University. Her research interests include visual communication, computers and writing, and creative nonfiction. Her publications include *Visual Communication: A Writer's Guide* (2nd ed., 2002, with Tharon Howard); *Literacy and Computers: The Complications of Teaching and Learning with Technology* (1994, with Cynthia L. Selfe); and a chapter in *Feminist Cyberspaces: Mapping Gendered Academic Spaces* (with Joanne Addison, in Blair & Takayoshi, Eds., 1999).

Amy C. Kimme Hea is an assistant professor in the Rhetoric, Composition, and Teaching of English Program and Associate Director of the Writing Program at University of Arizona. Her research interests include Web and wireless teaching and learning, teacher training, and professional writing theory and practice. Her current research project is a forthcoming edited collection with Hampton Press, *Going Wireless: A Critical Exploration of Wireless and Mobile Technologies for Composition Teachers and Scholars*. She has published on articulation theory and methodology, visual rhetoric, Web design, hypertext theory, and service learning projects. Her work appears in the anthologies and journals including *Computers and Composition, Kairos, Educare,* and *Reflections: A Journal of Writing, Service-Learning, and Community Literacy*.

Jacklyn Lopez is an undergraduate at Kean University studying for a BA in secondary English education. She has been playing video games as long as she can remember and is self-taught in Web site publishing.

Janice McIntire-Strasburg is an associate professor of English at Saint Louis University, and completed her graduate work at University of Nevada, Las Vegas. She has published articles in *The Writing Instructor, Kairos,* and *Studies in American Humor,* and has completed an online scholarly edition of *Modern Chivalry* at University of Virginia's Electronic Text Center.

Heidi McKee is an assistant professor of English at Miami University (Oxford, Ohio). Her work has appeared in *College Composition and Communication, Computers and Composition, Computers and Composition Online,* and *Pedagogy*. With Dànielle Nicole DeVoss, she co-edited the 20th-anniversary issues of *Computers and Composition* (20.4 & 21.1). Her work in progress includes a co-researched and co-authored study with James Porter on the ethics of digital writing research.

Iswari Pandey is a doctoral candidate in rhetoric and composition at the University of Louisville, where his interests include literacy studies, cultural rhetorics, global/postcolonial studies, and writing technologies. His work has appeared or is forthcoming in edited collections and journals such as the *Journal of Kentucky Studies* and *Computers and Composition*.

James E. Porter is a professor in the Department of Writing, Rhetoric, and American Cultures at Michigan State University, where he also serves as Co-Director of the Writing in Digital Environments (WIDE) Research Center. His teaching at MSU includes graduate and undergraduate courses in rhetoric theory and history and in professional/technical writing. His research—which explores connections between rhetoric theory, professional/technical communication, and digital writing—includes recent and forthcoming publications on digital communication ethics (particularly the ethics of digital research methodology); the economics and politics of digital delivery and distribution; issues in intellectual property and digital writing; and the impact of copying, downloading, and filesharing technologies, laws, and policies on writers' composing processes.

Colleen A. Reilly is an assistant professor of English at the University of North Carolina Wilmington where she teaches courses in professional writing. Her research and teaching interests include writing and technology, writing about science, electronic publication, and intersections of genders, sexualities, and technologies. She has recently published articles in *Computers and Composition* and in the peer-reviewed, Web-based journal *Innovate* and has been a co-editor of the Praxis section of *Kairos* since Fall 2001.

Rebecca J. Rickly is an associate professor at Texas Tech University where she serves as Co-Director of the Interactive Composition Online (ICON) program. At the center of her work is what she calls "applied rhetoric," which includes such diverse applications as technology, feminisms, methods and methodologies, literacy study, and administration. She has served on the Conference on College Composition and Communication Committee on Computers and Composition, NCTE's Assembly on Computers in English, and she has chaired NCTE's Instructional Technology Committee; she currently serves as Chair of the CCCC Basic Data Project Task Force. Her publications include *The Online Writing Classroom* (with Susanmarie Harrington and Michael Day, 2000), and her work has appeared in numerous edited collections, as well as *Computers and Composition*, *CMC Magazine*, *The ACE Journal*, and *Kairos*. Currently, she is working on an edited collection (with Krista Ratcliffe) entitled *Feminism and Administration in Rhetoric and Composition Studies*.

Julia Romberger is an assistant professor in the Professional Writing Program at Old Dominion University. She graduated from Purdue University in 2004; her dissertation investigated the rhetorical environment of Microsoft Word and its implications for users. She has taught classes in multimedia writing, business and technical writing, visual rhetoric, and composition. She also has a forthcoming co-authored article entitled "Designing Efficiencies: The Parallel Narratives of Distance Education and Composition Studies" that will appear in a special issue of *Computers and Composition*.

Filipp Sapienza is an assistant professor of Communication at the University of Colorado–Denver and Health Sciences Center. He teaches courses in technical communication, Web site design, usability, and content management. Sapienza's research interests include transnational cultures online, usability, structured content development, and Russian cultural theory. He has published research on these topics in the journals *Technical Communication, Journal of Technical Writing and Communication, Javnost'*, and *Philosophy and Rhetoric*.

Michelle Sidler is an assistant professor at Auburn University, where she teaches undergraduate and graduate courses in composition, technological literacy, and professional communication. Her research interests include the rhetoric of biological science, internet research, and electronic communication across the curriculum. She has published essays in journals such as *Computers and Composition, Rhetoric Review*, and *The WAC Journal*. She is currently writing a book about science literacy, biotechnology, and the future of writing-across-the-curriculum programs.

Shaun Slattery is an assistant professor at DePaul University where he researches and teaches in the related fields of composition, rhetoric, information technology, and writing across the curriculum. His research looks at how technical writers coordinate multiple texts (source documents, notes, emails, etc.) to help them produce a new "target" document, and how information technology helps and hinders this textual coordination.

Beatrice Quarshie Smith is an associate professor of Literacy Studies in the Department of Curriculum and Instruction at Illinois State University where she is also the Director of the Center for Reading and Literacy. Her research interests include explorations of the relationships among globalization, gender, literacy and work practices. Her most recent work has appeared in the *Journal of Adolescent and Adult Literacy*. She is currently working on a book-length manuscript tentatively titled *Globalization, Technology and Work Practices in Outsourcing*.

Christine Tulley is an assistant professor at the University of Findlay. Her research and teaching interests include digital rhetorics, visual rhetorics (including the link between cyberspace and film theories), women's studies and composition. Her work has appeared in *Journal of Advanced Composition, Computers and Composition*, and in the edited collection *Teaching Writing with Computers* (2003). Most recently, a collaborative book review of James Paul Gee's *What Video Games Can Teach Us About Learning* *and Literacy* with her senior Web Writing for English Majors course was featured in *Computers and Composition Online.*

Sean Williams is an associate professor of Professional Communication at Clemson University where he also directs Clemson's Multimedia, Authoring, Teaching and Research Facility. His research has recently taken a turn toward user experience design and new forms of usability that consider the role affective and emotional components play in an online product's success. His prior publications on industry/academy collaborations, information design, digital literacy, and computers and writing have appeared in journals including *Technical Communication, Technical Communication Quarterly, Intercom,* the *Journal of Advanced Communication, Business Communication Quarterly, Reflections,* and *Computers and Composition.*

REFERENCES

Abu-Lughod, Lila. (1991). Writing against culture. In Richard G. Fox (Ed.), *Recapturing anthropology: Working in the present* (pp. 137–162). Santa Fe, NM: School of American Research Press.

ACLU letter to Senator Feinstein addressing abuses of the Patriot Act by the government. (2004, April 4). Retrieved March 3, 2005, from http://www.aclu.org/news/NewsPrint.cfm?ID = 17911&c = 206

Addison, Joanne. (1997). Data analysis and subject representation in empowering composition research. *Written Communication, 14*, 106–128.

Addison, Joanne, & Hilligoss, Susan. (1999). Technological fronts: Lesbian lives "on the line." In Kristine Blair & Pamela Takayoshi (Eds.), *Feminist cyberscapes: Mapping gendered academic spaces* (pp. 21–40). Stamford, CT: Ablex.

Addison, Joanne, & McGee, Sharon. (1999). *Feminist empirical research: Emerging perspectives on qualitative and teacher research.* New York: Heinemann Boynton/Cook.

Afifi, Walid A., & Johnson, Michelle L. (2005). The nature and functions of tie-signs. In Valerie Manusov (Ed.), *The sourcebook of nonverbal measures: Going beyond words* (pp. 189–198). Mahwah, NJ: Erlbaum.

Agar, Michael. (1994). *Language shock: Understanding the culture of conversation.* New York: William Morrow & Co.

Agar, Michael. (1996). *The professional stranger: An informal introduction to ethnography* (2nd ed.). San Diego, CA: Academic Press.

Aguillo, Isidro F. (1996). De IMPACT II a INFO 2000. Construyendo la Sociedad Global de la Información. *Métodos de Información, 3*(11–12), 47–49.

Aguillo, Isidro F. (2003). Cybermetrics: Definitions and methods for an emerging discipline. Presentation at the European Indicators, Cyberspace and the Science-Technology-Economy System. Retrieved October 28, 2004, from http://www.eicstes.org/EICSTES_PDF/PRESENTATIONS/Cybermetrics%20(Aguillo).PDF

Albers, Michael J. (2000). The technical editor and document databases: What the future may hold. *Technical Communication Quarterly, 9*(2), 191–206.

Alcorn, Marshall W. (1994). Self-structure as a rhetorical device: Modern ethos and the divisiveness of self. In James S. Baumlin & Tita French Baumlin (Eds.), *Ethos: New essays in rhetorical and critical theory* (pp. 3–37). Austin, TX: Southern Methodist University Press.

Alexander, Jonathan. (1997). Out of the closet and into the network: Sexual orientation and the computerized classroom. *Computers and Composition, 14*, 207–216.

Alexander, Jonathan. (2002a). Digital spins: The pedagogy and politics of student-centered e-zines. *Computers and Composition, 19*, 387–410.

Alexander, Jonathan. (2002b). Ravers on the Web: Resistance, multidimensionality, writing (about) youth cultures. *Kairos: A Journal of Rhetoric, Technology, and Pedagogy, 7*(3). Retrieved March 31, 2005, from http://english.ttu.edu/kairos/7.3/binder2.html?coverweb/RaveWrite/index.htm

Alexander, Jonathan. (2005). *Digital youth: Emerging literacies on the World Wide Web.* Cresskill, NJ: Hampton Press.

Alexander, Jonathan, & Banks, William. (2004). Sexualities, technologies, and the teaching of writing: A critical overview. *Computers & Composition, 21*, 273–293.

Allen, Christina. (1996). *Virtual identities: The social construction of cybered selves.* Unpublished doctoral dissertation, Northwestern University, Evanston, IL.

Allen, Nancy. (2002). *Working with words and images: New steps in an old dance.* Greenwich, CT: Ablex.

Alverman, Donna E. (Ed.). (2002). *Adolescents in a digital world* (vol. 7). New York: Peter Lang.

Amdur, Robert, & Bankert, Elizabeth. (2002). *Institutional review board: Management and function.* Boston: Jones and Bartlett.

American Association of University Women Educational Foundation. (2000). *Tech savvy: Educating girls in the new computer age.* New York: AAUW.

American Library Association. (2003, January). Resolution on the USA Patriot Act and related measures that infringe on the rights of library users. Retrieved March 20, 2005, from http://www.ala.org/ala/washoff/WOissues/civilliberties/theusapatriotact/alaresolution.htm

Amponsah, Kofi. (2003). Patterns of communication and the implications for learning among two distributed-education student teams. *Proceedings of the 21st*

Annual International Conference on Documentation (pp. 20–27). San Francisco: Association of Computing Machinery.

Anderson, Benedict. (1991). *Imagined communities: Reflections on the origin and spread of nationalism.* London: Verso.

Anderson, Paul. (1996). Ethics, institutional review boards, and the involvement of human participants in composition research. In Gesa R. Kirsch & Peter Mortensen (Eds.), *Ethics & representation in qualitative studies of literacy* (pp. 260–285). Urbana, IL: National Council of Teachers of English.

Anderson, Paul. (1998). Simple gifts: Ethical issues in the conduct of person-based composition research. *College Composition and Communication, 49,* 63–89.

Anderson, Paul V., Brockmann, John, & Miller, Carolyn R. (1983). *New essays in technical and scientific communication: Research, theory, practice.* Farmingdale, NY: Baywood Publishing Company.

Ankersmit, Frank. R. (1988). Historical representation. *History and Theory, 27*(3), 205–228.

Appadurai, Arjun. (1990). Disjuncture and difference in the global cultural economy. In M. Featherstone (Ed.), *Global culture* (pp. 295–310). London: Sage.

Appadurai, Arjun. (1996). *Modernity at large: Cultural dimensions of globalization.* Minneapolis: University of Minnesota Press.

Aristotle. (1991). *Rhetoric* (George A. Kennedy, Ed. & Trans.). Oxford: Oxford University Press.

Associazione Italiana di Biologia Teorica (ABT). (2004). Retrieved October 30, 2004, from http://www.biologiateorica.it/

Athanases, Steven Z., & Heath, Shirley Brice. (1995). Ethnography in the study of the teaching of English. *Research in the Teaching of English, 29*(3), 263–287.

Baake, Ken. (2003). *Metaphor and knowledge: The challenges of writing science.* Albany: State University of New York Press.

Bahadur, Gary, Chan, William, & Weber, Chris. (2002). *Privacy defended: Protecting yourself online.* Indianapolis, IN: Que.

Baik, Martin J., & Shim, Rosa J. (1993). "Yes, we have no bananas": English negative tags in cross-linguistic communication. *Studies in the Linguistic Sciences, 23*(1), 43–59.

Bailey, Brian P., Gurak, Laura J., & Konstan, J.A. (2002). Trust in cyberspace. In Julie Ratner (Ed.), *Human factors and web development* (2nd ed., pp. 311–322). Mahwah, NJ: Erlbaum.

Bakardjieva, Maria, & Feenberg, Andrew. (2000). Involving the virtual subject. *Ethics and Information Technology, 2,* 233–240.

Bakeman, Roger. (2005). Analysis of coded nonverbal behavior. In Valerie Manusov (Ed.), *The sourcebook of nonverbal measures: Going beyond words* (pp. 375–381). Mahwah, NJ: Erlbaum.

Barber, John F., & Grigar, Dene. (2001). *New worlds, new words: Exploring pathways for writing about and in electronic environments.* Cresskill, NJ: Hampton Press.

Barbieri, Marcello. (2003). *The organic codes: An introduction to semantic biology.* Cambridge: Cambridge University Press.

Barlow, John Perry. (1996). A declaration of the independence of cyberspace. Retrieved January 1, 2000, from http://homes.eff.org/ ~ barlow/Declaration-Final.html

Barnes, Susan B. (2001). *Online connections: Internet interpersonal relationships.* Cresskill, NJ: Hampton Press.

Barrios, Barclay. (2004). Reimagining writing program Web sites as pedagogical tools. *Computers and Composition, 21,* 73–87.

Barry, Anne Marie. (1997). *Visual intelligence: Perception, image, and manipulation in visual communication.* Albany: State University of New York Press.

Barthes, Roland. (1972). Writers and authors. In *Critical essays* (Richard Howard, Trans.) (pp. 143–149). Evanston, IL: Northwestern University Press.

Barton, Ben F., & Barton, Marthalee. (1993). Ideology and the map: Toward a postmodern visual design practice. In Nancy Blyer & Charlotte Thralls (Eds.), *Professional communication: The social perspective* (pp. 49–78). Newbury Park, CA: Sage.

Barton, David, & Hamilton, Mary. (1998). *Local literacies: Reading and writing in one community.* London: Routledge.

Barton, Ellen. (2002). Inductive discourse analysis: Discovering rich features. In Ellen Barton & Gail Stygall (Eds.), *Discourse studies in composition* (pp. 19–42). Cresskill, NJ: Hampton Press.

Barton, Ellen. (2004). Linguistic discourse analysis: How the language in texts works. In Charles Bazerman & Paul Prior (Eds.), *What writing does and how it does it: An introduction to analyzing texts and textual practices* (pp. 57–82). Mahwah, NJ: Erlbaum.

Bassett, E. H., & O'Riordan, Kathleen. (2001). Ethics of internet research: Contesting the human subjects research model. In Charles Ess (Ed.), *Internet research ethics.* Retrieved May 1, 2005, from http://www.nyu.edu/projects/nissenbaum/projects_ethics.html

Bateson, Gregory. (1979). *Mind and nature: A necessary unity.* New York: E. P. Dutton.

Baudrillard, Jean. (1994). *Simulation and simulacra* (Sheila Faria Glaser, Trans.). Ann Arbor: University of Michigan Press.

Baugnet, Julie. (2003). The weaving of design and community. In Steven Heller & Veronique Vienne (Eds.), *Citizen designer: Perspectives on design responsibility* (pp. 95–99). New York: Alworth Press.

Bazerman, Charles. (1988). *Shaping written knowledge: The genre and activity of the experimental article in science.* Madison: University of Wisconsin Press.

Bazerman, Charles. (1994). *Constructing experience.* Carbondale: Southern Illinois University Press.

Bazerman, Charles. (1999). *The languages of Edison's light.* Cambridge, MA: MIT Press.

Bazerman, Charles, & Prior, Paul. (Eds.). (2004). *What writing does and how it does it: An introduction to analyzing texts and textual practices.* Mahwah, NJ: Erlbaum.

Bazerman, Charles, & Russell, David R. (2003). *Writing selves/writing societies: Research from activity perspectives.* Fort Collins, CO: WAC Clearinghouse. Retrieved January 2, 2005, from http://wac.colostate.edu/books/selves_societies/

Behar, Ruth. (1993). *Translated woman: Crossing the border with Esprenza's story.* Boston: Beacon Press.

Behar, Ruth., & Gordon, Deborah A. (Eds.). (1995). *Women writing culture.* Berkeley: University of California Press.

Belmont Report. (1979, April 18). The National Commission for the Protection of Human Subjects of Biomedical and Behavioral Research. Retrieved August 8, 2004, from http://www.hhs.gov/ohrp/humansubjects/guidance/belmont.htm

Benbunan-Fich, Raquel. (2001). Using protocol analysis to evaluate the usability of a commercial web site. *Information & Management, 39,* 151–163.

Berger, Arthur. (2000). *Media and communication research methods: An introduction to qualitative and quantitative approaches.* Thousand Oaks, CA: Sage.

Berkenkotter, Carol. (2002a). Analyzing everyday texts in organizational settings. In Laura J. Gurak & Mary M. Lay (Eds.), *Research in technical communication* (pp. 47–66). Westport, CT: Praeger.

Berkenkotter, Carol. (2002b). *Asylum notes and patient identities: The historical antecedents of psychiatric case histories.* Paper given at the annual convention of the National Communication Association, New Orleans, LA.

Berkenkotter, Carol. (2004). *Recontextualizing Dora: Freud's rhetorical uses of reported speech.* Paper given at the annual convention of the National Communication Association, Chicago, IL.

Berkenkotter, Carol, & Huckin, Thomas. (1993). You are what you cite: Novelty and intertextuality in a biologist's experimental article. In Nancy Roundy Blyer & Charles Thralls (Eds.), *Professional communication: The social perspective* (pp. 109–127). Newbury Park, CA: Sage.

Berkenkotter, Carol, & Huckin, Thomas. (1995). *Genre knowledge in disciplinary communication: Cognition, culture, power.* Hillsdale, NJ: Erlbaum.

Bernhardt, Stephen A. (1993). The shape of text to come: The texture of print on screens. *College Composition and Communication, 44,* 151-175.

Berry, David M. (2004). Internet research: Privacy, ethics, and alienation—an open source approach. *Studies in Social and Political Thought, 9,* 53–71.

Beserra, W. C. (1986). *Effect of word processing upon the writing processes of basic writers.* Doctoral dissertation, New Mexico State University. *Dissertation Abstracts International, 48,* 34-A.

Besthorn, Fred H., & McMillen, Diane Pearson. (2002). The oppression of women and nature: Ecofeminism as a framework for an expanded ecological social work. *Families in Society: The Journal of Contemporary Human Services, 83*(3), 221–232.

Bhabha, Homi K. (1990). DissemiNation: Time, narrative, and the margins of the modern nation. In Homi Bhabha (Ed.), *Nation and narration* (pp. 291–322). New York: Routledge.

Bhabha, Homi K. (1994). *The location of culture*. London: Routledge.

Biber, Douglas. (1988). *Variation across speech and writing*. Cambridge: Cambridge University Press.

Birdsell, David S., & Groarke, Leo. (1996). Toward a theory of visual argument. *Argumentation and Advocacy, 33,* 1–10.

Bishop, Wendy. (1999). *Ethnographic writing research: Writing it down, writing it up, and reading it*. Portsmouth, NH: Boynton/Cook.

Blair, J. Anthony. (1996). The possibility and actuality of visual arguments. *Argumentation and Advocacy, 33,* 23–39.

Blair, Kristine. (1998). Literacy, dialogue, and difference in the "electronic contact zone." *Computers and Composition, 15,* 317–329.

Blakeslee, Ann M., Cole, Caroline M., & Conefrey, Theresa. (1996). Constructing voices in writing research: Developing participatory approaches to situated inquiry. In Peter Mortensen & Gesa E. Kirsch (Eds.), *Ethics & representation: In qualitative studies of literacy* (pp. 134–154). Urbana, IL: National Council of Teachers of English.

Blakeslee, Ann M., & Spilka, Rachel. (2004). The state of research in technical communication. *Technical Communication Quarterly, 13,* 73–92.

Blakesley, David. (2004). Defining film rhetorics: The case of Hitchcock's *Vertigo*. In Charles A. Hill & Marguerite Helmers (Eds.), *Defining visual rhetorics* (pp. 111–134). Mahwah, NJ: Erlbaum.

Blakesley, David, & Brooke, Collin. (2001). Introduction: Notes on visual rhetoric. *Enculturation, 3*(2). Retrieved October 20, 2004, from http://enculturation. gmu.edu/3_2/introduction.html

Bleich, David. (1993). Ethnography and the study of literacy: Prospects for socially generous research. In Anne Ruggles Gere (Ed.), *Into the field: Sites of composition studies* (pp. 176-192). New York: MLA.

Bloch, Joel. (2001). Plagiarism and the ESL student: From printed to electronic texts. In Diane Belcher & Alan Hirvela (Eds.), *Linking literacies: Perspectives on L2 reading–writing connections* (pp. 209–228). Ann Arbor: University of Michigan Press.

Blythe, Stuart. (2004). IText, professional identity, and campus-community partnerships. *Journal of Business and Technical Communication, 18,* 270–293.

Bodker, Suzanne. (1997). Computers in mediated human activity. *Mind, Culture and Activity, 4,* 149–158.

Boese, Christine. (1999). A virtual locker room in classroom chat spaces: The politics of men as "other." In Kristine Blair & Pamela Takayoshi (Eds.), *Feminist cyberscapes: Mapping gendered academic spaces* (pp. 195–227). Stamford, CT: Ablex.

Bogdan, Robert C., & Biklen, Sara K. (2003). *Qualitative research for education: An introduction to theories and methods* (4th ed.). Boston, MA: Pearson Group.

Bolter, Jay David. (2001). *Writing space: Computers, hypertext, and the remediation of print* (2nd ed.). Mahwah, NJ: Erlbaum.

Bolter, Jay David, & Grusin, Richard. (1999). *Remediation: Understanding new media*. Cambridge, MA: MIT Press.

Bomberger, Ann M. (2004). Ranting about race: Crushed eggshells in computer-mediated communication. *Computers and Composition, 21*(2), 197–216.

Boren, M. Ted, & Ramey, Judith. (2000). Thinking aloud: Reconciling theory and practice. *IEEE Transactions on Professional Communication, 43*, 261–278.

Bowie, Jennifer. (2004). *Exploring user/webtext interactions: A feminist examination of gender and sex differences in web use.* Unpublished Ph.D. Dissertation, Texas Tech University, Lubbock, TX.

Braddock, Richard, Lloyd-Jones, Richard, & Schoer, Lowell. (1963). *Research in written composition.* Urbana, IL: National Council of Teachers of English.

Bradley, Candice. (1997). Keeping the soil in good heart: Women weeders, the environment, and ecofeminism. In Karen Warren (Ed.), *Ecofeminism: Women, culture, nature* (pp. 290–299). Bloomington: Indiana University Press.

Brady Aschauer, Ann. (1999). Tinkering with technological skill: An examination of the gendered uses of technologies. *Computers and Composition, 16*(1), 7–23.

Brail, Stephanie. (1996). The price of admission: Harassment and free speech in the wild wild West. In Lynn Cherny & Elizabeth Reba Weise (Eds.), *Wired women* (pp. 141–157). Seattle, WA: Seal Press.

Braine, George. (2001). A study of English as a foreign language (EFL) writers on a local-area network (LAN) and in traditional classes. *Computers and Composition, 18*, 275–292.

Brandt, Deborah. (1990). *Literacy as involvement: The acts of writers, readers and texts.* Carbondale: Southern Illinois University Press.

Brandt, Deborah. (1995). Accumulating literacy: Writing and learning to write in the twentieth century. *College English, 5*, 649–668.

Brandt, Deborah. (2001). *Literacy in American lives.* Cambridge, MA: Cambridge University Press.

Brasseur, Lee. (2003). *Visualizing technical information: A cultural critique.* Amityville, NY: Baywood.

Brasseur, Lee. (2005). Florence Nightingale's visual rhetoric in the Rose Diagrams. *Technical Communication Quarterly, 14*(2), 161–182.

Brettell, Caroline. (Ed.). (1993). *When they read what we write: The politics of ethnography.* Westport, CT: Bergin and Garvey.

Bridwell-Bowles, Lillian. (1989). Designing research on computer-assisted writing. *Computers and Composition, 7*1), 79–90.

Bridwell, Lillian S., Nancarrow, P. R., & Ross, D. (1984). The writing process and the writing machine: Current research on word processors relevant to the teaching of composition. In Richard Beach & Lillian S. Bridwell (Eds.), *New directions in composition research* (pp. 381–398). New York: Guilford Press.

Brin, Sergey, & Page, Lawrence. (1998). The anatomy of a large scale hypertextual Web search engine. *Computer Networks and ISDN Systems, 30*, 107–117.

Brooke, Robert. (1987). Underlife and writing instruction. *College Composition and Communication, 38*, 141–153.

Brown, Stephen, & Dobrin, Sidney. (2004). Introduction: New writers of the cultural sage, from postmodern theory shock to critical praxis. In Stephen Brown &

Sidney Dobrin (Eds.), *Ethnography unbound: From theory shock to critical praxis* (pp. 1–10). Albany: State University of New York Press.

Brownfield, Peter. (2004, February 13). White House under fire for outsourcing proposal. *Fox News*. Retrieved October 25, 2005, from http://www.foxnews.com/story/0,2933,111287,00.html

Bruce, Bertram C. (1997). Critical issues. Literacy and technology: What stance should we take? *Journal of Literacy Research, 29*, 289–309.

Bruce, Bertram C. (1999). Speaking the unspeakable about 21st century technologies. In Gail Hawisher & Cynthia Selfe (Eds.), *Passions, pedagogies and 21st century technologies* (pp. 221–228). Logan: Utah State University Press.

Budd, John M. (1999). Citations and knowledge claims: Sociology of knowledge as a case in point. *Journal of Information Science, 25*(4), 265–274.

Buege, Douglas. (1997). Epistemic responsibility and the Inuit of Canada's Eastern Arctic: An ecofeminist appraisal. In Karen Warren (Ed.), *Ecofeminism: Women, culture, nature* (pp. 99–111). Bloomington: Indiana University Press.

Bull, Michael, & Black, Les. (2003). Introduction: Into sound. In Michael Bull & Les Black (Eds.), *Auditory culture reader* (pp. 1–18). New York: Oxford.

Buller, David B. (2005). Methods for measuring speech rate. In Valerie Manusov (Ed.), *The sourcebook of nonverbal measures: Going beyond words* (pp. 317–324). Mahwah, NJ: Erlbaum.

Bump, Jerome. (1990). Radical changes in class discussion using networked computers. *Computers and the Humanities, 24*, 49–65.

Burgess, Robert G. (1984). *In the field: An introduction to research.* London: Allen & Unwin.

Burns, Hugh. (1979). *Stimulating rhetorical invention in English composition through computer-assisted instruction.* Unpublished dissertation. Austin: University of Texas.

Bush, Vannevar. (1945). As we may think. *Atlantic Monthly, 176*, 101–108.

Buskirk, T. D., & Steeh, C. G. (2004, March). *R U there? Using text messaging as a method of contact.* Paper presentation at the Wireless German Online Research Conference, University of Duisburg-Essen, Germany.

Campbell, Jeremy. (1982). *Grammatical man: Information, entropy, language, and life.* New York: Simon and Schuster.

Campbell, John Angus. (1986). Scientific revolution and the grammar of culture: The case of Darwin's *Origin*. *Quarterly Journal of Speech, 72*, 351–376.

Campbell, John Angus. (1990). Scientific discovery and rhetorical invention: The path to Darwin's *Origin*. In Herbert W. Simons (Ed.), *The rhetorical turn: Invention and persuasion in the conduct of inquiry* (pp. 58–90). Chicago: University of Chicago Press.

Carspecken, Phil F. (1996). *Critical ethnography in educational research: A theoretical and practical guide.* New York: Routledge.

Castells, Manuel. (1996). *The rise of the network society.* Oxford: Blackwell.

Cavanagh, Allison. (1999). Behaviour in public?: Ethics in online ethnography. *Cybersociology, 6*. Retrieved May 1, 2005, from: http://www.socio.demon.co.uk/magazine/6/cavanagh.html

CCCC Executive Committee. (2004). Guidelines for the ethical conduct of research in composition studies. *College Composition and Communication, 55*, 779–784.

Chang, N. (2003). How democracy dies: The war on our civil liberties. *Lost liberties: Ashcroft and the assault on personal freedom* (pp. 33–51). New York: New Press.

Chatterjee, Partha. (1993). *The nation and its fragments: Colonial and postcolonial histories*. Princeton, NJ: Princeton University Press.

Cherney, Lynn. (1995). "Objectifying" the body in the discourse of an object-oriented MUD. *Works and Days, 25/26*(1), 151–173.

Chiseri-Strater, Elizabeth. (1996). Turning in ourselves: Positionality, subjectivity, and reflexivity in case study and ethnographic research. In Peter Mortensen & Gesa Kirsch (Eds.), *Ethics and representation in qualitative studies of literacy* (pp. 115–134). Urbana: National Council of Teachers of English.

Clark, David. (2004). What if you meet face to face? A case study in virtual/material research ethics. In Elizabeth A. Buchanan (Ed.), *Readings in virtual research ethics* (pp. 246–261). Hershey, PA: Idea Group Publishers.

Clifford, James. (1992). Traveling cultures. In Lawrence Grossberg, Cary Nelson, & Paula Treichler (Eds.), *Cultural studies* (pp. 96–116). New York: Routledge.

Clifford, James. (1997). Spatial practices: Fieldwork, travel, and the disciplining of anthropology. In Akhil Gupta & James Ferguson (Eds.), *Anthropological locations* (pp. 185–222). Berkeley: University of California Press.

Clifford, James, & Marcus, George E. (Eds.). (1988). *Writing culture: The poetics and politics of ethnography.* Berkeley: University of California Press.

Cole, Eric. (2002). *Hackers beware: The ultimate guide to network security.* Indianapolis, IN: New Riders.

College Board. (2004). *Writing: A ticket to work . . . Or a ticket out. A survey of business leaders.* Retrieved June 4, 2005, from http://www.writingcommission.org/prod_downloads/writingcom/writing-ticket-to-work.pdf

CollegeNET. (2005a). *CollegeNET online applications and free financial aid search.* Retrieved March 20, 2005, from http://www.collegenet.com/

CollegeNET. (2005b). *Intelligent connections: Take the tour!* Retrieved March 20, 2005, from http://corp.collegenet.com/depts/higher_ed/admissions/index/

CollegeNET. (2005c). *Wireless triggers: Take the tour!* Retrieved March 20, 2005, from http://corp.collegenet.com/depts/higher_ed/admissions/index/

CollegeNET. (n.d.). *About CollegeNET*. Retrieved March 20, 2005, from http://www.collegenet.com/about/cninfo/results

Collot, Milena, & Belmore, Nancy. (1996). Electronic language: A new variety of English. In Susan C. Herring (Ed.), *Computer-mediated communication: Linguistic, social and cross-cultural perspectives* (pp. 13–28). Amsterdam /Philadelphia: John Benjamins Publishing Company.

Comstock, Michelle & Addison, Joanne. (1997). Virtual complexities: Exploring literacies at the intersections of computer-mediated social formations. *Computers and Composition, 14*, 245–255.

Conference on College Composition and Communication. (2004). *CCCC position statement on teaching, learning, and assessing writing in digital environments.*

Retrieved December 20, 2003, from http://www.ncte.org/about/over/positions/category/assess/115775.htm

Conley, Verena Andermatt. (1997). *Ecopolitics: The environment in poststructuralist thought.* New York: Routledge.

Conner, Tamlin. (2004). *Experience sampling resource page.* Department of Psychology, Boston College. Retrieved July 4, 2004, from http//www2bc.edu/∼connert/esm.htm

Conner, Tamlin, Feldman Barrett, Lisa, Bliss-Moreau, Eliza, Lebo, Kirsten, & Kaschub, Cynthia. (2003). A practical guide to experience-sampling procedures. *Journal of Happiness Studies, 4,* 53–78.

Conway, Glenda. (1995). "What are we doing today?" High school basic writers collaborating in a computer lab. *Computers and Composition, 12,* 79–95.

Cooks, Leda. (2001). From distance and uncertainty to research and pedagogy in the borderlands: Implications for the future of intercultural communication. *Communication Theory, 11,* 339–351.

Cooper, Charles, & Odell, Lee. (1978). *Research on composing: Points of departure.* Urbana, IL: National Council of Teachers of English.

Cooper, Joel, & Weaver, Kimberly. (2003). *Gender and computers: Understanding the digital divide.* Mahwah, NJ: Erlbaum.

Cooper, Marilyn M. (1986). The ecology of writing. *College English, 48,* 364–375.

Cooper, Marilyn. (1999). Postmodern pedagogy in electronic conversations. In Gail E. Hawisher & Cynthia L. Selfe (Eds.), *Passions pedagogies and 21st century technologies* (pp. 140–161). Logan: Utah State University Press.

Cooper, Marilyn M., & Holtzman, Michael. (Eds.). (1989). *Writing as social action.* Portsmouth, NH: Boynton-Cook, Heinemann.

Cooper, Marilyn M., & Selfe, Cynthia L. (1990). Computer conferences and learning: Authority, resistance, and internally persuasive discourse. *College English, 52,* 1–23.

Cope, Bill, & Kalantzis, Mary. (Eds.). (2000). *Multiliteracies: Literacy learning and the design of social futures.* London: Routledge.

Corby, Katherine. (2001). Method or madness? Educational research and citation prestige. *Portal: Libraries and the Academy, 1*(3), 279–288.

Correll, Shelley. (1995). The ethnography of an electronic bar: The lesbian café. *Journal of Communication, 24,* 270–298.

Craig, Terry, Harris, Leslie, & Smith, Richard. (1998). Rhetoric of the "contact zone": Composition on the front lines. In Todd Taylor & Irene Ward (Eds.), *Literacy theory in the age of the Internet* (pp. 122–145). New York: Columbia University Press.

Creswell, John. (1998). *Qualitative inquiry and research design: Choosing among five traditions.* Thousand Oaks, CA: Sage.

Cross, Geoffrey. (1990). Left to their own devices: Three basic writers using word processing. *Computers and Composition, 7*(2), 47–58.

Crumpton, Amy. (1999). Secrecy in science. *Professional Ethics Report, 12.* Retrieved March 1, 2005, from http://www.aaas.org/spp/sfrl/per/per16.htm

Csikszentmihalyi, Mihaly, & Larson, Reed. (1987). Validity and reliability of the experience-sampling method. *Journal of Nervous and Mental Disorders, 175,* 526–536.

Csikszentmihalyi, Mihaly, Larson, Reed, & Prescott, S. (1977). The ecology of adolescent activity and experience. *Journal of Youth and Adolescence, 6,* 281–294.

Cubbison, Laurie. (1999). Configuring Listserv, configuring discourse. *Computers and Composition, 16,* 371–381.

Cullen, R. (1988). Computer-assisted composition: A case study of six developmental writers. *Collegiate Microcomputer, 6,* 202–212.

Curtain, Deane. (1997). Women's knowledge as expert knowledge: Indian women and ecodevelopment. In Karen Warren (Ed.), *Ecofeminism: Women, culture, nature* (pp. 82–98). Bloomington: Indiana University Press.

Curtis, Marcia, & Klem, Elizabeth. (1992). The virtual context: Ethnography in the computer-equipped classroom. In Gail E. Hawisher & Paul LeBlanc (Eds.), *Reimagining computers and composition: Teaching and research in the virtual age* (pp. 155–172). Portsmouth, NE: Boynton/Cook.

Cushman, Ellen. (1996). The rhetorician as an agent of social change. *College Composition and Communication, 47,* 7–28.

Cushman, Ellen. (1998). *The struggle and the tools: Oral and literate strategies in an inner city community.* Albany: SUNY Press.

Czerwinski, Mary, Horvitz, Eric, & Wilhite, Susan. (2004). A diary study of task switching and interruptions. *Proceedings of the 2004 Conference on Human Factors in Computing Systems, CHI2004 6.1* (pp. 175–182). Vienna, Austria: ProCHI.

Danette, Paul, Charney, Davida, & Kendall, Aimee. (2001). Moving beyond the moment: Reception studies in the rhetoric of science. *Journal of Business and Technical Communication, 15*(3), 372–399.

de Certeau, Michel. (1984). *The practice of everyday life* (Steven Rendall, Trans.). Los Angeles: University of California Press.

Delanty, Gerard. (1999). Self, other and world: Discourses of nationalism and cosmopolitanism. *Cultural Values, 3,* 365–374.

Deleuze, Gilles, & Guattari, Felix. (1987). *A thousand plateaus: Capitalism and schizophrenia* (Brian Massumi, Trans.). Minneapolis: University of Minnesota Press.

Deming, M. P. (1987). *The effects of word processing on basic college writers' revision strategies, writing apprehension, and writing quality while composing in the expository mode.* Doctoral dissertation, Georgia State University. *Dissertation Abstracts International, 48,* 2263-A.

Denzin, Norman. (1970). *The research act: A theoretical introduction to sociological methods.* Chicago: Aldine Publishing Company.

Derrida, Jaques. (1988). *Limited inc.* Evanston, IL: Northwestern University Press.

DeVoss, Dànielle, Cushman, Ellen, & Grabill, Jeffrey T. (2005). Infrastructure and composing: The when of new-media writing. *College Composition and Communication, 57,* 14–44.

DeVoss, Dànielle, Hawisher, Gail E., Jackson, Charles, Johansen, Joseph, Moraski, Brittney, & Selfe, Cynthia L. (2004). The future of literacy. In Cynthia L. Selfe &

Gail E. Hawisher (Eds.), *Literate lives in the information age: Narratives of literacy from the United States* (pp.183–211). Mahwah, NJ: Erlbaum.

DeVries, Will T. (2003). Protecting privacy in the digital age. *Berkeley Technology Law Journal: Annual Review, 18*(1), 283–311.

DeWitt, Scott Lloyd. (1996). The current nature of hypertext research in computers and composition studies: An historical perspective. *Computers and Composition, 13*(1), 69–84.

DeWitt, Scott Lloyd. (1997). Out there on the Web: Pedagogy and identity in face of opposition. *Computers and Composition, 14*, 229–243.

DeWitt, Scott Lloyd, & Strasma, Kip. (Eds.). (1999). *Contexts, intertexts, and hypertexts*. Cresskill, NJ: Hampton Press.

Dey, Ian. (1999). *Grounding grounded theory: Guidelines for qualitative inquiry*. San Diego: Academic Press.

Dias, Patrick, Freedman, Aviva, Medway, Peter, & Paré, Anthony. (1999). *Worlds apart: Acting and writing in academic and workplace settings*. New York: Teacher's College Press.

Dibbell, Julian. (1993). *A rape in cyberspace or how an evil clown, a Haitian trickster spirit, two wizards, and a cast of dozens turned a database into a society*. Retrieved August 20, 2001, from http://ftp.game.org/pub/mud/text/research/VillageVoice.txt

Dibbell, Julian. (1998). *My tiny life: Crime and passion in a virtual world*. New York: Holt.

Digital Divide. (2002). *American wireless Web usage nears 10 million*. Retrieved August 15, 2003, from http://www.digitaldividenetwork.org/content/news/index.cfm?key=739

Dobbert, Marion L. (1984). *Ethnographic research: Theory and application for modern schools and societies*. New York: Praeger.

Doheny-Farina, Stephen. (1989). A case study of one adult writing in academic and nonacademic discourse communities. In Carolyn B. Matalene (Ed.), *Worlds of writing: Teaching and learning in discourse communities of work* (pp. 17–42). New York: Random House.

Doheny-Farina, Stephen. (1992). *Rhetoric, innovation, technology*. Cambridge, MA: MIT Press.

Dragga, Sam, & Voss, Dan. (2001). Cruel pies: The inhumanity of technical illustrations. *Technical Communication, 48*(3), 265–274.

Duguid, Paul, & Brown, John Seely. (2001). *The social life of information*. Cambridge, MA: Harvard Business School Press.

Durst, Russel K., & Cook Stanforth, Sherry. (1996). "Everything's negotiable": Collaboration and conflict in composition research. In Peter Mortensen & Gesa E. Kirsch (Eds.), *Ethics & representation: In qualitative studies of literacy* (pp. 58–76). Urbana, IL: National Council of Teachers of English.

Eble, Michelle, & Breault, Robin. (2002). The primetime agora: Knowledge, power, and "mainstream" resource venues for women online. *Computers and Composition, 19*, 315–329.

Edminster, Jude, & Moxley, Joe. (2002). Graduate education and the evolving genre of electronic theses and dissertations. *Computers and Composition, 19,* 89–104.

Ehrmann, Stephen C. (1998, July). The flashlight project: Tools for monitoring the progress of our hopes and fears about technology in education. *The Technology Source.* Retrieved October 20, 2004, from http://web.archive.org/web/1999 0423075544/horizon.unc.edu/TS/cases/1998-07.asp

Electronic Frontier Foundation. (2004). EFF analysis of Patriot II. Retrieved January 12, 2005, from http://www.eff.org/Censorship/Terrorism_militias/patriot-act-II-analysis.php

Elgesem, Dag. (2001).What is special about the ethical issues in online research? In Charles Ess (Ed.), *Internet research ethics.* Retrieved May 1, 2005, from http://www.nyu.edu/projects/nissenbaum/projects_ethics.html

Ellen, R. F. (Ed.). (1984). *Ethnographic research: A guide to general conduct.* Orlando, FL: Academic Press.

Emig, Janet. (1971). *The composing process of twelfth graders.* Urbana, IL: National Council of Teachers of English.

Engestrom, Yrjö. (1987). *Learning by expanding: An activity-theoretical approach to developmental research.* Helsinki: Orienta-Konsultit.

Eri, Frederick. (1996). On the evolution of qualitative approaches in educational research: From Adam's task to Eve's. *Australian Educational Researcher, 23*(2), 1–15.

Ericsson, K. A., & Simon, Herbert A. (1984). *Protocol analysis: Verbal reports as data.* Cambridge, MA: MIT Press.

Ess, Charles. (Ed.). (2001). *Internet research ethics.* Retrieved May 1, 2005, from http://www.nyu.edu/projects/nissenbaum/projects_ethics.html

Ess, Charles, & the AoIR Ethics Working Committee. (2002). *Ethical decision making and Internet research: Recommendations from the AOIR ethics working committee.* Retrieved May 1, 2005, from http://www.aoir.org/reports/ethics.pdf

Euben, Donna R. (2000). Corporate interference in research. *Academe, 86,* 85.

Erikson, Fredrick. (1986). Qualitative research. In Merlin Wittrock (Ed.), *The handbook of research on teaching* (3rd ed., pp. 119-161). New York: Macmillan.

Ewing, Margaret S., Hyde, Adrienne E., Kaufman, Judith S., Montgomery, Diane M., & Self, Patricia A. (1999). The hard work of remembering: Memory work as narrative research. In Joanne Addison & Sharon McGee (Eds.), *Feminist empirical research: Emerging perspectives on qualitative and teacher research* (pp. 112–126). Portsmouth, NH: Heinemann.

Eyman, Douglas, & Reilly, Colleen. (2004, March 25). *"If a tree falls": The impact of online publications on writing scholarship.* Paper presented at the Conference on College Composition and Communication, San Antonio, TX.

Facer, Keri, & Furlong, Ruth. (2001). Beyond the myth of the "cyberkid": Young people at the margins of the information revolution. *Journal of Youth Studies, 4,* 451–469.

Faden, Ruth R., & Beauchamp, Tom L. (1986). *A history and theory of informed consent.* New York: Oxford University Press.

Faigley, Lester. (1986). Nonacademic writing: The social perspective. In Lee Odell & Dixie Goswami (Eds.), *Writing in nonacademic settings* (pp. 231–248). New York: Guilford.

Faigley, Lester. (1992). *Fragments of rationality: Postmodernity and the subject of composition.* Pittsburgh: University of Pittsburgh Press.

Faigley, Lester, George, Diana, Palchik, Anna, & Selfe, Cynthia. (2003). *Picturing texts.* New York: Norton.

Fairclough, Norman. (1989). *Language and power.* New York: Longman.

Fairclough, Norman. (1992). *Discourse and social change.* Malden MA: Blackwell.

Feenberg, Andrew. (1991). *Critical theory of technology.* New York: Oxford University Press.

Feenberg, Andrew. (1995a). *Alternative modernity: The technical turn in philosophy and social theory.* Los Angeles: University of California Press.

Feenberg, Andrew. (1995b). Subversive rationalization: Technology, power, and democracy. In Andrew Feenberg & Alastair Hannay (Eds.), *Technology & the politics of knowledge* (pp. 3–22). Bloomington: Indiana University Press.

Feenberg, Andrew. (1999). *Questioning technology.* New York: Routledge.

Feenberg, Andrew. (2002). *Transforming technology: A critical theory revisited.* New York: Oxford University Press.

Finders, Margaret J. (1997). *Just girls: Hidden literacies and life in junior high.* New York: Teachers College Press.

Finemel, Sybil. (2003). Privacy and posting student information on school Web sites. *Library Media Connection, 21*(7), 2.

Fleckenstein, Kristie S. (2005). Faceless students, virtual places: Emergence and communal accountability in online classrooms. *Computers and Composition, 22,* 149–176.

Fleckenstein, Kristie, Spinuzzi, Clay, Rickly, Rebecca, & Papper, Carole. (2005). *Researching rhetorically: An ecological metaphor for the research process.* Unpublished manuscript.

Florio-Ruane, Susan, & McVee, Mary. (2002). Ethnographic approaches to literacy research. In Michael L. Kamil, Peter B. Mosenthal, P. David Pearson, & Rebecca Barr (Eds.), *Methods of literacy research* (pp. 77–86). Mahwah, NJ: Erlbaum.

Flower, Linda. (1994). *The construction of negotiated meaning: A social cognitive theory of writing.* Carbondale: Southern Illinois University Press.

Flower, Linda S., & Hayes, John R. (1981). A cognitive process theory of writing. *College Composition and Communication, 32,* 365–387.

Foucault, Michel. (1984). What is an author? In Paul Rabinow (Ed.), *The Foucault reader* (pp. 101–120). New York: Pantheon.

Fox, Helen. (1994). *Listening to the world: Cultural issues in academic writing.* Urbana, IL: National Council of Teachers of English.

Frankel, Mark S., & Siang, Sanyin. (1999). *Ethical and legal aspects of human subjects research on the internet: A report from the American Association for the Advancement of Science.* Retrieved August 8, 2004, from http://www.aaas.org/spp/sfrl/ projects/intres/report.pdf

Freeman, M., Csikszentmihalyi, Mihaly, & Larson, Reed. (1986). Adolescence and its recollection: Toward an interpretive model of development. *Merrill Palmer Quarterly, 32*, 167–185.

Fu, Danling. (1995). *"My trouble is my English": Asian students and the American dream.* Portsmouth, NH: Heinemann-Boynton/Cook.

Funkhouser, Edward T. (1996) The evaluative use of citation analysis for communication journals. *Human Communication Research, 22*(4), 563–574.

Gadamer, Hans-Georg. (1976a). *Hegel's dialectic: Five hermeneutical studies* (P. Christopher Smith, Trans.). New Haven, CT: Yale University Press.

Gadamer, Hans-Georg. (1976b). *Philosophical hermeneutics* (David E. Linge, Ed. & Trans.). Berkeley: University of California Press.

Gadamer, Hans-Georg. (1980). *Dialogue and dialectic: Eight hermeneutical studies on Plato* (P. Christopher Smith, Ed. & Trans.). New Haven, CT: Yale University Press.

Gadamer, Hans-Georg. (1989). *Truth and method* (2nd ed; Joel Weinsheimer & Donald G. Marshall, Ed. & Trans.). New York: Crossroad.

Gates, Bill. (1999). Everyone, anytime, anywhere. *Forbes.* Retrieved November 15, 2004, from http://www.microsoft.com/presspass/ofnote/10-04forbes.asp

Gee, James Paul. (1992). What is literacy? In Patrick Shannon (Ed.), *Becoming political: Readings and writings in the politics of literacy education* (pp. 21–28). Portsmouth, NH: Heinemann.

Gee, James Paul. (2003). *What video games have to teach us about learning and literacy.* New York: Palgrave Macmillan.

Geertz, Clifford. (1973). *The interpretation of cultures.* New York: Basic Books.

Geisler, Cheryl. (1994). *Academic literacy and the nature of expertise: Reading, writing and knowing in academic philosophy.* Hillsdale, NJ: Erlbaum.

Geisler, Cheryl. (2001). Textual objects: Accounting for the role of texts in the everyday life of complex organizations. *Written Communication, 18*, 296–325.

Geisler, Cheryl. (2003). When management becomes personal: An activity-theoretic analysis of palm technologies. In Charles Bazerman & D. Russell (Eds.), *Writing selves/writing societies: Research from activity perspectives.* Fort Collins, CO: WAC Clearinghouse. Retrieved August 14, 2005, from http://wac.col ostate.edu/books/selves_societies/

Geisler, Cheryl. (2004). *Analyzing and streams of language: Twelve steps to the systematic coding of text, talk, and other verbal data.* New York: Pearson/Longman.

Geisler, Cheryl, Bazerman, Charles, Doheny-Farina, Stephen, Gurak, Laura, Haas, Christina, Johnson-Eilola, Johndan, et al. (2001). IText: Future directions for research on the relationship between information technology and writing. *Journal of Business and Technical Communication, 15*, 269–308.

Gelsey, Zara. (2002). Who's reading over your shoulder? *Humanist, 62*(5), 38–39.

George, Diana. (2002). From analysis to design: Visual communication in the teaching of writing. *College Composition and Communication, 54*(1), 11–39.

Gerber, Stanford. (1986). *Russkoya celo: The ethnography of a Russian-American community.* New York: AMS Press.

Gere, Anne Ruggles (1987). *Writing groups: History, theory, and implications.* Carbondale: Southern Illinois University Press.

Gere, Anne Ruggles. (Ed.). (1993). *Into the field: Sites of composition studies.* New York: Modern Language Association.

Gere, Anne Ruggles. (1997). *Intimate practices: Literacy and cultural work in U.S. women's clubs, 1880–1920.* Urbana-Champagne: University of Illinois Press.

Gerrard, Lisa. (2002). Beyond "scribbling women": Women writing (on) the web. *Computers and Composition, 19,* 297–314.

Gilbert, G. Nigel, & Mulkay, Michael. (1984). *Opening Pandora's Box: A sociological analysis of scientific discourse.* Cambridge: Cambridge University Press.

Gilbert, Laurel, & Kyle, Crystal. (1996). *Surfergrrrls: Look Ethel! An Internet guide for us!* Seattle, WA: Seal Press.

Gillette, David. (1999). Pedagogy, architecture, and the virtual classroom. *Technical Communication Quarterly, 8,* 21–36.

Goody, Jack. (1986). *The logic of writing and the organization of society.* Cambridge: Cambridge University Press.

Götz, Aly, Chroust, Peter, & Pross, Christian. (1994). *Cleansing the fatherland: Nazi medicine and racial hygiene.* Baltimore: Johns Hopkins University Press.

Grabill, Jeffrey T. (1998). Utopic visions, the technopoor, and public access: Writing technologies in a community literacy program. *Computers and Composition, 15,* 297–315.

Grabill, Jeffrey T. (2001). *Community literacy programs and the politics of change.* Albany: SUNY Press.

Grabill, Jeffrey. (2003). On divides and interfaces: Access, class, and computers. *Computers and Composition, 20,* 455–472.

Grabill, Jeffrey T., & Hicks, Troy. (2005). Multiliteracies meet methods: The case for digital writing in English Education. *English Education, 37,* 301–311.

Grant-Davie, Keith. (1992). Coding data: Issues of validity, reliability, and interpretation. In Gesa Kirsch & Patricia A. Sullivan (Eds.), *Methods and methodology in composition research* (pp. 270–286). Carbondale: Southern Illinois University.

Green, Judith L., Dixon, Carol N., & Zaharlick, Amy. (2003). Ethnography as a logic of inquiry. In James Flood, Diane Lapp, James R. Squire, & Julie M. Jensen (Eds.), *Handbook of research on teaching the English Language Arts* (2nd ed., pp. 1–53). Mahwah, NJ: Erlbaum.

Gregory, Judy. (2004). Writing for the Web versus writing for print: Are they really so different? *Technical Communication, 51*(2), 276–285.

Gross, Alan G. (1990). *The rhetoric of science.* Cambridge, MA: Harvard University Press.

Gross, Alan G., & Keith, William M. (1997). *Rhetorical hermeneutics: Invention and interpretation in the age of science.* Albany: State University of New York Press.

Gruber, Sibylle. (2002). Special issue: Power and the World Wide Web. *Computers and Composition, 19*(3).

Guba, Egon G., & Lincoln, Yvonna S. (1994). Competing paradigms in qualitative research. In Norman K. Denzin & Yvonna S. Lincoln (Eds.), *Handbook of qualitative research* (pp. 105–117). Thousand Oaks, CA: Sage.

Guerrero, Laura K. (2005). Observer ratings of nonverbal involvement and immediacy. In Valerie Manusov (Ed.), *The sourcebook of nonverbal measures: Going beyond words* (pp. 221–236). Mahwah, NJ: Erlbaum.

Gunnarson, Britt Louise. (1997). The writing process from a sociolinguistic viewpoint. *Written Communication, 14*(2), 139–188.

Gurak, Laura J. (1996). The multi-faceted and novel nature of using cyber-texts as research data. In Teresa M. Harrison & Timothy D. Stephen (Eds.), *Computer networking and scholarly communication in the 21st century* (pp. 151–165). Albany: State University of New York Press.

Gurak, Laura J. (2001). *Cyberliteracy: Navigating the Internet with awareness.* New Haven: Yale University Press.

Gurak, Laura J. (2003). Internet studies in the twenty-first century. In David Gauntlett (Ed.), *Web.studies: Rewiring media studies for the digital age* (2nd ed., pp. 24–33). London: Arnold.

Gurak, Laura J., & Duin, Ann Hill. (2004). The impact of the Internet and digital technologies on teaching and research in technical communication. *Technical Communication Quarterly, 13,* 187–198.

Gurak, Laura J., & Lay, Mary M. (Eds.). (2002). *Research in technical communication.* Westport, CT: Greenwood Press.

Gurak, Laura J., & Silker, Christine M. (1997). Technical communication research: From traditional to virtual. *Technical Communication Quarterly, 6,* 403–419.

Gurak, Laura J., & Silker, Christine M. (2002). Technical communication research in cyberspace. In Laura J. Gurak, & Mary M. Lay (Eds.), *Research in technical communication* (pp. 229–248). Westport: Praeger.

Haas, Angela, Tulley, Christine, & Blair, Kristine. (2002). Mentors versus masters: Women's and girls' narratives of (re)negotiation in Web-based writing spaces. *Computers and Composition, 19,* 231–249.

Haas, Christina. (1994). Learning to read biology: One student's rhetorical development in college. *Written Communication, 11,* 43–84.

Habermas, Jurgen. (2001). *The postnational constellation: Political essays* (Max Pensky, Ed. & Trans.). Boston: MIT Press.

Hagood, Margaret C. (2003). New media and online literacies: No age left behind. *Reading Research Quarterly, 38*(3), 387–391.

Halio, Marcia. (1990). Student writing: Can the machine maim the message? *Academic Computing, 4,* 16–19.

Hall, Stuart. (1985). Signification, representation, ideology: Althusser and the post-structuralist debates. *Critical Studies in Communication, 2,* 91–114.

Halliday, M. A. K., & Hassan, Ruqaiya. (1976). *Cohesion in English.* New York: Longman.

Halloran, S. Michael. (1982). Aristotle's concept of ethos, or if not his somebody else's. *Rhetoric Review, 1*(1), 58–63.

Halpern, Jeanne W., & Liggett, Sarah. (1984). *Computers and composing: How the new technologies are changing writing.* Carbondale: Southern Illinois University Press.

Handa, Carolyn. (2001). Letter from the guest editor: Digital rhetoric, digital literacy, computers, and composition. *Computers and Composition, 18*, 1–10.

Handa, Carolyn. (Ed.). (2004). *Visual rhetoric in a digital world: A critical sourcebook.* Boston: Bedford/St. Martin's.

Haraway, Donna. (1991a). A cyborg manifesto: Science, technology, and socialist-feminism in the late twentieth century. In *Simians, cyborgs and women: The reinvention of nature* (pp. 149–181). New York: Routledge.

Haraway, Donna. (1991b). *Simians, cyborgs, and women: The reinvention of nature.* New York: Routledge.

Haraway, Donna. (1991c). Situated knowledges. In *Simians, cyborgs, and women: The reinvention of nature* (pp. 183–202) New York: Routledge.

Haraway, Donna. (1992). The promise of monsters: A regenerative politics for inappropriate/d others. In Lawrence Grossberg, Cary Nelson, & Paula Treichler (Eds.), *Cultural studies* (pp. 295–337). New York: Routledge.

Haraway, Donna. (1995). Situated knowledges: The science question in feminism and the privilege of partial perspective. In Andrew Feenberg & Alastair Hannay (Eds.), *Technology & the politics of knowledge* (pp. 175–194). Bloomington: Indiana University Press.

Haraway, Donna. (1997). *Modest witness@second_millenium: FemaleMan©_meets_OncoMouse™: Feminism and technoscience.* New York: Routledge.

Harding, Sandra. (1987). Introduction: Is there a feminist method? In Sandra Harding (Ed.), *Feminism and Methodology* (pp. 1–14). Bloomington: Indiana University Press.

Harper, Richard P. (1998). *Inside the IMF: An ethnography of documents, technology, and organizational action.* San Diego: Academic Press.

Harris, Lesley Ellen. (1998). *Digital property: Currency of the 21st century.* New York: McGraw-Hill Ryerson.

Hart-Davidson, William. (2002). Turning reflections into technology: Leveraging theory and research in the design of communication software. *Proceedings of the International Professional Communication Conference* (pp. 455–467). Portland, OR: IEEE.

Hart-Davidson, William. (2003). Seeing the project: Mapping patterns of intra-team communication events. *Proceedings of the 21st Annual International Conference on Documentation* (pp. 28–34). San Francisco: Association of Computing Machinery.

Hart-Davidson, William et al. (2004). Re: The future of computers and writing: A multivocal textumentary. *Computers and Composition, 21*, 147–159.

Harter, Stephen P. (1996). The impact of electronic journals on scholarly communication: A citation analysis. *The Public-Access Computer Systems Review, 7*(5). Retrieved October 28, 2004, from http://info.lib.uh.edu/pr/v7/n5/hart7n5.html

Harter, Stephen P. (1998). Scholarly communication and electronic journals: An impact study. *Journal of the American Society for Information Science, 49*(6), 507–516.

Harter, Stephen P., & Ford, Charlotte E. (2000). Web-based analyses of e-journal impact: Approaches, problems, and issues. *Journal of the American Society for Information Science, 51*(13), 1159–1176.

Harter, Stephen P., & Kim, Hak Joon. (1997). Electronic journals and scholarly communication: A citation and reference study. *The Journal of Electronic Publishing, 3*(2). Retrieved October 28, 2004, from: http://www.press.umich.edu/jep/archive/ harter.html.

Haug, Frigga. (1987). *Female sexualization: The collective work of memory* (E. Carter, Trans.). London: Verso.

Havelock, Eric A. (1988). *The muse learns to write: Reflections on orality and literacy from antiquity to the present.* New Haven, CT: Yale University Press.

Hawisher, Gail E. (1986). Studies in word processing. *Computers and Composition, 4*(1). Retrieved October 10, 2003, from http://www.hu.mtu.edu/%7Ecandc/archives/v4/4_1_html/4_1_1_Hawisher.html

Hawisher, Gail E. (1988). Research update: Writing and word processing. *Computers and Composition, 5*(2), 7–27.

Hawisher, Gail E. (1989). Research and recommendations for computers and composition. In Gail E. Hawisher & Cynthia L. Selfe (Eds.), *Critical perspectives on computers and composition instruction* (pp. 44-69). New York: Teachers College Press.

Hawisher, Gail E., & Fortune, Ron. (1989). Word processing and the basic writer. *Collegiate Microcomputer, 5,* 275–287.

Hawisher, Gail E., & Selfe, Cynthia L. (1991). The rhetoric of technology and the electronic writing class. *College Composition and Communication, 42,* 55–65.

Hawisher, Gail E., & Selfe, Cynthia L. (2000). *Global literacies and the World-Wide Web.* London: Routledge.

Hawisher, Gail, & Selfe, Cynthia. (2002). Collaborative configurations: Researching the literacies of technology. *Kairos: A Journal of Rhetoric, Technology, and Pedagogy, 7*(3). Retrieved October 20, 2003, from http://english.ttu.edu/kairos/7.3/binder2.html?coverweb/hawisher/index.htm

Hawisher, Gail E., & Sullivan, Patricia. (1998). Women on the networks: Searching for e-spaces of their own. In Susan Jarratt & Lynn Worsham (Eds.), *Feminism and composition studies* (pp. 172–197). New York: Modern Language Association.

Hawisher, Gail E., & Sullivan, Patricia. (1999). Fleeting images: Women visually writing the web. In Gail E. Hawisher & Cynthia L. Selfe (Eds.), *Passions, pedagogies and 21st century technologies* (pp. 268–291). Logan: Utah State University Press.

Hawisher, Gail E., LeBlanc, Paul, Moran, Charles, & Selfe, Cynthia L. (1996). *Computers and the teaching of writing in American higher education, 1979-1994: A history.* Norwood, NJ: Ablex.

Hawisher, Gail E., Selfe, Cynthia L., Moraski, Brittany, & Pearson, Melissa. (2004). Becoming literate in the information age: Cultural ecologies and the literacies of technology. *College Composition and Communication, 55,* 642–692.

Hayes, John R., & Flower, Linda. (1983). Uncovering cognitive processes in writing: An introduction to protocol analysis. In Peter Mosenthal, Lynne Tamor, & Sean A. Walmsey (Eds.), *Research on writing: Principles and methods* (pp. 206–220). New York: Longman.

Hayles, N. Katherine. (1999). *How we became posthuman: Virtual bodies in cybernetics, literature, and informatics*. Chicago: University of Chicago Press.

Hayles, N. Katherine. (2002). *Writing machines*. Cambridge, MA: MIT Press.

Hays, Janice N. (Ed.). (1983). *The writer's mind: Writing as mode of thinking*. Urbana, IL: National Council of Teachers of English.

Headland, Thomas N., Pike, Kenneth L., & Harris, Marvin. (Eds.). (1990). *Emics and etics: The insider/outsider debate*. Thousand Oaks, CA: Sage.

Heath, Shirley Brice. (1983). *Ways with words: Language, life and work in communities and classrooms*. Cambridge, UK: Cambridge University Press.

Heba, Gary. (1997). HyperRhetoric: Multimedia, literacy, and the future of composition. *Computers and Composition, 14,* 19–44.

Hedetoft, Ulf, & Hjort, M. (Eds.). (2002). *The postnational self: Belonging and identity*. Minneapolis: University of Minnesota Press.

Hefter, Laurence R., & Litowitz, Robert D. (1999). *What is intellectual property?* Retrieved October 10, 2003, from http://usinfo.state.gov/products/pubs/intel-prp/homepage.htm

Heidegger, Martin. (1969). *Discourse on thinking*. New York: Harper Perennial.

Heidegger, Martin. (1977). *The question concerning technology and other essays*. New York: Harper and Row.

Heidegger, Martin. (1982). *On the way to thinking*. San Francisco: Harper.

Heidegger, Martin. (1987). *Being and time*. Oxford: Blackwell.

Heller, Steven, & Vienne, Veronique. (Eds.). (2003). *Citizen designer: Perspectives on design responsibility*. New York: Alworth Press.

Henderson, Peter A. (2003). *Practical methods in ecology*. Malden, MA: Blackwell Publishing.

Henry, Julie. (2003; June 29). Outrage as Oxford bans student for being Israeli. *Telegraph.co.uk*. Retrieved October 30, 2004, from http://www.telegraph.co.uk/news/main.jhtml?xml = /news/2003/06/29/noxf29.xml&sSheet = /portal/2003/06/29/ixportal.html

Herndl, Carl G. (1991). Writing ethnography: Representation, rhetoric, and institutional practices. *College English, 53,* 320–332.

Herndl, Carl G., & Nahrwold, Cynthia A. (2000). Research as social practice: A case study of research on technical and professional communication. *Written Communication, 17,* 258–296.

Herring, Susan, C. (1994). Politeness in computer culture: Why women thank and men flame. In Mary Bucholtz, Anita Liang, Laurel Sutton, & Caitlin Hines (Eds.), *Cultural performance: Proceedings of the third Berkeley Women and Language Conference* (pp. 278–294). Berkeley, CA: Berkeley Women and Language Group.

Herring, Susan C. (1996). Two variants of an electronic message schema. In Susan C. Herring (Ed.), *Computer-mediated communication: Linguistic, social and cross-*

cultural perspectives (pp. 81–108). Amsterdam/Philadelphia: John Benjamins Publishing Company.

Herring, Susan Davis. (1999). The value of interdisciplinarity: A study based on the design of Internet search engines. *Journal of the American Society for Information Science, 50*(4), 358–365.

Herring, Susan Davis. (2002). Use of electronic resources in scholarly electronic journals: A citation analysis. *College and Research Libraries, 63*(4), 334–340.

Herrington, Anne J. (1993). Reflections on empirical research: Examining some ties between theory and action. In Lee Odell (Ed.), *Theory and practice in the teaching of writing: Rethinking the discipline* (pp. 47–60). Carbondale: Southern Illinois University Press.

Herrington, Tyanna K. (2001). *Controlling voices: Intellectual property, humanistic studies, and the Internet.* Carbondale: Southern Illinois University Press.

Herrmann, Andrea. (1990). Computers and writing research: Shifting our "governing gaze." In Deborah H. Holdstein & Cynthia L. Selfe (Eds.), *Computers and writing: Theory, research, practice* (pp. 124–134). New York: Modern Language Association.

Hess, Mickey. (2002). A nomad faculty: English professors negotiate self-representation in university Web space. *Computers and Composition, 19,* 171–189.

Heylighen, Francis, & Joslyn, Cliff. (1995). Systems theory. In Robert Audi (Ed.), *The Cambridge dictionary of philosophy* (pp. 784–785). New York: Cambridge University Press.

Hillocks, George. (1986). *Research on written composition: New directions for teaching.* Urbana, IL: NCTE.

Hine, Christine. (2000). *Virtual ethnography.* Thousand Oaks, CA: Sage.

Hocks, Mary E. (2003). Understanding visual rhetoric in digital writing environments. *College Composition and Communication, 54,* 629–656.

Hocks, Mary E., & Kendrick, Michelle R. (2003). *Eloquent images: Word and image in the age of new media.* Cambridge, MA: MIT Press.

Holland, John H. (1975). *Adaptation in natural and artificial systems: An introductory analysis with applications to biology, control, and artificial intelligence.* Ann Arbor: University of Michigan Press.

Holmevik, Jan Rune, & Haynes, Cynthia. (2000). *MOOniversity: A student's guide to online learning environments.* New York: Longman.

Howard, Tharon. (1997). *A rhetoric of electronic communities.* Stamford, CT: Ablex.

HR 3162 RDS, 107th Congress, 1st Session (2001). Uniting and strengthening America by providing appropriate tools required to intercept and obstruct terrorism (USA PATRIOT ACT) Act of 2001. Retrieved March 1, 2004, from http://www.fincen.gov/hr3162.pdf

Huckin, Thomas N. (1992). Context-sensitive text analysis. In Gesa Kirsch & Patricia A. Sullivan (Eds.), *Methods and methodology in composition research* (pp. 84–104). Carbondale: Southern Illinois University Press.

Huckin, Thomas. (2004). Content analysis: What texts talk about. In Charles Bazerman & Paul Prior (Eds.), *What writing does and how it does it: An introduction to analyzing texts and textual practices* (pp. 13–32). Mahwah, NJ: Erlbaum.

Huws, Ursula. (2003). *The making of a cybertariat: Virtual work in a real world.* New York: Monthly Review Press.

Hymes, Dell. (Ed.). (1965). *The use of computers in anthropology.* The Hague, Netherlands: Mouton.

Hymes, Dell. (1974). *Foundations of sociolinguistics.* Philadelphia: University of Pennsylvania Press.

Hymes, Dell. (1982). What is ethnography? In Perry Gilmore & Allan A. Glathorn (Eds.), *Children in and out of school: Ethnography and education* (pp. 21–32). Washington, DC: Center for Applied Linguistics.

Ingwersen, Peter. (1998). The calculation of web impact factors. *Journal of Documentation, 54*(2), 236–243.

Inman, James. (2004). *Computers and writing: The cyborg era.* Mahwah, NJ: Erlbaum.

Institute of Ecology Studies. (n.d.). *Defining ecology: The IES definition of ecology.* Available: http://www.ecostudies.org/definition_ecology.html

Intille, Stephen. (2003). Open-source context-aware experience sampling tool. Massachusetts Institute of Technology. Retrieved January 10, 2004, from http://web.media.mit.edu/~intille/caes/

IText Working Group: Geisler, Cheryl, Bazerman, Charles, Doheny-Farina, Stephen, Gurak, Laura, Haas, Christina, Johnson-Eilola, Johndan, Kaufer, David, Lunsford, Andrea, & Miller, Carolyn. (2001). IText: Future directions for research on the relationship between information technology and writing. *Journal of Business and Technical Communication, 15*(3), 269–309.

Jacob, Evelyn. (1982). Combining ethnographic and quantitative approaches: Suggestions and examples from a study in Puerto Rico. In Perry Gilmore & Allan A. Glathorn (Eds.), *Children in and out of school: Ethnography and education* (pp. 124–147). Washington, DC: Center for Applied Linguistics.

Jaeger, Paul, McClure, Charles, Bertot, John Carlo, & Snead, J. T. (2004, April). The USA Patriot Act, the foreign intelligence surveillance act, and information policy research in libraries: Issues, impacts, and questions for libraries and researchers. *Library Quarterly, 74*(2), 99–121.

Jameson, Fredric. (1991). *Postmodernism or, the cultural logic of late capitalism.* London: Verso.

Jazri, Peter. (1994). On the author effect: Contemporary copyright and collective creativity. In Martha Woodmansee & Peter Jazri (Eds.), *The construction of authorship: Textual appropriation in law and literature* (pp. 29–56). Durham, NC: Duke University Press.

Johanek, Cindy. (2000). *Composing research: A contextualist paradigm for rhetoric and composition.* Logan: Utah State University Press.

Johns, Mark D., Chen, Shing-Ling Sarina, & Hall, G. Jon (Eds.). (2004). *Online social research: Methods, issues, and ethics.* New York: Peter Lang.

Johnson, Doug. (2005). Student privacy and technology: Has 1984 arrived? Presentation. Retrieved January 25, 2006, from http://www.doug-johnson.com/pres.html

Johnson, Robert. (1998). *User-centered technology: A rhetorical theory for computers and other mundane artifacts*. Albany: State University of New York Press.

Johnson, Steven. (1997). *Interface culture: How new technology transforms the way we create and communicate*. San Francisco: Harper Collins.

Johnson-Eilola, Johndan. (1997). *Nostalgic angels: Rearticulating hypertext writing*. Norwood, NJ: Ablex.

Johnson-Eilola, Johndan. (1998). Wild technologies: Computer use and social possibility. In Stuart A. Selber (Ed.), *Computers and technical communication: Pedagogical and programmatic perspectives* (pp. 97–128). Greenwich, CT: Ablex.

Johnson-Eilola, Johndan. (1999). Space | action | movement: Understanding composition as architecture. Retrieved August 15, 2003, from http://www.clarkson.edu/ ~ johndan//read/architecture/welcome.html

Johnson-Eilola, Johndan, & Kimme Hea, Amy C. (2004). After hypertext: Other ideas. *Computers and Composition, 20,* 415–425.

Joint AHA-OAH Policy Statement on Regulations for the Protection of Human Subjects. (2004, June). American Historical Association & Organization of American Historians. Retrieved October 28, 2004, from http://www.historians.org/Perspectives/Issues/2004/0409/0409new4.cfm

Jones, Stefanie, Carrère, Sybil, & Gottman, John M. (2005). Specific affect coding system. In Valerie Manusov (Ed.), *The sourcebook of nonverbal measures: Going beyond words* (pp. 163–172). Mahwah, NJ: Erlbaum.

Joyce, Michael. (1995). *Of two minds: Hypertext pedagogy and poetics*. Ann Arbor: University of Michigan Press.

Kaplan, Nancy, & Nelson, Michael. (2000). Determining the publication impact of a digital library. *Journal of the American Society for Information Science, 51*(4), 324–339.

Kapoor, Priya. (2000). Ferment and transition in the New Europe: Intercultural imperatives for a Europe in transition. In Laura Lengel (Ed.), *Culture and technology in the New Europe: Civic discourse in transformation in post-Communist nations* (pp. 23–31). Stamford, CT: Ablex.

Kaptelinin, Viktor. (1997). Computer-mediated activity: Functional organs in social and developmental contexts. In Bonnie A. Nardi (Ed.), *Context and consciousness: Activity theory and human-computer interaction* (pp. 45–68). Cambridge, MA: MIT Press.

Kaptelinin, Viktor, & Nardi, Bonnie. (1997). *Activity theory: Basic concepts and applications*. Association for Computing Machinery Special Interest Group on Computer-Human Interaction. Retrieved July 10, 2004, from http://www.acm.org/sigchi/chi97/proceedings/tutorial/bn.htm

Keller, Christopher. (2004). Unsituating the subject: "Locating" composition and ethnography in mobile worlds. In Stephen Brown & Sidney Dobrin (Eds.), *Ethnography unbound: From theory shock to critical praxis* (pp. 201–218). Albany: State University of New York Press.

Kellner, Douglas. (2000). New technologies/new literacies: Reconstructing education for the new millennium. *Teacher Education, 11*(3), 245–265.

Kilker, Julian A., & Kleinman, Sharon S. (1997). Researching online environments: Lessons from the history of anthropology. *The New Jersey Journal of Communication, 5*, 66–83.

Kim, Hak Joon. (1998). *The hyperlinking process in scholarly electronic journals: A comparison of hyperlinking and citing practices*. Unpublished doctoral dissertation, Indiana University, Bloomington, IN.

Kim, Hak Joon. (2000). Motivations for hyperlinking in scholarly electronic articles: A qualitative study. *Journal of the American Society for Information Science, 51*(10), 887–899.

Kimme Hea, Amy C. (2002). Articulating (re)visions of the web: Exploring links among corporate and academic web sites. In Nancy Allen (Ed.), *Working with words and images: New steps in an old dance* (pp. 231–255). Westport, CT: Ablex.

Kingsolver, Ann E. (1992). Contested livelihoods: "Placing" one another in Cedar Kentucky. *Anthropological Quarterly, 65,* 128–136.

Kirkpatrick, David. (2004, October 4). It's hard to manage if you don't blog. *Fortune Magazine*, p. 46.

Kirsch, Gesa E. (1999). *Ethical dilemmas in feminist research: The politics of location, interpretation, and publication*. Albany: State University of New York Press.

Kirsch, Gesa E., & Ritchie, Joy S. (1995). Beyond the personal: Theorizing a politics of location in composition research. *College Composition and Communication, 46*, 7–29.

Kirsch, Gesa E., & Sullivan, Patricia A. (1992). *Methods and methodology in composition research*. Carbondale: Southern Illinois University Press.

Kitalong, Karla Saari. (1998). A web of symbolic violence. *Computers and Composition, 15*, 253–263.

Kleinberg, Jon M. (1999). Authoritative sources in a hyperlinked environment. *Journal of the ACM, 46*(5), 604–632.

Knadler, Stephen. (2001). E-racing difference in e-space: Black female subjectivity and the Web-based portfolio. *Computers and Composition, 18*, 235–255.

Kolko, Beth. (1995). Building a world with words: The narrative reality of virtual communities. *Works and Days, 25/26*(1), 105–126.

Kolko, Beth E., Nakamura, Lisa, & Rodman, Gilbert B. (Eds.). (2000). *Race in cyberspace*. New York: Routledge.

Kolko, Beth. (2000). Erasing @race: Going white in the (inter)face. In Beth E. Kolko, Lisa Nakamura, & Gilbert B. Rodman (Eds.), *Race in cyberspace* (pp. 213–232). New York: Routledge.

Kostelnick, Charles, & Hassett, Michael. (2003). *Shaping information: The rhetoric of visual conventions*. Carbondale: Southern Illinois University Press.

Kramarae, Cheris. (2001). *The third shift: Women learning online*. Washington, DC: American Association of University Women.

Krebs, Charles. (2001). *Ecology: The experimental analysis of distribution and abundance* (5th ed.). San Francisco: Benjamin Cummings.

Kress, Gunther, & van Leeuwen, Theo. (1996). *Reading images: The grammar of visual design*. London: Routledge.

Kress, Gunther, & van Leeuwen, Theo. (2001). *Multimodal discourse*. New York: Oxford University Press.

Kress, Gunther. (2003). *Literacy in the new media age*. London: Routledge.

Kubey, Robert, Larson, Reed, & Csikszentmihalyi, Mihaly. (1996). Experience sampling method applications to communication research questions. *Journal of Communication, 46*, 99–119.

Kuhn, Thomas. (1996). *The structure of scientific revolutions* (3rd ed.). Chicago: University of Chicago Press.

Kuhn, Virginia. (2005). Picturing work: Visual projects in the writing classroom. *Kairos: A Journal of Rhetoric, Technology, and Pedagogy, 9*(2). Retrieved October 20, 2004, from http://english.ttu.edu/kairos/9.2/index.html

Kuutti, Kari. (1991). The concept of activity as the basic unit of analysis for CSCW research. *Proceedings of the Second European Conference on CSCW* (pp. 249–264). Amsterdam, The Netherlands: Kluwer.

Kuutti, Kari. (1996). Activity theory as a potential framework for human-computer interaction research. In Bonnie Nardi (Ed.), *Context and consciousness: Activity theory and human–computer interaction* (pp. 17–44). Cambridge, MA: MIT Press.

Laclau, Ernesto. (1982). *Politics and ideology in Marxist theory: Capitalism, fascism, populism*. London: Verso.

Landow, George P. (1992). *Hypertext: The convergence of contemporary critical theory and technology*. Baltimore: Johns Hopkins University Press.

Landow, George P. (Ed.). (1995). *Hyper/text/theory*. Baltimore: Johns Hopkins University Press.

Lanham, Richard A. (1993). *The electronic word: Democracy, technology, and the arts*. Chicago: University of Chicago Press.

Lanham, Richard A. (1994). *The economics of attention*. Retrieved January 13, 2005, from http://ie.search.msn.com/en-us/srchasst/srchasst.htm

Lankshear, Colin, & Knobel, Michele. (2003). *New literacies: Changing knowledge and classroom learning*. New York: McGraw-Hill.

Larson, Reed. (1989). Beeping children and adolescents: A method for studying time use and daily experience. *Journal of Youth and Adolescence, 18*, 511–530.

Larson, Reed, & Csikszentmihalyi, Mihaly. (1983). The experience sampling method. In H. Reis (Ed.), *Naturalistic approaches to studying social interactions* (pp. 41–56). San Francisco: Jossey-Bass.

Larson, Reed, Csikszentmihalyi, Mihaly, & Freeman, M. (1984). Alcohol and marijuana use in adolescents' daily lives: A random sample of experiences. *International Journal of Addiction, 19*, 367–381.

Larson, Reed, & Lampman-Petraitis, C. (1989). Daily emotional states as reported by children and adolescents. *Child Development, 60*, 1250–1260.

Latour, Bruno. (1992). Where are the missing masses? The sociology of a few mundane artifacts. In Wiebe Bijker, Thomas Hughes, & Trevor Pinch (Eds.), *Shaping technology/building society: Studies in sociotechnical change* (pp. 225–258). Cambridge, MA: MIT Press.

Latour, Bruno. (1993). *We have never been modern* (Catherine Porter, Trans.). Cambridge, MA: Harvard University Press.

Latour, Bruno, & Woolgar, Steve. (1979). *Laboratory life: The social construction of scientific facts.* Beverly Hills, CA: Sage.

Lauer, Janice M., & Asher, J. William. (1988). *Composition research: Empirical designs.* New York: Oxford University Press.

Laurel, Brenda K. (1991). *Computers as theatre.* Reading, MA, Addison-Wesley.

Law, John. (2004). *After method: Mess in social science research.* New York: Routledge.

Lawrence, Steve, & Giles, C. Lee. (1999). Accessibility of information on the web. *Nature, 400,* 107–109.

Lea, Martin, O'Shea, Tim, Fung, Pat, & Spears, Russell. (1992). "Flaming" in computer-mediated communication: Observations, explanations, implications. In Martin Lea (Ed.), *Contexts of computer-mediated communication* (pp. 89–112). New York: Harvester Wheatleaf.

Leander, Kevin M. (2003). Writing travelers' tales on new literacyscapes. *Reading Research Quarterly, 38*(3), 392–397.

LeCourt, Donna. (1998). Critical pedagogy in the computer classroom: Politicizing the writing space. *Computers and Composition, 15,* 275–295.

LeCourt, Donna, & Barnes, Luann. (1999). Writing multiplicity: Hypertext and feminist textual practices. *Computers and Composition, 16,* 55–71.

Lefebvre, Henri. (1991). *The production of space* (Donald Nicholson-Smith, Trans.). Malden, MA: Blackwell Publishing.

LeFevre, Karen Burke. (1987). *Invention as a social act.* Carbondale: Southern Illinois University Press.

Lemke, Jay L. (1998). Metamedia literacy: Transforming meanings and media. In David Reinking, Michael C. McKenna, Linda D. Labbo, & Ronald D. Kieffer (Eds.), *Handbook of literacy and technology: Transformations in a post-typographic world* (pp. 283–301). Mahwah, NJ: Erlbaum.

Levitt, Peggy. (2001). *The transnational villagers.* Berkeley: University of California Press.

Lin-Lui, Jen, & Watzman, Haim. (2003, November 21). World beat. *Chronicle of Higher Education,* p. A33.

Lincoln, Yvonna, & Guba, Egon G. (1994). Competing paradigms in qualitative research. In Norman K. Denzin & Yvonna Lincoln (Eds.), *Handbook of qualitative research* (pp. 105–118). Thousand Oaks, CA: Sage.

Lister, Martin, Dovey, Jon, Giddings, Seth, Grant, Iain, & Kelly, Kieran. (2002). *New media: A critical introduction.* London: Routledge.

Litman, Jessica. (2001). *Digital copyright.* Amherst, NY: Prometheus Books.

Loer, Joseph. (1997). Ecofeminism in Kenya: A chemical engineer's perspective. In Karen Warren (Ed.), *Ecofeminism: Women, culture, nature* (pp. 279–289). Bloomington: Indiana University Press.

Lofland, John, & Lofland, Lyn H. (1984). *Analyzing social settings.* Belmont, CA: Wadsworth.

Lohse, Gerald, & Johnson, Eric J. (1996). A comparison of two process tracing methods for choice tasks. *Proceedings of the 29th Annual Hawaii International Conference on System Science, 4*, 86–97.

Luke, Carmen. (2000). Cyber-schooling and technological change: Multiliteracies for new times. In Bill Cope & Mary Kalantzis (Eds.), *Multiliteracies: Literacy learning and the design of social futures* (pp. 69–91). London: Routledge.

Luke, Carmen. (2003). Pedagogy, connectivity, multimodality, and interdisciplinarity. *Reading Research Quarterly, 38*(3), 397–403.

Luria, A. (1983). The development of writing in the child. In M. Martlew (Ed.), *The psychology of written language: Developmental and educational perspectives* (pp. 237–278). New York: Wiley.

Mackey, Margaret. (2003). Researching new forms of literacy. *Reading Research Quarterly, 38*(3), 403–407.

MacNealy, Mary Sue. (1999). *Strategies for empirical research and writing*. Boston: Allyn & Bacon.

Mailloux, Steven. (1988). *Rhetorical power*. Ithaca, NY: Cornell University Press.

Maitra, Kaushiki, & Goswami, Dixie. (1995). Response of American readers to visual aspects of a mid-sized Japanese company's annual report: A case study. *IEEE Transactions on Professional Communication, 38*(4), 197–203.

Mann, Chris, & Stewart, Fiona. (2000). *Internet communication and qualitative research: A handbook for researching online*. London: Sage.

Marcus, George. (Ed.). (1996). *Connected: Engagements with media*. Chicago: University of Chicago Press.

Markowitz, Fran. (1995). Criss-crossing identities: The Russian Jewish diaspora and the Jewish diaspora in Russia. *Diaspora, 4*(2), 201–210.

Matsuda, Paul Kei. (2002). Negotiation of identity and power in a Japanese online discourse community. *Computers and Composition, 19*, 39–55.

Mayers, Tim, & Swafford, Kevin. (1998). Reading the networks of power: Rethinking "critical thinking" in computerized classrooms. In Todd Taylor & Irene Ward (Eds.), *Literacy theory in the age of the internet* (pp. 146–157). New York: Columbia University Press.

McAllister, Carole, & Louth, Richard. (1988). The effect of word processing on the quality of basic writers' revisions. *Research in the Teaching of English, 22*, 417–427.

McCarron, Carolyn. (2003). Visual communications as a catalyst for change. In Steven Heller & Veronique Vienne (Eds.), *Citizen designer: Perspectives on design responsibility* (pp. 42–46). New York: Alworth Press.

McCloud, Scott. (1994). *Understanding comics: The invisible art*. New York: HarperPerennial.

McConaghy, Cathryn, & Snyder, Ilana. (2000). Working the Web in Australia. In Gail Hawisher & Cynthia Selfe (Eds.), *Global literacies and the World Wide Web* (pp. 74–92). New York: Routledge.

McKee, Heidi. (2002). "YOUR VIEWS SHOWED TRUE IGNORANCE!!!": (Mis)Communication in an online interracial discussion forum. *Computers and Composition, 19*(4), 411–434.

McKee, Heidi. (2003). Changing the process of institutional review board compliance. *College Composition and Communication, 54*(3), 488–493.

McKee, Heidi. (2004). "Always a shadow of hope": Heteronormative binaries in an online discussion of sexuality and sexual orientation. *Computers and Composition, 21,* 315–340.

McKee, Heidi, & Porter, James. (2006). The ethics of digital writing research: A rhetorical approach. Unpublished manuscript.

McKiernan, Gerry. (1996). CitedSites(sm): *Citation indexing of web resources.* Retrieved October 28, 2004, from http://www.public.iastate.edu/~CYBER-STACKS/Cited.htm

McMillan, S. J. (2000). The microscope and the moving target: The challenge of applying content analysis to the World Wide Web. *Journalism and Mass Communication Quarterly, 77,* 80–99.

McPherson, Tara. (2000). I'll take my stand in dixie-net: White guys, the south, and cyberspace. In Beth E. Kolko, Lisa Nakamura, & Gilbert B. Rodman (Eds.), *Race in cyberspace* (pp. 117–132). New York: Routledge.

McQuade, Donald, & McQuade, Christine. (2005). *Seeing and writing* (3rd ed.). New York: Bedford/St. Martin's.

Merchant, Carolyn. (1980). *The death of nature: Women, ecology, and the scientific revolution.* San Francisco: Harper Row.

Michener, William. (2000). Research design: Translating ideas to data. In William Michener & James Brunt (Eds.), *Ecological data: Design, management and processing* (pp. 1–24). Malden, MA: Blackwell Science.

Mided, Jon. (2000). The Internet and the public sphere: What kind of space is cyberspace? In Laura Lengel (Ed.), *Culture and technology in the New Europe: Civic discourse in transformation in post-Communist nations* (pp. 63–75). Stamford, CT: Ablex.

Mirel, Barbara. (1987). Designing field research in technical communication: Usability testing for in-house documentation. *Journal of Technical Writing and Communication, 17*(4), 347–354.

Mitra, Ananda. (1998). Virtual commonality: Looking for India on the Internet. In Steven Jones (Ed.), *Virtual culture: Identity and communication in cybersociety* (pp. 55–79). London: Sage.

MIT. (2003). Context-Aware Experience Sampling Tool (CAES). Available: http://web.media.mit.edu/~intille/caes/caesindex.htm

Mitchell, W. J. T. (1994). *Picture theory: Essays on verbal and visual representation.* Chicago: University of Chicago Press.

Monroe, Barbara. (2004). *Crossing the digital divide: Race, writing, and technology in the classroom.* New York: Teachers College Press.

Moran, Charles. (1999). Access: The "A" word in technology studies. In Gail E. Hawisher & Cynthia L. Selfe (Eds.), *Passions, pedagogies, and 21st century technologies* (pp. 205–220). Logan: Utah State University Press.

Moriarty, Sandra, & Rohe, Lisa. (2005). Cultural palettes in print advertising: Formative research design method. In Ken Smith, Sandra Moriarty, Gretchen

Barbatsis, & Keith Kenney (Eds.), *Handbook of visual communication: Theory, methods, and media* (pp. 117–126). Mahwah, NJ: Erlbaum.

Mortensen, Peter, & Kirsch, Gesa. (1996). *Ethics and representation in qualitative studies of literacy.* Urbana, IL: National Council of Teachers of English.

Moss, Beverly. J. (1992). Ethnography and composition: Studying language at home. In Gesa Kirsch & Patricia Sullivan (Eds.), *Methods and methodology in composition research* (pp. 153–171). Carbondale: Southern Illinois University Press.

Moss, Pamela. (1994). Can there be validity without reliability? *Educational Researcher, 23,* 5–12.

Moulthrop, Stuart. (1994). Rhizome and resistance: Hypertext and the dreams of a new culture. In George Landow (Ed.), *Hyper/text/theory* (pp. 299–319). Baltimore: The Johns Hopkins University Press.

Moulthrop, Stuart. (2000). Error 404: Doubting the Web. In Andrew Herman & Thomas Swiss (Eds.), *The World Wide Web and contemporary cultural theory: Magic, metaphor, power* (pp. 259-276). New York: Routledge.

Murray, Janet H. (1997). *Hamlet on the Holodeck: The future of narrative in cyberspace.* New York: Free Press.

Myers, Greg. (1990). *Writing biology: Texts in the social construction of knowledge.* Madison: University of Wisconsin Press.

Myers, Miles. (1985). *Teacher–researcher: How to study writing in the classroom.* Urbana, IL: National Council of Teachers of English.

Nakamura, Lisa. (2002). *Cybertypes: Race, ethnicity, and identity on the Internet.* New York: Routledge.

Nardi, Bonnie. (1996). *Context and consciousness: Activity theory and human-computer interaction.* Cambridge, MA: MIT Press.

Nardi, Bonnie. (1996). Studying context: A comparison of activity theory, situated action models, and distributed cognition. In Bonnie Nardi (Ed.), *Context and consciousness: Activity theory and human–computer interaction* (pp. 69–102). Cambridge, MA: MIT Press.

Nelson, Theodor. (1982). *Literary machines.* New York: Mindful Press.

Newkirk, Thomas. (1996). Seduction and betrayal in qualitative research. In Peter Mortensen & Gesa E. Kirsch (Eds.), *Ethics & representation in qualitative studies of literacy* (pp. 3–16). Urbana, IL: National Council of Teachers of English.

Nixon, Helen. (2003). New research literacies for contemporary research into literacy and new media? *Reading Research Quarterly, 38*(3), 407–413.

Noddings, Nel. (1984). *Caring, a feminist approach to ethics and moral education.* Berkeley: University of California Press.

Noddings, Nel. (1999). Two concepts of caring. *Philosophy of Education Yearbook.* Retrieved October 30, 2004, from http://www.ed.uiuc.edu/eps/PES-Yearbook/1999/1999toc.asp

Nold, Ellen. (1975). Fear and trembling: A humanist approaches the computer. *College Composition and Communication, 26,* 269–273.

Norman, Donald. (2004). *Emotional design: Why we love (or hate) everyday things.* New York: Basic Books.

North, Stephen. (1987). *The making of knowledge in composition: Portrait of an emerging field.* Portsmouth, NH: Boynton/Cook Publishers.

Norton, David, Zimmerman, Beverly B., & Lindeman, Neil. (1999). Developing hyperphoric grammar to teach collaborative hypertexts. In Scott Lloyd DeWitt & Kip Strasma (Eds.), *Contexts, intertexts, and hypertexts* (pp. 177–202). Cresskill, NJ: Hampton Press.

Nuremburg Code. (2002). In R. Amdur & E. Bankert (Eds.), *Institutional review board: Management and function* (pp. 490–491). Boston: Jones and Bartlett.

O'Keefe, Barbara J., & Wartella, E. (Eds.), *Rethinking communication Vol. 2. Paradigm issues* (pp. 329–345). London: Sage.

O'Sullivan, Mary F. (1999). Worlds within which we teach: Issues for designing World Wide Web course material. *Technical Communication Quarterly, 8,* 61–72.

Odell, Lee. (1983). Written products and the writing process. In Janet Hays (Ed.), *The writer's mind: Writing as mode of thinking.* Urbana, IL: National Council of Teachers of English.

Oelschlaeger, Max. (1991). *The idea of wilderness: From prehistory to the age of ecology.* New Haven, CT: Yale University Press.

Ogbu, John U. (1974). *The next generation: An ethnography of education in an urban neighborhood.* New York: Academic Press.

Ogbu, John U. (1978). *Minority education and caste: The American system in cross-cultural perspective.* New York: Academic Press.

Ogbu, John U. (1982). Cultural discontinuities and schooling. *Anthropology and Education Quarterly, 13*(4), 290–307.

Olson, Gary A. (1998). Encountering the other: Postcolonial theory and composition scholarship. *Journal of Advanced Composition, 18*(1), 45–55.

Ong, Walter. (1982). *Orality and literacy: The technologizing of the word.* London: Methuen.

Open Archives Initiative Protocol for Metadata Harvesting (2004). Retrieved November 10, 2005, from http://www.openarchives.org/OAI/openarchivesprotocol.html

Ortega, Lourdes. (1997). Process and outcomes in networked classroom interaction: Defining the research agenda for L2 computer-assisted classroom discussion. *Language Learning & Technology, 1*(1), 82–93. Retrieved October 20, 2004, from http://web.archive.org/web/19980504002425/http://polyglot.cal.msu.edu/llt/vol1num1/ortega/default.html

Paccagnella, Luciano. (1997). Getting the seat of your pants dirty: Strategies for ethnographic research on virtual communities. *Journal of Computer Mediated Communication, 3*(1). Retrieved October 1, 2003, from http://www.ascusc.org/jcmc/

Pagnucci, Gian S., & Mauriello, Nicholas. (1999). The masquerade: Gender, identity, and writing for the web. *Computers and Composition, 16,* 141–151.

Palen, Leysia, & Salzman, Marilyn. (2002). Beyond the handset: Designing for wireless communications usability. *ACM Transactions on Computer–Human Interaction, 9*(2), 125–151.

Pandey, Iswari, Pandey, Laxman, & Shreshtha, Angish. (in press). Learning to play: Class, culture, and literacy learning in the post-national interface. In Gail Hawisher & Cynthia Selfe (Eds.), *Gaming as literacy.* McMillan Palgrave.

Patton, Michael Q. (2002). *Qualitative evaluation and research methods* (3rd ed.). Newbury Park, CA: Sage.

Paye, Jean Claude. (2006, Fall). From the state of emergency to the state of exception. *Telos, 136,* 154-166.

Pecorari, Diane. (2003). Good and original: Plagiarism and patch writing in academic second language writing. *Journal of Second Language Writing, 12*(4), 317-345.

Peters, Brad, & Swanson, Diana. (2004). Queering the conflicts: What LGBT students can teach us in the classroom and online. *Computers and Composition, 21*(3), 295-313.

Plumwood, Val. (1993). *Feminism and the mastery of nature.* New York: Routledge.

Porter, James. (1992). *Audience and rhetoric: An archaeological composition of the discourse community.* Upper Saddle River, NJ: Prentice-Hall.

Porter, James. (1998). *Rhetorical ethics and internetworked writing.* Stamford, CT: Ablex.

Porter, James. (2002). Why technology matters to writing: A cyber writer's tale. *Computers and Composition, 20,* 375-394.

Potiguara, Eliane. (1997). The earth is the Indian's mother, Nhãndecy (Leland Robert Guyer, Trans.). In Karen Warren (Ed.), *Ecofeminism: Women, culture, nature* (pp. 140-153). Bloomington: Indiana University Press.

Potter, W. J., & Levinne-Donnerstein, D. (1999). Rethinking validity and reliability in content analysis. *Journal of Applied Communication Research, 27,* 258-284.

Powell, Katrina, & Takayoshi, Pamela. (2003). Accepting roles created for us: Reciprocity, *kairos,* and feminist research methodology. *College Composition and Communication, 54,* 394-422.

Pratt, Mary Louise. (1991) The arts of the contact zone. *Profession, 91,* 33-40.

Prelli, Lawrence J. (1989). *A rhetoric of science: Inventing scientific discourse.* Columbia: University of South Carolina Press.

Prior, Paul. (1998). *Writing/disciplinarity: A sociohistoric account of literate activity in the academy.* Mahwah, NJ: Erlbaum.

Prior, Paul. (2004). Tracing process: How texts come into being. In Charles Bazerman & Paul Prior (Eds.), *What writing does and how it does it: An introduction to analysis of text and textual practice* (pp. 167-200). Mahwah, NJ: Erlbaum.

Prior, Paul, & Shipka, Jody. (2003). Chronotopic lamination: Tracing the contours of literate activity. In Charles Bazerman & David Russell (Eds.), *Writing selves/writing societies: Research from activity perspectives* (pp. 180-238). Fort Collins, CO: The WAC Clearinghouse.

Randall, Marilyn. (2001). *Pragmatic plagiarism: Authorship, profit, and power.* Toronto: University of Toronto Press.

Ravotas, Doris, & Berkenkotter, Carol. (1998). Voices in the text: The uses of reported speech in a psychotherapist's notes and initial assessments. *Text, 18,* 211-239.

Ray, Ruth. (1993). *The practice of theory: Teacher research in composition.* Urbana, IL: National Council of Teachers of English.

Regan, Alison. (1993). "Type normal like the rest of us": Writing, power, and homophobia in the networked composition classroom. *Computers and Composition, 10*(4), 11-23.

Resnick, Elizabeth. (2003). *Design for communication: Conceptual graphic design basics.* New York: Wiley.

Rheingold, Howard. (2002). *Smart mobs.* New York: Basic Books.

Rheinharz, Shulamit. (1992). *Feminist methods in social research.* New York: Oxford.

Richardson, Elaine. (2002). *African-American literacies.* New York: Routledge.

Rickly, Rebecca. (1999). The gender gap in computers and composition research: Must boys be boys? *Computers and Composition, 16*(1), 121–140.

Ricoeur, Paul. (1981). The model of the text: Meaningful action considered as a text. In John B. Thompson (Trans. & Ed.), *Hermeneutics and the human sciences* (pp. 197–221). Cambridge, MA: Cambridge University Press.

Ries, Nancy. (1997). *Russian talk: Culture and conversation during Perestroika.* Ithaca, NY: Cornell University Press.

Rist, Ray. (1980). Blitzkreig ethnography: On the transformation of a method into a movement. *Educational Researcher, 9*(2), 8–10.

Rodrigues, Raymond J., & Rodrigues, Dawn W. (1984). Computer-based invention: Its place and potential. *College Composition and Communication, 35,* 78–87.

Romano, Susan. (1993). The egalitarianism narrative: Whose story? Which yardstick? *Computers and Composition, 10*(3), 5–28.

Romano, Susan. (1998). Tracking composition research on the World Wide Web. In Christine Farris & Chris M. Anson (Eds.), *Under construction: Working at the intersections of composition theory, research, and practice* (pp. 179–195).Logan: Utah State University Press.

Romano, Susan. (1999). On becoming a woman: Pedagogies of the self. In Gail E. Hawisher & Cynthia L. Selfe (Eds.), *Passions, pedagogies and 21st century technologies* (pp. 249–267). Logan: Utah State University Press.

Romberger, Julia E. (2004). *The ecology of a digital environment: Using ecofeminist theory to understand Microsoft Word's rhetorical design.* Unpublished doctoral dissertation, Purdue University, West Lafayette.

Rose, Jeanne Marie. (2004). "B seeing U" in unfamiliar places: ESL writers, email epistolaries, and critical computer literacy. *Computers and Composition, 21,* 237–249.

Rose, Shirley K. (1999). The role of scholarly citations in disciplinary economies. In Lise Buranen & Alice M. Roy (Eds.), *Perspectives on plagiarism and intellectual property in a postmodern world* (pp. 241–249). Albany: State University of New York Press.

Rose, Shirley K. (1996). What's love got to do with it? Scholarly citation practices as courtship rituals. *Language and Learning Across the Disciplines, 1*(3), 34–48.

Rousseau, Ronald. (1997). Sitations: An exploratory study. *Cybermetrics, 1*(1). Retrieved October 28, 2004, from http://www.cindoc.csic.es/cybermetrics/articles/v1i1p1.html

Rouzie, Albert. (2001). Conversation and carrying-on: Play conflict, and serio-ludic discourse in synchronous computer conferencing. *College Composition and Communication, 53*(2), 251–299.

Rouzie, Albert. (2005). *At play in the fields of writing: A serio-ludic rhetoric.* Cresskill, NJ: Hampton Press.

Russell, David R. (1997). Rethinking genre in school and society: An activity theory analysis. *Written Communication, 14*, 504–554.

Russell, David R. (2002). *Writing in the academic disciplines: A curricular history* (2nd ed.). Carbondale: Southern Illinois University Press.

Sachs, Colin, & Winther, Doug. (1987). *Intellectual property rights in an age of electronics and information.* Malabar, FL: Robert E Krieger.

Sachs, Colin, & Winther, Doug. (1998). *Dangers of student publishing on the Web.* Paper presentation #3733 at TESOL 98, Seattle, WA. Retrieved July 10, 1999, from http://www.tesolweb.net/Colin/present/dangers/98Presentation.htm

Sadker, Myra, & Sadker, David. (1994). *Failing at fairness: How our schools cheat girls.* New York: Simon and Schuster.

Sánchez, Raúl. (2005). *The function of theory in composition studies.* Albany: State University of New York Press.

Sapienza, Filipp. (2001). Nurturing translocal communication: Russian Immigrants on the World Wide Web. *Technical Communication, 48*, 435–448.

Schemo, Diane Jean. (2003, July 2). Oxford investigates scientist who denied Israeli application. *The New York Times*, p. A9.

Schmidt, Michael. (2003). Responsibility answers absurdity. In Steven Heller & Veronique Vienne (Eds.), *Citizen designer: Perspectives on design responsibility* (pp. 115–118). New York: Alworth Press.

Schneider, Suzanne P., & Germann, Clark G. (1999). Technical communication on the Web: A profile of learners and learning environments. *Technical Communication Quarterly, 8*, 37–48.

Schwartz, Helen. (1982). Monsters and mentors: Computer applications for humanistic education. *College English, 44*, 141–152.

Sclove, Richard E. (1995). Making technology democratic. In James Brooks & Iain A. Boal (Eds.), *Resisting the virtual life: The culture and politics of information* (pp. 85–104). San Francisco: City Lights.

Scott, Joan W. (1986). Gender: A useful category of historical analysis. *The American Historical Review, 91*(5), 1053–1075.

Scott, Joan W. (1988). *Gender and the politics of history.* New York: Columbia University Press.

Selber, Stuart. (1997). Hypertext spheres of influence in technical communication instructional contexts. In Stuart Selber (Ed.), *Computers and technical communication: Pedagogical and programmatic perspectives* (pp. 17–43). Greenwich, CT: Ablex.

Selfe, Cynthia L. (1999a). Technology and literacy: A story about the perils of not paying attention. *College Composition and Communication, 50*, 411–436.

Selfe, Cynthia L. (1999b). *Technology and literacy in the 21st century: The importance of paying attention.* Carbondale: Southern Illinois University Press.

Selfe, Cynthia L., & Hawisher, Gail E. (Eds.). (2004). *Literate lives in the information age: Narratives of literacy from the United States.* Mahwah, NJ: Erlbaum.

Selfe, Cynthia L., & Selfe, Richard J. (1994). The politics of the interface: Power and its exercise in electronic contact zones. *College Composition and Communication, 45*, 480–504.

Selfe, Cynthia L., & Wahlstrom, Billie J. (1989). Computer-supported writing classes: Lessons for teachers. In Cynthia L. Selfe, Dawn Rodrigues, & William R. Oates (Eds.), *Computers in English and language arts: The challenge of teacher education* (pp. 257–268). Urbana, IL: National Council of Teachers of English.

Sellen, Abigail, & Harper, Richard. (2001). *The myth of the paperless office.* Cambridge, MA: MIT Press.

Shami, Seteney. (1988). Studying your own: The complexities of a shared culture. In Soraya Altorki & Camilla Fawzi El- Solh (Eds.), *Arab women in the field* (pp. 115–138). Syracuse, NY: Syracuse University Press.

Sherman, Aliza. (1998). *Cybergrrl: A woman's guide to the World Wide Web.* New York: Ballantine.

Shkedi, Asher. (2004). Narrative survey: A methodology for studying multiple populations. *Narrative Inquiry, 14*, 87–112.

Shome, Raka, & Hegde, Radha. (2002). Culture, communication, and the challenge of globalization. *Critical Studies in Mass Communication, 19*(2), 172–189.

Silva, Tony. (1997). Differences in ESL and native-English-speaker writing: The research and its implications. In Carol Severino, Juan C. Guerra, & Johnnella E. Butler (Eds.), *Writing in multicultural settings* (pp. 209–219). New York: Modern Language Association.

Simons, Herbert W. (1990). *The rhetorical turn: Invention and persuasion in the conduct of inquiry.* Chicago: University of Chicago Press.

Sinclair, Carla. (1996). *NetChick: A smart-girl guide to the wired world.* New York: Henry Holt.

Slack, Jennifer Daryl. (1989). Contextualizing technology. In B. Dervin, L. Grossberg, B. J. O'Keefe, & E. Wartella (Eds.), *Rethinking communication* (Vol. 1). Thousand Oaks, CA: Sage.

Slack, Jennifer Daryl. (1996). The theory and method of articulation in cultural studies. In David Morley & Kuan-Hsing Chen (Eds.), *Stuart Hall: Critical dialogues in cultural studies* (pp. 112–130). London: Routledge.

Slade, Robert, Harley, David, & Gattiker, Urs. (2001). *Viruses revealed.* New York: Osbourne.

Slatin, John et al. (1990). Computer teachers respond to Halio. *Computers and Composition, 7*, 73–79. Retrieved January 14, 2005, from http://www.hu.mtu.edu/%7Ecandc/archives/v7/7_3_html/7_3_7_Slatin.html

Slattery, Shaun. (2003). Research methods for revealing patterns of mediation. *Proceedings of the 21st Annual International Conference on Documentation* (pp. 35–38). San Francisco: Association of Computing Machinery.

Slattery, Shaun. (2005). *Experiencing technical writing as textual coordination.* Paper presented at the 52nd Annual Conference of the Society for Technical Communication, Seattle, WA.

Slattery, Shaun. (2006). *The role of mediating artifacts in rhetorical techne: An activity-based study of textual coordination.* Unpublished doctoral dissertation, Rensselaer Polytechnic Institute, Troy, NY.

Sloane, Sarah J. (1999). The haunting story of J: Genealogy as a critical category in understanding how a writer composes. In Gail E. Hawisher & Cynthia L. Selfe

(Eds.), *Passions, pedagogies, and 21st century technologies* (pp. 49–65). Logan: Utah State University Press.

Smagorinsky, Peter. (Ed.). (2006). *Research on composition: Multiple perspectives on two decades of change*. New York: Teachers College Press.

Small, Henry. (1999). A passage through science: Crossing disciplinary boundaries. *Library Trends, 48*(1), 72–108.

Smart, Graham. (1999). Storytelling in a central bank: The role of narrative in the creation and use of specialized economic knowledge. *Journal of Business and Technical Communication, 13*, 249–273.

Smart, Graham. (2003). A central bank's "communications strategy": The interplay of activity, discourse genres, and technology in a time of organizational change. In Charles Bazerman & D. Russell (Eds.), *Writing selves/writing societies: Research from activity perspectives*. Fort Collins, CO: WAC Clearinghouse. Retrieved May 9, 2005, from http://wac.colostate.edu/books/ selves_societies/

Smith, Alistair. G. (2004). Web links as analogues of citations. *Information Research, 9*(4). Retrieved October 28, 2004, from http://informationr.net/ir/9-4/paper188.html

Smith, Beatrice. (2004). Teaching with technologies: A reflexive auto-ethnographic portrait. *Computers and Composition, 21*, 49–62.

Smith, C. (2002). Click on me! An example of how a toddler used technology in play. *Journal of Early Childhood Literacy, 2*, 2–20.

Smith, Ken, & Price, Cindy. (2005). Content analysis of representation: Photographic coverage of blacks in nondaily newspapers. In Ken Smith, Sandra Moriarty, Gretchen Barbatsis, & Keith Kenney (Eds.), *Handbook of visual communication: Theory, methods, and media* (pp. 127–137). Mahwah, NJ: Erlbaum.

Soja, Edward W. (1989). *Postmodern geographies: The reassertion of space in critical social theory*. London: Verso.

Sorapure, Madeline. (2003). Five principles of new media: Or, playing Lev Manovich. *Kairos: A Journal of Rhetoric, Technology, and Pedagogy, 8*(2). Retrieved November 21, 2005, from http://english.ttu.edu/kairos/8.2/index.html

Sorapure, Madeleine, Inglesby, Pamela, & Yatchisin, George. (1998). Web literacy: Challenges and opportunities for research in a new medium. *Computers and Composition, 15*, 409–424.

Spilka, Rachel. (Ed.). (1993). *Writing in the workplace: New research perspectives*. Carbondale: Southern Illinois University Press.

Spilka, Rachel. (2005). Technical communication research: A call for action. Keynote address delivered at the 2005 Council of Programs in Technical and Scientific Communication Conference, Lubbock, TX.

Spinuzzi, Clay. (2000). Investigating the technology-work relationship: A critical comparison of three qualitative field methods. In *IEEE PCS/ACM SIGDOC 2000 Conference Proceedings* (pp. 419–432). New York: ACM.

Spinuzzi, Clay. (2001). "Light green doesn't mean hydrology!": Toward a visual–rhetorical framework for interface design. *Computers and Composition, 18*, 39–53.

Spinuzzi, Clay. (2002). Toward integrating our research scope: A sociocultural field methodology. *Journal of Business and Technical Communication, 16*(1), 3–32.

Spinuzzi, Clay. (2003). *Tracing genres through organizations: A sociocultural approach to information design.* Cambridge, MA: MIT Press.

Spinuzzi, Clay. (2005a). Lost in the translation: Shifting claims in the migration of a research technique. *Technical Communication Quarterly, 14*(4), 411-446.

Spinuzzi, Clay. (2005b). The methodology of participatory design. *Technical Communication, 52*(2), 163–174.

Spinuzzi, Clay, Bowie, Jennifer L., Rodgers, Ida, & Li, Xiangyi. (2003). Open systems and citizenship: Designing a departmental Web site as an open system. *Computers and Composition, 20,* 168–193.

Spinuzzi, Clay, Hart-Davidson, William, & Zachry, Mark. (2004). Modeling knowledge work. *Computer Writing and Research Lab White Paper Series,* #040505-1. Austin: University of Texas and the CWRL. Retrieved September 4, 2005, from http://www.cwrl.utexas.edu/research/whitepapers/2004/040505-1.pdf

Spivak, Gayatri S. (1999). *A critique of postcolonial reason.* Cambridge, MA: Harvard University Press.

Spradley, James P. (1980). *Participant observation.* New York: Holt, Rinehart & Winston.

Stanley, Liz, & Wise, Sue. (1990). Method, methodology, and epistemology in feminist research processes. In Liz Stanley (Ed.), *Feminist praxis: Research, theory and epistemology in feminist sociology* (pp. 20–60). London: Routledge.

Statistical Abstract of the United States: 2004–2005. (2004). Washington, DC: U.S. Census Bureau.

Sternglass, Marilyn. (Ed.). (1997). *Time to know them: A longitudinal study of writing and learning at the college level.* Mahwah, NJ: Erlbaum.

Strauss, Anslem, & Corbin, Juliet. (1998). *Basics of qualitative research: Techniques and procedures for developing grounded theory.* Thousand Oaks, CA: Sage.

Street, Brian. (Ed.). (1984). *Literacy in theory and practice.* Cambridge, MA: Cambridge University Press.

Street, Brian. (Ed.). (1993). *Cross-cultural approaches to literacy.* Cambridge, MA: Cambridge University Press.

Strenski, Ellen. (1995). Virtual staff meetings: Electronic tutor training with a local e-mail listserv discussion group. *Computers and Composition, 12,* 247–255.

Stringer, Ernest T. (1999). *Action research: A handbook for practitioners* (2nd ed.). Thousand Oaks, CA: Sage Publications.

Sturgeon, Noël. (1997). *Ecofeminist natures: Race, gender, feminist theory and political action.* New York: Routledge.

Suchman, Lucy. (1987). *Plans and situated actions: The problem of human-machine communication.* Cambridge: Cambridge University Press.

Sujo de Montes, L. E., Oran, Sally M., & Willis, Elizabeth M. (2002). Power, language, and identity: Voices from an online course. *Computers and Composition, 19,* 251–271.

Sullivan, Laura L. (1997). Cyberbabes: (Self-)representation of women and the virtual male gaze. *Computers and Composition, 14,* 189–204.

Sullivan, Patricia A. (1992). Feminism and methodology in composition studies. In Gesa Kirsch & Patricia A. Sullivan (Eds.), *Methods and methodology in composition research* (pp. 37–61). Carbondale: Southern Illinois University Press.

Sullivan, Patricia A. (1996). Ethnography and the problem of the "other." In Peter Mortensen & Gesa E. Kirsch (Eds.), *Ethics & representation in qualitative studies of literacy* (pp. 97–114). Urbana, IL: National Council of Teachers of English.

Sullivan, Patricia, & Porter, James E. (1993). On theory, practice, and method. In Rachel Spilka (Ed.), *Writing in the workplace: New research perspectives* (pp. 220–237). Carbondale: Southern Illinois University Press.

Sullivan, Patricia, & Porter, James E. (1997). *Opening spaces: Writing technologies and critical research practices.* Greenwich, CT: Ablex.

Sullivan, Patricia, & Takayoshi, Pamela. (2007). *Labor, technologies, and the shaping of composition in the academy.* Cresskill, NJ: Hampton Press.

Sun, Huatong. (2004). *Expanding the scope of localization: A cultural usability perspective on mobile text messaging use in American and Chinese contexts.* Unpublished dissertation. Rensselaer Polytechnic Institute.

Sunnstein, Bonnie. (1996). Culture on the page. In Peter Mortensen & Gesa Kirsch (Eds.), *Ethics and representation in qualitative studies of literacy* (pp. 177–203). Urbana: National Council of Teachers of English.

Swales, John M. (1990). *Genre analysis: English in academic and research settings.* Cambridge, UK: Cambridge University Press.

Swarts, Jason. (2004). Technological mediation of document review: The use of textual replay in two organizations. *The Journal of Business and Technical Communication, 18*, 328–360.

Syverson, Margaret A. (1999). *The wealth of reality: An ecology of composition.* Carbondale: Southern Illinois University Press.

Takayoshi, Pamela. (2000). Complicated women: Examining methodologies for understanding the uses of technology. *Computers and Composition, 17*, 123–138.

Takayoshi, Pamela, Huot, Emily, & Huot, Meghan. (1999). No boys allowed: The World Wide Web as a clubhouse for girls. *Computers and Composition, 16*, 89–106.

Tansey, Frank. (2005, March). Getting personal. *Campus Technology, 18*, 34–39.

Thatcher, Barry. (2005). Situating L2 writing in global communication technologies. *Computers and Composition, 22*, 279–295.

The Code of Federal Regulations, Title 45 Public Welfare, Part 46 Protection of Human Subjects (45 CFR 46). (1991, November 13). Department of Health and Human Services, Office of Human Research Protections. Retrieved July 15, 2004, from http://www.hhs.gov/ohrp/humansubjects/guidance/45cfr46.htm

Thelwall, Mike. (2003). What is this link doing here? Beginning a fine-grained process of identifying reasons for academic hyperlink creation. *Information Research, 8*(3). Retrieved October 28, 2004, from http://informationr.net/ir/8-3/paper151.html

Thomas, Jim. (1996). When cyberresearch goes awry: The ethics of the Rimm "cyberporn" study. *The Information Society, 12*, 189–198.

Thomas, Sari. (1994). Artifactual study in the analysis of culture: A defense of content analysis in a postmodern age. *Communication Research, 21*. Retrieved November 29, 2001, from http://search.epnet.com/direct.asp?an = 96102342 78&db = ufh

Tiemens, Robert. (2005). A content analysis of political speeches on television. In Ken Smith, Sandra Moriarty, Gretchen Barbatsis, & Keith Kenney (Eds.), *Handbook of visual communication: Theory, methods, and media* (pp. 385–404). Mahwah, NJ: Erlbaum.

Titscher, Stefan, Meyer, Michael, Wodak, Ruth, & Vetter, Eva. (2000). *Methods of text and discourse analysis* (Bryan Jenner, Trans.). Newbury Park, CA: Sage.

Tulley, Christine, & Blair, Kristine. (2002). Ewriting spaces as safe, gender-fair havens: Aligning political and pedagogical possibilities. In Pamela Takayoshi & Brian Huot (Eds.), *Teaching writing with computers: An introduction* (pp. 55–66). Boston: Houghton-Mifflin.

Tusing, Kyle James. (2005). Objective measurement of vocal signals. In Valerie Manusov (Ed.), *The sourcebook of nonverbal measures: Going beyond words* (pp. 393–402). Mahwah, NJ: Erlbaum.

University of Oxford. (2003, July 4). *"Professor Andrew Wilkie."* Retrieved October 30, 2004, from http://www.admin.ox.ac.uk/po/wilkie2.shtml

van der Aalst, Will, Weijters, Tom, & Maruster, Laura. (2004). Workflow mining: Discovering process models from event logs. *IEEE Transactions on Knowledge and Data Engineering, 16*(9), 1128–1142.

Van Gelder, Lindsey. (1996). The strange case of the electronic lover. In Rob Kling (Ed.), *Computerization and controversy: Value conflicts and social choices* (pp. 533–546). San Diego: Academic Press.

van Manen, Max. (1997). *Researching lived experience: Human science for an action sensitive pedagogy.* Albany: State University of New York Press.

Vehovar, V., & Belak, E. (2004, October). *The influence of mobile phone usage on survey data collection.* Paper presentation at 14th Annual Statistical Days, Radenci, Republika Slovenije.

Vygotsky, L. (1978). *Mind in society.* Cambridge, MA: Harvard University Press.

Vygotsky, L. (1986). *Thought and language* (Alex Kozulin, Trans.). Cambridge, MA: MIT Press.

Wahlstrom, Billie J. (1994). Communication and technology: Defining a feminist presence in research and practice. In Cynthia L. Selfe & Susan Hilligoss (Eds.), *Literacy and computers: The complications of teaching and learning with technology* (pp. 171–185) New York: Modern Language Association.

Walther, Joseph. (2001). Research ethics in internet-enabled research: Human subjects issues and methodological myopia. In Charles Ess (Ed.), *Internet research ethics.* Retrieved May 1, 2005, from: http://www.nyu.edu/projects/nissenbaum/projects_ethics.html

Ward, Katie. (1999). Cyber-ethnography and the emergence of the virtually new community. *Journal of Information Technology, 14*, 95–105.

Ware, Paige D. (2004). Confidence and competition online: ESL student perspectives on web-based discussions in the classroom. *Computers and Composition, 21*(4), 451–468.

Warnick, Barbara. (2002). *Critical literacy in a digital era: Technology, rhetoric, and the public interest.* Mahwah, NJ: Erlbaum.

Warren, Karen. (Ed.). (1997). *Ecofeminism: Women, culture, nature.* Bloomington: Indiana University Press.

Warren, Karen. (2000). *Ecofeminist philosophy: A western perspective on what it is and why it matters.* Lanham, MD: Rowman and Littlefield.

Watkins, Steve. (1996). World WideWeb authoring in the portfolio-assessed, (inter)networked composition course. *Computers and Composition, 13,* 219–230.

Weare, C., & Lin W. Y. (2000). Content analysis of the World Wide Web. *Social Science Computer Review, 18,* 272–292.

Weintraub, Daniel. (2004, October 12). Pundits in pajamas are biting more than ankles. *Sacbee.* Retrieved October 21, 2004, from http://www.sacbee.com/content/politics/columns/weintraub/story/11063698p-11980559c.html

Wertsch, James. (1991). *Voices of the mind: A sociocultural approach to mediated action.* Cambridge, MA: Harvard University Press.

Whitaker, Reg. (2003). After 9/11: A surveillance state? In Cynthia Brown (Ed.), *Lost liberties: Ashcroft and the assault on personal freedom* (pp. 63–66). New York: New Press.

White, Cindy H., & Sargent, Jack. (2005). Researcher choices and practices in the study of nonverbal communication. In Valerie Manusov (Ed.), *The sourcebook of nonverbal measures: Going beyond words* (pp. 3–21). Mahwah, NJ: Erlbaum.

White, Hayden. (1973). *Metahistory: The historical imagination in nineteenth-century Europe.* Baltimore: Johns Hopkins University Press.

White, Howard D., & McCain, Katherine W. (1998). Visualizing a discipline: An author co-citation analysis of information science, 1972–1995. *Journal of the American Society for Information Science, 49*(4), 327–355.

White, Michelle. (2001). Representations or people? In Charles Ess (Ed.), *Internet research ethics.* Retrieved May 1, 2005, from http://www.nyu.edu/projects/nissenbaum/projects_ethics.html

White, Michele. (2002). Regulating research: The problem of theorizing community on LambdaMOO. *Ethics and Information Technology, 4,* 55–70.

Wickliff, Greg, & Yancey, Kathi. (2001). The perils of crating a class Web site: It was the best of times, it was the... *Computers and Composition, 18,* 177–186.

WIDE Research Center Collective. (2005). Why teach digital writing? *Kairos: A Journal of Rhetoric, Technology, and Pedagogy, 10*(1). Retrieved August 2005, from http://english.ttu.edu/kairos/10.1/binder2.html?coverweb/wide/index/html.

Wilkie, Andrew O. M. (2001). Genetic prediction: What are the limits? *Studies in History and Philosophy of Biological and Biomedical Sciences, 32,* 619–633.

Witte, Stephen P. (1987). Pre-text and composing. *College Composition and Communication, 38*(1), 397–425.

Wolfe, Janice L. (1999). Why do women feel ignored? Gender differences in computer-mediated classroom interactions. *Computers and Composition, 16,* 153–166.

Woodland, Randal. (1999). "I plan to be a 10": Online literacy and lesbian, gay, bisexual, and transgender students. *Computers and Composition, 16*(1), 73–87.

World Medical Association Declaration of Helsinki Ethical Principles for Medical Research Involving Human Subjects. (2002). In R. Amdur & E. Bankert (Eds.), *Institutional review board: Management and function* (pp. 499–500). Boston: Jones and Bartlett.

Worth, Robert L. (2002, July 22). In New York tickets, Ghana sees orderly city. *The New York Times,* pp. A1, A17.

Writing in Digital Environments (WIDE) Research Center Collective. (2005). Why teach digital writing? *Kairos: A Journal of Rhetoric, Technology, and Pedagogy, 10*(1). Retrieved January 2, 2006, from http://english.ttu.edu/kairos/10.1/binder 2.html?coverweb/wide/index.html

Wysocki, Anne Frances. (1998). Monitoring order. *Kairos: A Journal of Rhetoric, Technology, and Pedagogy, 3*(2). Retrieved October 20, 2004, from http://english.ttu.edu/kairos/3.2/binder.html?features/wysocki/mOrder0.html

Wysocki, Anne Frances. (2001). Impossibly distinct: On form/content and word/image in two pieces of computer-based interactive multimedia. *Computers and Composition, 18,* 137–162.

Wysocki, Anne Frances. (2002). A bookling monument. *Kairos: A Journal of Rhetoric, Technology, and Pedagogy, 7*(3). Retrieved October 20, 2004, from http://english.ttu.edu/kairos/7.3/binder2.html?coverweb/wysocki/index.html

Wysocki, Anne Frances. (2002). With eyes that think, and compose, and think: On visual rhetoric. In Pamela Takayoshi & Brian Huot (Eds.), *Teaching writing with computers* (pp. 182–201). Boston: Houghton Mifflin.

Wysocki, Anne Frances. (2005). awaywithwords: On the possibilities in unavailable designs. *Computers and Composition, 22,* 55–62.

Wysocki, Anne Frances, & Jasken, Julia I. (2004). What should be an unforgettable face. *Computers and Composition, 21,* 29–48.

Wysocki, Anne Frances, Johnson-Eilola, Johndan, Selfe, Cynthia L., & Sirc, Geoffrey. (2004). *Writing new media: Theory and applications for expanding the teaching of composition.* Logan: Utah State University Press.

Yair, Gad. (2000). Educational battlefields in America: The tug-of-war over students' engagement with instruction. *Sociology of Education, 73,* 247–269.

Yancey, Kathleen Blake. (2004a). Looking for sources of coherence in a fragmented world: Notes toward a new assessment design. *Computers and Composition, 21*(1), 89–102.

Yancey, Kathleen Blake. (2004b). Made not only in words: Composition in a new key. *College Composition and Communication, 56*(2), 297–328.

Yates, JoAnne. (1993). *Control through communication: The rise of system in American management.* Baltimore: Johns Hopkins University Press.

Young, Richard, Becker, Alton, & Pike, Kenneth. (1970). *Rhetoric: Discovery and change*. New York: Harcourt Brace.

Yuan, Yi. (2003). The use of chat rooms in an ESL setting. *Computers and Composition, 20,* 194–206.

Zaharlick, Amy, & Green, Judith. (1991). Ethnographic research. In James Flood, Diane Lapp, James R. Squire, & Julie M. Jensen (Eds.), *Handbook of research in teaching the English language arts.* (pp. 205–225). New York: Macmillan.

Zetter, Kim. (2005, April 6). Patriot Act gets a hearing. *Wired News*. Retrieved June 1, 2005, from http://www.wired.com/news/privacy/0,1848,67141-2,00.html?tw = wn_story_page_next1

Zettl, Herbert. (2005). Aesthetics theory. In Ken Smith, Sandra Moriarty, Gretchen Barbatsis, & Keith Kenney (Eds.), *Handbook of visual communication: Theory, methods, and media* (pp. 365–384). Mahwah, NJ: Erlbaum.

Zhang, Yin. (1998). The impact of Internet-based electronic resources on formal scholarly communication in the area of library and information science: A citation analysis. *Journal of Information Science, 24*(4), 241–254.

Zittrain, Jonathan. (2002, July 2). *Beware the cyber cops*. Forbes.com. Retrieved July 28, 2002, from http://64.233.187.104/search?q = cache:DXZNHcprqcMJ:www.forbes.com/forbes /2002/0708/062.html + cyber + cops&hl = en

SUBJECT INDEX